EXPLOITED CHILDREN

A Comprehensive Blueprint for Child Labour Rehabilitation

Exploited Children

A Comprehensive Blueprint for Child Labour Rehabilitation

Edited by

M. KOTESWARA RAO

KANISHKA PUBLISHERS, DISTRIBUTORS
NEW DELHI-110 002

KANISHKA PUBLISHERS, DISTRIBUTORS
4697/5-21A, Ansari Road, Daryaganj
New Delhi -110 002
Phones : 2327 0497, 2328 8285
Fax : 011-2328 8285
E-mail : kanishka_publishing@yahoo.co.in

First Published: 2000
Second Edition: 2011

ISBN : 978-81-7391-342-0

PRINTED IN INDIA

Published by Madan Sachdeva for Kanishka Publishers, Distributors, 4697/5-21A, Ansari Road, Daryaganj, New Delhi-110 002, Typeset by Sunshine Graphics, Delhi, and Printed at Rajdhani Printers, Delhi.

Introduction

As any nation's future lies in today's children, they are to be equipped with health and education for them to be more useful to the nation. In any case, half of the children are wasting their time, while a significant fraction of them are breaking their backs to earn a meagre living. Making, the nation ultimately pay the price for its negligence of children.

Though eradication of child labour has been recommended in various national and international seminars, it has been increasing at an alarming rate throughout the world. In Naples, millions of children are employed in leather industry. In Spain more than a hundred thousand children work in Orchards and Plantations. In the USA, millions of young hands are employed in farms and plantations. Thus child labour has been increasing at a higher rate in Africa and South Asia, than elsewhere.

The problem of child labour is insignificant when compared with the problems in the developed countries. The low level of child labour in developed countries was achieved mainly by laws governing the employment of children, by recognizing the need to educate children by increasing real income of parents due to industrial and social development. Besides, with industrial development, children were increasingly substituted by machines from the peripheral jobs, which were the children's major education, establishment of orphanages and homes for destitutes etc., also would have assisted in reducing the employment of these children. The near absence of child labour in the developed countries has resulted in excluding children below 14 years of age from the labour force.

In many cases, child labour is not an insignificant problem for developing countries like India. Though it has been in practice in the Indian Society since times immemorial, children have been helping their parents in the household chores and their family occupations. On the basis of historical experience, the problem of child labour lies in the process of industrial revolution.

According to the National Committee on Labour, "the employment of children is non-existent in organized industries. It presents in varying degrees in unorganized industries". Ironically India's child labour laws prohibit children from being employed in factories with high wages, but not in cottage industries, restaurants, in households and agricultural sector, where wages are comparatively low. In fact the agricultural sector stands out as the biggest single employer of child labour in India.

Article 24 of Indian Constitution prohibits employment of children below 14 years of age, in any factory, mine or any other hazardous industry, as also so many such Acts also prohibiting employment of children. Inspite of all these best efforts, the incidence of child labour has increased to 11.29 millions by 1991. The authenticity data is also disputable as unofficial figures of child labour in India are in the range of 44 to 144 million.

Given the nature of modern technology and abundance of unskilled labour in developing countries, child labour is found in both the 'formal' and 'informal' sectors of the urban economies. But it is the 'informal' sector where children are found to be generally employed earning direct wages in cash or kind or as unpaid family labour. The conditions of work at the place of their employment are highly unsatisfactory, especially in unregulated factories and other informal sector enterprises as they are subject to exploitation by making them work for long hours in absolutely unhealthy environment. Consequently, the children are also denied formal or even informal education.

Though there are a number of other reasons for child labour as social, traditional, psychological and political, the Economic Factors are the main cause for the prevalence of child labour in India. Utter Poverty, Unemployment or intermittent employment and Under-employment of the parents in the family etc., and the various economic factors. The child work exerts a negative influence on the child's personality and his well-being. The absence of harmonious family life, particularly if the child is employed on an external job, without the due attention and care of his parents and when the child is fully occupied in his work, he is without any opportunity for his physical or psychological development. In case of jobs accomplished in the streets, the child sometimes engaged in unsuitable, unhygienic surroundings is exposed to social evils, which may include even crime, drugs and prostitution.

Even though the use of child labour is deplorable, in actual practice it has become neither feasible nor desirable to have stringent measures to enforce existing child labour law. It is felt that for the time being i.e., till the economic condition of the country improves, efforts will have to be made to organize better conditions of work to eliminate abuse, exploitation and health hazards due to this child labour.

It is high time to review the nature, causes and consequences of child labour in the developing countries, like India in the context of recent restructuring of Indian Economy. In this context, the present book aims to deal with various aspects of child labour in India.

The contents of the book have been divided into Five parts.

Part I deals with the dimensions of child labour in India. By including the broad trends of child labour, as also multi-dimensional approaches to study this problem. The nature, magnitude, working conditions, causes and consequences, exploitation and rights of child labour are also discussed here at length.

Part II broadly deals with extent and problems of child labour in various states, districts and cities of India.

Part III presents the position of child labour in different industries such as Diamond cutting and polishing, Brick and Tiles industry, Garbage units and Handloom industry in different parts of the country.

Part IV analyses socio-economic characteristics of this problem, such as age and sex, caste, education, levels of living, levels of earning and impact on household incomes. Various aspects of migrant child workers are discussed. Further, this part also explains the nature and extent of labour, contribution of children to the rural farm household and determinants of it. This emphasises the effect of land holding on child labour and schooling of children.

Part V depicts the curbing of child labour in India. It discusses the number of Acts and Legislations, namely, constitutional provisions and legal provisions which were enacted to curb the child labour. The two strategies to eliminate the problem of child labour namely, the pull strategies and push strategies are examined. An attempt is also made in this section to give a blueprint of a time-bound 'SCOOP' Programme for eliminating the child labour in India.

The editor wishes to express his gratitude to all the contributors of articles as well as to the Kanishka Publishers for publication of this book.

M. Koteswara Rao

Contents

Section II
Child Labour in Indian Industries

Section III
Child Labour in Different Industries

Section V
Curbing Child Labour

List of Contributors

1. A. C. Komala, Lecturer in Economics, Government College for Boys, Kolar, (Karnataka).
2. A.D. Saramma, Associate Professor, Department of Economics, Bhavnagar University, Bhavnagar, (Gujarat).
3. Ajit S. Bhatia, Deptt. of Economics Punjabi University, Patiala, (Punjab).
4. A. K. Verma, Faculty Member, Institute of Applied Manpower Research, I.P. Estate, Ring Road, New Delhi, (Delhi).
5. Ambumani, Associate Professor, Bharatiar University, Coimbatore, (TN).
6. A. Prasad, 'H' Block — 18, S. V. University, Tirupathi, (A.P.).
7. C. Mathuraja, Annujo College, Teachers' Colony, Virahanoor, Madurai, (TN).
8. E. Singa Rao, Research Scholar, Deptt. of Economics, Nagarjuna University, Nagarjuna Nagar, Guntur District, (A.P.).
9. Smt. Gouradeve Katnalli, Deptt. of Economics, S.S. Margal College of Arts, Science, Commerce, Shahabad, Gulberga, (Karnataka).
10. (Mrs.) Gurubachan Kaur, Associate Professor, Punjabi University, Patiala, (Punjab).
11. Harindra Kishore Mishra, Deptt. of Economics, Nagendra Jhamavila, Laheriasarai, Darbhanga, (Bihar).
12. Harvinder Kaur, Lecturer in Economics Deptt. of Correspondence Course, Punjabi University, Patiala, (Punjab).
13. I. Narendra Kumar, 'H' Block — 18, S. V. University, Tirupathi, (A.P.).
14. I. Satya Sundaram, Associate Professor, Dr. No. 12/354-I, Rustumbada, Machilpatnam, Krishna District, (A.P.).

15. K. Gangadhara Rao, Lecturer, Deptt. of Economics, C.S.R. Sarma College, Ongole, Prakasam District, (A.P.).
16. Kalyani Mohanti, Faculty Member in HRM & IM Area, Bhubaneswar, (Orissa).
17. Kanchan Pd. Srivastava, Faculty Member, Deptt. of Economics, Magadh University, Bodh-Gaya, (Bihar).
18. K. Sreelakshmamma, Lecturer, Deptt. of Political Science, V.S.R. & N.V.R. College, Tenali, Guntur District, (A.P.).
19. L. D. Vaikunthe, Reader, Deptt. of Economics, Karnataka University, Dharwar, (Karnataka).
20. Matrin Patric, Senior Lecturer, Maharaja's College, Earnakulam, (Kerala).
21. M. Koteswara Rao, Associate Professor, Deptt. of Economics, Nagarjuna University, Nagarjuna Nagar-522510, Guntur District, (A.P.).
22. Mohan Prasad Shrivastava, Professor, Deptt. of Economics, Budh-Gaya, (Gaya), (Bihar).
23. Narendra Prasad, Professor of Economics, Magadh University, Bodh-Gaya, (Bihar).
24. Smt. Nira Kumari, Faculty Member, Deptt. of Economics, Magadh University, Budh-Gaya, (Bihar).
25. N. Narayana, Deptt. of Economics, University of Botswana, Private Bag-0022, Gaborone, Botswana, (Africa).
26. P.C. Tiwari, Reader, Deptt. of Economics, Handia P.G. College, Handia, Allahabad, (U.P.).
27. P. Venu Gopal, Lecturer, Deptt. of Economics, Hindu College, Guntur, Guntur District, (A.P.).
28. Raghuraman Narayan, D-288, Pandian St., Alagapan Nagar, Madhrai, (TN).
29. R.C. Talati, Principal Anand Arts College, Anand, (Gujarat).
30. R. Nagarajan, Lecturer, Gokhale Institute of Political and Economics, Pune, (MS).
31. Sangeetha Nagaiah, Research Associate, Deptt. of Economics, Punjabi University, Patiala, (Punjab).
32. S. Ganesan, Research Scholar, Deptt. of Economics, Bharathaiar University, Coimbatore, (TN).
33. Shakuntala Gupta, Reader, Deptt. of Economics, Punjabi University, Patiala, (Punjab).
34. Shyam Nath Nandkeoliyar, Professor, Deptt. of Economics, P.G. Centre, Gaya College, Gaya, (Bihar).

35. Silvia M. De-Mendonca C Noronha, Reader, Deptt. of Economics, Goa University, Taligao Platean, Goa, (Goa).
36. S.K. Patel, P.G. Deptt. of Economics, Sardar Patel University, Valiabh—Vidyanagar, (Gujarat).
37. Sriman Narayanan, Lecturer in Economics, Madura College, Madurai, (TN).
38. Sukhjinder Singh Tiwana, Head, Deptt. of Public Admn., Punjabi University, Patiala, (Punjab).
39. S. Velayudha Perumal, Professor and Head, Deptt. of Labour Studies, Madurai-Kamaraj University, Madurai, (TN).
40. T. Karunakaran, Lecturer, Deptt. of Sociology, Madura College, Madurai, (TN).
41. Vipla Chopra, Reader in Economics, Deptt. of Correspondence Course, Punjabi University, Patiala, (Punjab).
42. Virendra Prasad, Professor, Deptt. of Economics, Magadh University, Bodh-Gaya, (Bihar).

Section - I

DIMENSIONS OF CHILD LABOUR IN INDIA

1

Trends of Child Labour in India: A Review

—M. Koteswara Rao

Historical Background

Child Labour is an unfortunate product of industrial revolution originated in England and embraced not only other industries in independent countries but also the colonies captured by imperial powers during the period from 1760 to 1860. It is the story of one hundred years which gives us an account of increased wealth, increased productivity with the help of machines, profit-oriented activities of factory owners, migration of poor serfs and artisans from rural areas and hundreds of children who became victims of new capitalist economy. Children used to work 16 hours a day—from 5 am to 9 pm. History of child labour in factories during the 19th century gives us dreadful events of their poor conditions, about the serfs in labour market sent by landlords as well as growing richness of the millioneer millowners. The condition of working children in England was thus very bad due to poor conditions of parents, unemployment and lack of ideological background. However, later on Factory Legislation introduced by the liberal leadership regulated working hours for children and women. Many writers and trade union leaders in India have done a great deal in recent years to create public awareness of the wretched conditions in which millions of our poorest children work.[1]

Definition of Child Labour

Child Labour means the employment of children (5 to 14 years of age) in gainful occupations, which are injurious to their physical, mental, moral and social development. The child labour is, at times, used as synonym for 'employed child' or 'working child'. But a working child is one who subjects himself or herself to work, unpaid or free, instead of being at the school at a tender and formative stage of his or her life. The Operation Research Group (ORG) in India defines a working children as ". . . . a child falling within the 5-15 age bracket and who is at remunerative work, may be paid or unpaid and busy at any hour of the day within or outside the family . . . . . ."[2] The children belonging to meagre family income are compelled to join the labour force to supplement the family income. Generally, people from lower strata of our society send their children for work instead of sending them to school for education. Hence the children's intellectual growth is hampered by depriving them of educational opportunities, minimising their chances for vocational training and condemning them to low wages all their lives as unskilled labourers.[3] The growing number of child labourers all over the globe causes serious concern to those who are interested in the child welfare both in developed and developing countries. It is recognised that during the process of industrialization child labour grows in a big way in the unorganised sectors and it is intensified more with rapidly growing population. The employment of child is more or less a global phenomenon. In every country irrespective of its economic system, childrens are working in one form or the other to contribute significantly to the income of their families in all countries. The incidence is heaviest in south Asia. In these countries, employment of child labour has become a "conspicuous problem".[4]

Magnitude of the Problem

The world's population of working children has yet to be counted accurately. Because it is often illegal and clandestine, child labour lies beyond the reach of conventional labour statistics. New survey methods are penetrating the screen of obscurity which for too long has concealed the problem from public view. The findings reveal a tragedy of far greater magnitude than earlier. Some 61 per cent of this total or nearly 153 million are found in Asia; 32 per cent

Table 1.1

Child Labour at World Level, 1995

Asia	*Per cent*	*Africa*	*Per cent*	*Latin America*	*Per cent*	*Europe, Oceania, Middle East*	*Per cent*
Bhutan	55.10	Mali	25.30	Haiti	25.30	Portugal	1.76
East Timor	45.39	Burkina	51.05	Guatemala	16.22	Albania	1.11
Nepal	45.18	Burundi	48.97	Brazil	16.09	Italy	0.38
Bangladesh	30.12	Uganda	45.31	Dominican	16.06	Hungary	0.17
Pakistan	17.67	Niger	45.17	Bolivia	14.36	Rumonia	0.17
Thailand	16.22	Ethiopia	42.30	Nicaragua	14.05	Solomon Islands	28.89
India	14.37	Kenya	41.27	Paraguay	7.87	Papua New Guinea	19.31
China	11.55	Senegal	31.36	Mexico	6.73	Polynesia	3.67
Indonesia	9.55	Zimbabwe	29.44	Colombia	6.62	Turkey	24.00
Vietnam	9.12	Nigeria	25.75	Costa Rica	5.48	Yemen	20.15
Philippine	8.04	Cameroon	25.25	Argentia	4.53	Syrian Arab Rep.	5.78
Malayasia	3.16	CoteD' voire	20.46	Peru	2.48	Iran	4.71
Hong Kong	0.00	Zambia	16.27	Uruguay	2.08	Iraq	2.95
Japan	0.00	Ghana	13.27	Venezuela	0.95	Jordan	0.68
		Egypt	11.23	Chile	0.00	Saudi Arabia	0.00
		Morocco	5.61	Cuba	0.00		
		Algeria	1.63				
		South Africa	0.00				
		Tunisia	0.00				

Source : Economically active population, Estimates and projections, 1950-2010. Fourth edition (Unpublished data available from the ILO Bureau of Statistics), International Labour Office, Geneva, as reported in ILO, World of Work, No. 16, 1996, p.13

Note : Labour Force Participation Rages (age-group 10-14 years) for India, according to NSS 50th Round, 1993-94, were 11.4 per cent for Males and 10.5 per cent for Females.

or 80 million are in Africa and 7 per cent or 17.5 million, live in Latin America. These estimates are based on a new and more accurate methodology recently tested by the ILO's Bureau of Statistics in Ghana, India, Pakistan, Senegal and Turkey[5]. Child Labour as a per cent of child population (age group 10-14 years and in some cases 10-16 years) in different parts of the world as per ILO's estimates for 1995 is reported in Table 1.1. The proportions in Africa are generally higher than those in Asia and elsewhere. Within Asia the range is quite large from virtually zero in Japan to over 45 per cent in Nepal and East Timor.

It is difficult to give a prestige estimate of the overall magnitude of child labour in India on account of numerous limitations, such as, the predominance of the informal and unorganized nature of the labour market, multiplicity of concepts, methods of estimation and sources of data etc. However, as per the data furnished in Table 1.2 the child labour estimates are 10.74 million in 1971. By 1996 the estimated figure has gone upto 140 million. The reasons for variation in the estimation of the magnitude of child labour are many as stated above.

Table 1.2
Magnitude of Child Labour as Estimated by Different Organizations

Year	*Extent of Child Labour*	*Organization*
1971	10.74 Million	Census
1972-73	16.33	27th Round of N.S.S.
1975	15.10	I.L.O.
1981	13.60	Census
1983	17.36	38th Round of N.S.S.
1983	44.00	ORG, Baroda
1985	111.00	Balai Manila
1987-88	17.02	43th Round of N.S.S.
1991	23.02	D.P. Chaudhari
1994	20.00	Labour Ministry
1995	74.80	CACL
1996	140.00	Rashmi Sehgal
1996	35.00	UNICEF
1997	73.00	UNICEF

Source : Quoted in R.R. Patel, "Eliminating Child Labour: Some National and International Limitations", *Social Change*, Vol. 27, No. 3-4, Sept-Dec. 1997, p. 174.

In India the size of child labour force is not only large but it has been increasing from year to year inspite of ILO's conventions, labour legislation and India's commitment to universal and compulsory education upto the age of 14 years. According to the report of the committee on child labour (1979) child labour is not a new phenomena to our age. It has existed in one form or the other in all historical time[6]. The extent of child labour in India could be examined by analysing the census data presented in Table 1.3. It is evident that the percentage of child labour to total population is almost stable during 1961-81, but it is declining in case of rural areas and increasing in urban areas. Similarly, the percentage of

Table 1.3
Child Labour in India

Census year	*Rural*	*Urban*	*All*
	A. Percentage of Child Population to Total Population		
1961	34.02	7.01	41.03
1971	34.25	7.77	42.02
1981	30.88	8.66	39.54
	B. Percentage of Child Workers to Total Child Population		
1961	7.59	0.45	8.04
1971	4.33	0.34	4.67
1981	4.77	0.40	5.17
	C. Percentage of Child Workers to Total Workers		
1961	7.25	0.42	7.67
1971	5.53	0.43	5.96
1981	5.13	0.43	5.66

Source : Census of India, 1961, 1971, 1981.

child labour to child population declined from 8.04 per cent to 5.17 per cent during 1961-81. Though this sign is observed as prosperity sign for Indian nation, it is evident that the total percentage of child worker to total child population rose from 4.67 per cent to 5.17 per cent during 1971-81. This indicates the lessening of the economic opportunities of poor people in rural areas. Though the percentage of child labour to total workers declined by 2 per cent during 1961-81, the absolute number is increasing. The percentage distribution of child workers in India, by State is furnished in Table 1.4 for the period 1971-91. It can be observed from the table that Andhra Pradesh (14.63%) stands first for the last two decades in terms of percentage of child labour to total child workers in India followed by Uttar Pradesh (12.41%) and Madhya Pradesh (11.90%). The

Table 1.4

State-wise Distribution of Child Labour in India (%)

State	*1971*	*1981*	*1991*
Andhra Pradesh	14.97	14.24	14.63
Assam	2.20	—	2.88
Bihar	9.75	8.04	8.29
Gujarat	4.77	4.50	4.61
Haryana	1.27	1.42	0.96
Himachal Pradesh	0.66	0.73	0.50
Karnataka	7.44	8.26	8.59
J&K	0.65	1.89	—
Kerala	1.03	0.68	0.31
Madhya Pradesh	10.23	12.40	11.90
Maharashtra	9.09	11.37	9.40
Manipur	0.15	0.15	0.15
Meghalaya	0.36	0.33	0.30
Nagaland	0.13	0.19	0.15
Orissa	4.53	5.13	3.98
Punjab	2.14	1.58	1.26
Rajasthan	5.40	5.98	6.81
Sikkim	0.14	0.06	0.05
Tamilnadu	6.56	7.12	0.51
Tripura	0.16	0.18	0.15
Uttar Pradesh	12.21	10.47	12.41
West Bengal	4.71	4.12	6.26
A&N Island	0.01	0.01	0.01
Arunachal Pradesh	0.16	0.13	0.11
Chandigarh	0.01	0.01	0.02
D&N Haveli	0.03	0.03	0.04
Delhi	0.16	0.19	0.24
Daman & Diu	0.07	0.07	0.01
Goa	0.04	0.01	—
Lakshdeep	0.01	0.01	0.01
Mizoram	—	0.05	0.14
Pondicherry	0.01	0.03	0.02
Total	100.00	100.00	100.00

Source : Census Reports of 1971, 1981 and 1991, Government of India, New Delhi.

Child Labour Force Participation Rates (LFPR) for boys and girls for the major states for the period 1961-91 are given in Table 1.5. The variations in labour force participation rates and the states for both boys and girls given are apparent in the table. The data indicates that LFPR have substantially reduced during 1961-91 in the states such as Andhra Pradesh, Rajasthan, Bihar, Madhya Pradesh, Uttar Pradesh, Orissa, Punjab, Tamilnadu, Maharashtra and Karnataka etc. Abundant literature had emerged on the problem, causes and consequences of child labour and the elimination of child labour in India. The principle causes that are noticed in majority of the major studies of child labour are : poverty, illiteracy and ignorance of parents, large size of family, unemployment and under-employment of parents, absence of schemes for family allowance, child labour is cheap, death of parents and other economic and sociological reasons.

Table 1.5
Child Labour Participation Rates
(Percentage in Labour Force)

State	1961		1971		1981		1991	
	Male	*Female*	*Male*	*Female*	*Male*	*Female*	*Male*	*Female*
Andhra Pradesh	24.0	17.4	17.8	10.2	14.2	10.6	9.1	9.4
Bihar	14.9	9.6	10.0	2.8	6.4	2.3	4.7	1.9
Gujarat	11.9	10.6	9.3	4.0	6.8	3.3	4.7	2.7
Haryana	12.3	6.0	7.5	1.0	5.8	1.6	3.0	1.0
Himachal Pradesh	9.3	13.8	6.5	8.9	4.3	6.3	2.2	2.8
Karnataka	18.3	12.6	14.1	5.6	12.1	7.1	8.2	6.5
Kerala	3.4	3.0	2.1	1.8	1.1	1.1	0.5	0.4
Madhya Pradesh	19.3	18.3	12.4	7.3	11.0	7.9	6.6	5.2
Maharashtra	13.6	14.1	8.7	5.8	8.1	7.1	4.1	4.5
Orissa	18.9	10.5	13.5	2.3	10.5	3.5	5.6	2.8
Punjab	14.6	7.1	11.6	0.2	7.6	0.4	4.9	0.5
Rajasthan	21.4	19.8	11.2	4.2	7.8	4.1	4.4	4.3
Tamilnadu	14.5	10.6	9.7	4.6	8.4	6.6	4.4	4.3
Uttar Pradesh	13.3	6.7	8.3	2.3	6.3	1.4	4.6	1.3
West Bengal	7.8	2.0	7.0	1.0	5.6	1.3	5.1	1.8
All India	14.6	10.6	9.9	4.0	8.0	4.4	5.2	3.4

Source: Same as Table 1.4.

The higher the rate of child unempolyment the lower is the rate of adult employment. In many studies it is also observed that the market value of children's labour is less than half the value for adults. Apart from employment and earnings child labour is directly related to child health and exerts a negative effect on it. It seriously affects children's education and healthy personality development[7]. Further, it results in loss of schooling, mental retardation, physical strain and deprivation of avenues, which are vital for the normal growth of child. Hence, it may be said that child labour is economically unsound as it undercuts adult labour, reduces wages and increases adult unemployment. Consequently, child labour perpetuates poverty—it does not reduce it as it condemns one generation after another to its vicious circle.[8]

The future of the nation depends on the present day children. So every effort need to be made to provide the children a pleasent present and a bright future. Elimination of child labour in India has been attempted by NGOs and the government. National Policy on Child Labour was formulated in 1987, which envisages general developmental programmes for the benefit of child labour. "India has lately set up a National Authority on Elimination of Child Labour (NAECL) and Rs. 850 crores have been earmarked to abolish child labour in hazardous industries by 2000 A.D. The ILO sponsored International Programme for Elimination of Child Labour (IPEC) has given the country Rs. 3.6 million for implementing projects to eliminate child labour. The government also involves non-governmental organisations with grant-in-aid funds to strengthen its national Child Labour Projects (NCLPs)"[9].

Inspite of all these steps the plight of children remains the same. It may be noted that India can have the maximum number of child labour in the world by the end of 2000 AD. Hence certain measures have to be taken to remove children from the labour force. Such measures should be of two types:

(1) immediate and interim measures, and
(2) long term measures.[10]

The immediate and interim measures could be:

(i) prohibition or banning child labour through strict enforcement of Child Labour Act of 1986 and the Bonded Labour (Abolition) System Act 1975,
(ii) ratification of the ILO Convention 138 and Article 32 of the UN Rights of Child,
(iii) withdrawing/stopping all subsidies to industries employing children,
(iv) opening the residential schools for children withdrawn from jobs to give them education and training in vocations of their choice,
(v) providing the families of such children with substitute sources of income,
(vi) compulsory schooling for children in non-hazardous jobs,
(vii) continuous monitoring of the enforcement of law and

the implementation of projects seeking to provide substitute income for the families.

The long term measures for total elimination of child labour from the Indian society could be the following:

(a) creation of employment opportunities for adult unemployed,
(b) introduction of compulsory primary education upto the age of 14 as per Article 45 of the Constitution,
(c) extensive and intensive rural and urban community development programmes that create gainful employment for adults,
(d) entrepreneurial development through financial assistance and training to the poor and those interested/willing to set up their own enterprises or take to self-employment,
(e) opening up of free vocational and industrial training institutes for poor children after they complete compulsory primary education.

References

1. Sudha Kaldate, "Restoring Child Labour Rights to Child Labour", *Social Change,* Sept.-Dec., '97, Vol. 27, Nos. 3-4, p. 67.
2. Rehman, M.N. (1992), *Society, Economy and Education of Deprived,* Anupama Publishers, Delhi.
3. Subramanian, M.S. "Work Force Participation of Child Labour in the Rural Economy of India", *The Indian Journal of Labour Economics,* Vol. 33, No. 4, 1990, p. 263.
4. U.N. (1981), "Economic and Social Survey of Asia and the Pacific".
5. K. Suman Chandra, "Problems and Issues on Child Labour in India", *Social Change,* Sept.-Dec., 1997, Vol. 27, Nos. 3-4, p. 34.
6. Bhangood, K.S. "Child Labour in India", *Social Change,* Vol. 20, No. 3, Sept. 1990, p. 24.
7. Panigrahi, D.K., "Child Labour in India: A Point of View", *Social Change,* Dec. 1997, Vol. 27, Nos. 3-4, p. 52.
8. Bhatty, Kiran, "Child Labour: Breaking the Vicious Circle", *Economic and Political Weekly,* Feb. 17, 1996, p. 385.
9. Pande, Reeti, "Elimination of Child Labour: Use on Abuse", *Indian Journal of Industrial Relations,* October, 1996, Vol. 32, No. 2, p. 218.
10. B. R. Patil, "Eliminating Child Labour: Some National and International Initiatives", *Social Change,* Sept.-Dec., 1997, Vol. 27, Nos. 3-4, p. 176.

2

Child Labour in India: An Appraisal

—Sukhjinder Singh Tiwana

The problem of child labour in India has attracted considerable attention amongst the social scientists, government and voluntary organisations in the mid-eighties. The debate on the subject was initiated when Government enacted Child Labour (Prohibition and Regulation) Act, 1986 to deal with the problem. Many seminars, workshops, research studies were conducted in different areas with an objective to comprehend the problem. As the Government of India acceded to the U.S. Convention on the Rights of the Child on December 11, 1992, it has now become obligatory for the Government of India to undertake measures to eliminate child labour which has assumed serious proportions in recent years (Dixit, 1993, p. 20). The issue of child labour has become more significant in view of the judgement of the Supreme Court on December 10, 1996 in a writ petition (civil) in which it has given certain directions regarding the manner in which the childrens working in hazardous occupations are to be withdrawn from work and rehabilitated (Sharma, 1997, p. 11).

However the problem of children working in the unorganised sector in rural areas has not received similar attention. Even after draft Agricultural Workers Bill, the successive Union Governments failed to enact a Central legislation for agricultural workers. In

1982, the Congress Government directed the State Governments to plan appropriate legislation to regulate the working conditions and to provide for the welfare of the agricultural workers. Subsequently, only one state Tripura enacted a legislation: Tripura Agricultural Workers Act, 1986. Tripura thus became the second State to have a legislation for agricultural workers, the other State being Kerala which passed its Agricultural Workers Act in 1974 (John, 1997, p. 5).

Hazards of Child Labour: A Global View

As the experience of several countries in Africa, Asia and Latin America shows, legislative measures have failed to eliminate child labour even from those occupations considered hazardous. New industries and fields are being affected by the menace of child labour. Following are a few examples of the menace:

(a) Mining

Child labour is used in small scale mines in many countries in Africa, Asia and Latin America. Child miners work long hours without adequate protective equipments, clothing or training. They are also exposed to high humidity levels and extreme temperatures. Mining hazards include exposure to harmful dusts, gases and fumes that cause respiratory diseases that can develop intosilicosis, pulmonary fibrosis, asbertos and emphysema after some years of exposure. Child miners also suffer physical strain, fatigue and musculo-skeletal disorder as well as serious injuries from falling objects. Children working in gold mines are endangered by mercury poisoning.

(b) Ceramics and Glass Factory Work

Child labour in these industries is common in Asia but also can be found in other regions. Children carry molten loads of glass dragged from tank furnaces at a temperature of 1500-1800 degrees centigrade. They also work for long hours in rooms with poor lightning and little or no ventilation. The noise level from glass-pressing can be as high as 100 decibles or more, causing hearing impairment.

The main hazards in this industry are exposure to high temperatures leading to heat stress, cataracts, burns and lacerations, injuries from broken glass and fly glass particles, hearing impairment from noise, eye injuries and eye strains from poor lightning and exposure to silica dust, lead and toxic fumes such as carbon monoxide and sulpher dioxide (N.A., 1997, p. 16).

(c) Matches and Firework Industry

Production of matches normally takes place in small cottage units or in small scale village factories where the risk of fire and explosion is present all the time. Children as young as three years of age are reported to work in match factories in unventilated rooms where they are exposed to dust, fume, vapours and airborne concentrations of hazardous substances—asbestos, potassium chlorate, antimony tri-sulphide, amorphous red phosphorous mixed with sand or powdered glass, tetraphosphorus trisulphide intoxication and dermatitis from these substances are frequent.

(d) Deep-Sea Fishing

In many Asian countries especially Myanmar (Burma), Indonesia, the Philippines and Thailand, children are working in muro-amifishing which involves deep-sea diving without the use of protective equipment. Children are used to bang on coral reefs to scare the fish into nets. Each fishing ship employs up to 300 boys between 10 and 15 years old recruited from poor neighbourhoods. Divers reset the nets several times a day, so that the children are often in the water for up to 12 hours. Dozens of children are killed or injured each year from drowning or from decompression illness or other fatal accidents from exposures to high atmospheric pressure. Predatory fish such as Sharks, barracudad, needly-fish and poisonous sea snakes also attack the children (*Ibid.*, p. 16).

(e) Child Domestic Workers

Child domestic service is a widespread practice in many developing countries, with employers in cities often recruiting children from villages through family friends and contacts. Violence and sexual abuse are among the most serious and frightening hazards facing children at work, especially those in domestic service. Such abuse leads to permanent psychological and emotional damages.

There are no estimates on how many children are employed in domestic service because of "hidden" nature of the work, but the practice, especially in the case of girls, is certainly extensive. For example, studies in Indonesia estimate that there are around 4,00,000 child domestic workers in Jakarta and up to 5 million in the country as a whole. In Brazil, 22 per cent of all working children are in domestic service, and in Venezuela, 60 per cent of all working girls between 10 and 14 years are in domestic service (Geeta, 1985, p. 212).

(f) Construction

Children undertaking heavy work, carrying massive loads and maintaining awkward body positions for a long time can develop deformation of the spinal column. Sometimes, the pelvis can also be deformed, because of excessive stress being placed on the bones before the epiphysis has fused. Children working in construction and other fields are exposed to other toxic and carcinogenic substances, including asbestos, one of the best known of human carcinogens.

Child Labour in India

Though the practice of child labour is widely prevalent in many of the Third World Countries such as China, Pakistan, Bangla Desh, Nepal and Brazil, India has come to acquire the nasty distinction of possessing the largest child labour force. Large scale employment of the children below the age of 14 is predominantly found in glass, carpet-weaving, match and fireworks, beedis, bangle and also in rural such as construction, brick, iron ore and red oxide mines, tile manufacturing units (*Ismail*, 1995, p. 29).

According to 1981 Census, the estimated figure of working children was 13.6 million whereas in 1991, it was reduced to 11.28 million as is indicated in Table 2.1.

The state with the highest child labour population in the country is Andhra Pradesh which had 1.66 million working children. Other states where child labour population is more than one million are Madhya Pradesh, Maharashtra and Uttar Pradesh. More than 90 per cent of the child labour is engaged in rural areas, in agriculture and allied employments like—cultivation, agricultural labour, livestock, forestry and fisheries.

Table 2.1
State-wise Distribution of Working Children According to 1981 and 1991 Census

State/Union Territories	*1981*	*1991*		
	Workers	*Main Workers*	*Marginal Workers*	*Total Workers*
1. Andhra Pradesh	1,951,312	1,537,293	124,647	1,661,940
2. Assam	*	259,953	67,645	327,598
3. Bihar	1,101,764	795,444	146,801	942,245
4. Gujarat	616,913	373,027	150,558	523,585
5. Haryana	194,189	89,030	20,661	109,691
6. Himachal Pradesh	99,624	30,771	25,667	56,438
7. Jammu & Kashmir	258,437	*	*	*
8. Karnataka	1,131,530	818,159	158,088	976,247
9. Kerala	92,854	28,590	6,210	34,800
10. Madhya Pradesh	1,698,597	997,940	354,623	1,352,563
11. Maharashtra	1,557,756	805,847	262,571	1,068,418
12. Manipur	20,217	13,478	3,015	16,493
13. Meghalaya	44,916	30,730	3,903	34,633
14. Nagaland	16,235	16,106	370	16,476
15. Orissa	702,293	325,250	127,144	452,394
16. Punjab	216,939	132,414	10,454	142,868
17. Rajasthan	819,605	490,522	283,677	774,199
18. Sikkim	8,561	5,254	344	5,598
19. Tamilnadu	975,055	523,125	55,764	578,889
20. Tripura	24,202	13,506	2,972	16,478
21. Uttar Pradesh	1,434,675	1,145,087	264,999	1,410,086
22. West Bengal	605,263	593,387	118,304	711,691
23. Andaman & Nicobar Island	1,309	758	507	1,265
24. Arunachal Pradesh	17,950	11,632	763	12,395
25. Chandigarh	1,986	1,839	31	1,870
26. Dadra & Nagar Haveli	3,615	2,677	1,739	4,416
27. Delhi	25,717	26,670	681	27,351
28. Daman and Diu	9,378	741	200	941
29. Goa	*	3,938	718	4,656
30. Lakshadweep	56	17	17	34
31. Mizoram	6,314	6,391	10,020	16,411
32. Pondicherry	3,606	2,565	115	2,680
Total	13,640,870	9,082,141	2,203,208	11,285,349

* Cencus could not be conducted.

Source: *Annual Report of the Ministry of Labour 1996-97*, New Delhi, Government of India Publication, p. 100.

Constitutional Provisions and Policy Framework

India has followed a proactive policy in the matter of tackling the problem of child labour. India has always stood for constitutional, statutory and developmental measures that are required to eliminate child labour. Six International Labour Organisation (ILO) conventions relating to child labour have been ratified and three of them as early as first quarter of the 20th century. The framers of the Indian Constitution consciously incorporated relevant provisions in the Constitution to secure compulsory universal elementary education as well as labour protection for children.

Article 24 states, "No child below the age of fourteen years shall be employed to work in any factory or mine or engaged in any other hazardous employment."

The Constitution of India in its Directive Principles of State Policy in Article 39(e) and (f) pledged that (e) the health and strength of workers, men and women, and the tender age of children are not abused and that citizens are not forced by economic necessity to enter avocations unsuited to their age or strength; and that (f) children are given opportunities and facilities to develop in a healthy manner and in conditions of freedom and dignity and that childhood and youth are protected against exploitation and against moral and material abandonment.

Article 45 states that, "state shall endeavour to provide, within a period of ten years from the commencement of this Constitution, free and compulsory education for all children until they complete the age of fourteen years" (Sachdeva, 1992, p. 612).

The policy of the Government is to ban employment of children below the age of 14 years in factories, mines and hazardous employments and to regulate the working conditions of children in other employments. The Child Labour (Prohibition & Regulation) Act, 1986 seeks to achieve this basic objective. Through a notification on May 26, 1993 the working conditions of children have been regulated in all employments which are not prohibited under the Child Labour (Prohibition and Regulation) Act, 1986 (T.T., 1993 p. 6.)

Evolution of India's Child Labour Policy

Labour Commissions and Committees have gone into the problem of child labour and made extensive recommendations. The various laws adopted by Indian Government to check the evil of child labour have a pragmatic foundation and are consistent with International Labour Conference Resolution of 1979 which calls for a combination of prohibitory measures and measures of humanising child labour wherever the same cannot be outrightly eliminated in the short run.

The question of the regulation of the conditions of work for labour was first broached in 1875 by the appointment of a Committee by the Bombay Government. It only provided for the regulation of the working hours of the children below twelve years of age and it prohibits the employment of the children below seven years (Gupta, 1987, p. 91). In 1891 another Act was passed which applied to units having 50 or more workers. The minimum age for children was fixed at nine and hours of work were seven for children between nine and fourteen years of age. However, the smaller units where the worst child abuses existed, were not covered by the Act.

India became one of the founder members of the International Labour Organisation (ILO) and was a signatory to the first convention on the prohibition of child labour in 1919. Since than a number of Acts have been passed in India dealing with child Labour. The ILO has adopted 18 conventions and 16 recommendations with regard to child labour so far.

Legislation relating to the regulation of child labour concentrates mainly on four basic issues, which are:

(a) Minimum age for employment of children;
(b) Maximum period of work per day and forbidding work at night;
(c) Prohibition of employment of young persons as trimmers and stokers in vessels or ports; and
(d) Compulsory medical examination of children and young persons employed at sea.

The Children (Pledging of Labour) Act, 1933

This Act prohibits the pledging of labour of children for employment. It also prescribes penalty for persons and guardians pledging child labour. The penalty will be Rs. 200 on employer and Rs. 50 on guardians. A child is defined in the Act as a person who is under the age of fifteen years.

The Employment of Children Act, 1938

To prevent employment of children in hazardous employments and those injurious to health, the Employment of Children Act, 1938 prohibits their employment in certain occupations. It prohibits the employment of children below 15 years in certain occupations connected with the transport of passengers, goods or mails by railways connected with port authority within the limits of any port or connected with any work of railway premises.

The Factories Act, 1948

The Factories Act 1948 prohibits the employment of children below 14 years in factory. The Act requires persons between the age of 14 years to 18 years to obtain a certificate of fitness from a certifying surgeon and periodical examination. The Act prohibits employing children between 14 and 17 years at night (between 10 p.m.—6 a.m.) between 14 and 15 years for not more than 4½ hours in any day, only one shift and in one factory. The Act prohibits employing children in certain processes within factories. They shall not be allowed to work on machines which are considered dangerous. They shall not clean, lubricate or adjust any part of prime mover or of any transmission machinery while it is in motion or if they stand the risk of injury. They shall not be employed to press cotton if a cotton opener is at work in that area (Pandhe, 1979, p. 2).

Adoption and Enactment of the Constitution of India 1949, by the Constituent Assembly

In 1949, the Constituent Assembly of India adopted and enacted a Constitution of India, 1949 which was enforced on January 26, 1950. The Indian Constitution prohibits the employment of children below 14 years of age in factories, mines and hazardous employments in terms of Fundamental Rights and Directive Principles laid down against the abuse of the tender age of the children until 14 years of age.

National Labour Commission, 1969

The National Labour Commission in its report submitted to the Union Government in 1969 recommended combination of work with education and flexible employment hours which would not inhibit education.

Report of Gurupadswamy Committee, 1979

Gurupadswamy Committee in its report submitted in 1979 recommended:

(a) Setting up of Child Labour Advisory Boards,
(b) Fixation of minimum age of entry to any establishment;
(c) Strengthening of enforcement machinery;
(d) Formulation of effective educational policy with emphasis on integration of educational requirements with local crafts.

Establishments of the Central Child Labour Advisory Board, 1981

Following the recommendations of the Gurupadswamy Committee on Child Labour, the Government of India established a special Central Child Labour Advisory Board in March, 1981 to:

(a) Review the implementation of the existing laws;
(b) To suggest legislative and administrative measures for working children;
(c) To review progress of welfare measures; and
(d) To recommend industries where child labour should be eliminated.

The Child Labour (Prohibition and Regulation) Act, 1986

The objective of the Child Labour (Prohibition and Regulation) Act, 1986 was to ban employment of children below the age of 15 years in factories, mines and hazardous employment and to regulate the working conditions of the children in other employment. The Act defines "Child" as a person who has not completed his fourteen years of age. The Act provides for the setting up of the "Child Labour Technical Advisory Committee" for the purpose of addition of occupations and processes to the Schedule. A notice of atleast three months will be given by Central Government before adding any occupation or process to the Schedule (S, 1988, p. 12).

The Child Labour (Prohibition and Regulation) Act, 1986 does not ban child labour even in hazardous industries but only in hazardous processes. Domestic labour, family labour, agricultural labour or hotel labour is not banned at all. The Act does not prohibit children working in match box and firework industry in

Sivakasi, glass factory in Ferozabad or carpet industry in Mirzapur and Kashmir, but only in hazardous processes in them. The Act, in fact, offers little protection to the children (Dhagamwar, 1997, p. 33).

National Policy on Child Labour, 1987

The Government announced the National Policy on Child Labour in August, 1987. The action plan under the National Child Labour Policy comprises:

(a) A legislative action plan;
(b) Focussing of general development programmes for benefitting children wherever possible; and
(c) Projection-based action plans in areas of high concentration of child labour engaged in wage and quasi-wage employment.

Under the project based action plan, 12 National Child Labour Projects (NCLP) were started in Andhra Pradesh (Jaggampet and Markapur), Bihar (Garwah), Madhya Pradesh (Mandsaur), Maharashtra (Thane), Orissa (Sambalpur), Rajasthan (Jaipur), Tamilnadu (Sivakasi), and Uttar Pradesh (Varanasi-Mirzapur-Bhadoi, Moradabad, Aligarh and Ferozabad).

A major activity undertaken under the NCLP is the establishment of special schools to provide non-formal education, vocational training, supplementary nutrition, stipend, health care etc. to children withdrawn from employment. In the Eighth Five Year Plan, Rs. 15 crores were provided for the scheme.

With a view to fulfilling the constitutional mandate, a major programme was launched on August 15, 1994 for withdrawing child labour working in hazardous occupations and rehabilitating them through special schools.

National Authority for the Elimination of Child Labour (NAECL)

It was constituted on September 26, 1994 under the Chairmanship of Union Labour Minister. The functions of NAECL are:

(a) To lay down policies and programmes for elimination of child labour particularly in hazardous employments;

(*b*) To monitor the progress of implementation of programmes, projects and schemes for elimination of child labour; and
(*c*) To co-ordinate implementation of child labour related projects of the various sister Ministries of the Government of India to ensure convergence of services for the benefit of the families of child labour.

Secretaries to Government of India in the Ministries of Labour, Information and Broadcasting, Welfare, Rural Development, Textiles and the Departments of Expenditure, Education, Health, Family Welfare and Women and Child Development are members of the National Authority for the Elimination of Child Labour. The NAECL in its meeting on January 16, 1995 adopted a programme of securing convergence of services of the Ministries of Government of India and Departments of the State Governments which implement child related programmes at the national, state and field levels (*Ibid.*, p. 101).

Response of Judiciary against the Practice of Child Labour

The need for concerted action on the part of all social partners has been emphasised by the Supreme Court. The Supreme Court, in its judgment on December 10, 1996 in a writ petition (civil) No. 465/1986 has given certain directions regarding the manner in which the children working in the hazardous occupations are to be withdrawn from work and rehabilitated as also the manner in which the working conditions of the children working in non-hazardous occupations are to be regulated and improved upon. The important directions given in the judgment include payment of compensation amounting to Rs. 20,000 by the offending employer for every child employed in contravention of the provisions of the Act, constitution of the child Labour Rehabilitation-cum-Welfare Fund, giving alternative employment to an adult member of the family in place of the child withdrawn from the hazardous occupation or payment of an amount of Rs. 5,000 for each child employed in hazardous employment, by the appropriate government, completion of the survey of children working in hazardous employments within a period of six months, payment of interest on the corpus of Rs. 25,000 (Rs. 20,000 to be paid by the employer and Rs. 5,000 to be paid by the appropriate Government) to the family of the child withdrawn from work, provision of education in a suitable institution for the child withdrawn from work, constitution of a separate cell in the Labour Department of the appropriate Government for the purpose of monitoring etc. (T.I., 1996 p. 1).

As a follow up of the directions of the Supreme Court, all the State Governments have sent detailed guidelines on December 26, 1996 indicating the manner in which the directions of Supreme Court could be given effect to. A meeting of the NAECL was convened on December 31, 1996 to discuss the directions of Supreme Court on child Labour. It was, *inter alia,* decided in the meeting that the Ministry of Labour should immediately release funds to the State Governments so as to enable them to conduct surveys of working children before June 10, 1997 and Ministry of Labour would keep the Supreme Court informed of the action taken by the Central and the State Governments from time to time (I.E., 1997, p. 1).

Despite various measures undertaken by the Government to tackle the exploitation of children, India has the dubious distinction of having the largest child labour force in the world.

India has failed to tackle the problem of child labour due to wrong policies adopted by the successive Union Governments. Systematic destruction of rural life, menacing spread of urbanisation, commercialisation of education, callous attitude towards various poverty alleviation schemes etc. are the causative factors behind the alarming spread of child labour, forced labour and bonded labour. The various acts enacted by the Government in India to tackle the problem of child labour have remained unoperative due to the following reasons.

(a) Since dire poverty and destitution are the main causes of child labour, Labour inspectors feel sympathetic to the problems of the families. They find themselves in a kind of moral dilemma because the parents, more than the employers, plead that their children should be allowed to bring some little relief to their miserable conditions. Even if the child does not work, he will not be better off; he will starve and be the target of the wrath and frustration of adults.

(b) Besides, the schools also do not offer any relief from this miserable condition—no food, no play, no sympathy. On

the contrary, children of the economically and socially backward sections are treated in a discriminatory manner by teachers and school authorities.

(c) Most children work in the unorganised sector. There is no official record of the number of children working and no proof of the extended working hours, absence of holidays and hazardous working conditions (Alam, 1995, p. 8).

Indian law prohibits the employment of children below 14 years in factories, but there is no law protecting children from working in cottage industries, family households, restaurants or in agriculture or from rotting on the streets and in the slums. Why has the state not taken prohibitive action when the Indian Constitution calls for a ban on child labour and for compulsory primary school education? Poverty of the parents is cited as the main cause. Government officials and even social workers argue that it would be inhuman not to allow an extremely poor family that little bit of extra income which a child can bring. But why couldn't steps be taken in as long a period as 50 years and with as many as Eight Five-Year Plans, to improve the economic conditions of the majority, if not of all people? Why could not adults be given enough jobs with proper wages so that their children do not have to supplement the family income?

Suggestions to Combat Child Labour in India

1. India should have a statutory National Minimum Wage (a living wage) equal atleast to the first-day wage of the lowest paid government employee. Subsequent revision due to inflation etc. should also be linked simultaneously. State governments must guarantee all citizens employment at a National Minimum Wage for at least 200 days in a year or productive infrastructure building projects. While computing the cost of production of farm produce such as wheat, paddy, sugarcane, cotton etc., the government should calculate National Minimum Wage as the basis for all human labour. This will mean not only economic justice to the poorest sections but also greater unity between the farmers and agricultural labourers, leading towards social integration.
2. All means of mass communication, particularly

Doordarshan and Akashvani should disseminate all aspects of National Minimum wage in all languages and dialects on a regular basis. This will empower the voiceless and unorganised labour to galvanise and unionise themselves and fight for a rightful place in the society.

3. For combating child labour, it is suggested that Indian Government should give national priority to education and social services. Government should commit itself to universalisation of free and compulsory elementary education for all children upto the age of fourteen years with training in productive skills.
4. Some educationists and trade unionists have suggested a compromise between the needs for education and child labour, that the school hours be adjusted so as to make it possible to work and learn. But the danger is that whenever there is a conflict, education will be sacrificed and not work. Either the children will not attend the school at all, or he or she will be too tired to learn anything. Moreover, we should make out our objective to discourage long hours of work for children. There are of course special cases. Helping the family farming is one—it may be necessary to adjust school hours in the busy agricultural season (Dharma, 1988, p. 35).

In order to attract all the child labour to schools and to guard against drop-outs, a Food for Education Scheme should be launched with atleast one kilogram of rice or wheat to every child for every day of schooling. This scheme will provide the poor parents food security and also strength for fighting against the social evil of child labour.

To conclude, the experience of several countries of the Third World shows that legislative measures have failed to eliminate child labour. In India the child labour force is the highest in the world due to wrong policies adopted by successive Union Governments in India. Poverty has been identified as a major factor compelling parents to send their children to work. Lack of awareness and educational opportunity and ineffective enforcement of child labour related laws contribute to the existence and acceptance of this social evil. Basically, it is the exploitation of cheap labour which motivates large-scale employment of the children. Unless the Government realises its responsibility, the practice of child labour cannot be eliminated. There is an urgent need to mount a massive onslaught against poverty and ignorance. The improvement in the living and working conditions of parents and improvement in their economic conditions is considered crucial to the elimination of child labour.

It is the duty of the Government to convert working children into productive and participative members of the society. For fulfillment of this objective, the Government should pay more attention towards rehabilitation measures. Proper education facilities should be provided to the children. NGOs, trade unions and grassroot workers belonging to various political parties should also be involved in accomplishing this task.

Notes and References

Alam, Jayanti, (1995), "Child Labour: Compulsory Schooling is the Only Solution," *Mainstream,* Vol. XXXIII, No. 16, March 11, p. 8.

Dixit, J.N., (1993), "Government Promoting Rights of the Child," *Mainstream,* Vol. XXXI, No. 47, p. 20.

Indian Express, (1997), Chandigarh, June 11, p. 1.

Ismail, A.R.M., (1995), "Child Labour in India," *Mainstream,* Vol. XXXIII, No. 52, November 18, p. 29.

John, J. (1997), "Recognising Labour Rights of Agricultural Workers: The Ignominious Delay," *New Age,* February 23—March 1, p. 5.

Kumar, Dharma (1988), "What Can We Do," *Seminar,* No. 350, October, p. 35.

Ministry of Labour, (1996-97), *Annual Report,* New Delhi, Government of India Publication, p. 101.

Ibid., p. 101.

New Age, 1997, February 16-22.

Ibid., p. 16.

Seminar (1988), No. 350, October, p. 12.

Sharma, P.D. (1997), "Hideous World of Child Abuse", *The Tribune,* May 30, p. 11.

The Times of India, (1996), New Delhi January 11, p. 1.

The Tribune, (1993), Chandigarh, May 27, p. 6.

Vasudha Dhagamwar, (1997), "Childhood Denied Under the Law", *Mainstream,* Vol. XXXV, No. 37, August 23, p. 33.

Gupta, Manju (1987), "Labour Laws—Brief Description and How They Affect Children," Gupta, Manju and Voll, Klaus (eds.), *Young Hands at Work: Child Labour in India,* Delhi, Atma Ram and Sons, p. 91.

Gupta, Menon (1985), "Health Problems of Working Children: Some Observation", Naidu, Usha and Kamini, R. (eds.), *Child Labour and Health: Problems and Prospects*, Bombay, Tata Institute of Social Sciences, p. 212.

Pandhe, M.K., (1979), *Child Labour in India*, Calcutta, Indian Book Exchange p. 2.

Sachdeva, D.R., (1992), *Social Welfare Administration in India*, Allahabad, Kitab Mahal, p. 612.

3

Multi-Dimensional Approach to Child Labour in India

—Harindra Kishor Mishra

Children are the most lovely creation of nature. They are universally recognised as the greatest assets of any nation and are also the future of the nation. They are flowers of our national garden. Every child is an asset to the society and the future welfare of the society depends on the welfare of the child. Jawaharlal Nehru once said, "But somehow the fact that ultimately everything depends on the human factor, gets rather lost in our thinking of plans and schemes of national development in terms of factories and machinery and general schemes. It is all very important and we must have them, but ultimately of course, it is the human being that counts, and if human being counts, well, he counts much more as a child than as a grown up."[1]

The system of child labour is a measuring rod of any economy, curse for children and slur for modern and civilised society. Child labour is a global phenomenon. The problem has assumed serious dimensions in developing countries. In India the system of child labour is very old. The process exists till today and childhood of crores of children is being crushed in the dark race of modernity. Children were required to do some work either at home or in the field alongwith their parents from ancient times. We find in Manusmriti and Arthashastra that the king made education of every child, boy or girl, compulsory and Kautilya prohibited the trade of children, who were purchased and converted to slaves by some people. The problem of child labour marked as a grave problem in the 19th century when the first factory was started in the mid-19th century.

Concept

The term 'Child labour' is at times, used as a synonym for employing child or working child. The children who are engaged in employment at the age of fourteen years or below the age of fourteen deprived them the opportunities of development, are called child labour. Generally there are two kinds of child labour: traditionally to assist in work by the children alongwith their parents and works done by the children outside the family for kind or cash remuneration to raise the income of the family. According to V.V. Giri, "the term child labour is commonly interpreted in two different ways: *First,* as an economic practice and *secondly,* as a social evil."[2]

The committee on child labour constituted under the Chairmanship of Sri Gurupadaswamy observed that, "labour becomes an absolute evil in the case of the child when he is required to work beyond his physical capacity, when hours of employment interferes with his education, recreation and rest, when his wages are not commensurate with the quantum of work done and when the occupation in which he is engaged endangers his health and safety."[3]

The definition provided by the International Labour Organisation seems to be more comprehensive. "Child labour includes children primarily leading adult lives, working long hours for low wages under conditions damaging to their health and to their physical and mental development, sometimes separated from their families, frequently deprived of meaningful educational and training opportunities that could open up for them a better future."[4]

Causes of Child Labour

The socio-economic conditions play a significant role in giving rise to the problem of child labour. It is generally considered that illiteracy, ignorance, low wages, unemployment, low standard of living and social life all are the root cause of child labour. Parents believe that 'more children mean more earning' also help to fast increase in child labour. The low income of parents which is not adequate to meet the basic needs of the family, force the children to work and supplement the family income. In this way poverty compels parents to send their children to distant places to work. The abject poverty and unemployment forces the children to take up un-remunerative jobs which results into many social evils. "Economic compulsions weigh heavily on the consciousness of the poor parents and they would not mind colluding with their children's employers in violating the law and putting their children under the risk of inhuman exploitation. Parents want their children to fend for themselves as early as possible, much better, if they become a source of income to the family."[5]

At an early age the child is put to adult role. They also marry early and breed early thus increasing his family liabilities and liabilities of the whole nation. A recent study conducted in three big cities of Tamilnadu by the students of Madras School of Social Work revealed that "55% of children employed belonged to families with less than Rs. 300 per month and 72% of total children had sought employment to augment the family income."[6] Many employers prefer to engage children because the child labour is cheap, on account of which the employers are encouraged to exploit them. According to an estimate, "If all children are eliminated from the work force in India, there will be additional employment opportunities for atleast 15 million adult unemployed persons."[7] A survey also conducted by National Institute of Public Co-operation and Child Development in Bombay revealed that "the contribution of children to the income of the family in 52% of the families in the monthly income range of Rs. 25 to Rs. 50 was 23%."[8]

Another cause of child labour is the lack of primary educational facilities especially in rural areas. Estimates show that "of the 82 million children in India in the age group of 6 to 14, fewer than half attend school. Of every 10 children who enter the first standard only four complete the first four years of schooling. The net result is that every 18th child in the country becomes a child labourer."[9] A Government report also acknowledges that the incidence of child labour is closely related to the school dropout rate. "At the primary level, the dropout rate is 47% which increases to 64% at the middle school level and a major chunk of these dropouts finds wage employment of somekind."[10]

The most significant cause of employing child labour is a beneficial proposition as it subsidises the cost of production. They are easily available for monitoring and control. The committee on child labour has pointed out that "the main cause of child labour are the tradition to engage children in family occupations, chronic poverty, preference of employers to engage children as they are more amenable to discipline and control and are cheaper."[11]

Magnitude

In India, many attempts have been made by various international agencies like the United Nations, International Labour Organisation and the Red Cross Society, the Government (Census, National Sample Survey, Planning Commission) and many other voluntary organisations to estimate the extent of child labour. Inspite of such efforts, accurate and detailed statistics relating to the number of children employed in agriculture, trade, industry, mining, transport, etc. are not available.

The assumption that child labour goes on only in the poor nations is a myth but in rich nations it is surprisingly high. The U.K. and U.S.A. have registered a rise in the number of children entering their work force. The UNICEF report on the state of the world's children says that "in the United Kingdom, the most reliable estimates available show that between 15 and 26 per cent of children aged 11 years and between 36 and 66 per cent of children aged 15 years are working. And the US general accounting office showed a 250 per cent increase in child labour violations between 1983 and 1990. In a three day operation in 1990, the US department of labour discovered more than 11,000 children working illegally."[12] Industrialised nations always claim that having completely eradicated the harsher forms of child labour and thus preach the poorer nations that they should follow their example seems totally false. According to the latest International Labour Organisation report, "Child Labour figures to an astounding 250 million. Out of the 250 million, about 120 million are working full-time while 130 million work part time. The report, *'Child Labour:* Targetting the Intolerable' says Asia accounts for 153 million working children; Africa about 80 million and Latin America about 17.5 million."[13]

This social malaise is fast assuming appalling proportions throughout the developing world. According to the International Labour Organisation report, "a shocking 125 million children toil in hazardous employment such as in the production of glass, brass, locks, fireworks, matches, carpets and bidis in industrial units scattered across much of Asia, Africa and Latin America. India alone has over 100 million such children."[14]

In Calcutta, Fourth Asian Conference on Child Exploitation and Abuse was organised by the Institute of Psychological and Educational Research (IPER), in collaboration with the Government of India and West Bengal besides the UNICEF. The conference will have delegates from Asian countries and social activists from European countries. IPER provided statistics which was based on Times International show that "India heads the list of Asian countries having child labour ranging between 73 million and 115 million. Pakistan accounts for 8 m., Nepal 5.7m., China 5m., Bangladesh 2.8m., Indonesia 2.4m., Thailand 1.1m. and Srilanka 5 lakh."[15]

India harbours the largest number of children in servitude. In India the highest number of children working in organised and unorganised sector. Official estimates put the number of child workers at around 25 million, but NGOs insist that it is atleast 55 million. After studying the situation recently in major areas where child labour is prevalent in hazardous industries. The National Human Rights Commission focussed on the Ferozabad district in U.P. "Where about 50,000 children are working in the glass/ bangles industry. The NHRC is extremely pessimistic whether it would be possible to free two million children in such industries from bondage by 2000. India's carpet industry, concentrated around Varanasi, employs about 3,00,000 children. Besides, there is a large army of children employed over a wide spectrum from agriculture to hotel industry to domestic work."[16]

According to 1991 census, the number of working children are 11.28 million. As per 1991 census, the state with the highest child labour population in the country is Andhra Pradesh which had 1.66 million working children. Other states where child labour population is more than one million are Maharashtra, Madhya Pradesh and U.P. More than 90% of the child labour is engaged in rural areas, in agriculture and allied employments like cultivation, agricultural labour, forestry, livestock and fisheries. According to the 1981 census, about 86.4% of child workers are employed in agriculture and allied activities.

Systems of bonded child workers continue to exist in different parts of India. Most often children enter the stage of bondage to pay off parents petty debts, sometimes in the range of Rs. 500 to

Rs. 2,000. According to the study, "there are 3.25 lakh child workers (over 50 per cent bonded) in the bidi industry, which has a turnover of Rs. 4,000 crores; 10,000 bonded children in the Steel Industry in Salem (Tamilnadu) which has a turnover of Rs. 50 lakhs; several thousands in the leather industry, which has an annual earning of 2.5 billion; 1.6 lakhs (over one lakh bonded) in the gem cutting trade which has a turnover of Rs. 10 crores; 2.5 lakhs in the silk industry, having earning of $ 650 million. Agriculture accounts for over half of the bonded child workers."[17]

Evils of Child Labour

Though our country is celebrating its fiftieth year of independence, there are so many grave problems that are still existing in our society. Child Labour is one of them. While some health-work in childhood may be a social good and a national gain, child labour is a great social ill and a national waste as "the economic necessity for wage earning to support the family deprives the child an opportunity for education, wholesome play and recreation; stunts his physical growth, interferes with the normal development of his personality and thwarts his preparation for adult responsibility."[18]

According to the International Labour Organisation, "Worldwide, as many as 200 million children from the ages of 10 to 14 are working in jobs that are dangerous, unhealthy and often inhumane."[19]

India is facing increasingly the problem of child labour with growing urbanisation. They are engaged in the manufacture of glass, locks, fireworks, bangles, carpet and in making 'bidis'. Few people are aware that "the children are working in 3,600 authorised and 30,000 unauthorised slaughter houses in cities and towns."[20]

Working in the hazardous occupations like carpet, brassware, lock, matches, pottery, gems, fireworks, powerloom, handloom, etc; the children contract various diseases like tuberculosis, acid burns, asthma, acute headaches, breathlessness, sillicosis, pneumonia, eye defects, muscle wastage etc. Besides children who work with dangerous machines and chemicals and furnaces with high temperatures run the risk of getting involved in accident. Sivakasi is a classic example of children work in horrendous conditions. In 8,000 match units in Sivakasi region, 80,000 children comprise half the number of employees in these factories. These children literally play with fire every minute of their lives. They have to work for 10 to 12 hours for just Rs. 5 to 7 per day. They inhale toxic fumes and suffer from intense heat."[21]

In glass factories and carpet industries, child labour suffers from immense pitiable condition. "The glass factories of Firozabad in U.P. which produce glass jars, bangles, beads, bulbs, containers, employ more than 60,000 children. These children work barefoot in a temperature of 1,400°C near the furnaces. And in the carpet industry of Mirzapur, Bhadoi, Palamau and Varanasi, about 1,00,000 child labourers work from 12 to 16 hours at a stretch. They only get Rs. 7 to 10 per day. Meagre wages combined with high craftsmanship kept these children far away from the world's crafts."[22]

The same shabby story of innocent and helpless children exists in Moradabad brassware, bidi making units in U.P. and in lock industries of Aligarh, Karnataka and Tamilnadu. They also work in shops, restaurants and homes from dawn to dusk.

The working conditions for child labourers are awful. The child workers are not openly abused but many times tortured and beaten by their employers. They are forced to work overtime in poorly ventilated places, dimly-lit dirty surroundings and emerging metal gases. These make them prematurely old and even drag them towards death before time. The wages of child workers are also very low—generally 30% to 50% of the wages of adults. "In tea plantations, the wages of children have been between 37 p. to 50 p. per day in Assam and between 50 p. to 62 p. in South India. In coffee plantations, the wages of children have now been fixed at 60 p. per day, while formerly they were only 25 p. per day. In Coffee plantations in Mysore, children get 48 p. per day and in rubber plantations, between 37 p. to 42 p. per day. In shellac industry, the wages have been about 50 p. and in bidi industry 20 p. to 37 p. per day."[23] It is evident that the wages of children are extremely low. The situation has not changed much since then.

The problem of sexual harassment of girl child is very alarming. A recent report from Manila said that in Asia alone there are more than one million children in prostitution. UNICEF made violence against women and girls as the main thrust of its fifth annual report because sexual violence is a major obstacle to social and economic development and has corrosive effects on children. "It is every where, in every conceivable form, from assault, rape, sexual slavery and domestic abuse to torture, mutilation and disfigurement, even murder."[24]

The problem of exploitation of the girl child in flesh trade has come with the growing urbanisation on the Indian scene. The spurt in tourism has given encouragement to child prostitution. India has four lakhs child prostitutes including 40,000 in Mumbai alone. In rural areas when the girl child goes for fuel collection and even for natural call in the open field they are harassed physically as well as sexually by local hudlooms and anti-social elements. Generally minor girls from weaker sections of the society are the main victims of this social system.

Rights of the Child and Legislative Measures

In India protection of rights of the child is not a new concept. In March 1931 Lahore session of the Congress, Mahatma Gandhi presided over 20 resolutions to protect the rights of children. The framers of the constitution were consciously aware about the rights of the child. It was enshrined in our constitution in its directive principles.

"Article 24 prohibits the employment of children in factories etc. It also says that no child below the age of fourteen years shall be employed to work in any factory or mine or engaged in any other hazardous employment.

Article 39 says that the state shall, in particular, direct its policy towards securing (e) that the health and strength of workers, men and women, and the tender age of children are not abused and that citizens are not forced by economic necessity to enter into a vocation unsuited to their age or strength. And (f) that children are given opportunities and facilities to develop in a healthy manner and in conditions of freedom and dignity and that childhood and youth are protected against exploitation and against moral and material abandonment.

Article 45 has the provision for free and compulsory education for children. It also says that the state shall endeavour to provide, within a period of ten years from the commencement of this constitution, for free and compulsory education for all children until they complete the age of fourteen years."[25]

Human rights organisation, child right activists, religious organisations, consumers, politicians, governments, international organisations like I.L.O., UNICEF, are coming forward to protect the rights of children and stop exploitation of child labour. Internationally, the principle was stated in the Geneva Declaration of 1924 on the Rights of the child. In 1948 it was revised and amplified. In its turn, it formed the basis of the ten-point Declaration on the Rights of the child adopted by the UN General Assembly on November 20, 1959. On November 20, 1989 a convention on the Rights of the child, with which the international community had been involved for several years, came to be adopted by the United Nations General Assembly. "The various articles which are of paramount importance for the mental, physical, emotional, intellectual and educational development of the child are enshrined in Articles 13, 17, 18, 28 and 29 of the UN convention on the Rights of the Child 1989."[26] India has joined the comity of nations in the successive reaffirmations of global commitment to improve the status of children with a vigorous drive and adopted a plan of action.

In India many legislations have been passed from time to time to protect and solve the problem of child labour. They are—The Children (pledging of labour) Act, 1933; The Employment of Children Act, 1938; The Bidi and Cigar Workers (Conditions of Employment) Act, 1966; The Factories Act, 1948; The Mines Act, 1952; The Motor Transport Workers Act; The Child Labour (Prohibition and Regulation) Act, 1986; The Plantations Labour Act, 1951; Minimum Wages Act, 1948. These legislations regulates the working conditions, working hours, wages and services of child labours. The Child Labour (Prohibition and Regulation) Act, 1986 is more effective. Except in the process of family based work or recognised school-based activities, children are not permitted to work in occupations connected with carpet weaving, cement manufacturing, cloth printing, dyeing, weaving, manufacture of matches, explosives, fireworks, Mica cutting, splitting, Wool cleaning, Bidi making, catering establishments in Railway, premises of port limits, building operations, construction, cinder picking, cleaning of ash pits, passenger and goods mail transport by Railway. In occupations and processes, work by children is permissible only for six hours between 8.00 am and 7.00 pm with one day weekly rest. Occupier of establishment employing children to give notice to local inspector and maintain prescribed register. No child shall be required or permitted to work overtime etc. In the present Bill a provision has been made for the Appointment of the Child Labour Technical Advisory Committee and Appointment of inspectors for the purpose of securing compliance with the Provisions of this Bill.

Court's Verdicts

The conditions of the children continue to remain deplorable despite constitutional safeguards. The problem is so grave that the Apex court has shown its concern from time to time for child workers by bringing occupations or processes under the courts order by the direct application of constitutional provisions. Some landmark judgement can be cited.

In *Sheela Barse* Vs *Secretary, Children Aid Society and Others,* 1987, the Supreme Court held, "If there be no proper growth of children of today, the future of the country will be dark. It is the obligation of every generation to bring up children who will be citizens of tomorrow in a proper way. Today's children will be leaders of tomorrow who will hold the country's banner high and maintain the prestige of the nation."[27]

In *M.C. Mehta* Vs *State of Tamilnadu,* 1991, the Supreme Court has not allowed children to work in a prohibited occupation. According to the judges, "the provisions of Article 45 in the Directive Principles of State Policy has still remained a far cry and though according to this provision all children upto the age of 14 years are sponsored to be in school, economic necessity forces grown up children to seek employment. Children can, therefore, be employed in the process of packing but packing should be done in an area away from the place of manufacture to avoid exposure to accident."[28]

On a petition filed by environmentalist lawyer M.C. Mehta the Supreme Court of India. In its judgement dated December 10, 1996 ordered that compensation be paid to each child labourer in nine major industries across the country, is perhaps the most dramatic judicial intervention on the issue in Indian legal history. The Supreme Court recalled Tagore's words in this context, "let the child of the 21st century find himself into that heaven of freedom of which our poet-laureate Rabindra Nath Tagore has spoken in Gitanjali. "The court has directed that every offending employer must play a compensation of Rs. 20,000 to each child under the provisions of the Child Labour (Prohibition and Regulation) Act, 1986. The amount is to be deposited in a Child Labour Rehabilitation cum-Welfare Fund. In addition, the state has been asked to ensure that atleast one adult member of the working child family be employed, failing which Rs. 5,000 be contributed to the fund which is aimed at educating the child. The court said, "We have the fond hope that the closing years of the 20th century would see us keeping the promise made to our children by our constitution about a half century ago."[29] The Court had directed the state governments to complete the survey of working children before 10 June, 1997. It is really a historic judgement as no previous judgement has ever set a time frame for action.

Remedial Steps

The child labour is the most pressing moral issue of the late 20th century. World bodies like the United Nations, ILO, UNICEF, World Bank and World Health Organisation have played an important role in the gradual elimination of Child Labour. But sorry to say little is done in favour of them. Indian Government is determined to root out the problem. Many remedial steps have been taken by the Government and NGOs. India has adopted many meaningful legislations and declarations at policy level. Various committees have been set up from time to time to look into the working conditions and related problems of working children. But the real fact is that every third labour in India is a child. Due to the seriousness of the problem, the Apex Court has also intervened to protect Child Labour. Inaugurating the first regional labour minister's conference of eastern and northern region, Union Labour Minister Mr. Aruna Chalam said, "the whole world is watching our commitment and real efforts for the elimination of Child Labour from the country during the next five years. There is no room for complacency on the part of the Government."[30]

In April 1947, India adopted a resolution on National Policy for children. The Government of India introduced the Integrated Child Development services on 2nd October, 1975. The draft Five Year Plan 1978-83 stated that special attention would be devoted to the problem of children, including prevention of the exploitation of the child Labour. Economic backwardness necessitating recourse to child labour to supplement the family income and lack of educational facilities are primarily responsible for employment of children. Greater priority in the plan on universal primary education and increasing employment opportunities for the adults would enable parents to allow the children to devote more time to school. In 1979 the National Committee on Child Labour had even recommended more and more survey to be done on child labour to help, understand the problem and suggest remedial measures. The Draft Sixth Five Year Plan observed that in the immediate future total abolition of Child Labour with all its socio-economic ramifications does not seem to be a feasible proposition. It also felt that child labour has to be seen distinctly in the categories of wage earning employed, paid family workers and apprentices in traditional crafts. The Seventh Five Year Plan also stated that the ultimate goal of abolition of child labour can only be achieved when there is sufficient improvement in the conditions of living of families whose children are compelled to work.

The Central Advisory Board on child labour was constituted on 4-3-1981. The terms of reference of the Board are following—review the implementation of the existing legislation administered by the Central Government, suggest legislative measures as well as welfare of working children, review the progress of welfare measures for working children and recommend the industries and areas where there must be a progressive elimination of child labour.

The Government of India formulated a National Child Labour Policy in 1987 in pursuance of constitutional directives and legal provisions. The basic thrust of the policy is to co-ordinate and intensify ongoing development programmes for income generation and employment in areas prone to Child Labour.

The National Authority for the Elimination of Child Labour (NAECL) was constituted on September 26, 1994 under the Chairmanship of Labour Minister. Its functions are: to lay down policies and programmes for elimination of Child Labour, particularly in hazardous employments, to monitor the progress of implementation of programmes, projects and schemes for elimination of child labour, to co-ordinate implementation of child labour related projects of the various sister ministries of the Government of India.

A special programme has been evolved with an outlay of Rs. 800 crore to take an estimated two million children out of hazardous employment. During the Eighth Plan a provision of Rs. 15 crore was made for child labour elimination programmes. During the year 1995-96, out of the budget allocation of rupees 34.40 crore, an expenditure of Rs. 34.29 crore was incurred on Child Labour related programmes. For 1996-97 the allocation was Rs. 56 crore.

Under the drive initiated by the labour and employment ministry of the Indian Government, the Government of Bihar had started special schools to eliminate child labour. The labour and employment minister said that "under the national child labour policy, altogether 173 special schools had been opened so far in eight districts of the State in collaboration with the union government to impart education and training to child labourers, in which 10,094 child labourers had been enrolled so far. The Central Government had been paying Rs. 100 to each student of these schools as monthly scholarship, alongwith Rs. 50 per student per month for stationaries and mid-day meal free of cost. The health of the students studying in these schools was being checked up regularly."[31]

The Government has launched a scheme 'Education for All by the year 2000' giving free education upto primary level. State and district education committees with focus on rural areas have also been set up for better implementation of programmes. But the goal of universalisation of primary education by the turn of this century seems only a dream.

Many welfare projects for working children are run by NGOs. They are providing health care, supplementary nutrition, non-formal education and vocational/skilled training. On March 31, 1997, at the end of a public hearing attended by 1,000 children employed in various fields, an eight-member jury called for the abolition of the practice of employing children upto the age of 14. The hearing was organised in New Delhi by the campaign against Child Labour (CACL), an umbrella organisation of about 700 NGOs. The jury made 11 recommendations on the basis of depositions by child labourers, the presentations by CACL and information from other sources. The main recommendations of the jury are "that no child should be made to work in any capacity as a labourer till the completion of 14 years of age; that free, compulsory, relevant and quality elementary education should be provided to all children and that state laws be enacted for this purpose; that special measures be taken to safeguard the well being of the girl child in the matter of schooling and in society; that the Child Labour (Prohibition and Regulation) Act, 1986 should be amended to prohibit the employment of children upto the age of 14 in all sectors, including employment in private dwelling houses or employment carried on with the aid of the family, and generally to fulfill India's commitment under international instruments, that the recent Supreme Court judgment in *M.C. Mehta* Vs the *State of Tamilnadu* (1996) should be strictly enforced and that citizens groups should be actively involved; etc."[32]

The CACL reiterated its commitment to the eradication of

child labour in all sectors. Criticising the New Economic Policy (NEP) launched in 1991, the CACL said, "The NEP with its market dominated paradigm has ensured deregulation of labour laws, accelerated retrenchment, led to the informalisation of labour, depression in adult wages and higher inflation."[33]

Effects are already on to link child labour to international trade. In 1992, American Senator Tom Harkin introduced the Child Labour Deterrence Act which called for ban on the import of goods produced by children under the age of 15. These days another campaign is "Rugmark". The campaign to sell carpets made without child labour is being co-ordinated in Germany by the Economic Workshop a church based centre in Heidelberg in Southern Germany. The marked difference is that the Harkin's bill prescribes outright rejection of products based on child labour and the 'Rugmark' approach attempts towards achieving a mean between market compulsions and social obligations. German importers have their "Care and Fair" fund, into which they pay one per cent of the value of imports for the welfare of the children working in the carpet industry.

Conclusion and Suggestion

India is facing pressure of over-population, mounting poverty, increasing unemployment, under development and abject backwardness. About 330 million children constituting 17% of the total population, 30% of which live below poverty line, certainly pose a great challenge. In India the root cause of child labour is poverty. The Government has initiated various economic programmes to solve the problem of poverty from both the urban and rural areas. But the abolition of poverty is an utopian idea. The UNICEF report emphasises that "the end of hazardous child labour should not wait for poverty to end". World poverty cannot be eliminated by the end of the decade. But hazardous child labour and the grave violation of the rights of the children involved can be.

The Government has taken some steps either to prohibit or regulate employment of children through legislation. The superfluity of protective legislations, as now exists, means little in the absence of the political will to implement them. There are various loopholes in these laws. In May, 1995, three-day workshop on "combating child labour" organised by the PHD Chamber of

Commerce and Industry was told "that only 4,000 people were convicted for using child labour. 'About 3500 of the accused were let off and fined only Rs. 150, suggesting that the law is lax, not effective enough to combat the menace. There is need to rationalise these laws. At present through legislation child labour cannot be totally abolished. It will be achieved when total change in the attitude of the society towards child labour takes place. In India, efforts are on to eradicate child labour in a phased manner. The Bangladesh example can be an eye-opener under pressure from the Western importers. The Bangladesh Garment Manufacturers and Exporters Association (BGMEA) "responded on an emergency basis and induced garment factories to lay off thousands of young workers. The result was more, not less, distress for children. With no place to go-UNICEF later found some of the children ended up becoming prostitutes and welders. The BGMEA had to reverse its decision. Later, a tripartite agreement was worked out among BGMA, ILO and UNICEF. Taking recourse to inherent ambiguity, the agreement stipulated that child labour will be phased out of the garment industry "at an early date" but no children will be retrenched without being rehabilitated."[34]

Access to free and compulsory education is being shown up as the key weapon to end child labour. There is an urgent need for enforcement of universalisation of primary education. The country cannot afford to wait until incomes rise to make primary education universal and compulsory. "Half the battle will be won when free and compulsory education becomes available to all children upto the age of 14. In states like Kerala where the 'education for all' mantra has been made a reality, child labour is unheard of. Yet in India the Government is far more committed to the universalisation of education for the age 11-14. It must realise that only way to contain child labour is to ensure that children do not enter the job market in the first place. If this is not done, today's illiterate child workers will become tomorrow's illiterate and unskilled adults."[35]

In India the Government has to generate additional resources to fulfil the target of compulsory education to all. National Children Welfare Fund be created to be placed at the disposal of The President of India. In consultation with the Ministry of Finance donations/contributions made to this fund be treated tax free and donors may not be asked to disclose the sources of income. Instead of politicians the President of India should appeal the people within India and abroad to contribute liberally to make it a success and effective instrument for eradication of child labour and other physical and mental disabilities facing the children. At the same time suitable mechanism be created to monitor the fund to win the confidence of the donor in particular and people in general.

Some employers of carpet industry are firmly convinced that the work for which they employ children cannot be done by adults ("nimble fingers" theory). So it is impractical for the Government to remove child workers from the carpet industry. A study covering the carpet weavers in India concludes that the argument of "nimble fingers" often advanced in defence of retaining children in employment in the carpet weaving industry is a fictitious one. "Over 2,000 weavers showed that some of the best carpets, with the greatest density of small knots, were actually woven by adults. It had more to do with dexterity than the size of the fingers."[36]

India is facing over-population. No society can prosper without checking population. In this context the concept of small family is the best remedy to eliminate child labour. Keeping in view small family, proper facilities can be availed for the development of the children. Initially let us plan for zero rate of population growth which means every couple should produce two children to maintain the present population at a static level even though it is very-very high and not sustainable. Some incentive as well as mild punitive measures can also be initiated to make this movement success. For example, the couple who is in service and if they produce one child they must get some extra incentive in forms of cash benefit, promotion, etc. Similarly, if the couple produce more than two children and they are in job in that case few increments can be stopped or promotion may be denied or government accommodation may not be preferred for them. But for all those couples who are not in service and they also co-operate in this movement, either in terms of cash or subsidised items should be made available to them. But all those who are not with the movement they may be deprived of certain facilities, example given, ration cards, various kinds of subsidies and grants of loan, etc.

In rural areas these children are less unfortunate as they live with their parents in the open surroundings while their counter parts in the Urban Centres are deprived, deserted, isolated and completely rootless living under various strains and stresses in the most inhospitable and unhygienic conditions doing more fatal jobs.

The problem has a global dimensions, hence global initiative and policy measures are required to create awareness among the nations to accept the challenge to apply correctives within time frame to offer effective solution. The battle against the enslavement and abuse of children is acquiring an international dimension.

Three groups of children and activists who work to end child labour and child abuse have set out from Manila in the Philippines, Sao Paulo in Brazil and the Cape of Good Hope in South Africa on a Global March to Geneva. The marchers reached Geneva by June 3, 1998 for the non-governmental organisation that will be held parallel to the International Labour organisation convention on Child Labour. The children from India had joined in the Asian segment of the march. The three groups will pass through five continents and 80 countries, and will cover 80,000 km. The aim of the global march is to create an awareness among the people about child labour, its causes and to identify effective measures to eradicate these; "to urge nation-states to ratify, enforce and monitor compliance with the international conventions on abolishing child labour; to introduce, strengthen and implement within a strict time-frame national laws and programmes consistent with international obligations; to increase national and international funding for primary education; to promote effective strategies to send all working children to school; to produce goods without the use of child workers; to replace child workers with adults; and to broaden efforts to combat poverty and exploitation."[37] It is the largest social movement in support of the 250 million working children of the world.

Though various steps have been taken by the external agencies governmental and NGOs are coming forward to help the poor children in various ways directly and indirectly but thanks to the rat race for material acquisition these schemes are failures. The old addage is that 'where there is a will, there is a way'. Nothing is impossible, the things are to be taken in right earnestness and pursued honestly and vigorously in the missionary zeal. There may be better and brighter prospect in the future if we are sincere and honest. Substantial progress may be made in this direction when the people of this country take it as a patriotic duty to help the nation in fulfilling this laudable objective in a given time frame. Multi-pronged attacks on this problem, externally as well as internally, are urgently called for to meet the target of eradicating this social evil from the map of the world.

References

1. *Yojna,* May 1-15, 1990, p. 12.
2. Giri, V.V., 1958, "Labour Problems in Indian Industries", Asia Publishing House, Bombay, p. 360.
3. *Yojna,* May 15, 1994, pp. 15-16.
4. Bhatia, S.C. (edited), "Children in India", *Indian University Association for Continuing Education,* University of Delhi, 1990, p. 13.
5. *Ibid.,* p. 14.
6. *Ibid.,* p. 15.
7. Dr. Bhagoliwal, T.N., "Economics of Labour and Industrial Relations", Sahitya Bhawan, Agra, 1984, p. 796.
8. *Ibid.,* pp. 796-97.
9. *Rashtriya Sahara,* May 1994, p. 54.
10. *Yojna,* December 31, 1994, p. 24.
11. Saxena, R.C., "Labour Problems and Social Welfare", K. Nath & Co., Meerut, 1981, p. 790.
12. *The Times of India,* Patna, December 27, 1996, p. 5.
13. *The Economic Times,* Calcutta, November 14, 1996, p. 10.
14. *The Hindustan Times,* Patna, December 12, 1996, p. 7.
15. *The Hindustan Times,* Patna, November 24, 1996, p. 11.
16. *The Economic Times,* Calcutta, November 22, 1996, p. 9.
17. *Frontline,* January 24, 1997, p. 85.
18. Dr. Bhagoliwal, T.N., p. 796.
19. *Yojna,* January 1996, p. 61.
20. *Ibid.,* p. 60.
21. *Rashtriya Sahara,* May 1994, p. 54.
22. *Ibid.*
23. Saxena, R.C., p. 797.
24. *The Times of India,* Patna, July 24, 1997, p. 7.
25. *Rashtriya Sahara,* March 1997, p. 23.
26. *Yojna,* November 30, 1993, p. 18.
27. *Yojna,* May 31, 1994, p. 23.
28. *Ibid.*
29. *The Times of India,* Patna, December 11, 1996, p. 01.
30. *The Times of India,* Patna, October 18, 1996, p. 06.
31. *The Times of India,* Patna, January 3, 1997, p. 03.
32. *Frontline,* May 2, 1997, p. 112.
33. *Ibid.,* p. 113.
34. *The Times of India,* Patna, November 14, 1996, p. 08.
35. *The Times of India,* Patna, April 8, 1997, p. 06.
36. *The Hindustan Times,* Patna, November 12, 1996, p. 06.
37. *Frontline,* April 24, 1998, p. 102.

4

Child Labour in India: A Multi-Dimensional Problem

—*S. K. Patel & R. C. Talati*

The existence of child labour is a slur on a modern welfare state which seeks to promote the all-round development of its citizens, children are the future hope of the society. They are like buds which need to be properly nursed and well-taken care of so that they bloom fully and grow into able human-beings and contribute their worth to the future development of the society. On the contrary, instead of being sent to schools and properly educated, they are made to work, which amounts to squeezing the bud before it blooms. It not only thwarts the development of children, but of the society as well, since only able citizens can put the society on sound footing. Thus, child labour has become a chronic problem and has entered deep into the Indian Social Fabric. The problem of child labour is a burning problem of the world which has constantly engaged the minds of jurists, legislators, social thinkers, politicians, economists and philanthropists from time immemorial. The problem has changed its venues and from public platforms, it has reached the inner circle of legislative, executive and judicial chambers.

The children are subjected to work at a tender age, when they require the utmost love, affection, care and proper education. They are the direct victim of the existing exploitative set-up and due to denial of minimum basics, they are forced to join labour force. They are subjected to toil for some work and they are devoid of opportunities to grow. It is a sad commentary against civilized society where children are living miserable, cheerless lives, toiling endlessly toward off starvation, totally deprived of all conforts and opportunities for self-growth and development. The phenomenon of child labour robs the child of his youthful life, restricts opportunities for better earning in future due to lack of education. Child labour not only harms the physical and intellectual growth of the child, but stunted growth of children ultimately affects nation's future growth. Thus, child labour is a curse to the society, a malady that may wreck the economic backbone of a country and it is a drag on the development of human civilization.

In this paper, therefore, an attempt is made to analyse the meaning of child labour, history of child labour, causes of child labour, effects of child labour, extent of child labour, educational status of child labour, workforce participation of child labour in the rural economy of India, rights of the child, health of children, laws protecting the child, policy prescriptions etc. etc.

Definitional Aspect of Child Labour

First of all, it is interesting to analyse the meaning of child labour as a variety of definitions are given for child labour. Child labour has been defined differently, and therefore, there is no universally accepted definition of child labour is available at present. In India, the definition of child labour in terms of age has differed from year to year under different legislations.

The Factories Act, 1948 prohibits children below the age of 14 years from working in any factory, the minimum age in the Mines Act (1952) is 15 years and it is 12 years in the Plantations Labour Act (1951).

If we go back into the history of child labour legislation, we find that the Factories Act, 1881, defined child as a person below 12 years, minimum age of employment was 7 years and hours of work for the age 7 to 12 years, were fixed at 9 with rest interval and holidays. Factories Act, 1891, raised the minimum age of employment to 9 years, and the hours of work for age 9 to 14 years, were fixed at 7 hours a day restricted to day light. Factories Act, 1911, put the hours of work to 6 in textile mills and employment of labour between 7.00 p.m. and 5.30 a.m. was prohibited, Factories Act, 1922, declared persons below the age of 15 years as children; hours of work were limited to 6 with rest interval of half an hour, minimum age of employment was raised from 9 to 12 years. Factories Act, 1934 fixed the minimum age of employment at 12 and persons between 12 to 15 years were to be treated as children. Factories Act, 1948, raised the minimum age of employment to 14 years, a working day of 4½ hours with a spread over of 5 hours was prescribed. Employment during night and on hazardous occupations is prohibited. So the history of child labour legislation in India is the history of exploitation of child labour as work for the child moved out from home and the village field to work in factories.

Article 24 of the constitution of India states: "No child below the age of 14 years shall be employed to work in any factory or mine or engaged in any other hazardous employment." The most recent legislation: "The Child Labour (Prohibition and Regulation) Act, 1986, defines child labour as a person who has not completed his fourteenth year of age."

Homer Folks (the Chairman of the United States National Child Labour Committee) defines Child Labour as . . ."any work by children that interferes with their full physical development, their opportunities for a desirable minimum of education or their needed recreation".

Dr. V. V. Giri has distinguished the term child labour in two senses. *First,* as an economic practice and *second,* as a social evil. The first signifies employment of children in gainful occupation with a view to adding income of the family, and the second aspect takes into account the dangers to which the children are exposed which means the denial of opportunities of development.

Taking into account the consequences of labour on children, the definition given by International Labour Organization (ILO) seems to be more comprehensive. According to ILO, "child labour includes children primarily leading adult lives, working long hours for low wages under conditions damaging to their health and to their physical and mental development, sometimes separated from their families, frequently deprived of meaningful educational and training opportunities that could open up for them a better future."

The *convention* stipulates in the very first article that all persons under 18 are to be treated as children. However, the Article grants the discretion to individual countries to determine by law whether childhood should cease at 12, 14, 16 or whatever age they find appropriate. In this case, the country play mischief by ractifying the convention. The country may reduce the age upto 12 or 14 and thereby deny the benefits of the convention.

B. D. Gula *et al.* (Tahir Hussain, 1991) defined child labour "as any work done by children in order to economically benefit their family or themselves directly or indirectly, at the cost of their physical, mental or social development."

M. S. Subramanian (1991) defines child labour thus: "child labour means the employment of children (5 to 14 years of age) in gainful occupations, which are injurious to their physical, mental, moral and social development."

According to Indradeo Sharma (1991), "child labour includes all those aged 14 years or below, who are engaged in some productive work, whether paid or not, within the family or outside."

Thus, a variety of definitions of child labour have been given by various authors and various Acts have prescribed different age limits for child labour. Therefore, the owners of the factories or industrialists have under one pretext or the other, exploited child labour and even today this practice has been continued with.

History of Child Labour

The prevalence of child labour has been found more or less in all periods of time though varied in its nature and dimensions, depending on the existing socio-economic structure of the society. In the past, child labour has been part of the social organization in which all members pooled their labour to produce for the subsistence and survival. This was, and is, particularly true of rural subsistence farming where the work of the child formed part of the labour necessary for the reproduction of the system and value of labour taken as part of child's socialization for reproduction of the labour power. Child labour in the feudal society was seen differently. To some extent parents' obligations were very often involved in working for the landlord on such low wages that it created conditions for the child to work on the farms for wages and often remained as bonded labour in the landlord's house alongwith the parents to repay or to minimize the debt. In pre-capitalist society, the work place of the child was often confined to the family environment, relationships were very informal and the child was not exposed to hazardous environment. Work was considered as the central aspect of their socialization and training. This conception, however, underwent a dynamic change with the advent of capitalism in industrialization in several European countries particularly England where industrial revolution took place first during the 18th century and child labour designated as a social problem.

This uneven development of industrialization gave a new turn to the history of mankind and brought a change in the overall socio-economic order. Family based economy continued to be destroyed and a large number of people became wage earning labourers and, as a result, the children were in a situation where they had to earn wages for themselves as well as for their families. The working hours were from morning to night, but the earnings remained quite low. Conversely, this trend shows that child labour was not destined to disappear in the transaction from the more 'savage' to the more advanced forms of capitalist accumulation and unevenly replicated in the dependent capitalist economy of the Third World countries, whereas high as 90 per cent of the child labour of the world was concentrated.

The absence of any sponsored scheme of family allowance to enable poor parents to secure for their children an adequate and balanced diet and living conditions had forced them to join the industrial establishments. Besides, there was no compulsion on their part to get education upto a certain age limit and thus the children were let free to accept certain occupations at tender age. According to Labour Investigation Committee, "slow process of protective legislation accompanied with inadequate inspection machinery to enforce these provisions caused growth in employment of child labour in different industries at different times."

Thus, the history of child labour can be traced even in ancient India. In ancient India trade with children of down-trodders did exist. Kautilya in his "Arthashastra" pointed out that the trade of children as slaves was not prohibited in mlechchas as they were backward and uncivilized. Thus, in ancient India the child labour did exist. However, this problem has been aggravated in recent years, because their number has increased considerably and their economic position is miserable.

The Magnitude of Child Labour

The problem of child labour has been a worldwide problem. Industrialization on large scale leads to many mal-adjustments and one such mal-adjustment is the employment of children in factories, workshops and in other unregulated occupations.

According to one estimate, more than 100 million children live abondoned by their families on the streets of the world's cities. The number of such children according to the Report of ILO prepared for the "Commission on Human Rights" was 52 million, out of which 38 million is found in Asia. India contributes one-third of Asia's child labour and a fourth of the world's working children. According to the estimate of Planning Commission in March 1983, there were 15.70 million child labour (14.3 million in rural areas and 1.67 million in urban areas) in the age group 10-14 years and 17.36 million in the age-group 5-14 years. Another estimate put the number at 44 million in 1985. The seriousness of the problem can be judged from the observation made by UNO in its study, "The Child in India-1979" which says "If workers under 18 years of age could be withdrawn from the labour force and diverted to educational institutions, some 15 to 20 million unemployed adults would be able to find jobs on standard wages."

Thus, the estimates of total number of child labour in India widely vary. According to 1971 census, child labour in India was 14 millions, i.e. about 4.66 per cent of the total child population. The National Sample Surveys placed it at 15.1 million in 1979. Planning Commission put it at 17.3 million. According to Child Labour Board, the number is around 18 million. 90 per cent of the children work in unorganized sector. According to one estimate, in India there were 16.66 million child labourers in 1986.

Thus, India has the largest number of working children. As a percentage to all children in 10-14 years age group, working children in India stood at 20% which was next to Tanzania (29.9), Mozambique (28.1) and Thailand (25.4). Moreover, the quantum of child labour in India is increasing both in absolute and relative term. In absolute term, the number has gone up from 10.74 million in 1971 to 13.59 million in 1981. In relative terms, the percentage of child labour to total child population has risen from 4.66 in 1971 to 5.17 in 1981. In 1990, the number of child labour is estimated at 18.2 millions. It is also estimated that in the age group of 10-14 years, every third child in the rural area and every eighth child in the urban area is a working child. All-India Survey of Operation Research Group, 1983, had estimated 44 millions child workers in India.

Thus, the magnitude of child labour in India vary from source to source. But it can be conveniently said that the number of child labour in India is alarming and needs immediate corrective measures.

Nature of Work

Now, it is pertinent to discuss the nature of work which these children are engaged in. During the period from 1961 to 1981, 41 per cent of the child labour was working as cultivators, 36 per cent as agricultural labourers, 7.4 per cent in mining, quarrying, livestock, forestry, fishery, hunting, plantation, orchards and allied activities, 8.87 in manufacturing, processing, services and repairs, 0.57 per cent as construction workers, 1.8 per cent in trade and commerce, 0.36 per cent in transport, communication and storage and 4.23 per cent in others on an average.

Table 4.1 depicts the share of child labour in total workforce of different industries during 1961-1981. The share of child labour was 5.58 per cent in cultivation, 9.46 per cent in agriculture, 16.34 per cent in mining, quarrying, livestock, fishing, forestry, hunting, plantation, orchards and allied activities, 5.44 per cent in manufacturing, processing, service and repairs, 2.72 per cent in construction work, 1.96 per cent in trade and commerce, 0.76 per cent in transport, communication and storage, and 4.05 per cent in others, on an average during 1961 to 1981.

Table 4.1

Percentage of Child Labour to Total Labour-force Engaged in Different Industry Groups

Industry groups	*1961*	*1971*	*1981*	*Averages*
Cultivators	7.42	5.97	4.34	5.58
Agricultural labourers	10.13	9.66	8.06	9.46
Mining, quarrying, livestock, forestry, fishing, hunting, plantation, orchards and allied activities	19.92	12.42	11.68	16.34
Manufacturing, processing, services, repairs	8.62	3.85	3.84	5.44
Construction	3.23	2.69	2.23	2.72
Trade and commerce	2.01	2.11	1.76	1.96
Transport, storage and Communications	0.78	0.95	0.56	0.76
Others	4.47	2.57	5.12	4.05

Source : Social Change, Vol. 20, Number 3, September 1990, p. 27.

In India child labour is so widespread that it accounts for the largest number of the world's working children. Census 1971 and

1981 throw important searchlight on the work participation rate. The percentage of boys and girls (0-14 age group) among main workers are 5.46 and 2.95 respectively in 1981, while the corresponding percentages in 1971 were 6.44 and 2.57. While among boys the work participation rate has decreased, it has increased in case of girls. In fact, among boys, the number of workers during 1971-81 has declined by 3.5 per cent, and that among girls, it has increased by 3.2 per cent. This clearly shows that more and more female children are brought into the labour force. The work participation rate among male children in the rural areas (6.30) is higher than that in the urban areas (2.46). The same trend is also noticeable in respect of work participation rate of female children; it is 3.3 in rural areas as against 0.88 in urban areas. The problem of child labour is thus more acute in rural than the urban areas. Children constitute about 19 per cent of male marginal workers and 9 per cent of female marginal workers.

From Table 4.2, it is clear that Jammu & Kashmir has the highest percentage of child labour (10.5). The other States which have percentage of child labour higher than the country's figure of 5.2, are Himachal Pradesh (5.9), Karnataka (7.6), Madhya Pradesh (7.9), Meghalaya (7.9), Nagaland (5.7), Rajasthan (5.6) and Sikkim (6.8). Kerala has the lowest percentage of child labour (1.1). According to the 1971 census, Andhra Pradesh also had a high percentage of workers among children. It was 9.2 per cent of total children—11.8 per cent among boys and 6.6 per cent among girls.

Educational Status of Child Workers

The practice of child labour can be attributed to socio-economic compulsion of the parents and guardans who opt their children to be employed as child labour rather than sending them to schools. The Table 4.3 clearly pinpoints that the educational levels are low and illiteracy persists predominantly in the child labour. The level of education is certainly higher in urban areas as compared to rural areas. Similarly, the education level of male children is higher as compared to female children. Two inferences can be drawn from this : *Firstly*, it may be pointed out that the Indian psychology has not changed much to break the barriers in order to get the fruits of education, *Secondly*, the relatively higher educational levels in the case of male children may be largely due to the higher preferences accorded to educate the male children in our society. The relatively lower educational levels in the case of female children may be attributable to the social taboo that still exists in the minds of the parents and guardians of the child labour.

Table 4.2
Percentage of Total Workers Among Children for India/States/Uts—1981 Census

States/UTs	*Percentage of Total Workers Among Children*		
	P	*M*	*F*
	5.17	5.96	4.32
States:			
1. Bihar	3.74	5.96	4.32
2. Gujarat	4.70	5.27	4.09
3. Haryana	3.61	4.47	2.65
4. Himachal Pradesh	5.88	4.66	7.14
5. Jammu & Kashmir	10.53	10.48	10.58
6. Karnataka	7.64	8.74	6.52
7. Kerala	1.08	1.10	1.06
8. Madhya Pradesh	7.90	8.24	7.54
9. Maharashtra	6.42	6.18	6.67
10. Manipur	3.62	2.88	4.37
11. Meghalaya	7.92	8.85	6.99
12. Nagaland	5.69	5.01	6.39
13. Punjab	3.62	5.67	1.32
14. Rajasthan	5.64	6.00	5.27
15. Sikkim	6.83	5.75	7.96
16. Tripura	3.00	3.88	2.09
17. Uttar Pradesh	3.04	4.50	1.37
18. West Bengal	2.83	4.34	1.27
Union Territories:			
1. Andaman & Nicobar Islands	1.75	2.53	0.92
2. Arunachal Pradesh	7.21	6.14	8.33
3. Chandigarh	1.32	2.00	0.54
4. Dadra & Nagar Haveli	8.21	7.33	9.12
5. Delhi	1.16	1.87	0.37
6. Goa, Div & Daman	2.45	2.07	2.85
7. Lakshadweep	0.34	0.36	0.31
8. Mizoram	3.23	2.94	3.53
9. Pondicherry	1.63	2.11	1.51
1971 Census:			
Andhra Pradesh	9.24	11.81	6.62
Assam	3.41	6.04	0.74
Orissa	5.30	9.07	1.49
Tamilnadu	4.58	6.22	2.82

Source : *Social Change*, Vol. XXXIII, No. 2, May 1986.

Table 4.3
Sex-wise Distribution of Child Workers by Education Levels, Rural and Urban Areas (Percentages)

Educational Level	*Male*		*Female*	
	Rural	*Urban*	*Rural*	*Urban*
1. Illiterate	79.75	63.47	88.93	77.25
2. Literate (without educational level)	10.28	15.31	5.58	10.92
3. Primary	8.58	17.28	4.81	10.00
4. Middle	1.28	3.47	0.65	1.64
5. Matriculation/Secondary	0.10	0.43	0.03	0.19
6. Higher Secondary/ Intermediate/Pre-Univ.	0.01	0.03	0.00	0.00
7. Non-technical diploma or certificate not equal to degree	0.00	0.01	0.00	0.00
8. Technical diploma or certificate not equal to degree	0.00	0.00	0.00	0.00

Source : Census 1981.

When we look into the State-wise educational status, it is clear that Kerala leads in case of literacy with more than 70 per cent as compared to the all-India literacy rate of 36.2 per cent. In the age group of 5-9, 75 per cent of the children attend school in Kerala State and in the age-group of 10-14 about 86 per cent of children attend school. Sex-wise analysis shows that in the age-group 5-9, the percentage of school attendance is almost the same (75) for both the sexes. In the age group 10-14, 88 per cent among boys and 84 per cent among girls attend school. With such high percentage of school attendance, the percentage of child labour is very low. In Jammu & Kashmir, where the percentage of child labour is the highest, only about 41 per cent of children in the age group-5-14 attend school.

In the country as a whole, only 30 per cent of the children in the age group 0-14 attend school. The percentages are respectively 37 and 24 for males and females. In the rural areas, only 26 per cent of these children attend school. The low level of school attendance and literacy among working children may be due to the fact that children are not at all admitted in the school due to their diversion into the labour force and many of those admitted drop-out owing to poverty.

Inducing children to attend school is necessary, if we want to reduce the incidence of child labour. The Mid-Day Meals Programme and Nutrition Programme should be effectively implemented by the State Governments to promote school attendance. Parents should also be motivated to send their children to school rather than for job.

Working Conditions

Child labour is found more in the unorganized sector like agriculture rather than in organized sector, because in the organized sector number of laws prohibits employment of children. However, the occupational distribution of working children shows their concentration in the following occupations:

(1) Agriculture, (2) Plantations, (3) Mining and quarrying, (4) Beedi-rolling, (5) Glass and bangles, (6) Handloom and carpet weaving, (7) Match and fireworks, (8) Machine tools, repair shops and petrol pumps, (9) Zari and embroidery, (10) Gem cutting and weaving, (11) Cashew processing and manufacture of coir products, (12) Domestic worker, (13) Helpers in hotels, restaurants, canteens, tea stalls, shops and way-side establishments, (14) Rug picking, (15) Construction, (16) Hawkers, vendors, news-paper sellers, (17) Shoe-shining, (18) Coolies etc.

The working conditions of child labour are very harsh. They have to work under deplorable conditions. They are not paid adequately and are allowed to starve and suffer seriously from mal-nutrition.

So far as the working conditions of the children in agriculture and plantations are concerned, they are healthy as work is done outdoors, but they have to work both in fair and foul weather, in the scorching heat of the sun and in the driving rain of the monsoon. It is unorganized and organized sector of the industries that has caused much concern in respect of working conditions for the employed children. According to Whitely Commission, "In many cities, large numbers of young boys are employed for long hours and discipline is strict. Indeed, there is reason to believe that corporal punishment and other disciplinary measures of a reprehensible kind are sometimes resorted to in the case of smaller children. Workers as young as five years of age may be found in some of the places working without adequate meal intervals or weekly rest days, and 10 or 12 hours daily for sums as low as 2 annas in the case of those of tenderest years."

The Labour Investigation Committee had also reported that the working conditions were deplorable in different industries especially in the unorganized industries like 'bidi' making, glass bangles and match industries. To quote the committee in this respect: "In Bombay, the conditions of workshops, so far as sanitation, light and ventilation are concerned, beggars description. They are dark, dingy places with very few, if any, windows and the approaches are very insanitary. Workers are huddled together, men, women and in some cases children, and there is hardly some space to move." Similarly, in South India, "the most serious evil in the bidi industry is highly insanitary conditions of work places. The workshops are generally low-roofed, dark and ill-ventilated places with uneven mud floors."

The Labour Bureau's Study (1954) also revealed that the actual hours of work were found to be in excess of the prescribed working hours under different enactments. In cottage industries, children were required to work as long as adult workers, except where home-work system was prevalent. The working conditions for children in the bidi and glass industries continued to remain deplorable. However, a redeeming feature reported by the study was that children were assigned comparatively light work wherever employed in plantations, factories, cottage industries and small-scale industries.

According to the Labour Investigation Committee, "In most of the glass factories, the basic materials viz. silica, soda ash, calcium oxide, borax etc. are mixed by workers in closed rooms and the workers are provided with neither dirt respirators nor goggles nor hand-gloves. Again, there is almost no arrangement for the control of temperature and the results are particularly disastrous in the glass and shellac factories where children of tender age often have to work near open furnaces in the extreme heat of North India and cases of fainting are most common. In the glass factories small pieces of glass are scattered over the entire compound and red-hot electric wire is sometimes employed to act the tubings, but the children are supplied neither wooden sandals nor gloves and are often found to work with burns and cuts in their bodies." According to the Rege Committees Report on Labour Conditions, "In the glass industries it is almost impossible to describe sufficiently and accurately the wretched conditions in which labourers work. No wonder the children in the glass industry look emaciated, anaemic, myopic and gloomy and invariably suffer from rickets and eye-dieses."

However, the National Commission on Labour has observed that "employment of children is almost non-existent in organized industries. It, however, persists in varying degrees in the unorganized sector. Employment of children below the prescribed age is also reported to be continuing in far off places and in rural areas where enforcement of statutory provisions is more difficult."

Rights of and Laws for Children

Protection of basic Human Rights is now recognized as a primary obligation of every society irrespective of its political ideology or level of development. Arbitrary exercise of power and denial of equality, justice and dignity have been fought by individuals and groups through legal and political processes in country after country during the last fifty years in a scale unprecedented in human history.

One section of persons who are ordinarily not aware of their rights and do not possess the resources to seek their enforcement are children. Even among children, brothers have a superior status as compared to their sisters both in law and in society. Most of the children have to meet with social injustice despite all the guarantees and declarations in law and policy.

No doubt, there is increasing awareness of the "child dimension" in the development and implementation of social policies. Much has been done. A lot remains to be done. Law is supposed to protect the weak particularly against the strong for a just share of resources and for fair treatment in mutual relationships.

U.N. Convention on the Rights of Child

In international law, there are many conventions and covenants which proclaim standards for human rights protection with the legal systems of various countries. They are applicable to all individuals including children. However, taking into consideration, the physical and mental immaturity of children as well as their special needs and vulnerability, the United Nations as early as 1959 adopted a ten-point Declaration on the Rights of child. According to one study, there are over 80 international instruments that concern the situation of children. The 1989 convention on the Rights of the child is in response to the felt need for a comprehensive, recognizable and enforceable legal regime which can guarantee the welfare of the child in the 1990s. It recognizes three basic facts, namely

(a) children have special human rights which adults do not have,
(b) the human rights standards in relation to children are higher than those of adults, and
(c) that many of these rights cast obligations as much on parents themselves as on the State and society.

The rights of the child can be grouped into three heads, namely

(a) civil and political rights,
(b) social and economic rights, and
(c) cultural and developmental rights.

A. Civil and Political Rights:

1. The inherent right to life and the States obligation to ensure to child's survival and development.
2. Right to have a name from birth and the right to acquire a nationality.
3. Right of children to have their views heard in matters affecting them.
4. Right to freedom of expression, freedom of information, freedom of thought, conscience and religion.
5. Right to freedom of association and of peaceful assembly.
6. Right to protection from interference with privacy and right to reputation.
7. Right to be protected against torture and inhuman treatment, death or life improvement, and unlawful or arbitrary deprivation of liberty.
8. Right to legal assistance and treatment with dignity whilst deprived of liberty.
9. Right to protection and care during armed conflict and right not to be called for service in armed forces while under 15.
10. Right of child victims of armed conflicts, of torture, neglect or exploitation to receive appropriate rehabilitative treatment for their recovery and social re-integration.
11. Right of children accused of offence to benefit from all aspects of the due process of law including legal aid.
12. Right not to be subjected to judicial proceedings wherever appropriate and right to have alternatives to institutional treatment.

13. Right of children placed for care, protection or treatment to have all aspects of that placement evaluated regularly.

B. Economic Rights:

1. Right of children to benefit from social security.
2. Right for an adequate standard of living and to recover maintenance wherever necessary.
3. Right to be protected from work that constitutes a threat to health, education or development.
4. Right for appropriate regulation of the hours and conditions of employment.
5. Right to protection from all forms of exploitation.

C. Social and Cultural Rights:

1. Right to education, free and compulsory at the primary level.
2. Right to have such education which develops child's personality and talents, promote respect for human rights and child's own cultural and natural values.
3. Right to protection from all forms of maltreatment from parents or others responsible for care.
4. Right to the highest attainable standard of health and access to medical services.
5. Right to health education, preventive health care and to the abolition of harmful traditional practices.
6. Right of handicapped children to special care, education and training.
7. Right of refugee children for special protection.
8. Right of children of minorities to enjoy their own culture.
9. Right to protection from the use of narcotic and psychotropic drugs and from being involved in their production and distribution.
10. Right to protection from sexual exploitation and abuse including prostitution and pornography.
11. Right against being subjected to sale, trafficking and abduction.

Some important legislations providing protection to child have been passed by the government. Some of the important legislations are:

1. *The Children (Pledging of Labour) Act, 1933* prohibits the pledging of labour of children (child means person below 15 years of age),
2. *The Employment of Child Act, 1938* prohibits employment of children who have not completed 15 years of age in certain occupations like railway, ports etc.
3. *Factories Act, 1948* envisages that those who are under 14 years, are prohibited from entering in employment in factories and persons between 15 and 18 years of age may be employed in factories on fulfilling certain conditions such as after acquiring certificate of fitness etc.
4. *Minimum Wages Act, 1948* makes provision for fixation of minimum wages in certain employments.
5. *The Plantation Labour Act, 1951* applicable to plantations (where 30 or more persons are employed) prohibits employment of children under 12, and makes the provision of education as the responsibility of the employer and also for housing and medical and recreational facilities.
6. *The Mines Act, 1952* prohibits employment of children in any mine and also their presence in any part of the mine which is below ground or in any open cast working in which any mining operation is carried out.
7. *The Merchant and Shipping Act, 1958* prohibits employment of children under 15 years in a ship.
8. *The Motor Transport Workers Act, 1961* which is amended in 1986 prohibits employment of children under 14 in motor transport undertakings.
9. *The Apprentices Act, 1961* regulates the working conditions of the apprentices.
10. *Atomic Energy Act, 1962* prohibits the employment of persons who have not completed 18 years as radiation workers without prior written permission of the competent authority.
11. *The Bidi and Cigar Workers (Conditions of Employment) Act, 1966* prohibits the employment of children in premises wherein any manufacturing process connected with bidi or cigar making or both is being, or ordinarily carried on with or without the aid of power.

Besides these Central Acts, various State legislatures have also passed Acts for regulating conditions of employment in shops and commercial establishments.

12. Recently, the *Child Labour (Prohibition and Regulation) Act* has been passed in 1986. As per the provision of the Act no child can be employed or permitted to work in certain occupation or processes which are hazardous in nature. The Act prescribes heavy penalty, i.e. fine from Rs. 10,000 to Rs. 20,000 or imprisonment from 3 months to one year in case of violation of the provisions of the Act. The Child Labour Advisory Committee is to advise the government as to which other occupations should be added to the list of prohibited occupations.

Certain other Acts also have been passed by the government.

Besides legal Acts, the constitution also provides special Articles for the protect of child labour. Article 24 prohibits the employment of child below 14 years of age. Forced labour has been prohibited in Article 23. Articles 39(c); 39(f), 42 and 43 are related to the welfare of children.

The Directive Principles of State Policy embodied in the Constitution of India re-affirmed the policy of protection of children against exploitation. "The State shall, in particular, direct its policy towards securing that the health and strength of workers, men and women and the tender age of children are not abused and that citizens are not forced by economic necessity to enter a vocation unsuited to their age or strength, that childhood and youth are protected against exploitation and against moral and material abandonment." Article 24 of the constitution lays down that "no child below the age of 14 shall be employed to work in any factory or mine or engaged in any other hazardous employment."

The National Policy for children adopted in 1974 also envisaged the balanced growth of children and prohibits employment of children below 14 years in hazardous occupations.

This National Policy has emphasized the following points:

1. to extend educational facilities for child labour upto primary level.
2. to arrange technical training for child labour.
3. arrangement of establishing union of child labour.
4. to fix up (a) time of working hours, (b) holidays, and (c) wage.
5. to make independent Child Labour Union which should not come under the politically organized Union.
6. to implement all welfare measures which are mentioned in various Acts relating to child labour.

7. to prepare an environment which will give scope to the Child Labour Unions to discuss directly with the owners of the organization.

International organizations like UNO, UNICEF, ILO etc. are making efforts to protect child labour. The children's charter of rights, the UNO's principles, the ILO's conventions, the constitutional provisions and the Labour Laws have been passed to protect the child labour. Inspite of these sincere efforts, child labour still exists and the number is increasing. The ILO observes that while protective Laws have laid down conditions, the oversights and ambiguities in legal codes allow employers to circumvent them.

These Labour Laws do not cover 86% of child labour working in unorganized sectors. The child labour, below 14 years are out of scope of labour laws. If child labour is a must, laws are to be amended for regulating working conditions of child labour.

Inspite of these legal measures, many people believe that children are less protected and cared for today as compared to earlier times. Love and even care of one's own children are increasingly becoming scarce. Exploitation of child labour and sexual abuse of children are now widespread in the society. Education is the privilege of a few children only, children are lucky if they get nutritious food essential for their development. Health services are woefully inadequate. This sorry state of affairs, is not confined to third world countries alone, but also to other countries, the difference is that of degree only.

Causes of Child Labour

The causes of child labour are many and varied. Thus, a variety of factors can be attributed for the employment of child labour:

(1) Easy availability of child labour without many obligations for employers.

(2) Poverty is the single important reason for child labour. The poor parents in order to supplement their income allow the children to work even on unremunerative jobs. Abject poverty and unemployment forces the children to take up unremunerative jobs. Thus, "economic compulsions weigh heavily on the consciousness of the poor parents and they would not mind colluding with their children's employers in

violating the law and putting their children under the risks of inhuman exploitation. Parents want their children to fend for themselves as early as possible, much better, if they become a source of income to the family." Since the child is put to adult role at an early age, he/she also marries early and breeds early, thereby increasing the liabilities of his/her family and also of the whole nation. A recent study conducted in three big cities of Tamilnadu by the students of Madras School of Social Work revealed that 55% of the children employed belonged to families with the income less than Rs. 300 per month and 72 per cent of total children had sought employment to augment the family income.

(3) Many employers prefer to engage children, because they are cheap. Moreover, children tend to be less troublesome, more disciplined and highly adaptable.
(4) School drop-outs.
(5) Loss of an earning member of the family.
(6) Absence of any State sponsored scheme of family allowance in India.
(7) Non-existence of any general scheme of compulsory education upto a minimum age.
(8) Slow advance of protective labour legislation.
(9) The evasion of the existing laws for the protection of children.
(10) Introduction of the factory system.
(11) Death of mother.
(12) Death of parents.
(13) Ill habituated father spending money on drinking, etc.
(14) Illegitimacy of child.
(15) Sometimes social structure of the society becomes responsible for child labour. The social structure in our country is characterized by caste system. The members of low castes and down-trodden communities are supposed to be for the service of the upper castes. Thus, they are deprived of their aspirations.
(16) Ignorance of the parents.

Thus, the problem of child labour in India is rooted in the exploitative socio-economic set-up and poor and backward economy. Ignorance, lack of job opportunities and other socio-economic institutions perpetuate this evil. Mass awareness does not prevail in our society which is also an important cause of child labour.

Effects of Child Labour

While some healthy work in childhood may be a social good and a national gain. Child labour in general is a great social ill and a national waste, as the economic necessity for wage earning to support the family, deprives the child of an opportunity for education, play and recreation, stunts his physical growth, interferes with the normal development of child's personality and thwarts his preparation for responsibility. The hazards suffered by the child workers are of no one's concern. Among the main hazards is the health hazard which causes the following diseases in various occupations.

- *(a)* Tuberculosis and bronchitis
- *(b)* Muscle atrophy
- *(c)* Weakening and malformation of bones
- *(d)* Eye diseases
- *(e)* Stunted growth
- *(f)* Finger Artheritis
- *(g)* Damage to the finger nails
- *(h)* Excessive fatigue and malnutrition effects, functioning of endocrine glands

Economic and Social Evils:

- *(a)* Child labour gives birth to numerous economic problems such as the use of labour at its lowest productivity implying thereby an inefficient utilization of labour power.
- *(b)* The practice of employing children permits unfair competition with adult labour with the result that there may be an excessive unemployment of adult labour, low wages and less satisfactory working conditions.
- *(c)* Child labour tends to interfere with normal family life and encourages the breakdown of the social order, child used to early economic independence starts an early sex life acquiring general diseases and addition to intoxicants. Generally, he/she also marries young and starts early procreation.
- *(d)* The worst effect of child labour is that it interferes with their education and minimizes the chances for their vocational development. They neither acquire any skill nor do they

receive any education thereby condemning them to a status of illiterate, oppressed and trampled worker for the rest of their lives.

(e) The effects of poor and unsafe working conditions on working children take the form of fatal accidents or accidents that result in deformities. The vulnerability of children is increased by the high incidence of malnutrition and under-nourishment and making them less resistant to debilitating diseases.

(f) Children in some work situations are exposed to physical and mental abuse. This involves long and often permanent separation from parents and isolation, sometimes amounting to virtual imprisonment and physical cruelty. Child participation in labour force activity reduces the potential for schooling and educational development. Given the low educational or skill content of many of the jobs in which working children are involved, the possibilities for acquiring remunerative or satisfying skills become still more remote, children, thus, find themselves locked in unskilled, low paying situations and permanently disadvantaged in the labour market.

(g) There are also other kinds of deprivations from which labourers suffer, including the absence of clear and written contractual agreements, the dearth of feeding programmes, health care facilities and other welfare services and the lack of insurance and social security. The regulation of employment of children by law covers only a frings of these occupations and even where regulation has been sought, the enforcement is extremely half-hearted and tardy.

Unless a systematic evaluation is made from time to time in respect of jobs in which children are employed and certain purposeful policy decisions are taken to meet the deficiencies, the existing situation is not likely to undergo any dimentional, qualitative or quantitative change.

Remedial Measures

Effective policies aimed at the protection of child labour at work and the gradual elimination of child labour must be adjusted to the socio-economic situation of the country. Child labour cannot be approached as an isolated problem; its reduction and elimination will require a set of direct and indirect, *albeit*, inter-related measures.

1. *Removal of poverty and unemployment*: Child labour is rooted in poverty; the progressive elimination of unacceptable labour by those too young to undertake it, requires a general improvement in the economic condition of the country. If it is possible to take all children away from the labour market, it might be possible to eliminate the hard core of unemployment of able and willing workers available in the country between the age group of 15 to 59. In the long run the social costs borne by the society are far more substantial than what it gets from the working children in economic terms.

The problems of child labour cannot be eliminated in the presence of poverty and starvation. Child labour is due to economic necessity. In this connection *Paul Douglas* observes, "the most effective way in which society protects children is in providing their parents with sufficient income so that they can be brought up properly. It is foolish to expect wage earner with unduly low income to feed, cloth and rear their children in adequate fashion. Give a family of average intelligence sufficient money and it will be able to take care of its children. The most pressing obligation is for the industry to put its system of wage payment on an adequate basis and until this is done, social reform will swing against the child."

2. *Ensuring minimum wages*: If parents income increase, they will be less inclined to allow their children to do service. Effective enforcement of the minimum wages Act should be emphasized. Trade Union representatives and representatives of voluntary organizations had pointed out that if minimum wages are actually paid to the workers according to statutory provisions, the financial position will certainly be better and many amongst them will take better care about the future of their children.

The ILO report on the Protection of Children and Young Workers has rightly emphasized, "the problem of prohibition of child labour is inextricably mixed up with the problem of the maintenance of the child and the provision of a living wage for all employed persons adequate to maintain the family at an adequate standard." The fixation of a minimum and fair wage and a scheme of social insurance for industrial workers can solve this problem to a great extent. The society must take the responsibility of maintaining and educating the children in order to secure to all children the fullest possible opportunity for the development of their intellectual, moral and spiritual faculties so that when grown up, they may become efficient workers, intelligent citizens and responsible men and women, for their own greater good as well as that of society.

3. *Meaningful education policy*: Meaningful and effective policy for education of children is also important in solving the child labour problem. As a matter of policy, the education curriculum for each area should be drawn up keeping in view the basic requirements of the environment. This would also require a definite orientation towards greater decentralization in respect of implementation of education programmes. It would also be worthwhile to inject special literacy and vocation training system and also to strengthen existing apprenticeship opportunities by either providing support to existing ones or by introducing new ones. No doubt, existing formal vocational and technical institutions can have an important role to play in this regard. It should also be pointed out that a conscious effort is necessary to see that the children who are employed in a regulated sector, attain first certain minimum educational qualifications.

The role of elementary education in checking the evils of child labour is also important. It is, therefore, essential that extension of free and compulsory education should be given highest priority irrespective of finance and language difficulties. Compulsory and free education should be extended upto the age of 16. Besides, a thorough overhauling should be done in elementary and primary school curricula to give it a practical bias. The Gurupadswamy Committee Report on Child Labour has rightly pointed out that, "the major concern of the government should be with regard to evolving a meaningful policy for education of these children. It has suggested the need for change of curriculum and integration of educational requirements with local crafts, changes and adjustments in the schedule of vacation and holidays to coincide with environmental requirements."

4. *Medical and health support*: In order to ensure good health of working children a system should be evolved in such a way that every child worker is periodically checked. In the organized industries health checking should be made compulsory by enacting proper laws wherever it is not available. In case of unorganized sector, particularly in agriculture, this could be linked with the National Health Scheme. A drive to keep working environment hygienically clean and to provide any working place particularly for child workers should be attempted. The provision of

supplementary feeding programmes for children should be given a primary place in efforts directed at enhancing the nutritional status of children and the improvement of their working conditions.

5. *Proper housing facilities*: Lack of proper housing facilities affects adversely not only to the health and growth of children, but also drag them to join the group of undesirable elements leading to deliquent behaviour. Efforts should, therefore, be made to provide housing facilities with necessary basic amenities both in the organized and unorganized sectors. Attempts should also be made to provide library and reading facilities which they can make use of in their leisure time.

6. *Research and cultural activities*: If facilities for recreation and cultural activities are provided either at the place of work or at the place of residence, the workers can take advantage of these facilities and rejuvenate themselves. This will help in keeping the workers fresh and thereby increase their efficiency leading to increased production. This could also be integrated with a counselling programme for providing guidance to the working children.

7. *Family planning* : It is often found that large families exist in poor sections of the society who are unable to bear the burden of a large number of dependents and therefore, the children are compelled to join the labour force early. This increases the number of working children to a very large proportion. Therefore, a very well-organized family planning programme, both in the organized and unorganized sectors, is bound to give rich dividends in the years to come.

8. *Role of media*: Evils of child labour have so far been given a lip-sympathy. The community has yet to feel its shocking implications on the national development in the long run. There is a surprisingly high degree of ignorance about the consequences of child labour in general and the ill-effects of unsafe working conditions in particular. Child work is often accepted as part of the natural state of things, and the rights and needs of the child are not always fully appreciated. A great deal of effort, therefore, needs to be made to generate and promote public awareness of the consequences of child labour and the rights of the working child and to expose unacceptable conditions by mass media.

9. Efforts should also be made by the voluntary organizations to involve the local public and parents/guardians of child labour, so that they become aware of the efforts made by the government for the upliftment of child labour.

10. Trade Unions of Child Labour should be formed through which the child labour can raise their voice and can represent their problems to the employer directly.

11. At present there is no adequate and reliable information on the problem of child labour. Therefore, there is an urgent need to step up a permanent Board to study, identify and establish and catalogue the nature and extent of child employment and also to focus light on the needs and working conditions of children.

Moreover, the provisions of the Act prohibiting the employment of child labour should be strictly followed. According to *National Commission on Labour*, "Quite often, it is the feeling of sympathy rather than the desire to exploit which weights with employers in employing child workers. Ironically enough, it is the same feeling which makes the inspecting officers to take a lenient view of breaches of the legal provisions in this regard. It is most cruel form of hycrisy to pay insufficient wages to fathers of families and then to show sympathy by employing child workers and by contributing to child welfare agencies to feel that the duty has been done".

The Gurupadswamy Committee has also emphasized that "apart from strict enforcement of statutory provisions in existence, steps should be taken to make jobs safe, secure and healthy while dovetailing job opportunities with education, the process of integration of work with education should be pragmatic keeping in view the future prospects of the child. The major emphasis should be on education and training so that employment of children over the age of 15, help in creating a skilled adult, a technician and a master craftsman."

Thus, the problem does not need piecemeal efforts, but demands massive and co-ordinated attacks from all directions. Hence, there is the need for co-odinated and integrated effort to reduce the problem.

Concluding Remarks

The existence of child labour is a slur on a modern welfare state which seeks to promote the all-round development of its citizens. The problem of child labour is a burning problem of the world which has constantly engaged the minds of jurists, legislators, social thinkers, politicians, economists and philanthropists from time immemorial.

Different Acts have prescribed different age for child. But by and large, a person below the age of 15, is considered as children.

Different bodies have given different magnitudes of child labour in India and abroad.

The problem of child labour is everywhere, but it is more acute in the Third World Countries, particularly in India.

It has very bad social and economic impacts. It can be said that child labour is economically unsound, psychologically disastrous and physically as well as morally dangerous and harmful. It is a curse on the society, a malady that may wreck the economic backbone of a country and it is a drag on the development of human civilization.

Vaidya had observed that "the arms of law do not reach them, trade unions do not reach them or cover them and the public opinions take no heed of them."

Though there is reduction in the employment of children after independence, partly due to the expansion of educational facilities, implementation of child welfare programmes and enforcement of statutory provisions, the problem is still to be cured for the development of younger generation and country as a whole. How child labour could be regulated under the present circumstances is a crucial question. The National Commission on Labour has suggested that with the help of State Governments, work should be combined with schooling. This can be done in three ways : *(i)* after schooling hours, *(ii)* intermittently, and *(iii)* during school vacations. The legislation should be expanded to neglected areas of employment and implementation of the legislative measures should be geared up and there should be necessary changes in the implementation machinery. The State and Central Governments should provide adult workers with a family allowance to enable them to educate their children. Workers should also follow the family welfare programmes of the government and other social welfare organizations.

Summary

Among many hazards, health hazard is the main hazard which leads to many diseases such as tuberculosis, muscle atrophy, bronchitis, finger artharitis, so also child labour gives birth to economic problems such as the use of labour at its lowest productivity leading thereby to in-efficient utilization of labour power. It also leads to unfair competition, it interferes with the normal family life, it encourages the breakdown of the social order, their education is also adversely affected, they are abused both at mental and physical level.

A variety of remedial measures can be suggested for the removal or eradication of this ill, *e.g.*

(i) Removal of poverty and unemployment,
(ii) ensuring minimum wages,
(iii) meaningful education policy,
(iv) medical and health support,
(v) proper housing facilities,
(vi) family planning,
(vii) role of media and voluntary organizations,
(viii) effective implementation of child labour legislations etc.

Thus, it can be said that the existence of child labour is a slur on a modern welfare state. This is a serious problem not only for India, but also for the whole of the world. And, therefore, effective measures should be taken to reduce the extent of child labour, if it cannot be totally eradicated.

References

1. Mustafa and Sharma, (1996), *Child Labour in India: A Bitter Truth,* Deep and Deep Publications, New Delhi.
2. Bhatia, S.C., (1990), *Child in India,* University of Delhi, New Delhi.
3. Mamoria, C.B. and Mamoria, Satish, (1983), *Some Aspects of Industrial Labour in India,* Kitab Mahal, Allahabad.
4. S. N. Mehrotra, (1976), *Labour Problems in India,* S. Chand and Co., New Delhi.
5. T. N. Bhagoliwal, (1983), *Economics of Labour and Industrial Relations,* Sahitya Bhavan, Agra.
6. R. C. Saxena, (1981), *Labour Problems and Social Welfare,* K. Nath and Co., Meerut.
7. J.C. Kulshreshtha, (1978), *Child Labour in India,* Ashish Publishing House, New Delhi, pp. 1-10.
8. N. Mitra, (1980), *The Slave Children of Mandsaur,* Sunday, 8, 19 December.
9. Lai Ah-Eng., (1982), "The Little Workers: A Study of Child Labour in the Small Scale Industries of Penang", *Development and Change,* Vol. 13, No. 4, Oct., pp. 565-70.
10. Smitu Kothari, (1983), "There's Blood on those Matchsticks: Child Labour in Sivakasi", *Economic and Political Weekly,* Vol. XVIII, No. 27, July, pp. 1191-1202.
11. G.D. Gokhale, (1979), *Surat in Seventeenth Century,* Popular Prakashan, Bombay.

12. Elias Mendelievitt, (1979), *Child Labour International Labour Review,* Vol. 18, No. 5, Sept.-Oct., p. 212.
13. *Social Welfare,* Vol. XXXIII, No. 3, June, 1985, pp. 20-23 & 31-32.
14. *Social Welfare,* Vol. XXXIV, No. 2, May, 1986, pp. 4 to 9.
15. *Social Welfare,* Vol. XXXVIII, No. 6, Sept. 1991, pp. 14-16.
16. *Social Welfare,* Vol. 37, No. 3, Sept. 1990, pp. 33-38.
17. Tripathy, M.S., (1989), *Child Labour in India,* Discovery Publishing House, New Delhi.
18. Vaidya, S.A., (1983), "Child Lablour in the Unorganized Sectors" in *Encyclopaedia of Leading Articles,* Vol. II, Part F, Delhi, The Commercial Law Publications, p. 31.
19. *Government of India (1969),* "Report of National Commission on Labour", New Delhi: Ministry of Labour, Employment and Rehabilitation.
20. Dinesh, B.M. and Rayappa, P.H., "School and Work: Are They Compatible?", *Indian Journal of Social Work,* Vol. XLVII, No. 2, July 1986.
21. *The Indian Journal of Labour Economics,* Vol. 33, No. 4, Oct.-Dec., 1990. See Articles by:
    (a) Subramanian, M.S., "Workforce Participation of Child Labour in the Rural Economy of India", pp. 263-67.
    (b) Maya Prasad, "Problems of Child Labour in Indian Agriculture", pp. 267-71.
    (c) Sudama Singh and Maya Sinhal, "The Problem of Child Labour", pp. 272-76.
    (d) K. Shiv Prasad and B. Ramchandra Yogi, "Magnitude of Child Labour in India", pp. 277-82.
    (e) Bhagwan Pratap Singh, "Sad Plight of Child Labour and Need for Proper Deal", p. 325.
    (f) Biswanath Ray, "Child Labour in India—A Critical Survey of Literature", p. 326.
    (g) Usha Kundu, "Child Labour: An Economic Boon or a Social Malady", p. 328.
    (h) Tahir Hussain, "Present Position and Problems of Child Labour in India", p. 341.
    (i) Silvia M. de Noronha, "Child Labour in India", pp. 346-47.

5

Child Labour in India: Extent and Causes–A Case Study

—*Shakuntala Gupta & Sangeeta Nagaich*

Like women, children have always participated in economic and non-economic activities both within and outside their houses. The main determining factor of the relationship between child and work is the stage of economic development and the system of production prevalent in a country. So, it is only by a change in the economic system that brings about a change in the structure of labour and a corresponding change in the economic roles of children.

Actually, the advent of industrialisation in many parts of the world including India is mainly responsible for the origin of child labour. At present the problem of child labour has become a world-wide problem. According to the report of I.L.O. about 52 million children below the age of 15 years are engaged in odd jobs out of which about 29 million in South Asia, more than a million in East Asia, 9.7 million in Africa, 3.1 million in Latin America, 3 lakh in North America, 7 lacs in Europe and about 1 lac in Oceania. About 41.2 million children work without wages in fields, crafts or small industries. Recently, in its another report, ILO (The International Labour Organisation) has estimated the number of child workers to be around 100 million in the world as a whole. As its earlier report, most of child labour is concentrated in south and south East Asia. In case of India, although accurate and detailed data is not available, yet there has been a considerable quantity of child labour employed in industrial establishments. The Royal Commission (1931) estimated children aged 5 years working for 18 hours a day. According to Labour Investigation Committee (1946) one black spot of labour conditions in India is the illegal employment of children in certain industries.

According to 1971 census, over 10.7 million children were working in various activities in the country for their living. National Sample Survey Organisation estimated the child labour force as 16.25 million in 1978.[1] But in 1993, the number of children usually employed per 1000 children were found to be 73 males and 67 females in rural areas and 41 males and 16 females in urban areas (49th Round Jan.-June 1993). The Government of India (Planning Commission) acknowledges at least 17.5 million working children in 1983.[2] A Baroda based Operational Research Group estimated 44 million child working population in the country in 1985.[3] According to U.S. Labour Department Publication, India has the third largest number of urban and rural child workers in the world. Its one volume of the publication says and adds that estimates by various organisations range from 44 million to over 100 million children workers.[4]

According to recent International Labour Organisation sponsored study, every fourth child in the age group of 5 to 15 is employed in India. India is expected to have 50 per cent of the world's illiterate population by the year 2000, will undoubtedly have 78 million children between 6 and 11 years who do not go the school.

Among the states, Andhra Pradesh has the largest child labour population, according to 1991 Census. To support this thesis, the recent district level limited survey conducted on Supreme Court directive found 46,979 children working in the state's hazardous and non-hazardous industrial units.[5]

The states which crossed 1 million in 1981 are Bihar, Karnataka, Madhya Pradesh, Maharashtra, Rajasthan and Uttar Pradesh. These are the states where the literacy levels are low, rate of economic growth is slow, school drop out rates are very high, and people below the poverty line are in larger percentage.

Among the developed States, Punjab acknowledges 142830 working children only. Here the proportion of child labour force to total labour force declined significantly, from 4.10 per cent during 1981 to 2.20 per cent during 1991. Whereas, the proportion of working children combining school with work among total working children increased manifold i.e. from 1.12 per cent during 1981 to 5.53 per cent during 1991.

Among the metropolitan cities, the extent of child labour in Delhi is the highest. According to UNICEF study (1992), the number of child labour is 4 lakh in Delhi. That is about 18 per cent of the national capital's total population of children have to work for their survival. Infact, child labour problem is grave one.

There are several factors which play an important role causing child labour problem in India. The literacy/educational level of the parents and of children being one of them. A case study of Patiala City of Punjab confirm that nearly half of the sampled working children had no formal education.[6]

Orphanage is another factor which plays very crucial role in pushing children to the labour force. A large percentage of children start working because of being orphan, rejected by parents or because of broken families and other domestic problems. These children go into streets totally abandoned with no one to care for them. They always live at the mercy of others, who instead of providing them shelter/protection, try to exploit them in every possible way. Resulting, exploitation retards the physical and mental development of a child. The same study of Patiala City support that one-fifth of working children were of those who had lost either one parent or both the parents. Many children join labour force because they did not have anything else to do. So to make sensible use of their time and keep them away from vagrancy, theft, begging and other social evils, they had taken up the jobs. This fact is also supported by a number of key studies.

Occupational status of the parents is another reason for the persistence of child labour in India. Generally, the craftsmen train children in their hereditary crafts at a very early age because the nimble fingers and keen eyesight of easy childhood are an asset in the learning process. Carpet weaving, pottery, silk and cotton weaving, wood carving etc. are some of the traditional crafts taught to children within their houses. In the villages, the boys at the young age are made to handle a plough, reap the harvest, cut and bring fuel from the forest, graze the cattle, guard the crops against birds etc. while the girls help in weeding the fields, looking after younger siblings, sweeping the house etc. These activities may not be viewed as gainful activities, however, they do free the mother from working in the fields or in other remunerative activities.

Urbanisation and increasing poverty which compells the rural households/families to migrate to cities is another factor which induces children belonging to these families to take up work as assistants in shops and establishments, hotels and restaurants, small scale repair workshops and variety of other occupations in different establishments. Some of them enter into self-employment occupations such as vendors, shoe shiners, newspaper sellers, balloon sellers, hawkers etc.

Indebtedness is also the cause of child labour. Many parents secure advances from the landlords/employers and return the loans in terms of child labour. The reports by Prof. R.K. Mishra and Fact Finding Committee confirm the facts. According to the report based on sample survey conducted by Prof R.K. Mishra, Head of Human Right Cell, the number of children engaged in saree manufacturing in and around Varanasi is about 1 lakh. Here in Varanasi, there is a practice of taking advance (Rs. 2,000 to 5,000) by the parents of children from their employers against the services of their children. Here most of the children are found to be working under bonded conditions. The services of the children cannot be withdrawn so long as dues are not cleared. So there is a definite element of bondage involved in this practice.[7]

Similarly the report of the Fact Finding Committee (appointed by Supreme Court of India) of number of villages in Mirzapur area revealed that quite a large number of children are still working under bounded conditions. These number is 300 in Tiltih village, 130 in Balwabilwali and 100 in Harsinghpur. Increasing globalisation is also one of the factor causing child labour in developing countries.

In fact, poverty and economic considerations are the basic inducing factors compelling children to work for considerably long hours, thereby making significant contribution to the household income.

Studies conducted in Java (Indonesia) and Nepal[8], Nigeria[9] and Philippines[10] all confirm the economic contribution of the children to the household. In Nigeria, children enter into economic activities as early as five years of their age and in Philippines, children even less than five years of their age are found carrying messages and making small purchases.

Study of Dakshina Kannada, a district of Karnataka state also reveals that more than 55 per cent of the wage earning children contributed to household income[11]. Similarly, a study conducted in three big cities of Tamilnadu revealed that 72 per cent of the total children had sought employment to augment the income of their families. An all India survey of the Ministry of Labour also shows that 52 out of every 1000 working children were wage earners who augmented family income[12]. Economic compulsion as the cause of child labour has also been depicted by the studies of Muktsar district of Punjab[13] and of Chandigarh[14]. Though their earnings are quite meagre still it was found that children contributed nearly 30 per cent of the total income of their poverty striken families. A study by S. Murty on child labour working in the unorganised sector of Ujjain city reported that the share of children in the earning of their families ranged between 8 per cent and 40 per cent[15]. A study by Bal Krishan (1997) highlighted that in Punjab by sending their children to work, on an average, the rural households were able to increase their income by Rs. 596.[16]

Furthermore, inadequate, irregular or no family income is also the cause of child labour. This fact is supplemented by the study of Patna where poverty striken large size families with their immiserisation were a compelling factor for children to join labour force so as to supplement family income.[17]

Child labour as a symptom of poverty and unemployment is depicted by S.S. Mehta's study which shows a significant positive correlation (0.78) between number of child labour and the number of people below the poverty line and positive significant correlation between the number of child labour and number of unemployed on daily status basis.[18]

Except poverty and unemployment, high wage rate is also one of the important factors inducing child labour particularly in Punjab where due to tightness of labour market, wage rates are very high.

Punjab is the most developed and prosperous state of India. Here per capita income is very high due to good climatic conditions. Therefore, people of Punjab are very rich and enjoy good status. The living standards of these people are very high. The labour class gets influenced by their living standards. They also want to improve their living standards and want to avail all the facilities through hard work and hence they do not hesitate to force their kids to work. The kids who do not know the pro and cones of child labour, in order to lead easy life and for their own economic independence, they accept work happily. They also try to imitate the kids of well influenced persons. Some of them (low socio-economic strata children) even try to imitate hero and heroines of today's glamorous life.

So, in Punjab, economic compulsion is not the main factor behind child labour.

The case study conducted by Shakuntla Gupta of 5 villages i.e. of Shekhupura, Bahadurgarh, Raipur, Majri and Khedi of Patiala district based on 100 rural households supplying child labour support the above thesis (Appendix I and II).

The average size of the sampled rural households supplying child labour is 7 person, and their children number is 4 to 6. Total sample consists of 500 children. About 35 per cent has been found to be school going. Among the school going children, the proportion of males was somewhat higher as compared to females. Another 15 per cent children were neither working nor attending school. These children were found idle, they had nothing to do, except to join labour force. Even the parents of such children during the survey reported that whenever suitable work would be available, they would like to send their children to work.

Out of 250 sampled children, 150 were found child workers, i.e. 60 per cent of the child population was found to be engaged. Among these 150 child worker, 65 per cent were employed and were not attending school, another 20 per cent were combining the school with the work and 15 per cent were combining household with work. The rest 100 children left are mostly females who are engaged in household work and look after their small brother and sisters.

A majority of the rural children were working as wage earners and most of them were employed in agriculture and allied services (72 per cent). The employment of the children in services was found to be 18 per cent, in trade about 7 per cent and in manufacturing, construction and transport only 3 per cent.

The proportion of children in services particularly as domestic servants was found to be about 15 per cent. The detailed study of 20 children (most of them belonged to low income group) working in services, particularly as domestic servants in Punjabi University Campus and in Urban Estate, Patiala, clearly shows that more than 60 per cent of the children were employed on part time basis. However, those working on part time basis were mostly the school attending children explaining thereby that economic compulsion of the parents force the children to work.

But actually, this is not the case. It was found in the survey that about 30 per cent of child labour (as domestic servants) gave economic compulsion as the reason for taking up employment.

Rather about 70 per cent of the employed children shared no responsibility regarding their families. This concludes that in Punjab parents sent their children in labour market not only due to economic compulsion but for further increase in their income or for improving their living standard or for the economic independence of the children so that the children may get better education and may enjoy better facilities even. It was found during the survey that some of the children had bank balances also. Cause may be any one, from social point of view, it is curse on the part of the country and injustice to the child. It is deprivation of his right to education. So the government should prohibit child labour through laws. Steps like preferential coverage of child labour household under poverty alleviation programmes can prove useful. Voluntary agencies like N.G.O.'s, Mahila Mandals can also help to lower the incidence of child labour. International Labour Organisation movement, trade unions can also play an important role.

The protective laws on the age of employment, minimum wages, working hours, interval, weekly offs, life insurance of children working in hazards need to be enforced effectively. At the same time, there should be a provision of nutritional food to the working children.

In addition to that enforcement of universal compulsory education and the provision of training and scholarship schemes can play a significant role in education and elimination of child labour in India.

Alongwith this, parents of working children should be motivated through education, publicity and propaganda to send their children to school. There is also a need to change the attitude of the parents towards their children, because proper attitude and homely atmosphere in the family also affect the development of the children favourably.

References

1. *Times of India* (Delhi), September 7, 1981, p. 7.
2. *Indian Express* (Chandigarh), November 26, 1985, p. 5.
3. Khatu, K.K. *et al.*, *Working Children in India* (Baroda Operational Research Group), 1983, p. 69.
4. *The Tribune* (Chandigarh), June 8, 1996, p. 17.
5. *The Tribune* (Chandigarh), July 28, 1997, p. 8.
6. Sharma, B.K. and Mittar Vishwa, *Child Labour and Urban Informal*

Sector, Delhi, Deep & Deep Publications, 1990, p. 120.

7. Mustaja, Mohd. and Sharma, Onkar, *Child Labour in India: A Bitter Truth,* Delhi, Deep & Deep Publications, 1996, p. 195.
8. Nag, M. *et al.*, "An Anthropological Approach to the Study of Economic Value of Children in Java & Nepal," *Current Anthropology,* Vol. 19, No. 2, 1978, pp. 293–306.
9. Caldwell, J.C., "An Investigation Illustrated with Nigeria Data," *Population Studies,* Vol. 31, No. 1, 1977, pp. 5–27.
10. Dinesh, B.M., *Economic Activities of Children: Causes and Consequences* (Delhi, Daya Publishing House, 1988), p. 13.
11. Dinesh, B.M., *Ibid.*, p. 109.
12. *Indian Express* (Chandigarh); August 27, 1985, p. 8.
13. Kaur, Sukhbir, "An Economic Contribution of Child Labour of Landless Families in the Skilled Activities in Mukatsar Block," Unpublished M.Phil. thesis, Punjab Agricultural University, Ludhiana, p. 56.
14. Kumar, Rajan, "Problems of Unorganised Labour in a Planned City," Unpublished M.Phil. thesis, Punjab University, Chandigarh, p. 148.
15. Murty, S. "Child Labour in Unorganised Sector: A Case Study of Ujjain City," *The Indian Journal of Labour Economics,* Vol. 33, Oct.-Dec. 1990, p. 286.
16. Sharma, B.K., "Economic Aspects of Child Labour in Punjab: A Case Study of Patiala District," Unpublished Ph. D. thesis, Punjabi University, Patiala, 1997, p. 252.
17. Singh, Bhagwan Prasad, "Sad Plight of Child Labour and Need for Proper Deal," *Indian Journal of Labour Economics,* Vol. 33, No. 4, Oct.-Dec. 1990.
18. Mehta, S.S., "Why Child Labour? The Indian Case," in Hirway Indira, Cottoyn Jacqui.

APPENDIX I

Flow chart showing distribution of child population in Punjab (A case study of Patiala)

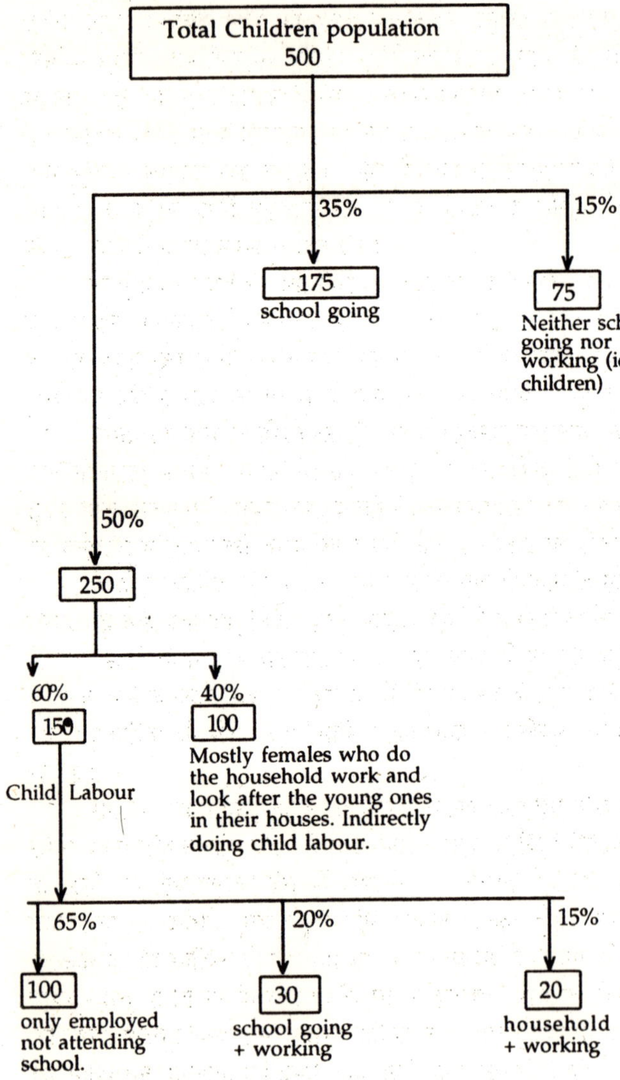

APPENDIX II

Statement of sample survey of Rural Children Involved in different occupations

Agricultural and allied	72 per cent
Services (Domestic, Social and Personal)	18 per cent
Trade	07 per cent
Manufacturing, Construction and Transport	03 per cent
Domestic and Personal Services	15 per cent (20 Children)
Basis of Employment	60 per cent regular/part time 40 per cent regular/full time
Reason for Employment	30 per cent –purely economic 70 per cent economic + other factors

6

Assessment of Incidence and Child Development Activities in India During Fifty Years of Independence

—*Mohan Prasad Shrivastava, Virendra Prasad,*
Kanchan Pd. Shrivastava & Nira Kumari

Introduction

Children constitute the nation's future human resource. Investment in child development is thus an investment in the country's future and in improving the nations quality of life. The early years of the children are very delicate period and require well designed programmes for the child's survival, growth and development. Deficiencies during this stage can lead to permanent retardation in physical and mental growth.[1] As children represent the human resources of a country, it is vital to have a well-planned strategy to aid them in their process. Efforts to save the lives of millions of children and aid the physical, mental and emotional development of many more must be viewed as a long-term investment in human resources. The fact that children have neither a voice nor a political constituency assigns a great responsibility to adults to plan for child development.

Child development is a scientific study of children and draws from Medicine, Psychology, Education, Social work, Home Science, Anthropology and Economics. It is the study of how and why children develop perception, thought process, emotional relations and patterns of social behaviour. It also provides knowledge that is important for advising parents, forming educational programmes creating government programmes for children making legal policies affecting children.

The phenomenon of child labour rolls the youthful life of the children and restricts the prospects of education which can enable him to reach a high level at a latter stage of life on the one hand and ultimately it harms the prosperity and progress of the nation on the other. Child labour requires a historic view and inter-sectoral linkage so as to lead to allround development of child, as child development is not merely an issue about launching programmes designed to provide isolated services for the child such as early education and nutrition.

Incidence of Morbidity and Mortality

The incidence of morbidity and mortality among children tells us about the state of their health as well as that of their mothers before, during and after pregnancy. Infant and early childhood mortality rate reflect the extent of awareness and knowledge of mothers about different aspects related to health nutrition needs of children. They also reflect the extent of immunisation of children, the availability of health services (particularly maternal and child health services), the food availability and distribution patterns in the family, accessibility to safe drinking water and sanitary living conditions, and the extent to which major causes of child morbidity and mortality have been tackled.

Causes of High Incidence of Child Labour

The reasons for the high incidence of child labour in rural areas are not hard to trace. These reasons are social, economic, educational and political. Children are expected to contribute to the subsistence of the family from an early age. Parents, particularly if they are illiterate do not attach much importance to schooling, more so in the case of girls.

Early dropout from school facilitates the process. Many parents do not think that there is anything wrong if a child is engaged in work. On the contrary, they think that it is useful of engaging a child who is not attending school. In any case, most parents can't afford to send a child to school which would incur expenditure on

Table 6.1

Per Capita GNP (Gross National Product) and Labour Force in India and Abroad (1996)

Countries	Population (in million)	Per Capita GNP (US $)	Labour Force					
			Agriculture				Industries	
			1980	1996	1980	1996	1980	1996
1. India	913.6	320	70	64	13	16	34	32
2. China	1190.9	530	62	59	13	13	51	51
3. Morocco	26.4	1140	56	45	20	25	34	35
4. Columbia	36.3	1670	40	24	21	23	25	25
5. Namibia	1.5	1970	56	49	15	15	40	40
6. South Africa	40.5	3040	17	14	35	32	35	37
7. Saudi Arabia	17.8	7050	43	18	16	20	8	12
8. New Zealand	3.5	8110	13	12	34	32	28	30
9. Australia	17.8	18000	6	6	32	26	36	42
10. United Kingdom	58.4	18340	3	2	38	29	39	43
11. Italy		19300	13	9	38	31	33	37
12. Kuwait	1.6	19420	2	1	32	25	40	44
13. France	57.9	23420	8	5	35	29	40	44
14. Germany,	81.5	25580	7	4	45	38	40	41
15. U.S.A.	260.6	25880	3	3	31	28	42	45
16. Japan	125.0	34630	11	7	35	34	38	40
17. Switzerland		37930	6	6	39	35	39	40
18. Belgium	10.1	22870	3	3	35	28	34	40
19. Singapore	2.9	22500	2	0	42	36	37	37

Source : World Development Report, 1996. Oxford University Press, New York.

Table 6.2
Statewise Selected Socio-Economic Indicators in India (1996)

	States	*Per capita Income (Rs.)*	*Density*	*Literacy*	*Work*
1.	Andhra Pradesh	1839	242	44.09	45.05
2.	Arunachal Pradesh	2493	10	41.59	46.24
3.	Assam	1915	286	52.89	36.09
4.	Bihar	1142	479	38.48	32.16
5.	Goa	4105	316	75.51	35.28
6.	Gujarat	2526	211	61.29	40.23
7.	Haryana	3456	372	55.85	31.00
8.	Himachal Pradesh	2074	93	63.86	42.83
9.	J & K	1687	N.A.	N.A.	N.A.
10.	Karnataka	2171	235	56.04	41.99
11.	Kerala	1886	749	89.91	31.43
12.	Madhya Pradesh	1588	149	44.20	42.82
13.	Maharashtra	3440	257	64.87	42.97
14.	Manipur	2002	82	59.89	42.18
15.	Meghalaya	1756	79	49.10	42.67
16.	Mizoram	N.A.	33	82.27	48.91
17.	Nagaland	1905	73	61.67	42.68
18.	Orissa	1652	203	49.09	37.53
19.	Punjab	3864	403	58.51	30.88
20.	Rajasthan	1717	129	38.55	38.89
21.	Sikkim	N.A.	57	56.94	41.51
22.	Tamilnadu	2056	429	68.66	43.31
23.	Tripura	N.A.	263	60.44	31.14
24.	Uttar Pradesh	1606	473	41.60	32.20
25.	West Bengal	2084	767	67.70	32.19

Source : Ibid.

books and uniform, etc. As is obvious from Table 6.1 that in most developing economies children are living miserable, cheerless lives and moving towards starvation. The extent and the nature of activities of child labour are influenced mainly by the socio-economic structure and level and pace of development in India and abroad. Table 6.1 illustrates the per capita GNP (Gross National Product); population (in million) and percentage of labour force in agriculture and industries in India and other countries like China, Morocco; Columbia, Namibia; South Africa; Saudi Arabia; New Zealand, Australia; United Kingdom; Italy; Kuwait; France; Germany; U.S.A.; Japan; Switzerland; Belgium and Singapore, etc.

On the basis of these indicators World Development Report, 1996 can easily be referred as "the problem of maintenance of child and the wage of adult wage-earner so that they should maintain the family at the adequate standard.[3] It is further referred that "a well educated healthy work force is essential for economic growth.[4]

Table 6.2 shows the statewise selected socio-economic indicators in India consisting of per capita income; density; literacy and the work. Similarly, Table 6.3 indicates the statewise percentage of participation rates of male and female children during 1961 to 1991 as labour force. Table 6.4(a) gives the picture of statewise participation rates of male and female children between 5 to 14 years in school during 1961 to 1991 census of both the male and female child. Table 6.4(b) presents the statewise child work participation rates in India of male and female child during the same year. These tables present the comprehensive picture of inter-state analysis.

Table 6.3
Statewise Percentage of Participation Rates of Male and Female Children in Labour Force (1961-91)

States	*Percent of Labour Force*							
	Male Children				*Female Children*			
	1961	*1971*	*1981*	*1991*	*1961*	*1971*	*1981*	*1991*
1	2	3	4	5	6	7	8	9
1. Andhra Pradesh	24	17.8	14.2	9.1	17.4	10.2	10.6	9.4
2. Bihar	14.9	10.0	6.4	4.7	9.6	2.8	2.3	1.9
3. Gujarat	11.4	9.3	6.8	4.7	10.6	4.0	3.3	2.7
4. Haryana	12.3	7.5	5.8	3.0	6.0	1.0	1.6	1.0
5. Himachal Pradesh	9.3	6.5	4.3	2.2	13.8	8.9	6.3	2.8
6. Karnataka	18.3	14.1	12.1	8.2	12.6	5.6	7.1	6.5
7. Kerala	3.4	2.1	1.1	0.5	3.0	1.8	1.1	0.4
8. M.P.	19.3	12.4	11.0	6.6	18.3	7.3	7.9	5.2
9. Maharashtra	13.6	8.7	8.1	4.1	14.1	5.8	7.1	4.5
10. Orissa	18.9	13.5	10.5	5.6	10.5	2.3	3.5	2.8
11. Punjab	14.6	11.2	7.6	4.9	7.1	0.2	0.4	0.5
12. Rajasthan	21.4	11.2	7.8	4.4	19.8	4.2	4.1	3.8
13. Tamilnadu	14.5	9.7	8.4	4.4	10.6	4.6	6.6	4.3
14. U.P.	13.3	8.3	6.3	4.6	6.7	2.3	1.4	1.3
15. West Bengal	7.8	7.0	5.6	5.1	2.0	1.0	1.3	1.8
All India	14.6	9.8	8.0	5.2	10.6	4.0	4.4	3.4

Source : Computed from Census of India (from 1961 to 1991) Registrar General of India. All India Education Survey : Third (73), Fourth (78), Sixth (93) NCERT, New Delhi.
Report of the Education Commission 1964-66, Supplementary Volume II Ministry of Education and Youth Service; Ministry of H.R.D.; Annual Reports, Deptt. of HRD of many years.

Table 6.4(a)
Statewise Participation Rates of Male and Female Children (5-14 years) in School (1961-91 Census)

States	*Percentage of Child Population in Schools*							
	Male Children				*Female Children*			
	1961	*1971*	*1981*	*1991*	*1961*	*1971*	*1981*	*1991*
1	2	3	4	5	6	7	8	9
1. Andhra Pradesh	35.9	33.3	48.7	55.2	19.3	20.5	32.0	41.5
2. Bihar	34.0	30.1	43.1	43.0	9.3	10.2	21.0	26.5
3. Gujarat	46.2	48.7	59.6	67.5	27.7	31.5	44.1	56.3
4. Haryana	42.3	46.9	58.2	66.6	21.7	21.2	33.6	54.6
5. H.P.	50.9	58.4	68.6	76.1	34.8	33.8	50.1	67.7
6. Karnataka	43.3	43.5	52.5	62.6	24.0	27.1	37.2	51.8
7. Kerala	66.3	73.0	81.7	86.4	57.7	66.5	79.9	86.6
8. M.P.	33.5	32.1	45.4	54.2	11.1	14.0	23.3	38.8
9. Maharashtra	49.7	53.9	64.9	70.3	27.2	35.0	49.0	61.2
10. Orissa	42.4	37.5	52.1	59.8	20.3	20.2	32.2	45.4
11. Punjab	42.5	48.3	62.2	66.1	31.0	37.1	52.8	60.1
12. Rajasthan	29.9	32.1	46.4	53.3	8.8	10.6	17.1	26.0
13. Tamilnadu	51.2	60.0	64.9	74.1	31.9	42.4	49.9	67.1
14. U.P.	28.7	35.8	44.1	45.5	8.0	16.1	20.9	29.0
15. All India	39.6	41.3	52.5	56.6	20.1	25.2	34.6	44.2

Source : Ibid.

Table 6.4(b)
Statewise Child Work Participation Rates in India of Male and Female Child (1981-91)

States	*Male Children*			*Female Children*		
	1981	*1991*	*% change*	*1981*	*1991*	*% change*
1. All India	8.7	5.7	3.4	12.8	10.5	3.3
2. Andhra Pradesh	12.8	9.4	3.4	12.8	10.5	3.3
3. Bihar	7.1	4.9	2.2	3.8	2.9	0.9
4. Gujarat	7.5	5.1	2.4	6.2	5.5	0.7
5. Haryana	6.5	3.2	3.3	3.8	1.8	2.0
6. H.P.	6.9	3.6	3.3	10.6	5.5	5.1
7. Karnataka	12.8	8.9	2.9	9.7	8.7	1.0
8. Kerala	1.5	0.6	0.9	1.5	0.5	1.0
9. M.P.	12.1	7.6	4.5	11.4	8.6	2.8
10. Maharashtra	9.0	4.9	4.1	9.8	6.6	3.2
11. Orissa	11.9	6.3	5.6	7.3	5.4	1.9
12. U.P.	6.6	5.0	1.6	2.2	2.5	–0.3
13. West Bengal	6.1	5.6	0.5	1.9	2.7	–0.8

Source : Ibid.

Table 6.5
Global Percentage of Primary and Secondary Education of Male and Female

Countries	Primary				Secondary			
	Female		Male		Female		Male	
	1981-82	'95-96	'81-82	'95-96	'81-82	'95-96	'81-82	'95-96
1	2	3	4	5	6	7	8	9
1. World	89	100	104	109	38	57	49	65
2. India	67	91	98	113	20	38	39	59
3. Low Income	80	98	108	112	26	42	42	55
4. Middle Income	101	102	107	105	48	63	53	65
5. Lower-Middle Income	99	101	107	105	49	62	55	64
6. Upper-Middle Income	103	—	106	—	47	—	48	—
7. Low and Middle Income	89	99	104	106	30	30	45	59
8. Sub Sahara	69	64	91	77	10	23	20	-
9. Europe and Central Asia	—	97	—	97	—	90	—	81
10. Middle-East and North Africa	74	91	98	104	32	51	52	—
11. Latin America and Caribbeans	105	—	108	—	41	98	40	97
12. High Income Economies	102	104	103	104	—	98	—	97
13. East Asia and Pacific Regions	103	115	117	119	38	53	51	61

14.	Pakistan	27	49	51	80	8	—	20	—
15.	Bangla Desh	46	105	76	128	9	12	26	26
16.	China	109	116	121	120	37	51	51	54
17.	Sri Lanka	100	105	105	106	57	78	52	71
18.	Mexico	121	110	222	114	46	58	51	58
19.	New Zealand	111	101	111	102	84	104	82	101
20.	U.K.	103	113	97	100	105	130	94	110
21.	Italy	100	99	100	98	70	82	73	81
22.	France	110	105	112	107	92	100	83	97
23.	Sweden	97	100	96	100	93	100	96	101
24.	France	99	98	90	97	92	100	96	98
25.	Japan	101	102	101	102	94	97	98	95
26.	Denmark	95	98	96	97	104	115	105	112
27.	United Arab Amirat	88	108	90	112	49	94	95	84

Source : World Development Report, 1996, pp. 194-95. Oxford University Press, New York.

Role of Education

Education plays a catalistic role in socio-economic development of the economy. To quote V.V. Giri, "Education is the principal tool of socio-economic development and unless all societies are provided with right type of education, adequate in quality and quantity, it will not be possible to tackle satisfactorily the problem of ignorance of health and poverty which afflicts the majority of human beings in the world."[5] Education is needed in all these areas to cope with and repair the destruction already introduced. It is also necessary for the economic modernisation of the society.[6] It is now universally acknowledged that the goal of plan efforts in human development is a necessary pre-requisite.[7] Education is the catalistic factor which leads to human resource development comprising better health and nutrition, improved socio-economic opportunities and more congenial and beneficial natural environment for all. The primary purpose of education system is to impart knowledge and skill and just as important to transmit certain values. The resulting education package will vary economically across countries and culture.[8] There is already enough evidence in India to show that high literacy rates, especially high female literacy rates, are associated with low rates of population growth, infant mortality and material mortality besides a higher rate of life expectancy.[9]

Illiteracy Problem of Child Labour in Global Perspective

Illiteracy and poverty are the global and fundamental problem of child labour. As is obvious from the Table 6.5 in addition to other causes, illiteracy is the root cause in developing nations particularly in India. The global percentage of primary and secondary education of male and female can easily be illustrated from this table. The primary purpose of education system is to impart knowledge and skills and just as important transmit certain values. The resulting education package will vary economically across countries and culture.[10] To refer World Development Report, 1996, "Reform of education is therefore, needed both to give workers more transferable, marketable skills and to develop informed citizens, capable of participating actively in civil society. Reforms of health care system is needed to raise the life expectancy and reduce the burden of disease and injury—contributing both to productivity and the quality of life."[11] Due to poverty and illiteracy, they think only about the present time which is their sole concern and worry;

Table 6.6

Statewise Literacy Rate in India of Male and Female (As per 1991 Census)

States	Total	Male	Female	Gross Enrolment					
				Primary (Class I-V)			Upper Primary (Class VI-VIII)		
	%	%	%	Boys %	Girls %	Total %	Boys %	Girls %	Total %
1. Andhra Pradesh	44.09	55.13	32.72	99.6	89.9	94.9	53.3	41.8	49.7
2. Assam	52.89	61.87	43.03	113	124	128.8	91.6	65.9	79.1
3. Bihar	38.48	52.49	22.89	93	55.4	75.1	47.5	21.9	35.3
4. Gujarat	61.29	73.13	48.64	158.3	106.8	131.4	81.1	61.5	71.6
5. Haryana	65.95	69.10	40.47	86.4	84.9	85.6	70.9	56.7	64.2
6. Karnataka	56.04	67.25	44.34	131.1	123.5	127.4	78.1	66.8	72.6
7. Kerala	89.81	93.62	86.17	98.4	95.4	96.9	105.1	101.5	103.3
8. M.P.	44.20	58.42	28.85	112.9	88.2	102.1	91.6	43.3	64.4
9. Maharashtra	64.87	76.56	52.32	125.5	120.2	122.9	92.4	77.2	85.0
10. Orissa	49.09	69.9	34.69	113.4	78.2	95.6	73.0	39.8	56.2
11. Punjab	58.51	65.66	50.41	92.4	90.7	91.5	70.0	65.0	69.7
12. Rajasthan	38.55	54.99	20.44	129.3	75.3	103.4	79.9	32.0	56.9
13. Tamilnadu	62.66	73.75	51.75	159.3	145.6	156.6	118.2	99.5	109.1
14. Uttar Pradesh	41.60	55.73	25.31	104.3	72.2	89.1	72.3	34.9	54.7
15. West Bengal	57.70	67.81	46.56	128.6	122.3	125.5	102.8	91.8	97.2
16. All India	62.00	64.13	39.29	114.5	93.3	104.3	79.5	54.9	67.6

Source : (a) Economic Survey: 1996-97, p. 185. Government of India, Ministry of Finance; New Delhi.
(b) Financial Population Total of 1991, Series-I, paper-2, 1992. Registrar General of India, New Delhi.
(c) Compiled from Ministry of Human Resource Development Report, 1996-97; Government of India; Department of Education; New Delhi.

Table 6.7
Statewise Literacy in India of Male and Female
(As per 1991 Census)

(in percentage)

States	*Total (%)*	*Male (%)*	*Female (%)*
1. Andhra Pradesh	44.09	55.13	32.72
2. Assam	52.89	61.87	43.03
3. Bihar	38.48	52.49	22.89
4. Gujarat	61.29	73.13	48.64
5. Haryana	65.95	69.10	40.47
6. Karnataka	56.04	67.26	44.34
7. Kerala	89.81	93.62	86.17
8. Madhya Pradesh	44.20	58.42	28.85
9. Maharashtra	64.87	76.56	52.32
10. Orissa	49.09	69.09	34.69
11. Punjab	58.51	65.66	50.41
12. Rajasthan	38.55	54.99	20.44
13. Tamilnadu	62.66	73.75	51.33
14. Uttar Pradesh	41.60	55.73	25.31
15. West Bengal	57.70	67.81	46.56
All India	52.20	64.13	39.29

Source : Economic Survey: 1996-97, p. 185. (Census Series I; Paper-2, Registrar General of India.)

they do never think of their future.[12] They feel themselves fully satisfied with what they are gaining by the earning of children. They ignore the participation of their children even in educational opportunities.[13] Consequently, child labour deprives the children of all the educational opportunities. It also affects their health and they are converted into labourers of low wages for all their lives.

Lack of provision of compulsory education is also a cause of child labour.[14] Non-availability of school going facilities tend children to do some jobs as an alternative. The gross ignorance on the part of parents in not sending their children to school is condemned by ILO.[15] The child labourers, today, will be paupers of tomorrow, they are the boys and girls who will grow up without either formal schooling or knowledge of a trade, sooner or later, their youthful energies exhausted, they will become dull, shiftless, driftless.[16] Tables 6.6 & 6.7 consist of statewise literacy rate of male and female child in primary and upper primary schools as per 1991 census and gross enrolment as well.

Historical Overview

Traditionally, children in need of care were looked after by the family, kin and caste groups. Religious institutions and centres learnings also provide child care services.

In the early part of the twentieth century, a voluntary effort took on an organised character. In the mid-twenties, voluntary organisations such as Indian Red Cross Society; All India Women's Conference; Kasturba Gandhi National Memorial Trust and Children's Aid Society etc. organised programmes in the areas of welfare, health, nutrition and education for children.

In 1920, a first organisation with the membership of children namely 'Balkanji Bari' for children was set up in India. Around this time several other organisations at local and regional levels were also set up. Among these All India Shia Orphanage, the Bai Dosabai Kotwali Parsi Orphanage etc. were running on the basis of religion. But these organisations remained more confined to only urban areas.[17]

The post independence period witnessed some marked changes in the approach and strategy of child development exhibiting deep concern for reaching rural poor and other depressed groups. Over the years, there has been a radical change during various plan periods in the child development approach. In the first two five year plans[18] the main focus was on provision on health and nutrition services only. Child development was left to voluntary agencies with grants-in-aid being sanctioned by the government. Investment in children really started in the third five year plan with the setting up of Demonstration Projects in each state to integrate all services of education, health and nutrition. A new cadre of workers, 'Balsevikas' was created during this plan. For evaluating the basic needs of children and giving necessary support to the demonstration Project the Child Care Committee was also set up.

Constitutional Provisions

The Indian Constitution provides several provisions for protection, development and welfare of children. Article 24 prohibits the children's employment in any mine or factory or in any other hazardous occupation. Article 39(e) and (f) lay[19] down that the state shall direct its policy in such a manner that the tender age of children is not abused, children are given opportunities to develop in a healthy manner and childhood is protected against exploitation and against moral and material abandonment.

Child Development Approach During 1950's (Fifties)

During fifties (1951-60) the First Five Year Plan acknowledged that the need of children should receive much greater consideration than is commonly given to them. According to Ist Plan the total responsibility of welfare had to be borne commulatively by the family, community and the state. Voluntary agencies could organise child welfare activities, as they had been engaged in this task even earlier without adequate state aid with their own resources. Voluntary organisations were sanctioned grants-in-aid by the state for strengthening, improving and extending the existing activities in the child and social welfare. To mobilise voluntary activities in all aspects of child development the first national level organisation "The Indian Council for Child Welfare" was established. In a significant development in 1953 'Central Social Welfare Board' was set up to assist voluntary organisations and mobilise their support. In 1954 the CSWB launched the WEP (Welfare Extention Project) to cater the rural population.

During Second Five Year Plan (1956-61)[21] the CSWB programmes were reviewed and it was decided to locate welfare Extension Projects in community development blocks and convert it into the Co-ordinated Pattern Projects. Demonstration Projects were set up in rural areas whose component consisted of education, health, nutrition and welfare. But these projects could not do well due to many unavoidable reasons.

In 1959 United Nations General Assembly[22] adopted UN Declaration of Rights of Children and accepted by the Indian Government. According to this declaration the children has the right to:

(i) affection, love and understanding;
(ii) adequate nutrition and medical care;
(iii) free education;
(iv) full opportunity for play and recreation;
(v) a name and nationality;
(vi) special care, if handicapped;
(vii) be among the first to receive relief in times of disaster;
(viii) develop individual ability;
(ix) be brought up in spirit of peace and universal brotherhood;

(*x*) enjoy these rights, regardless of race, colour, sex, religion, national or social origin.

Child Development Approach During Sixties (1960's)

During this decade also the emphasis on child welfare continued and the Children Act, 1960 came into effect which provided penalisation of offenders for cruel treatment of children, employment of children in begging; giving a child liqour or dangerous drugs and employing a person below 14 years in mines or factories. This Act[23] was ammended in 1978. On the basis of recommendations of WEP (Welfare Extension Programme) and the Evaluation Committee a new scheme of Family and Child Welfare was launched in 1967 which would provide integrated basic social services to children and promote cultural, educational and recreational activities for women and children. The ICCW was entrusted with the responsibility of providing trained personnel i.e. Mukhya Sevikas; Balsevikas and Grih Sevikas. In 1963 NCERT was established with the objective of conducting child studies and evolving methods of childhood education. In 1966 Kothari Commission was set up which recommended expansion of pre-school facilities to children from disadvantaged areas in particular. In 1967 the 'Ganga Saran Sinha Committee' was set up to identify the problems and needs of the child and suggest action programmes. In 1968 the 'National Policy of Education'[24] was announced which reiterated the recommendations of the Education Commission (1964-66).

Child Development Approach During Seventies (1970's)

During seventies 'National Policy for Children' was adopted on the basis of recommendations of 'Ganga Saran Sinha Committee.' It stated that State shall provide adequate services to children before and after birth during the period of growth to ensure their full physical, mental and social development.

The policy provided for a National Children's Board set up in 1974 and later reconstituted in 1978 to provide a forum to plan, review and co-ordinate the various services directed towards children. Under this policy, 'Bureau for Nutrition and Child Development' in the Ministry of Social Welfare was set up which was made responsible for the implementation of various programmes under this policy. National Children's Fund was also set up by the government for providing financial assistance to children and high priority during fourth five year plan. During this plan a special nutrition programme (SNP) was also launched to provide nutritional status of pre-school children, pregnant and lactaling mothers.

During Fifth Plan, ANP & SNP was transferred to state sector with fully funded by the government. Balwadi Nutrition Programme started with central government funding during fourth plan was another feeding programme. In the same year Prophylaxis Programme was launched to prevent nutritional anemia in children and expectant and nursing mothers. But this programme had marginal impact. Consequent upon this, ICDS[25] (Integrated Child Development Services) programme was initiated and 'National Institute of Public Co-operation and Child Development' (NPCCD) was set up in 1975 as an autonomous body. In 1979 'Child Labour Prohibition and Regulation' was passed and 'Gurupad Swamy Committee' was set up. A Child Labour Cell was also constituted in 1979 which is now under the Ministry of Labour. Child Labour Cell has been made responsible for the formulation, co-ordination and implementation of programmes and policies for protecting child labour from exploitation. It also provides grants to the voluntary organisations.

Child Development Approach During Eighties (1980's)

Programmes of services for children in health, nutrition, education, social services were expanded during eighties. In 1983 the National Health Policy[26] was adopted. Legislation pertaining the minimum age for employment of children, hours of work etc. were consolidated into a comprehensive law.

The Child Labour (Prohibition & Regulation) Act, 1986 came into effect which prohibits child labour in selected work areas and processes, and regulates it in some others. This Act prohibits employment of children in jobs that are hazardous to their lives or health working near dangerous machines, handling poisonous chemicals working at ports etc. According to this Act, children should not be employed in bidi making, carpet weaving, cement industries, tanneries, mica cutting and construction sites.

The new policy was adopted in 1987 comprising three trust areas: legal action, development programmes and child labour and project based Plan of Action. Interestingly, the Act permitted child labour in any industry, even if hazardous, where the contribution of children formed part of family labour. A Comprehensive National Education Policy on Education was adopted in 1986 under the leadership of late Prime Minister Rajiv Gandhi which intensified efforts in human resource development. The policy gave universalisation of elementary education, universal enrolment and retention of children upto 14 years in the school system and improvement in the quality of education. In 1987-88 Operation Black Board was launched and Navodya Vidyalayas were set up to cater the rural children. A scheme was initiated whereby voluntary organisations were provided central assistance for operating early childhood education centres in rural and backward areas.

The educational policy emphasised early childhood care and education (ECCE) and day care centres be made available as a support service for working woman and girls engaged in taking care of siblings. The policy suggested integration of ECCE with ICDC whereas possible. In 1987-88 ECCE was transferred from Department of Education to Department of Women and Child Development of Ministry of Human Resource Development. The Juvenile Justice Act, 1986[27] replaced Children's Act, 1960 and for the first time separated delinquent from neglected children. Under the Act children taken into custody in remand/observation homes or later sent by Juvenile courts/children's Board into institutional care, were treated as undertrail.

In order to upgrade and strengthen the available infrastructure for effective implementation of the juvenile justice Act, the scheme for Prevention and Control of Juvenile Social Maladjustment was initiated in 1986-87. During this decade efforts for safeguarding the rights of children were also under way at the regional level.

The Seventh Plan continued the strategy of promoting early childhood survival and development through programmes in different sectors, important among these being ICDS. In 1989-90 more than 82 per cent coverage was reported for DPT, OPV, BCG and about 70 per cent of measles and TT(PW). In 1988-89 about 27 million children were enrolled in class I to VIII. Of these, 96 million were in class I to V and 31 million in class VI to VIII. The enrolment ratio in 1988-89 was 99.6 per cent in class I to V (age group 6-11 years) and 56.9 per cent in class VI to VIII (age group 11-14).[28] The provision was made to augment training of ICDS functionaries and a system for decentralised monitoring and qualitative feedback have been developed.

Child Development Approach During Nineties (1990's)

During 1990's a large number of constructive efforts for the welfare and development of children and child labour have been initiated by the Government. During Eighth Plan the universal programme of immunisation was to be further expanded and strengthened. An attempt has been made for creating greater awareness about the need and importance of immunisation through mass media and non-formal channels. Child development programmes have been given high priority during eighth plan. A National Child Labour Programme has been taken up to make effective intervention for preventing exploitation of child labour in organised sector. During this plan 9 child labour projects have been launched. According to VIIIth Plan[29] "In regard to literacy, the emphasis would be on sustainability of literacy skills, gained and on the achievement of goals of remediation, continuation and application of skills to actual living and working conditions." Early childhood education programmes were to be strengthened. It was felt during this plan that "The problem of child labour is an unfortunate manifestation of economic compulsions as well as socio-cultural perceptions".

During this decade literacy has been a priority on national agenda as a tool of information and knowledge as an instrument of social change. The total literacy compaign (TLC) has become the principal strategy of the National Literacy Mission (NLM) for eradication of illiteracy throughout the country. The total literacy is targeted to be achieved by 2005 A.D. 442 districts have been covered under TLC and 215 districts under Postal Campaign. The Gross Enrolment Ratio (GER) in primary stage (Class I-V) increased from 42.6 per cent in 1950-51 to 90.5 per cent in 1996-97 and in the upper primary stage (Class VI-VIII) from 12.7 per cent to 62.3 per cent over the period. These changes have contributed to increasing the overall literacy rate from 18.3 per cent in 1951 to 52.2 per cent in 1991.

According to Economic Survey, 1997-98[30] "Concerted efforts have been made to achieve the goal of universalisation of Elementary Education. As a result, India has become the second largest country in the world with 151.5 million children in the age group of 6-14 years enrolled in 1996-97 covering about 81 per cent of children in this age group. The number of primary schools have increased from 0.14 lakh to 1.71 lakh. While universalisation of Elementary Education is the ultimate goal, it has been laid on enrolment and retention of the girl child schooling and recruitment of rural women as teachers. Special provisions have been incorporated in various schemes *e.g.* the revamped Blackboard Scheme provides that at least 50% of teachers recruited should be women under Non-formal Education Programme. 90% assistance is given for centres

Table 6.8
Revenue and Expenditure and Capital Expenditure on Education and Child Development Programme during 1995- 1997-98

(in Rs.)

Items	*1995-96*	*1996-97*	*1997-98*
1	2	3	4
1. Operation Black Board	279	268.26	279
2. Teacher's Training Programme	118	108	117
3. Non-Formal Education	158	153.50	158.25
4. Shiksha Karmi Project in Rajasthan	8.00	8.00	9.00
5. Bihar Education Project	30.00	30.00	25.00
6. Lok Jumbish	22.14	22.14	22.20
7. Distt. Primary Education	225.00	230.94	238.50
8. Nutrition Support to Primary Education	07.00	617.79	1400.00
9. Other Programmes	02.00	02.00	03.00
10. Total Elementary Education	651.90	1144.02	2264.68
11. NCERT	27.12	27.12	25.12
12. Kendriya Vidyalya	196.00	298.96	255.50
13. Navodaya Vidyalya	249.27	226.26	237.24
14. Vocational Education	82.00	82.00	82.00
15. Compulsory Education in Schools	47.00	27.00	40.00
16. Integrated Education for Disabled Children	4.70	4.70	4.70
17. Educational Technological Programme	22.88	17.88	22.88
18. Promotion of Science Laboratory	24.47	24.47	21.69
19. Open School Programme	5.34	5.19	5.34
20. Other Programmes	5.29	7.29	11.12
21. Total Secondary Education	670.23	727.97	713.41

Source : Demand and Expenditure Budget: 1996-97 to 1998-99. Ministry of Finance; Government of India, pp. 106-07 & 110-11.

exclusively for girls. Free education is provided to girls by various State Governments while education is free for girls up to class XII in Kendriya and Navodaya Vidyalayas. The central Plan allocation on elementary education programme has been raised from about 2265 crores in 1997-98 (R.E.) and on DPEP (District Primary Education Programme) Rs. 561 crores in the same year.

Table 6.9
Budgetary Allocation on Education During 1995-96, 1996-97 and 1997-98

(Rs. crores)

Items	*1995-96*	*1996-97*	*1997-98*
1	2	3	4
1. Early Childhood Education Assocation to Primary Organisations	3.45	3.55	3.55
2. NIPCCD (National Institute of Public Cooperation and Child Development)	5.83	5.83	5.96
3. Total Child Welfare	635.37	717.02	729.89
4. Day-care Centres	23.5	23.5	23.5
5. ICDS	00.44	00.44	00.44
6. Social Security and Child Welfare	2.63	3.36	3.10
7. Balwadi Nutrition Programme	3.72	9.72	9.72
8. Contribution to UNICEF	2.95	2.98	3.10
9. Other Schemes	2.58	2.59	2.61
10. Nutrition	5.75	5.84	6.06
Grand Total	774.89	868.25	896.07

Source : IBID pp. 106-07 & 110-11.

A new scheme "Balika Samriddhi Yojna" has been launched on October 2, 1997. Under this scheme, the mother of a girl child born on or after August 15, 1997 in a family below the poverty line in rural and urban areas will be given a grant of Rs. 500. Further, a scholarship will be given for education of the girl child when she attends school.

For holistic child development, Integrated Child Development Services Scheme (ICDS), the widely acclaimed and unique programme provides an integrated package of services comprising supplementary nutrition, immunisation, health check-up and referal services, pre-school, non-formal education and health to children

Table 6.10

Sources of Income of All Educational Institutions in India (%)

Years	*Govt. Funds Central and State Govts.*	*Local Bodies Fund*	*University Fund*	*Total Fund*	*Fees*	*Endowment Sources*	*Total*
1950-51	57.06	10.93	—	67.99	20.39	11.62	100.0
1960-61	67.97	6.57	—	47.50	17.14	8.35	100.0
1970-71	75.65	4.34	1.36	81.35	12.81	5.85	100.0
1980-81	81.70	4.71	1.37	87.78	8.20	4.02	100.0
1985-86	80.29	5.23	2.15	87.67	6.27	6.06	100.0
1989-90	83.00	9.89	0.04	92.93	3.94	3.13	100.0
1990-91	86.40	6.39	0.06	93.41	3.94	3.13	100.0
1992-93	86.63	6.94	0.09	92.95	3.99	3.24	100.0
1993-94	86.72	6.42	0.09	93.01	4.10	3.26	100.0
1994-95	86.76	6.48	1.01	93.04	4.11	3.29	100.0
1995-96	87.03	6.89	10.09	93.23	4.23	3.39	100.0
1996-97	87.01	6.83	1.02	93.20	4.15	3.30	100.0
1997-98	87.2	6.85	1.3	93.31	4.25	3.37	100.0

Source : Annual Report, Ministry of Human Resource Development; 1997-98, Government of India, New Delhi.
Economic Survey: 1997-98: Govt. of India, Ministry of Finance.

below six years started in 1975-76 with 33 projects, the scheme has expanded to 5614 ICDS projects covering 201 lakh children and 38 lakh mothers. Apart from ICDS, the other programmes for child development includes 'Early Childhood Education', 'Balwadi Nutrition Programme', 'Day Care Centres' for children below 5 years and belonging to the weaker sections of society.

In view of the importance of the national programme of nutritional support to primary education mid-day-meal programme launched since August 15, 1995 by the then Prime Minister Mr. P. V. Narasimha Rao for boosting universalisation of education and improving the nutritional level of students in primary class. The mid-day-meal programme[31] has been launched in all the states and union territories. Gujarat, Haryana, J&K, Kerala, M.P.; Orissa, Tamilnadu and Pondicherry are serving cooked meals. In the rest of the states/UTs foodgrains are being distributed.

According to the approach paper of the Ninth Plan[32], "There has been a significant shift in approach towards the well-being of women and the children from 'welfare during fifties' to 'development during seventies' and to "empowerment during nineties." During Ninth Plan investment of child development will be viewed not only as a desirable social investment for the nation's future but also as fulfilment of rights of every child for survival, protection and development so as to achieve their full potential.

The convention of child Right's ratified by the country in 1992 will become the guiding principles for formulating necessary policies and programmes of child development in the Ninth Plan. Following universalisation of ICDS and ensured availability of basic minimum services for the overall development of the child, emphasis will be on consolidation and content enrichment of ICDS through adequate nutrition, supplemented with necessary health check-up, immunization and referral services. For achieving this, ICDS will continue to be the mainstay of the Ninth Plan to promote all round development of the young child. Tables 6.8, 6.9, 6.10 & 6.11 reveal the revenue and expenditure, budgetary allocation on education and child development programme, sources of income of institutions.

As regards food and nutrition security to children during IXth Plan, the Government adopted a National Nutrition Policy in 1993 and initiated the National Plan of Action in 1995, food and nutrition security has been recognised as one of the primary objectives of the Ninth Plan. The following approach have been accorded for the Ninth Plan:

1. Major emphasis will be on long-term measures which aim at eradication of hunger and starvation by ensuring availability, accessibility and affordability of balanced food and nutrition for all.
2. Special efforts will be made to universalise the supplementary feeding programmes *viz;* SNP & MDM for pre-school and school going children respectively.
3. Additional measures such as augumenting food production and availability of essential food items, affordability through increasing purchasing power of those living below poverty line through employment and income generation programmes, accessibility through PDS and other basic minimum services, awareness amongst the people.
4. To tackle the problem of protein energy malnutrition (PEM) the primary focus will be on 'At Risk Group' who are living below the poverty line and women and child particularly girl child.
5. The micro-nutritional deficiencies of vitamin A, iron and iodine which are extremely important from point of view of their serious health consequences and wide geographical prevalence will receive priority.
6. Efforts will be made to cover all the remote and neglected pockets predominantly inhibited by SC & ST and primitive tribal group (PTGs).
7. A Nutritional Monitoring and surveillance system will be essential to facilitate flow of data and information on the regular and systematic manner based on selected nutritional indicators for the purpose of planning and monitoring.

Summing Up

On the basis of the above cited comprehensive and indepth observation it is concluded that:

(i) Child labour legislation should be organised and unified and should make clear distinction between hazardous and non-hazardous occupations aiming at abolition of child labour and should be made applicable to the faulty workers.

(ii) Existing laws should essentially and strictly be implemented.

(iii) Law enforcing officials should be sincere and honest in regulating laws regarding such problems.

(iv) Administrative machinery must be strengthened and an uniform attempt should be made.

(v) Compulsory primary education for all the children below the age of 14 years should be strictly reinforced.

(vi) School environment must be made attractive and interesting.

(vii) Education to all must be the great goal of socio-economic development.

(viii) Eradication of poverty and illiteracy must be the prime objectives of our society.

(ix) The movement of child labour should be intellectually equipped, ideologically sound and politically strong to challenge the present evils of our societies.

(x) A Statutory Commission on Child Labour should be established with immediate effect.

(xi) Government and society should take suitable measures to eradicate the social evils like poverty, unemployment, illiteracy and pity conditions of the children and should also focus attention on the protection, welfare, safety, security, rehabilitation and abolition of child labour.

References

1. Planning Commission, *Eighth Five Year Plan* (1992-97); Vol. II, p. 395, Government of India; New Delhi.
2. Mussen, *et. al.* (1990), IGNOU—*Development of Rural Children; Rural Social Development;* p. 16; New Delhi.
3. United Nations (1996), *World Development Report;* 1996.
4. *Ibid.*
5. Giri, V.V. (1997), *Yojna,* Vol. XIV, No. 76, September 1997.
6. Chandrashekhar, C.P. (1997), "The Economic Consequences of the Abolition of Child Labour: An Indian Case Study", *Journal of Peasant Studies,* Vol. 24, No. 3, pp. 137-79.
7. Balchandran, Geetha (1986), "Legislation on Child Labour", *Social Welfare;* Vol. 33, No. 3, June 1995; pp. 20-23.
8. Buragohain, T. (1997), "Child Labour and Demand for Education", *Journal of Educational Planning and Administration;* Vol. XI, No. 1; pp. 55-65.
9. Kumar, Biswas & Gita (1992), *Problems of Child Labour in India;* G.B. Pant Social Science Institute, Allahabad.

10. Gouri, John (1979), *UNICEF SCARV;* "Health and Basic Services", New Delhi, pp. 5-12.
11. United Nations (1996), *World Development Report, 1996, op. cit.*
12. Grootaert, G. & Kanbur, R. (1995), "Child Labour: An Economic Perspective", *International Labour Review,* Vol. 134, No. 2.
13. Khadria, Binod (1996), "Child Labour: Reform through a Fiscal Instrument", *Economic and Political Weekly,* Vol. 31, No. 30, July 27; pp. 2009-10.
14. Chaudhari, D.P. (1996), *A Dynamic Profile of Child Labour in India;* 1951-91; I.L.O., New Delhi.
15. Grootaert, G. (1996), *op. cit.*
16. Giri, V.V. (1997), *op. cit.*
17. Nagia, P. (1987), *Child Labour: Cause Effect Syndrame;* Janak Publishers, New Delhi.
18. Planning Commission, First and Second Five Year Plan; Government of India; New Delhi.
19. *Constitution of India;* Article 24; 39(E) & (F).
20. Planning Commission (1950-55), *First Five Year Plan.*
21. Planning Commission (1955-60), *Second Five Year Plan.*
22. United Nations, (1959), *United Nations Declaration of Rights of Children;* UN General Assembly.
23. Government of India (1960), *Children Act,* 1960.
24. Government of India (1968), *National Policy on Education, 1968* and *Education Commission (1964-66).*
25. Planning Commission, *Fifth Five Year Plan* and ICDS, 1975.
26. Government of India (1983), *National Health Policy.*
27. Government of India, *Juvenile Justice Act,* 1986.
28. Planning Commission (1992-97), *Eighth Five Year Plan,* Vol. II, *op. cit.*
29. *Ibid.*
30. Government of India (1998), *Economic Survey,* 1997-98; Ministry of Finance.
31. Narasimha Rao, P.V. (1995), Prime Minister's Broadcast to the Nation; 15th August, *on Independence Day,* 1995.
32. Planning Commission (1997-2002), *Approach to the Ninth Five Year Plan.*

7

Trends of Urban Child Labour in India: A Review

—*P.Venu Gopal & K. Sreelakshmamma*

The problem of Child Labour (those below the age of 14 years) in developed countries is insignificant when compared with the problem in less developed countries. The low level of child labour in former countries was achieved mainly by laws governing the employment of children, by recognizing the need to educate children and by increasing real incomes of parents due to industrial and social development. Besides, with industrial development, children were increasingly substituted by machines from the peripheral jobs, which were the children's major occupations.

As child labour is a universal phenomenon, eradication of child labour has been recommended in various forms at national and international level all over the world. The number of working children in the world has been increasing at an alarming rate, unabated; particularly in the third world countries of South Asia and Africa. In 1973, the ILO adopted the Minimum Age Convention No. 138 with a view to achieve the total abolition of Child Labour, but it was barely ratified by 33 countries out of the total 162 member countries of the ILO, as on January, 1986. Although the conventions and recommendations are adopted by the countries, the same are not implemented in the true spirit and the measures taken are half-hearted leaving enough scope for the system of child labour to persist and thrive. International Organisations are expected to guide but it is the national Government which has to take suitable measures. In India, Article 24 of Indian Constitution prohibits the employment of children below the age of 14, in any factory, mine or in any hazardous employment. The Child Labour (Prohibition and Regulation) Act of 1986 is a comprehensive Act which prohibits the employment of children under 14 years in specified occupations, and processes and regulates the conditions of work of children in occupation where their employment is not prohibited.[1]

The welfare measures of the Government in the form of free education, establishment of orphanages and homes for destitutes etc., also would have assisted in the reduction of employment of children. The near essence of child labour in the developed countries has resulted in excluding children below 14 years of age from the labour force.[2] Despite the significant progress made in industrial and social development, India has not yet been able to grapple with the problem of child labour.

Although the estimates of child labour provided by different sources differ significantly, yet the fact remains that the constituted a substantial proportion of India's labour force. In 1971 Census over 10.7 million children, the largest for any country were reported to be working for living.[3] National Sample Survey Organisation placed the child working population at 26.25 million in 1978.[4] Planning Commission worked the number of child workers at 17.56 million as on March 1, 1983.[5] According to Ministry of labour the Child Working population in the country is estimated at 1.5 crore.[6] Another Baroda based Research Group is estimated 44 million children in India's Labour Force.[7] Census 1981 placed the estimate at 13.6 million.[8] According to 1991 census there were 11.29 million child labour in India.[9] In 1996 ILO estimated 144 million child labour in India.[10] Under certain conditions child labour has been regarded as vital contribution to labour force. Being a cheap source of labour supply; the production of goods and services which might otherwise not to be produced, has been facilitated. Their alertness in handling certain jobs makes them more productive in some occupations even than adults. In present economies availability of child labour provides the household an access to many productive opportunities.[11] The availability of children's assistance in child care and house-keeping provides opportunity of women to undertake alternative productive employment.[12]

The empirical research on child labour shows that the child labour has been increasing in Urban areas from the last two decades. Hence, Trends of Urban Child Labour is purposively selected for the study.

This paper aims at providing a perspective of the situation regarding urban child labour in India. The term child labour applies to population 5-14 years age group as those in the 0-4 age category are not capable either physically or mentally to participate in any meaningful economic activity. Information will be given for those states in the Indian Union with more child labour according to 1991 census so as to examine regional variations.

In Urban areas higher proportion of children are expected to be in schools because of better educational facilities, high disposable income of parents and awareness of the beneficial aspects of schooling and education. Sex differences also affect work participation and hence information will be given separately for males and females.

The source of data for the study are mainly the Census of India for the period 1961 to 1991. This will be supplemented by information from various reports, articles and other sources.

Work Participation Rates

Work participation rates of the children are given in Table 7.1. The results show that Andhra Pradesh is having the highest percentage of child labourers right from 1961 to 1991, though it has been declined from 6.3 per cent to 3.9 per cent during 1961-91. It is observed that the percentage of male child labour has declined in case of Himachal Pradesh, Haryana, Kerala, Karnataka, Maharashtra, Madhya Pradesh, Uttar Pradesh, Rajasthan and Tamilnadu. The percentage is almost constant in the state of Punjab. The percentage of child labour has increased in case of Bihar, Gujarat, and West Bengal. The rates for female do show that Andhra Pradesh is having highest percentage during 1961-91. Karnataka is having highest percentage of girl child labourers (1991), though it has decreased from 2.8 per cent in 1981 to 2.2 per cent in 1991. The declining percentage is noticed among all states except in case of West Bengal. This has been increased from 0.2 per cent in 1961 to 1.2 per cent in 1991. However, the percentages have decreased for in both male and female at the National level.

Table 7.1
Percentage of Child Labour to Total Child Population

States	1961		1971		1981		1991	
	Boy	*Girl*	*Boy*	*Girl*	*Boy*	*Girl*	*Boy*	Girl
1. Andhra Pradesh	6.3	3.5	4.7	1.8	3.9	3.5	3.9	2.0
2. Bihar	3.9	1.2	2.8	0.6	2.1	1.2	2.3	0.5
3. Gujarat	2.1	0.9	2.2	0.5	2.1	0.9	2.4	0.5
4. Himachal Pradesh	3.0	0.9	3.1	0.5	1.3	0.9	1.3	0.7
5. Haryana	2.7	0.5	2.0	0.2	1.8	0.5	1.8	0.4
6. Kerala	2.2	1.8	1.3	1.4	0.7	1.8	0.5	0.4
7. Karnataka	5.9	2.8	4.4	1.6	4.0	2.8	4.5	2.2
8. Maharashtra	2.9	1.6	2.0	0.7	1.8	1.6	1.9	0.8
9. Madhya Pradesh	2.7	1.6	1.9	0.8	2.0	1.6	2.1	0.9
10. Orissa	5.0	2.0	3.6	1.0	3.2	2.0	2.4	1.0
11. Punjab	2.7	0.5	3.1	0.1	2.5	0.5	2.7	0.3
12. Rajasthan	3.2	1.7	2.4	0.5	2.2	1.7	2.1	0.8
13. Tamilnadu	4.4	2.8	3.0	1.4	3.4	2.8	3.1	1.9
14. Uttar Pradesh	3.8	0.6	3.2	0.3	2.7	0.6	3.5	0.5
15. West Bengal	2.2	0.2	2.1	0.5	1.0	0.2	2.3	1.2
All India	3.5	1.2	2.8	0.8	2.5	0.9	2.2	0.9

Source : Computed from Census of India, 1961, 1971, 1981 & 1991.

Distribution of Urban Children

The activity-wise distribution of urban children is furnished in Table 7.2. It can be observed from the table that the share of male students has increased from 60.80 per cent in 1961 to 69.7 per cent in 1991. On the other hand the share of child labour has decreased from 5.4 per cent in 1961 to 2.7 per cent in 1991.

Table 7.2
Percentage of Urban Child Labour

Child	1961		1971		1981		1991	
	Boy	*Girl*	*Boy*	*Girl*	*Boy*	*Girl*	*Boy*	Girl
Student	60.8	45.1	61.4	52.0	69.6	60.8	69.7	64.6
Child Labour	5.4	2.4	4.1	1.2	3.6	1.3	2.7	1.0
Now here	33.8	51.8	34.5	46.8	26.6	37.8	27.5	34.2
Marginal Workers	—	—	—	—	0.1	0.3	0.1	0.2
Total	100	100	100	100	100	100	100	100

Source : Same as Table 7.1.

In case of Females, the alarming growth of students is noticed was about 20 per cent growth. Female child labour were decreased from 2.4 per cent in 1961 to 1.0 per cent by 1991. Further, the number of children were also decreased from 51.8 per cent in 1961 to 34.2 per cent in 1991. Marginal Workers were decreased during 0.1 per cent between 1981–91.

Sectoral Allotment of Urban Child Labour

Sectoral allotment of urban child labour is shown in Table 7.3. The changes in the occupations of urban male child labour are evident 14.60 per cent of urban child labour were working in agricultural and allied activities by 1961, which has been the share is increased to 19.70 per cent by 1991. Manufacturing sector had lost its percentage by 7.90 between 1961 and 1991. There was a small growth in case of others by 3.30 per cent between 1961 and 1991. Others includes the industrial activities like Trade and Commerce. Transport, Construction and Service. Highest percentage of male child labour in urban areas are concentrated in these industries.

Table 7.3
Sectorial Allotment of Urban Child Labour

Child Labour	*1961*		*1971*		*1981*		*1991*	
	Boy	*Girl*	*Boy*	*Girl*	*Boy*	*Girl*	*Boy*	Girl
Cultivators	8.7	12.5	6.5	3.3	6.4	4.0	6.2	5.4
Ag. Labour	5.9	12.3	12.4	22.1	12.8	23.2	13.5	22.0
Manufacturing	13.1	31.5	8.0	17.7	7.9	17.5	5.2	13.5
Others	72.4	43.7	73.1	56.7	72.9	55.3	75.1	59.1
Total	100.0	100.0	100.0	100.0	100.0	100.0	100.0	100.0

Source : Same as Table 7.1.

In case of Urban Female Child Labour, about 60 per cent were working in 'others' category. There was 13.40 per cent growth between the census years 1961–1991. It can be observed from the table that the percentage of cultivators was decreased by 7.10 per cent and the percentage of Agricultural Labour was increased by 9.70 per cent by 1991. It can also be observed that the participation of child labour in Manufacturing activity has been decreased from 1961 onwards.

In sum it may be concluded that the problem of child labour both in organized and unorganized sectors is alarming in the developing countries like India. Millions of children are at work in various occupations. Even though the use of child labour in actual practice, it is neither feasible nor desirable to have stringent measures to enforce existing child labour law. It is felt that for the time being i.e. till the economic condition of the country improves, efforts will have to be made to organise better conditions of work that will eliminate abuse, exploitation and health hazards due to child labour.

References

1. I.S. Singh, (1992), 'Child Labour', Oxford & IBH Publishing Company Private Limited, New Delhi.
2. D. Radha Deve, 'Prevalence of Child Labour in India: A Secondary Data Analysis,' *Child Labour and Health Problems and Prospects* (eds.), Tata Institute of Social Sciences, p. 34.
3. *Census of India*, 1971.
4. *Times of India* (Delhi), Sept. 7, 1981, p. 7.
5. *Indian Express*, Nov. 26, 1985, p. 14.
6. *The Tribune*, June 2, 1985, p. 5.
7. *Indian Express* (Chandigarh), Aug. 27, 1985, p. 14.
8. *1981 Census.*
9. *1991 Census.*
10. *ILO Report*, 1996.
11. Terence H. Hill, 'Perspectives and Methods in the Study of Children's Work (Geneva, *ILO*, 1979), p. 2.
12. *Ibid.*, p. 4.

8

Explosive and Exploitative Scenario of Child Labour in India

—P.C. Tiwari

Introduction

The International Labour Organisation confirms the view that, "Child Labour includes Children prematurely leading adult lives working long hours for low wages under conditions damaging to their health and to their physical and mental development, sometimes separated from their families, frequently deprived of meaningful educational and training opportunities, that could open up for them a better future". "Adolescent" is a person who has completed his 15th year but has not completed his 18th year. A human resource below the age of 15, if employed for work is termed as child labour. The most recent "the child Labour Prohibition and Regulation Act 1986, defined" child "as a Labour who has not completed his 14 years of age. Whether part time/ full-time in any occupation, engagement of a child in labour force simply means a complete or partial denial of childhood to him". He is not merely deprived of the jobs and carefree life of a child, but also of desirable physical and mental developments. This is not only injustice to him as child, but also as adult throughout his life, for the foundation of his adulthood is built on extremely weak-structure of under-development.

The practice of employing child as a labour is not a tradition of India alone but almost all the countries of the world have had similar history varying in nature and magnitude. Even the advanced countries of today have not spared children in their exploitation. Therefore, the utilisation of children as a resource for present or future depends on the socio-economic parameters of a country.

Magnitude of Child Labour in India

Several estimates have been made about the magnitude of child labourers in India varying between 1.83 crores in 1971 and 1.74 crores in 1991. Every third house in India has a working child. Every fourth child in the 1 to 5 years age group is employed. Children are forced to drop out of school and accept meagre wage for working under inhuman conditions. Nearly 45 lacs children are employed in the carpet, glass and lock industries in the State of U.P.

Size and composition of child labour in India (1951-91), computed from Census and NSS Sources has been estimated. Estimated magnitudes for 1991 are, full time child workers (-14 years) 12.7 million, full time plus marginal child labour 23.3 million, non-students and non-workers 74.4 million and total child population 297 million. Child labour being a subset of child population is directly linked to another related subset namely non-working children whose number is atleast three times larger than child labour. Details pertaining to growth rates and sectoral shares, including projections to 2001 A.D.

The traditional agriculture sector employed 76% of child labour in 1991. Comparable figures for 1981 are 77% and 69% in 1961. The shares of manufacturing increase from 3.1% of total child labour in 1971 to 5.7% in 1991. The major part of the efforts of those who advocate a labour clause has targeted his latter segment which consists of about 0.65 million child workers. In absolute size in 1991, the number of full time waged based excluding children working on their own family farms child agricultural labourers was 5.4 million.

Wide diversity in the pace and pattern of child labour use, its growth and subsequent decline can be seen in the different regions in India. In half its states child labour is declining fast while in others it is declining slowly. Variations across states in labour participation rates of children are also enormous with Kerala at 1%

and A.P. at 17% for male children in 1981. Diversity can also be perceived between urban and rural development with the employment of child workers in the urban sector growing fast while concomitantly declining slowing in rural India. Inter-state variation in these outcomes is very large with Kerala reporting the lowest incidence and U.P. the highest increase of Urban Child labour. For activities registering fast growth between 1961 and 1991 are manufacturing, transport, storage and communication, trade and commerce and agricultural labourers. The bi-model groupings of the states in terms of economic development, structural change and the incidence of child labour is unmistakable. The leaders and leggards in 1961 retained their relative positions in 1991 suggesting the presence of mutually reinforcing virtuous and vicious circles. The incidence of child labour was negatively corrected with per capita income, infrastructure development, school enrolment ratios and female participation rate in non-agricultural work. It is positively correlated with incidence of poverty, illiteracy and the per cent of the labour force in agriculture.

Various case studies of child labour engagements in U.P. are as follows:

Carpet Industry

The carpet industry is one of the most notorious unit for employing child labour. According to the non-governmental organisations (NGOs) children constitute almost 80% of the total workforce of that factory/industry. However, according to survey conducted by the National Council for Applied Economic Research (NCAER), Child Labour accounted for 80% only. The UNICEF data claims" shocked with reports of Child labour, countries like Germany have stopped buying Indian carpet.

Working for more than 14 hours a day at a stretch and often even more than that, children became prone to occupational diseases like broncho-pneumonia, lung cancer, nasalsiruses, poor vision, T.B. and work infestation. Inspite of all the hard work, a child labour barely manages to earn Rs. 5 to Rs. 20 daily. Even though the owners of cush industries are aware that employing children violates the factories act and labours laws, they continue to hire children because the children have no unions, and practically have no bargaining capacity. In U.P. the Bhadohi district NGOs have estimated the child labour as 9.5 lacs. Every third carpet house in

Bhadohi district have 25 working children. Every 5th child in the 5-10 years age group is employed. Children are forced to drop out of school and accept meagre wage for working under inhuman conditions. Nearly 15 lacs children are employed in the carpet industries in Uttar Pradesh.

Child Labour in Glass and Lock Industry

In the glass industry small children sit a mere six inches away from the furnaces at 700° centigrade to 1800° centigrade temperature handling red hot glass blowing and cutting it into shape. Continuous exposure to heat besides causing burns and scolding often leads to dehydration and heat-exhaustion. In the lock industry in U.P., the working children are exposed to various occupational hazards. Lock industry in India specially in U.P. requires children to do electroplating, spray painting, cutting of various components, polishing etc. by hand processes. Inhalation of paints and thinners on the job damages children's lungs. Some face the danger of loosing their fingers, while working on heavy machines or suffers severe shock and electrocution while electroplating. They have to work with hazardous chemicals like potassium cyanide, tridum and phosphate for long stretches of time. Due to ignorance of these chemicals and their careless handling, many children workers die.

Child Labour in Plantation and Other Industries

The plantation industry legally permits the employment of child labour where the minimum age is 12 years. Children account for 6% of labours, while adolescents account for 3%. The actual number is 95,000 only. These children are made to work irrespective of the facilities like education, rehabilitation, medical benefits, limited hours or work provided to them. The bulk of child labour in the plantations are in West Bengal, Assam, Maharashtra, U.P. It is almost negligible in Tamilnadu, Pondicherry, Kerala and Karnataka.

Other industries employing, children as labour are Bidis, handloom, clothes and sari embroidery, match and fire works, cashew and coir products, fisheries, pottery, slate, brick-klin, gem-cutting, numerous small scale and cottage Industries, Many work as coolies, hawkers, vendors and newspaper sellers. The harsh reality is that child labour is prevalent mainly in the unorganised sectors of Industry, where even adult workers rarely receive the statutory minimum wages.

Child Labour and Wayward (Street) Children

The surveys conducted of the Lakhera or street children in different cities have revaluated that the children are neither delinquent nor wayward. They are on the street looking ways of supporting themselves and their families. In a sample of 2000 street children in Allahabad (U.P.) and Junction Railway Station 70% were working for living. Half of them were self-working as rag-pickers and petty traders of edible and non-edible items, 16% working in shops and servicing centres, 15% as casual labour carrying loads, cleaning and washing at marriage parties and doing other such work. Most of them worked 7 to 12 hours a day. Those who worked for lesser hours did part-time work after school or household.

Thirty eight per cent of the Allahabad City street kids earned less than Rs. 300 per month. Some working as apprentices to the tailors got a stipend ranging from Rs. 50 to Rs. 150 per month. The children engaged in rag-picking were able to earn Rs. 50 a day after putting 12 hours of labour. Voluntary organisations that have worked with street children known as Lakheras have found street urchins to be 'admirable survivors', potential entreperneurs and decent citizens.

Reasons for Growing Menace of Child Labour

Many reasons are attributed to the growing menace of child labour in India. Main factors are poverty, inequitable distribution of assets, insufficient legislative protection and absence of strong child labour unions. In India poverty is a major contributing factor for the child labour. In 1987-88 almost all the major states registered about 30% population below poverty line. Orissa and Bihar were roughly half with U.P. and Maharashtra, Andhra Pradesh, slightly behind, some states like Himachal Pradesh, Haryana, Punjab were better off with merely 10% population below poverty line, Large numbers of families below poverty are forced to involve their children as labour out of desperation and necessity.

The child labour force is directly related with the high percentage of dropouts from the school. The percentage of dropouts 1990-91 between class Ist to 8th, the average rate of dropouts is as high as 64% in India. Only 36% of our children continue upto High School level. In some states like Bihar, Tripura, U.P. the rate of dropouts touches nearly 80% of the total school going children.

The rate of dropouts is invariably a consequence of poverty. The second reason is, that in most places the schools are situated in remote areas or are inaccessible. In most places, the schools present state and dismal picture and hold little attraction for the children. Due to lack of funds and facilities many schools do not run regularly, with teachers absenting most of the time, schooling of the children is costly for the present too, and deprives them of the income that accrues from child labour.

India is ranked the lowest in the world as far as literacy is concerned. The average rate of literacy in India according to 1991 census was 52.1%. Some states like A.P., Bihar, M.P. etc. registered less than 40% literate population. The higher rate of illeteracy indicates the ignorance of the persons in realising their duties as guardians who push their children to join the child labour force. In India, the states with higher rate of illiteracy attributes to higher percentage of child labour, for instance Andhra Pradesh registers 15% child labour with M.P. and Karnataka 7.9% and 7.6% respectively. Some states like Bihar 3.5 and Rajasthan show lower (5.8) percentage of child labour inspite of low percentage of literacy. This may be due to migration of child labour force to other states.

Insufficient Protective legislation—The practice of engaging child labour is an indicator of the backwardness of rules and regulatory measures. India has passed laws for almost all the industries which engage children as labour, specifying their hours, terms and conditions of works, education, wages etc. But, no industry so far strictly adhered to the laws and rules and no administrative machinery has every undertaken to enforce the same on employers. Poor children get sandwitched in between the attrocities of both the sides. There is no organisational or institutional set up which can protect them from their miseries.

Lack of Unions and Inequitable Distribution of Land Assets

In some industries like Bidi's, glass, carpets, Lock, Handloom etc. children are preferred for more delicate and minute workmanship. But in general the most relevant factor for their employment is lack of organisational support to child labour. The child labour is not associated with any trade union, as such this section of working class has no voice and strength to fight for their rights and dues. There is no institutional set up which can apprise them of their rights and mandatory provisions. In the absence of proper guidance and partronage the child labour yields to deprivation and callousness.

In India merely 10% of the privileged class holds 90% of total agricultural land. The rest of the farmers are actually farm labourers who work for wages. Inspite of 49 years of enforcement of tenancy laws, there has been practically no reform at this front. Even today most of the tenant farmers alongwith their families are mortgaged to big land-holders and rich farmers. The slogan of "land to the tiller" has borne no fruit. The poor families on account of insufficient earnings compel their children to take up any jobs, this occurs as child labour force.

Remedies and Suggestions for Prohibiting Child Labour

Perhaps, India is the only country whose constitution specifically provides for prohibition of this dreadful practice. Article 24 of Indian Constitution prohibits engagement of child labour in any hazardous work. Article 39 guarantees protection against normal and material abandonment. Article 45 ensures free and compulsory education for all children till the age of 14.

In course of last 100 years, a wide gamut of legislations have been enacted prohibiting child labour. The International Labour Organisation has played a revolutionary role in changing the status of child labour. The International Labour Organisation has so far adopted 18 conventions mainly in respect of children and young persons concerning their minimum age entry to employment, education, medical examination and right to work. Besides International Labour Organisation has also adopted 9 recommendations on these topics. The convention and recommendations alongwith many others, from the international labour code. Perhaps, India is the only country whose constitution specifically provides for prohibition of this dreadful practice.

The Minimum Wages Act, 1948 prescribes minimum wages for different age groups and industries. The Factories Act, 1948 has fixed the minimum age for employment of children in different jobs. Section 68 of Factories Act adheres to certificate of fitness before employing any child or adolescent. Section 71 prohibits the employment of children at night and limits the working time to half hours only. Section 73 implies compulsory maintenance of register by the employers. Section 34(2) prescribes the maximum weight a child labour should carry.

The Plantation Labour Act, 1951, rectifies rules regarding age, education, weekly hours, night work if necessary, certificate of fitness, medical examination of the child labour in plantation and forestry jobs.

The Mines Act 1951, which was amended in 1983, prohibits employment of persons below eighteen years of age, to work in mines.

The Merchants Shipping Act 1958, has also fixed the minimum age to be fifteen years. It also states that no person below the age of eighteen years shall be engaged or carried to see to work as a trimmer or stoker in any ship.

The Motor Transport Worker Act, 1961, prohibits employment of child or adolescent in any motor transport undertaking.

The Apprentice Act 1961, has also specified age, working hours and conditions or work for children.

The Bidi-cigar workers condition and Employment Act, 1966 prohibits employment of children below fourteen year, and overtime work.

According to Child Labour Act, 1986, the penalty for violating the child labour laws is a fine from Rs. 1,000 to Rs. 20,000 and also imprisonment (Jail) for 3 months to one year with or without fine, to the employer and guardians. Inspite of such lofty constitutional provisions and legislative measures. More than 20 million children are forced to work in various industrial and non-industrial occupation at the cost of their childhood.

Suggestions

As said earlier, main causes of child labour is poverty and resourcefulness of the rural and urban families below the Poverty line. It is felt that efforts should be made to increase the family assets and income of the poor families. The important suggestions are as follows:

(*a*) Employment schemes like Jawahar Rojgar Yojna (JRY) Employment guarantee schemes and Integrated Rural Development Programme (IRDP) should be intensified and strictly carried out with the true spirit of service and proper identification of beneficiaries,

(*b*) vocational education should be given equal importance

alongwith the general education. State governments should give high priority to education, in their five years' plan allocation,

(c) The labour laws should be implemented more and more strictly. It is imperative to make the punishments more rigorous,

(d) More and more schools should be started for children, as well as for adults. Spread of education will help in changing and broadening the outlook of the parents towards children.

(e) All poverty eradication measures are equally important for raising the income and assets of the family for reducing the incidence of child labour. If poverty is removed, no child will be forced to work.

(f) Trade Unions should take child labour too, into their domain of activities. Political parties should consider inclusion of measures for solving child labour problem in their manifesto.

(g) Controlling the size of families through family welfare programme is essential for raising the standard of living and thereby ensuring healthy, proper and enjoyable childhood to the children. The children are the best human capital resources to ensure a healthy and prosperous future. There is need to evolve industry for specific projects for skill, education, health and nutrition for children.

References

1. Chaudhary, D.P. (1996), *Dynamic Profile of Child Labour in India,* CLASP, ILO, New Delhi, June.
2. GOI, (1986), *Child Labour Prohibition and Regulation Act,* Government of India, New Delhi.
3. ILO, (1993), *World at Work,* Special Issue on Child Labour, Global Offensive, No. 4, June.
4. NLI, (1992), "Special Issue on Child Labour, Legislation", *Awards Digest,* Vol. XVIII, Nos. 3-6, March, June.
5. UNICEF (1989), *Convention on the Right of the Child Labour,* United Nations, New York.

9

Child Labour: Beyond Legislation

—I. Satya Sundaram

The problem of child labour in India has received due attention in recent years as it has assumed ominous dimensions. Concerted efforts are needed to solve this problem as it has its roots in the socio-economic conditions of the country. Isolated efforts/attempts to solve the problem are not of any help. Child labour is a complex phenomenon. It is a symptom, not the disease. It is the product of grinding poverty and under-development of the economy (Sundaram, I. Satya 1994: 43). The problem certainly deserves a holistic approach.

There is no correlation between the incidence of poverty and child labour. Five Indian states, viz., Andhra Pradesh, Rajasthan, Tamilnadu, Karnataka and Maharashtra have the highest ranks in terms of child labour. Maharashtra and the three Southern states mentioned above have much higher intensity of child labour than the poor states like Uttar Pradesh, Bihar and Orissa.

Of course, poverty is a major cause for growing strength of child labour, but the evil cannot be attributed to poverty alone. There is a high percentage of child labour even in the industrialised countries. Non-economic factors too contributed to child labour (Kannan R., 1997).

It is argued that children starve, if they are not permitted to work. This argument lacks logic. Children can avoid starvation by working a few hours a day for survival. But, when the children work for long hours at very low wages, it is more an exploitation than work (Remington, Francoise 1996: 3354).

Incidence of Child Labour

There are 17 million child labourers in India while the ILO puts the figure at 44 million. Non-governmental organisations suggest a figure of 55 million. In Sivakasi in Tamilnadu, about one lakh children work in the match making industry.

In 1981 and 1991 census, without drawing any distinction between hazardous and non-hazardous nature of work, put the total number of working children in the country at 13 million and 11 million respectively. The Baroda-based Operations Research Group put the figure at 44 million in 1983.

According to the United Nations International Children's Emergency Fund (UNICEF), child labour in India accounts for over one-third of the 250 million children working as labourers world-wide. The situation is really alarming.

The child labourers in India contribute about 20 per cent of the country's GNP. They account for over eight per cent of the nation's work force. India has the dubious distinction of possessing the largest child labour force in the world.

The incidence of child labour is so rampant in India that the western countries have stopped import of goods made by using child labour. The worst victim is the carpet industry. Other goods affected are: furnishings/upholstry, garments, woollens and to some extent leather goods.

The I.L.O.'s recent report (1997), *Child Labour Targetting the Intolerable* came out with new figures for child labour. According to the report, some 250 million between the ages of 5 and 14 work in developing countries—with some 120 million working full-time and 130 million part-time.

An earlier I.L.O. survey in 1996 had put the number of child labourers (between ages 10 to 24) at some 73 million in some 100 countries. Of course, the report admitted that child labour is prevalent in many industrialised countries including Italy, Portugal, Spain, the United Kingdom and the United States.

According to the I.L.O. data and Indian census 1991, the child labour is more in use in rural areas. The I.L.O. study pointed out that

— 85 per cent of the working children do so to supplement household income;
— 75 per cent of parents consider working of their wards important for economic reasons and 50 per cent feel that the children's earnings are essential for the maintenance of the family; and
— 70 per cent would like to continue work even if they had a choice.

The ban on Indian exports by western countries simply because child labour is involved in their manufacture is not proper. In Asian countries, a 15-year or 16-year girl may be a married one. It is improper to ban them from work. Also, excluding certain types of activities which are more prevalent in the West for child workers is not fair. Moreover, Indian child labour is not the outcome of industrialisation, nor an urban phenomenon (Kaushal, H, 1996).

The number of bonded child labourers is also very large. There are about 200 million bonded child labourers in the world, of which, 80 million are in South Asia. In India, their number is around 5.5 million.

Past Efforts

The I.L.O. adopted a number of conventions relating to minimum age for admission to employment, medical examination and night work in respect of children, and young persons. Prohibition of the employment of children has been one of the basic tenets of the I.L.O. In fact, achieving the goal of complete abolition of child labour has been incorporated in the preamble of the I.L.O. itself.

The UN Convention on the Rights of the Child has also been ratified by India. Among these are the right "to education on the basis of equal opportunity (especially free and compulsory primary education)" the right "to protection from economic exploitation and from performing any work that is likely to be hazardous or interfering with the child's education and development."

The Government of India has been aware of the pernicious practice of child labour. According to Article 24 of the Constitution, children below the age of 14 are not to be employed in any factory or mine or engaged in any other hazardous employment. Article 39(e) directs the state to see that the tender age of children is not abused and that citizens are not compelled by economic circumstances to do work that is unsuited to their age or strength.

Again, Article 39(f) draws our attention to the need for protecting youth from exploitation. Of course, Article 45 directs the state to provide for free and compulsory education for all children until they complete the age of fourteen. The Employment of Children Act, 1938 was the first comprehensive Act which was repealed and substituted by the Child Labour (Prohibition and Regulation) Act, 1986. The Human Rights Commission had come forward with a convention on the Rights of the Child in 1989.

The convention admitted three things:

- that children need special safeguards beyond those provided to adults;
- that the best environment for a child's survival and development is within the protective and nurturing family setting, and
- the governments and the adult world in general should be committed to act in the best interests of children.

The National Commission on Labour (1969) recommended fixing the hours of employment of children so as to enable them to go to school. The Committee on Child Labour (1979) recommended banning of child labour only in hazardous areas and regulate and ameliorate the conditions of work in other areas.

The National Policy for Children Resolution adopted in August 1974, provided a policy framework for adequate services for children.

The Government of India constituted, on September 26, 1994, a National Authority for Elimination of Child Labour (NAECL). Its functions are:

- To lay down, policies and programmes for elimination of child labour, particularly in hazardous employments.
- To monitor the progress of implementation of programmes, projects and schemes for elimination of child labour.
- To co-ordinate implementation of child labour related projects of the various sister ministries of the Government of India.

However, the performance of NAECL is almost dismal. It has not been made a statutory body.

Problems and Consequences

Abolition of child labour is becoming increasingly difficult because of the mindset that accepts it as a part of life (Menon, Santosh 1997:11). For instance, in Sivakasi, nobody views child labour as a crime. It is an age-old practice. The factory owners feel that they are the saviours of children who do not have any alternative available. The government machinery too turns a Nelson's eye to this pernicious practice.

Law is not of much help in the eradication of child labour. In fact, inspections are confined to registered units only. The bigger industrial units source their products from the small cottage sector. The child labourers mostly work in the unorganised units. Even among the registered ones, the conviction rate is far from impressive (Menon, Santosh 1977: 11).

It is more appropriate to say that child labour perpetuates poverty—it does not reduce it as it condemns one generation after another to its vicious circle (Bhatty, Kiran 1996: 385).

According to the Gurupadswamy Committee Report, 1979, "Child labour assumes the character of a social problem in as much as it hinders, arrests or distorts the natural growth processes and prevents the child from attaining his full-blown manhood."

In one of its judgments (*Sheela Barse* Vs *Secretary, Children Aid Society and others,* 1987), the Supreme Court pertinently pointed out

> If there be no proper growth of children of today, the future of the country will be dark. It is the obligation of every generation to bring up children who will be citizens of tomorrow in a proper way. Today's children will be leaders of tomorrow who will hold the country's banner high and maintain the prestige of the nation.

In India, according to official figures, 90 per cent of children receive primary education. But, the drop-out rate is high. Hence, 75 million children do not go to school at all.

Even when children are not employed in hazardous work, the environment itself often puts them at risk. For instance, those who take up household employment are often beaten and sexually abused (Weiner, Myron 1996: 3009).

Children who work with dangerous machines chemicals and furnaces with high temperatures run the risk of getting involved in accidents. Children working in hazardous occupations like carpet, matches, brassware, lock, pottery, gems etc. contact various diseases like T.B., skin disorders, burn injuries and silicosis. Also, the social integration of such children becomes difficult (Kitchlu, T.N. 1994: 24).

It is also reported that 20 per cent of the prostitutes are minors. In a country like India, cyber pornography or child sex based tourism is also prevalent. The UNICEF's status report (1997) has observed:

> The underground nature of the multi-billion dollar illegal industry in commercial sexual exploitation of children makes it difficult to gather reliable data. Every year atleast one million girls are lured into the prostitution.

Measures Required

Children must be enabled to enjoy their childhood through better nutrition, easy learning, enough play and more importantly, affectionate environment in which they live (Joshi, Uma 1997: 28).

True, poverty is an important cause for child labour. But, the problem of child labour should not be allowed to persist till we completely eliminate poverty. As rightly observed by the UNICEF report, *The State of the World's Children 1997:*

> The end of hazardous child labour should not wait for poverty to end. The world poverty cannot be eliminated by the end of the decade. But, hazardous child labour and the grave violation of the rights of children involved can be.

Child labour has become a source of cheap labour. In fact, when minimum wages were stipulated by states, the wages for children become half that for adults (Debray, Bibek 1994). The suggested amendment to the 1986 Act includes: an equalisation of adult and child wages. This would eliminate the monetary incentive for employers in using child labour.

In the Indian context, law is not of much help in reducing the incidence of child labour. For instance, the December 10, 1996 Supreme Court order banning child labour in hazardous industries and making education conditional in non-hazardous jobs employing children, has had several factories in Noida and Okhla simply close the doors to children, for fear of prosecution and the reluctance to contribute to the Child Labour Rehabilitation-cum-Welfare Fund.

Of course, another notable aspect of the Supreme Court directive is that an adult member of the child's family has to be given employment.

Those who are better placed, like the landlords, businessmen and industrialists should also help financially in solving the problem of child labour. The parents too need to be educated about the harmful effects of child labour (Singh, S.P. 1997: 23).

Primary education in India involves high opportunity costs for the poor. In the developed countries, these costs are negligible as the illiterates cannot think of securing any worthwhile work. Mere improvement in the quality of education is not going to help reduce the incidence of child labour (Khadria, Binod 1996: 2009).

The best remedy for the problem of child labour is the effective implementation of provisions relating to universal primary education. At present, there is nothing in our schools to inspire the child. The schools are unattractive and poorly maintained. They lack even the essential learning materials. Even when the poor children are sent to schools, it is difficult to retain them in schools. The stress should be on vocational education. A learner-friendly environment should be there; particularly in rural schools. The elected leaders of local panchayats should take interest in solving the problem of child labour.

In an area like child labour, there ought to be rapport between government and non-government agencies.

The Committee on Child Labour has observed (Ministry of Labour, Government of India, December 1979: 43):

> Apart from the qualitative change in the curriculum of education, action is also called for to make certain adjustments in the schedule of vacations. It is well-known that at the time of sowing and harvesting, the farmers require maximum help. The children also get drafted to assist the family or to earn wages, during this period. If the schools, are not in vacation at this time, the children are compelled to miss their classes. In many cases due to this intermittent absence, which is unavoidable, the children eventually drop out from the schools. In some states, efforts have been to make the vacations coterminus with seasonal agricultural requirements. The system needs to be adopted on a nation-wide basis.

The National Policy for Children Resolution (August 1974) emphasized the importance of

— free and compulsory education for all children up to the age of 14;
— provisions of health and nutritional programmes and services;
— providing alternative forms of education for children unable to take full advantage of formal school education, and
— measures for protecting children against neglect, cruelty and exploitation.

The Government of India formulated a National Child Labour Policy in 1987. The basic thrust of the policy is to co-ordinate and intensify the on-going development programmes for income generation and employment in areas prone to child labour. A National Child Labour Technology Advisory Committee has been constituted to identify hazardous processes and industries and action programmes have also been formulated in ten selected industries.

India's seventh five year plan (1985-90) did admit that the ultimate goal of abolition of child labour can only be achieved when there is sufficient improvement in the conditions of living of families whose children are compelled to work.

A plan provision of Rs. 15 crore was made for child labour elimination programme during the eighth plan (1992-97). The budgetary allocation was substantially stepped up after the launching of the programme for rehabilitation of child labour working in hazardous occupations in August 1994. For the year 1995-96, the budget allocation was Rs. 34.40 crore, actual expenditure came to Rs. 34.29 crore. The allocation for 1996-97 was Rs. 56 crore (Mahapatra, Sevashree 1997: 25).

The UNICEF, in its 1997 State of the World's Children Report, has suggested the following measures to end child labour:

— the immediate elimination of hazardous child labour;
— free and compulsory education for all children;
— stringent anti-child labour laws and their vigorous enforcement;
— registration of all children at birth;
— data collection and monitoring (data on child labour is very scarce), and
— codes of conduct and procurement policies.

Rapid economic development appears to be a panace a for the

pernicious problem of proliferation of child labour. The ILO's recent report (1997) quoted earlier has observed:

> The fight against child labour has to go hand in hand with a campaign to create full, freely chosen and productive employment and ensure that this goal is considered as an ethical, social, political and economic imperative of mankind.
>
> Some of the specific measures suggested by the report include:
>
> — adopting a time-bound programme of action for eliminating child labour;
> — priority should be given to abolishing the worst and intolerable forms of child labour such as slavery and slave-like practices, all forms of forced labour including debt bondage and child prostitution, and child work in hazardous occupations and industries;
> — complete prohibition of work by young children—under 12 or 13 years—and the protection of girls; and
> — action against child labour should have a strong rehabilitative content.

The eradication of child labour should become an integral part of rural and urban development programmes. After all, the problem of child labour has its roots in the socio-economic and educational backwardness of a country (Francis, C 1996: 465).

Given the socio-economic conditions in India, there is no push-button solution to the problem of child labour. Concerted efforts are needed on various fronts to minimise the incidence of child labour in the short-run and completely eliminate it in the long-run.

References

Bhatty, Kiran, 1996, 'Child Labour: Breaking the Vicious Circle', *Economic and Political Weekly*, February 17.

Debroy, Bibek, 1994, 'Child Labour: A Labour of Hercules', *The Economic Times*, May 30.

Francis, C., 1996, 'Eradication of Child Labour: Need for an Integrated Approach', *Social Action*, October-December.

Joshi, Uma, 1997, 'Restoring Childhood to Child Labour', *Social Welfare*, April.

Kannan, R., 1997, 'Economy is Only One Dimension of Child Labour', *The Hindu*, February 18.

Kaushal, H., 1996, 'Dangers of Denying the Child an Honest Day's Work', *The Economic Times,* May 13.

Khadria, Binod, 1996, 'Child Labour: Reform Through a Fiscal Instrument', *Economic and Political Weekly,* July 27.

Kitchulu, T.N., 1994, 'Child Labour: Current Scenario', *Yojna,* May 31.

Mahapatra, Sevashree, 1977, 'Steps to Check Child Labour', *Yojna,* July.

Menon, Santosh, 1997, 'Matchless Exploitation' (Cheap Child Labour in Sivakasi), *The Economic Times,* July 6.

Ministry of Labour, Government of India, December 1979, *Report of the Committee on Child Labour* (Chairman: M.S. Gurupadswamy).

Remington, Francoise, 1996, 'Child Labour: A Global Crisis Without a Global Response', *Economic and Political Weekly,* December 28.

Singh, S.P., 1997, 'Child Labour: The Malady and the Remedy', *Yojna,* July.

Sundaram, I. Satya, 1994, 'Child Labour: Facing the Harsh reality', *Social Action,* July-September.

Weiner, Myron, 1996, 'Child Labour in India: Putting Compulsory Primary Education on the Political Agenda', *Economic and Political Weekly,* November 9-16.

Section - II

CHILD LABOUR IN INDIAN INDUSTRIES

10

Child Labour in Indian States

—Vipla Chopra & Harvinder Kaur

(An assessment of the magnitude and changes in the composition of child labour in India as a whole and in its four States, Punjab, Haryana, Bihar and Orissa, has been made in this paper for three census periods, 1971, 1981 and 1991. The rural-urban, inter-state and gender differentials in child labour have been examined and an attempt has also been made to analyse the possible determinants of inter-state differentials in the magnitude of child labour).

Introduction

Child labour, a global phenomenon, is conspicuously prevalent in the developing countries of the world. According to estimates of International Labour Organisation, nearly 250 million children between the ages of 5 and 14 are working in developing countries. Of this total, some 120 million children are working full-time and 130 million work part-time. About 61 per cent of child workers (or nearly 152 million) are found in Asia, 32 per cent (or 80 million) in Africa and 7 per cent (or 17.5 million) in Latin America.[1] India, Pakistan and Bangladesh together account for a percentage of child labour higher than that of the rest of the world.

The problem of child labour has recently come in the forefront. Children have been abused in various industrial and service establishments. They have also been made to work in various hazardous conditions in both organised and unorganised sectors mainly owing to poverty, illiteracy, ignorance, unemployment, low wages, large size of family etc. International Labour Organisation (ILO), through various conventions, recommendations and declarations, has been making rules and thus guiding the member countries (including India) for abolition of child labour through several measures. The Government of India has taken a number of legislative and executive steps to mitigate the evil of child labour. Article 24 of our Constitution lays down, "No child below the age of 14 shall be employed to work in any factory or mine or engaged in any other hazardous employment."[2] The Child Labour (Prohibition and Regulation) Act, 1986 also states that no child under the age of 14 shall be permitted to be engaged in hazardous occupations or to be made to undertake heavy work.[3]

The implementation of child labour Acts in our country is very ineffective. The main reasons for this are lack of adequate enforcement machinery, lack of political will, deliberate attempt of employers to flout the legal provisions and lack of consciousness within the minds of parents themselves who send their children to work. Keeping in view the pitiable conditions of child labour in India, the Government of India has endeavoured to expound national policy of 'Child Labour Welfare', which includes provision of free and compulsory education for all children up to the age of 14, alternative forms of education for those children who are unable to take full advantage of formal school education for whatever reasons; health and nutritional programmes and services for all children; and measures for protecting children against neglect, cruetly and exploitation. The national anti-poverty policies, the national education policy and the national policy on health-for-all and on nutrition are together expected to help in realising the objectives of the National Policy on Child Labour (NPCL), 1987. This is clear in the following paragraph of NPCL document: "The measures to promote employment-oriented development schemes both in rural and urban areas, and the all-round development and extension of adequate facilities for both formal and normal education, vocational education and training and in the coverage and extension of social security and family welfare should all go a long way to tackle the basic and root cause of child labour."[4]

But inspite of statutory provisions for prohibition and regulation of child labour, the problem still exists in alarming proportions in India. With around 23 million working children,

India shares one-third of the Asia's child labour and one-fourth of the world's unfortunate working children.[5]

From among the States of India, Andhra Pradesh has the highest number of working children (15.2 per cent of total child workers in the country) and Kerala the lowest (where it is only 1.8 per cent of the total labour force in 1981). Karnataka and Rajasthan States have 7.9 and 7.3 per cent, respectively, of the child labour of the total labour force.[6]

Problem

To assess the gravity of the child labour problem, an attempt has been made in this paper

(*i*) to examine the extent of child labour in India;
(*ii*) to assess the magnitude of child labour in four states of India, namely Punjab, Haryana, Bihar and Orissa; and
(*iii*) to identify the possible determinants of inter-state differentials in child labour.

Extent of Child Labour in India

As this study is based on census data, the figures of extent of child labour in India are under-estimated. Census data gives statistics regarding children working in the organised sector only. It does not give an account of children working in the unorganised sector of the country. According to official reports, there were 17.36 million working children in 1985, however, according to the estimates of non-governmental organisations, the figures could have been between 44 million and 100 million in 1985.[7] Thus whatever may by the actual figures on child labour, the important point is that the phenomenon of child labour is on the rise in India.

Table 10.1 shows the extent of child labour in India at three census points i.e. 1971, 1981 and 1991. Total population of the country was 548.16 million in 1971, out of which 42 per cent were children below 14 years of age. The proportion of child-population (296.93 million) to total population (836.16 million) declined to 35 per cent in 1991. Though, in absolute terms, both total population and child population have increased rapidly, in relative terms the rate of increase in total population is high. Further, the extent of child labour in India increased from 10.75 million in 1971 to 23.6

Table 10.1
Child Labour/Child Population in India (1971-1991)

Years	*Total (in millions)*				*Percentage of Child Workers to Total*			*Percentage of Child Population to Total Population*
	Population	*Children (0-14 years)*	*Workers*	*Child Workers*	*Population*	*Workers*	*Children*	
1971	548.16	230.33	180.49	10.75	1.96	5.96	4.67	42.02
1981	665.29	263.11	222.52	13.64	2.05	6.13	5.18	39.55
1991	836.61	296.93	314.90	23.16	2.77	7.35	7.80	35.49

Sources : 1. Census of India, 1971, Series I, Part III of 1972—Economic Characteristics of Population (Selected Tables).

2. Census of India, 1981, Series I, Part III A, General Economic Tables, Table B-3.

3. Census of India, 1991, quoted in D.P. Chaudhari, "Statistical Profile of Child Labour in India 1961-91," University of Wollongong.

million in 1991. In other words, the volume of child labour has more than doubled within 20 years. About 7 per cent of the total labour force of the country consists of child labour. Thus, the ratio of child workers to total workers turns out to be 1:14. On the whole, the situation emerges to be quite depressing as the share of child labour has increased by 41.33 per cent in total population and 67.02 per cent in total child population in 1991 as compared to 1971.

Table 10.2 depicts area-wise and sex-wise distribution of child labour in India. During 1991, 21.27 million (91.84 per cent) children were found to be working in rural areas as against 12.57 million (92.84 per cent) in 1981. Thus a very high majority of child workers is observed in rural areas. Further, disparities in the proportions of male and female child labour are also noticeable in both rural and urban areas. Out of 9.98 million child workers in rural India, 7.29 million (73 per cent) were males and 2.69 million (27 per cent) were females in 1971, whereas, in 1991, out of total 21.27 million rural child workers, 8.7 million (40 per cent) were males and 12.57 (60 per cent) were females. In urban India, during 1971, out of a total 0.77 million child workers, 0.61 million (80 per cent) were males and 0.16 million (20 per cent) were females and during 1991, 1.89 million were total working children and out of them, 1.15 million (68 per cent) were males and 0.74 million (32 per cent) were females. While taking sex-wise total figures of child workers, the proportion of male child labour fell sharply from 73.4 per cent in 1971 to 42.53 per cent in 1991. The corresponding figures of females have gone up tremendously from 26.6 per cent to 57.46 per cent. In urban India, more males than females work as child labour, though, in percentage terms, males are substantially lower in rural India.

In a nutshell, the incidence of child labour is quite high in the country and this is so particularly in the rural areas. Moreover, the trend in employment is shifting from male children to female children in rural as well as urban areas.

Extent of Child Labour in Indian States

As a large number of factors are responsibles for inter-state variations in the extent of child labour, it would be illuminating to examine the extent and nature of child labour in a few Indian states independently as well as in comparative perspective. To study these variations, we have selected four states, namely Punjab,

Table 10.2
Area-wise Distribution of Child Labour in India

Years	*Child Labour (in millions)*								
	Rural			*Urban*			*Total*		
	M	*F*	*T*	*M*	*F*	*T*	*M*	*F*	*T*
1971	7.29	2.69	9.98	0.61	0.16	0.77	7.89	2.86	10.75
1981	7.34	5.23	12.57	0.77	0.30	1.07	8.11	5.53	13.64
1991	8.70	12.57	21.27	1.15	0.74	1.89	9.85	13.31	23.16

Sources : 1. Census of India, 1971, Series I, Part III of 1972—Economic Characteristics of Population (Selected Tables).
2. Census of India, 1981, Series I, Part III A, General Economic Tables, Table B-3.
3. Census of India, 1991, quoted in D.P. Chaudhari, "Statistical Profile of Child Labour in India 1961-91," University of Wollongong.
4. M=Male, F=Female, T=Total.

Haryana, Bihar and Orissa, on the basis of difference in the level of their socio-economic development. Punjab and Haryana states are advanced compared to Bihar and Orissa in terms of both per capita income and literacy. In terms of per capita income, punjab and Haryana occupy the highest and the second highest positions, respectively, whereas Bihar and Orissa occupied the lowest and the third lowest positions among the Indian states during 1991-92.[8]

Similarly, in terms of literacy, Punjab and Haryana ranked 17th and 21st, respectively, whereas Bihar and Orissa ranked 30th and 23rd during 1991.[9] Table 10.3 reflects the quantum of population and of child labour in these states. The population of Bihar was the highest (863.7 lakhs), followed by Orissa (316.6 lakhs), Punjab (202.8 lakhs) and Haryana (164.6 lakhs) in 1991. Similar positions have been observed in the case of child labour in these states. The figures of child labour in absolute terms were 10.7 lakhs, 5.1 lakhs, 1.3 lakhs and 0.6 lakh for Bihar, Orissa, Punjab and Haryana, respectively, in 1991. Table 10.3 also depicts the growth rates of child labour in these states for the periods 1971-81 and 1981-91. It can be observed from this Table that both Punjab and Haryana have experienced a decline in the growth rate of child labour during these decades, though the rate of decline has been more in Haryana. This may be due to a sharp rise in the literacy rate of Haryana as the percentage increase in literacy rate of Haryana was 27.28 as compared to 21.47 in Punjab during 1981-91. On the other hand, Bihar and Orissa experienced positive growth rate during 1971-81 and negative growth rate during 1981-91. Bihar experienced the lowest rate of decline in child labour during 1981-91 among the four states under consideration.

Table 10.4 points out the percentage of child labour to total population, total labour force and total child population in the states under study for the period 1971-91. The percentages of child labour to total population fell from 2.24, 1.88, 1.72 and 1.37 in 1971 to 1.64, 1.24, 0.66 and 0.55 in 1991 in Orissa, Bihar, Punjab and Haryana respectively. These proportions were the highest for Orissa and the lowest for Haryana during the period under study. The percentage of child labour to total labour force has also shown a decreasing trend in all these four states. During 1971, these percentages in Haryana, Punjab, Bihar and Orissa were 5.2, 5.94, 6.06 and 7.18, respectively, and came down to 1.78, 2.14, 3.86 and 4.37, respectively, in 1991. A similar downward tendency has been observed in the case of proportions of child labour to total child

Table 10.3
Child Labour in Four States in India

States	*Total Population ('000) 1991*	*Child Labour ('000)*			*Computed Annual Growth Rate of Child Labour*	
		1971	*1981*	*1991*	*1971-81*	*1981-91*
Punjab	20,281.9 (2.40)	232.8	216.9	134.2	–0.7	–4.7
Haryana	16,463.6 (1.94)	240.6	194.2	90.9	–2.1	–7.3
Bihar	86,374.5 (10.21)	1059.4	1101.8	1073.3	0.4	–0.3
Orissa	31,659.7 (3.74)	492.5	702.3	518.7	3.6	-3.0

Sources : 1. Census of India, 1991 - Series I, Part II - B(i), Volume (ii).

2. D.P. Chaudhari, "A Dynamic Profile of Child Labour in India, CLASP, ILO, New Delhi, June 1996.

Note : The figures in parenthesis represent percentage to total population of India.

Table 10.4
Percentage Share of Child Labour in Four States of India

States	*Percentage of Child Labour to Total Population*			*Percentage of Child Labour to Total Labour Force*			*Percentage of Child Labour*to Total Child Population, Census Data Based Estimates (0-14 Years)*		
	1971	*1981*	*1991*	*1971*	*1981*	*1991*	*1971*	*1981*	*1991*
Punjab	1.72	1.29	0.66	5.94	4.10	2.14	6.07	5.16	2.85
Haryana	1.37	1.50	0.55	5.20	4.75	1.78	7.86	5.27	2.11
Bihar	1.88	1.58	1.24	6.06	4.87	3.86	6.55	5.57	4.55
Orissa	2.24	2.66	1.64	7.18	7.01	4.37	7.98	9.58	6.73

★ The percentage of child labour to total child population of the respective state is out of children of 5-14 age group.

Sources : Census of India, 1981, Primary Census Abstract General Population, Series-I, Part II, B(i).
Census of India, 1991, Series I, Part II, B(i) Volume (ii).

population. During 1991, these proportions were found to be 2.11, 2.85, 4.55 and 6.73 as against 7.86, 6.07, 6.55 and 7.98 during 1971 in Haryana, Punjab, Bihar and Orissa, respectively. One can infer from the above analysis that the share of child labour is diminishing at a faster rate in Punjab and Haryana than that in Bihar and Orissa which may be due to the fact that Punjab and Haryana have been placed better economically (in terms of income) and socially (in terms of education) than Bihar and Orissa.

Table 10.5 charts out sex-wise ard area-wise distribution of child labour during 1971-91. Out of the total child workers, an overwhelming majority of males is observed to be working in all the four states during the entire period. However, the percentage shares of male child workers dwindled from 98.7, 89.8, 79.3 and 85.9 in 1971 to 92.2, 78.5, 73.8 and 67.2 in 1991 in Punjab, Haryana, Bihar and Orissa, respectively. On the other hand, the percentages of female child workers went up tremendously in Punjab, Haryana, Bihar and Orissa from 1.3, 10.2, 20.7 and 14.1 in 1971 to 7.8, 21.5, 26.2 and 32.8 respectively in 1991. Thus, the share of female child workers shot up in all the four states. This may be due to lower female literacy rate than male literacy rate in all the four states. In Punjab, Haryana, Bihar and Orissa, the female literacy rates were 50 per cent, 40 per cent, 23 per cent and 31 per cent, respectively, which were quite lower than the corresponding male literacy rates of 68 per cent, 69 per cent, 53 per cent and 63 per cent during 1991.

Child labour prevails both in rural and urban areas throughout the country. Table 10.5 manifests that an overwhelming majority of child labourers is engaged in rural areas but their percentage has been found to be continuously sliding down in all the states throughout the study period. The percentages of child labour in rural areas of Punjab, Haryana, Bihar and Orissa stepped down from 90.8, 93.9, 96.2 and 96.5 in 1971 to 83.7, 87.7, 94.5 and 94.7 per cent, respectively, in 1991. On the other hand, the corresponding percentages of child labour in urban areas have recorded a steep rise from 9.2, 6.1, 3.8 and 3.5 in 1971 to 16.3, 10.3, 5.5 and 5.3, respectively, in 1991. Children in urban areas are working mainly in small manufacturing units as cheap labourers to supplement their family income.

Thus, from the above analysis, it can be concluded that the States of Punjab and Haryana are leading in reducing substantially the overall incidence of child labour (male and female taken

Table 10.5

Sex-wise and Area-wise Distribution of Child Labour (5-14 Years) in Four States of India

(Percentages)*

States	*1971*		*1981*		*1991*		*1971*		*1981*		*1991*	
	M	*F*	*M*	*F*	*M*	*F*	R	*U*	R	*U*	R	*U*
Punjab	98.7	1.3	95.5	4.5	92.2	7.8	90.8	9.2	87.0	13.0	83.7	16.3
Haryana	89.8	10.2	80.9	19.1	78.5	21.5	93.9	6.1	92.5	7.5	87.7	10.3
Bihar	79.3	20.7	75.5	24.5	73.8	26.2	96.2	3.8	95.0	5.0	94.5	5.5
Orissa	85.9	14.1	75.3	24.7	67.2	32.8	96.5	3.5	94.9	5.1	94.7	5.5

Sources : Computed from Census data available in D.P. Chaudhari, (1996), "A Dynamic Profile of Child Labour in India, 1951-91", CLASP, ILO, New Delhi, June 1996.

* The percentages are out of total child labour of the respective State.

M=Male, F=Female, R=Rural, U=Urban.

together) while Bihar and Orissa continue to have a rather sluggish decline. However, the majority of child labourers are still found in rural areas of these States.

Extent of Child Labour in Agriculture

Children are generally employed in agricultural and non-agricultural activities in the States under reference. We have categorized these activities into three groups, namely cultivators, agricultural labourers and others. Others include children engaged in manufacturing in household industry, mining and quarrying, manufacturing in other than household industry, construction, trade and commerce, and transport. It is clear from Table 10.6 that proportions of child labourers engaged in non-agricultural activities were meagre as compared to those in agricultural activities in all the four States (except female child workers in Punjab). In agricultural sector, child workers are predominantly employed as cultivators and as agricultural labourers. In Punjab, the share of male as well as female child cultivators have diminished, whereas their share as agricultural labourers has sky-rocketed throughout the period under study. More than half (51.1 per cent) of male child workers and 45.6 per cent of female child workers were employed as agricultural labourers in Punjab in 1991. Similar trend was observed in the case of male child labourers in Haryana. In Bihar and Orissa, the proportions of male agricultural child labourers were more than those of male child cultivators during 1971-91. Similarly, more female child workers were noted as agricultural labourers in Bihar and Orissa, though recently they have preferred doing cultivation.

Combining the above-mentioned two agricultural activities, one can infer that the proportion of male child workers engaged in agricultural sector has dropped slightly in Punjab (-3.8%) and Haryana (-0.1%), whereas the situation has been the opposite in the case of Bihar (+3.8%) and Orissa (+7.5%) during the study period.

The corresponding figures of female child workers absorbed in agricultural sector have risen by 38 per cent, 7 per cent, 1 per cent, and 24 per cent in Punjab, Haryana, Bihar and Orissa, respectively. Thus the number of female child workers engaged in agricultural sector in growing in all the States which fact needs serious attention.

Table 10.6
Child Labour Engaged in Agricultural Sector

States	Male Child Workers*1			Female Child Workers*2		
	1971	*1981*	*1991*	*1971*	*1981*	*1991*
Punjab						
Cultivators	44.9	37.4	26.5	9.4	3.7	12.1
Agricultural Labourers	35.8	44.0	51.1	32.3	50.0	45.6
Others*3	19.3	18.6	22.4	58.3	46.3	42.3
Haryana						
Cultivators	49.1	48.8	41.5	48.3	61.6	54.9
Agricultural Labourers	28.4	31.2	35.9	31.5	21.8	30.6
Others	22.5	20.0	22.6	20.2	16.6	14.5
Bihar						
Cultivators	34.6	36.2	37.6	14.0	23.7	32.4
Agricultural Labourers	52.3	50.0	52.6	77.6	66.0	60.2
Others	13.1	13.8	9.8	8.4	10.3	9.4
Orissa						
Cultivators	34.5	39.1	42.2	10.7	18.8	22.1
Agricultural Labourers	45.1	43.5	42.8	57.9	61.1	62.8
Others	20.4	17.4	15.0	31.4	20.1	15.1

Sources : Computed from Census data available in D.P. Chaudhari, "A Dynamic Profile of Child Labour in India, 1951-91," CLASP, ILO, New Delhi, June 1996.

★1 Out of total male child workers.

★2 Out of total female child workers.

★3 Others include manufacturing in household industry, mining and quarrying, manufacturing in other than household industry, construction, trade and commerce, transport.

Socio-Economic Development and Child Labour

The socio-economic indicators of development have a great bearing on the extent of child labour. Many studies lay great emphasis on the relationship between socio-economic indicators of development and child labour. Some of these studies are as under :-

In a survey of 200 families of four villages of Mohindergarh district of Haryana, S. Chander and L.Devi[10] have found that the maximum number of parents received child income as high as 26 to 50 per cent of the total family income. Moreover, all this income was coming from farming activities. Another study by Sukhbir Kaur[11], conducted in 6 selected villages of Mukatsar district of Punjab, finds that a majority of the families were sending their children for labour due to their economic backwardness. With the pooling of children's money with the family income, the bulk of families were able to provide better food to the members of the family. The study further found that 'poverty was the major factor responsible for the child labour participation.'

Another study by P.K. Mishra and B.N. Mishra[12] organised in Cuttack city of Orissa State points out, "Owing to poverty it becomes very difficult for their parents to bring them (children) up, but to engage them in some form of economic activity to earn their livelihood and support their families."

Yet another study made in Patna by Bhagwan Prasad Singh[13] on poverty-stricken families with large size noticed that their misery compelled them to join labour force so that they might supplement the family income. S.S. Mehta[14] has also pointed out "a highly significant positive correlation (+0.78 per cent) between the number of child labour and the number of people below poverty line in 1981." His study concludes that child labour is a symptom of poverty.

Many other studies have highlighted the issues concerning the problem of child labour - wage earning. Children contribute very significantly to their household income (B.M.Dinesh)[15]; as the earnings of family go up, the share of working children goes down faster, especially in the case of girls (S. Murty[16]); the percentage of households below the poverty-line dips owing to the income from child labour (B.K.Sharma and Vishwamittar[17]).

These studies lead us to the conclusion that low income/ poverty is the root cause of child labour. Illiteracy is another significant factor that generates child labour.

Education for children should be a basic right. It is also essential that prevention of child labour should be one of the major objectives of educational programmes. Giving priority to education is not only a way of combating child labour but also a sound economic investment. Numerous studies have examined the impact of education on the incidence of child labour. These studies, in general, agree that education does have a bearing on the prevalence of child labour (Kambargi and Kulkarni[18], Singh[19] and Kumar[20]). It is observed that most of the parents make a straight choice between education and work. The study by R. Sharma and R. K. Sharma[21] reveals a close link between education and incidence of child labour. The study finds out, "a correlation between the education of heads of the households and schooling of the child workers; these two variables have a positive correlation (r=.28). It means that "the higher the level of education of the head of the household, the higher would be the schooling of the child and consequently the lower would be the incidence of child labour."

In the study by Mahavir Jain[22], the relationship between literacy rate of the States and incidence of child labour has also been shown. It concludes, "In states having lower urban literacy rates, there is higher incidence of urban child labour."

The above studies spotlight that education also plays a significant role in reducing the extent of child labour.

Thus to identify the possible determinants of inter-state differentials in child labour in the four states under discussion, we have considered three determinants, namely population below poverty-line, per capita net domestic product and literacy rate.

Figures shown in Table 10.7 point out that population below poverty-line is much high in Bihar and Orissa as compared to that in Punjab and Haryana. However, the situation is improving in all the four states—Population below poverty-line turned out to be 65%, 43% and 45% in Orissa and 56%, 50% and 41% in Bihar for the years 1977-78, 1983-84 and 1987-88 respectively. On the other hand, the corresponding percentages were 16, 14 and 7 for Punjab and 25, 16 and 12 for Haryana. Thus comparatively larger number of population was observed to be below poverty-line in Bihar and Orissa. The figures of per capita net domestic product worked out to be Rs. 8,423, Rs. 7,516, Rs. 2,539 and Rs. 3,595 in 1991 as compared to Rs. 1,070, Rs. 877, Rs. 402 and Rs. 478 in 1971 for Punjab, Haryana, Bihar and Orissa, respectively. Thus the States

Table 10.7
Indicators of Economic Development in Four States of India

States	*Per Capita Net Domestic Product Current Prices (Rs.)*			*Literacy Rate*			*Population Below Poverty-Line*		
	1971	*1981*	*1991*	*1971*	*1981*	*1991*	*1977-78*	*1983-84*	*1987-88*
Punjab	1070	2620	8423	33.67	48.17	58.51	16.4	13.8	7.2
Haryana	877	2351	7516	26.89	43.88	55.85	25.2	15.6	11.6
Bihar	402	943	2539	19.94	32.05	38.48	56.3	49.5	40.8
Orissa	478	1173	3596	26.89	40.97	49.09	65.1	42.8	44.7

Sources : Computed from

1. CMIE, Basic Statistics Relating to the Indian Economy, Vol. 2, Various Issues.
2. Census of India, 1981, Series-I, Part II, B(i).
3. Census of India, 1991, Series I, Part II, B(i) Volume (ii).
4. D.P. Chaudhari, "A Dynamic Profile of Child Labour in India, 1951-91", CLASP, *ILO*, New Delhi, June 1996.
5. NSS Reports.
6. Economic Survey: 1994-95.

of Bihar and Orissa had almost less than half of the per capita income of Punjab and Haryana throughout the period 1971-91 (Table 10.7). Because of low per capita income and a comparatively high percentage of people living below poverty-line, the number of literates is also very low in Bihar and Orissa as compared to that of Punjab and Haryana. During 1991, the literacy rates were 58.81, 55.85, 38.48 and 49.09 per cent in Punjab, Haryana, Bihar and Orissa respectively.

One can infer from the above facts that people of Punjab and Haryana are more educated and enjoy higher per capita income than the people of Orissa and Bihar. As a result, the incidence of child labour is also plunging at a faster rate in comparatively advanced states of Punjab and Haryana.

The above analysis leads us to the conclusion that inter-state disparities in the incidence of child labour are mainly caused by poverty and illiteracy. The results suggest that if we really want to reduce the incidence of child labour and really want to build up a strong and developed India, efforts should be made to eradicate illiteracy and raise the level of education and income, particularly in those States where the problem is very acute.

In any case, the problem of child labour demands serious and immediate attention at the national level as it is one of the major problems of the country. The situation is rather grave in the rural areas. A growing percentage of female child labour out of total child labour has been found recently in the country. Thus, there is a dire need to give special attention to the welfare of female children.

References

1. ILO Report, "Child Labour : Targetting the Intolerable," *International Conference (Report VI (i) 86th Session,* 1998), ISBN 92-2-110328-5. International Labour Office, Geneva, 1996.
2. P.L. Mehta and S.S. Jaiswal, *Child Labour and the Law—Myth and Reality of Welfare Measures,* Deep & Deep Publications, New Delhi, 1996.
3. S. K. Tripathi, *Child Labour in India,* Discovery Publishing House, New Delhi, 1989.
4. "National Policy of Child Labour : 1987: 3," quoted in Mahavir Jain, *Ibid.,* p. 9.
5. Bipul Malakar and Tapa Roy, "Child Labour: Incidence, Causes

and Concerns in India," Indian Journal of Labour Economics, Vol. 40, No. 4, 1997.

6. S. K. Tripathi, *op. cit.*
7. Mahavir Jain, *Child Labour in India—A Select Bibliography,* Child Labour Cell, National Labour Institute, Noida, 1994.
8. Statistical Abstract of Pubjab, 1996.
9. *Census of India,* 1991, Series I, Part II—B(i) Volumes (ii).
10. S. Chander and L. Devi, "Child Workers in Haryana", *Social Welfare,* Vol. XVI (7), 1979.
11. Sukhbir Kaur, *An Economic Contribution of Child Labour of Landless Families in the Skilled and Unskilled Activities in Muktasar,* Block PAU, Ludhiana, M.Phil thesis, 1984-85.
12. P. K. Mishra and B.N. Mishra, "Child Labour: A Study in Cuttak City", *Indian Journal of Labour Economics,* Vol. 33, No. 4, 1990, p. 291.
13. Bhagwan Prasad Singh, "Sad Plight of Child Labour and Need for Proper Deal", *The Indian Journal of Labour Economics,* Vol. 33, No. 4, Oct.-Dec. 1990.
14. S.S. Mehta, "Why Child Labour? The Indian Case", in Hirway India and others (ed.), *Towards Eradication of Child Labour—An International View,* IBH Publishing Co., New Delhi, 1991.
15. B.M. Dinesh, *Economic Activities of Children: Dimension, Causes and Consequences,* Daya Publishing House, Delhi, 1988.
16. S. Murty, "Child Labour in Unorganised City", *Indian Journal of Labour Economics,* Vol. 33, No. 4, Oct.-Dec., 1990.
17. B.K. Sharma and Vishwamittar, *Child Labour and Urban Informal Sector,* Deep & Deep Publications, New Delhi, 1990.
18. R. Kanbargi and P.M. Kulkarni, "Child Labour, Schooling and Fertility", in Stoeckel and Jain (eds.), *Fertility in Asia: Assessing Impact of Development Projects,* France Printers, London, 1986.
19. A.N. Singh, *Child Labour in India: Socio-Economic Perspectives,* Shipra Publication, Delhi, 1990.
20. Sudhir Kumar, "Child Labour in Education," in Singh & others (eds.) *Children at Work: Problem and Policy Options,* B.R. Publishing Corporation, Delhi, 1993.
21. R. Sharma and R.K. Sharma, "Education and Child Labour: The Case of Class Bangle Industry of Firozabad," *Indian Journal of Labour Economics,* Vol. 40, No. 4, 1997.
22. Mahaveer Jain, *op. cit.*

11

Child Labour in Bihar

— *Narendra Prasad*

Children constitute the most important asset of any nation. Jawaharlal Nehru once said "The Nation walks on the tiny feet of its children". Children are the future of the nation. They are flowers of our national garden.

Child labour is a global problem. It is more common in under-developed countries or region. Child labour by and large, is a problem of poor and destitute families, where either parent cannot afford education of their children or have to depend on the earning of their children. The prevalence of Child Labour is a blot on the conscience of society. It is a national disgrace that millions of children in this country have to spend a major part of their daily routine in hazardous works while millions of youth and able bodied men go without employment.

The problem of child labour in India may seem to result from traditional attitudes—urbanisation, industrialisation, migration, lack of schools or reluctance of parents to send their children to school and so on. However, its causes are extreme poverty. Despite tremendous amount of awareness generated by intellectuals, media men, social workers and voluntary organisations over the last few years about the seriousness of the problem, little effort has been made towards correctly analysing the problem of child labour in Bihar.

The term 'Child Labour' a convenient expression for 'the labour of children', has a well recognised though rather vague meaning. Child Labour is at times, used as synonym for 'Employed Child' or 'Working Child'. In this sense it is co-extensive with any work done by a child for gain. Homer Falks, The Chairman of United State National Child Labour Committee, defined child labour as: "..... any work by children that interferes with their full physical development, their opportunities for a desirable minimum of education or their needed recreation".[1] V.V. Giri has distinguished two senses of the term 'Child Labour'.[2] The term child labour is commonly interpreted in two different ways: *first,* as an economic practice and *secondly,* as a social evil.

In the *first* context it signifies employment of children in gainful occupations with a view to adding to the Labour income of the family. It is in the *second* context that the term child labour is now more generally used. The mention of Child Labour is intended to cover children under the age of fifteen engaged in work or employment with the aim of earning livelihood for themselves or for their families.[3] A comprehensive definition of Child Labour is "any work done by the children in order to economically benefit their family or themselves directly or indirectly at the cost of their physical, mental or social development".[4] Thus, the term child labour not only applies to the children working in industries but also to the children working in all forms of non-industrial occupations which are injurious to their physical, mental, moral and social development.

The data on child labour in the country as a whole or the states in particular is not every accurate because: Child Labourers are scattered widely in unorganised sectors as family workers or as hired workers. Some states include children with permanent job duty in the labour force. School going children are frequently excluded from child labour statistics though they work outside school hours. Employers do not always provide accurate data on child labour in order to avoid legal restrictions. Management, efficiency and capability are badly lacking in the State statistical and census offices and staff. But inspite of all these pitfalls, the data available from secondary sources give some idea about the range of estimates rather than any accurate data on child labour. Table 11.1 gives the picture of growth rate of child population and child labour in Bihar and All India 1961-91.

The size of child population and child labour is computed from census and NSS sources and it indicates that child population is declining slowly and child labour is marginally rising in Bihar.

The child labour is positively correlated with incidence of poverty, illiteracy and the per cent of the labour force in agriculture. The incidence of child labour was negatively correlated with per capita income, infrastructural development, school enrolment ratios and female participation rates in non-agricultural work.

Table 11.1

Year	*Child Population*		*Child Labour*	
	All India	*Bihar*	*All India*	*Bihar*
1961-71	2.5	2.0	—2.9	—3.7
1971-81	1.3	2.0	0.4	—1.7
1981-91	1.2	1.4	1.2	1.8

Source : Census of India 1961, 1971, 1981 and Projections to 2001 A.D.

The phenomenon of child labour robs the child of his youthful life, restricts the prospects of education which can enable him to reach a higher level at a later stage of life on the one hand and ultimately, it harms the progress and prosperity of the nation. John has rightly observed "Starve a child of food, of affection, of freedom, of education and you produce an adult who is stunted as an individual and holds back progress forward development rather than accelerate it".[5] This is exactly happening in Bihar. When put the children to work at a tender age in reduces their physical growth, lowers their efficiency, scale of intellectual growth and ultimately their ability and thereby nation's growth in future. Thus, child labour is economically unsound, psychologically disastrous and physically as well as morally dangerous and harmful. It is inefficient utilisation of labour power at a lowest productivity level which precludes full development of children's potentialities and ultimately harms economic development. It is rightly remarked by Mustafa H. Nagi about the sad plight of child labour that "One of the paradoxical features which characterise developing nations is the existence of a relatively large child labour force at a time when unemployment problem of men and women in the economically productive age groups is soaring".[6]

Most of the child workers belong to poor, landless and semi-landless families whose income is otherwise insufficient to keep the family alive. The children are therefore forced to work to supplement the meagre income of the family. Most of the village artisans and crafts-men cannot make a living unless their children work with them and thereby supplement their income. It is primarily on account of poverty that poor parents fail to send their children to schools. In Bihar lower socio-economic groups of population are illiterates. They only think about the present time which is their sole concern and worry. They never think of future. They are fully satisfied with what they gain by the earnings of their children. It is ignored by them that their children may participate even in educational opportunities, they do not think that the child labourers today will be the paupers of tomorrow, they are the boys and girls who will grow up without either formal schooling or knowledge of a trade, sooner or later, their youthful energies exhausted they will become dull, shiftless and driftless.

Child labourers are generally found engaged in a number of economic activities like brick kilns, stone quarries, construction, carpet weaving, handlooms, matches and fireworks, glass, bangles, diamond cutting and polishing, lock making, household activities, hotels and restaurant and the like. Children are known to work for 12 to 20 hours sometimes and are subjected to all sorts of abuse reminiscent of what Karl Marx wrote of the early phase of capitalism. Children suffer from long, bone and muscle disorders in brass making units. All in all, the end result on economic system is one of hitting at the base of human capital formation if children are allowed to work for long hours in unhygenic conditions on low wages. In Bihar the incidence of child labour is the highest in the rural sector. A majority of child labour are employed in the unorganised and informal sectors. The highest number of child labour is found in agriculture and allied activities. The long working hours, low wages, absence of holidays, absence of social security, poor working environment, all these adversely affect the children's health. Its impact on the future of the State and on the social dimension is adverse.

In Bihar gender discrimination continues. Gender discrimination is a patent fact not only among adults but also among children in Bihar. Parents favour male children as boys are more economically valuable than girls. The comparative economic advantage accounts for the sex bias in favour of boys over girls in Bihar, where agriculture is the main source of employment and income for most of the people. In Bihar girl child is a daughter of denial in traditional culture and gender discrimination is conspicious and appalling. The prevalence of mass scale poverty and illiteracy in rural areas compel a large number of female child to take part in some kind of gainful activity. The prevalence of female child labour is an index of under-development of the society. Usually the girl child helps her mother to perform different household activities. In Bihar as a whole specially in south Bihar and tribal areas, girls help their mother in working in fields and forests. Female child labour is a said reflection of the state of the society's social and economic health.

Thus, in Bihar child labour is prevalent and inspite of several acts enacted to protect the children against exploitation, the evil of child labour is flourishing because of the non-uniformity and various loopholes in the laws. In the past no serious attention has been paid by the Government to implement the enacted laws to remove the blot on the conscience of society. Despite the number of legislations, the exploitation of child labour continues unabated. Undoubtedly child labour is embedded in the fabric of our society and this is one of the serious problems facing the state. What is required is the right environmental change of behaviour and attitudes. Legislation must be enacted forcefully and should be associated with punitive treatment and action. Children are like buds which need to be properly nursed and well taken care of so that they bloom fully, grow into able human beings and contribute their worth to the future development of the state. It must be accepted that the problem of child labour cannot be solved by legislation alone. It calls for multi-dimensional approach, the major dimensions being economic, educational and legal. For this the strong political will power for eradication of child labour is essential.

References

1. Stein, E. and Davis, T. (1940), *Labour Problem in America,* New York.
2. Giri, V.V., (1958), *Labour Problem in Indian Industry,* Asia Publishing House, Bombay.
3. International Labour Office, (1986), *Child Labour,* Geneva.
4. Gupta, B.D. & Maheshwari, R.K., (1988), *Child Labour,* Indian Academy of Pediatrics, Jodhpur.
5. John Orun, (1979), UNICEF SCARU, *Health and Basic Service,* New Delhi.
6. Nagi, M. Mustafa, (1972), *Rural Sociology,* Vol. 37 (623).

12

Problem of Child Labour in India: A Case Study of Patiala in Punjab

—Ajit S. Bhatia & (Mrs.) Gurbachan Kaur

Both the developed and developing countries, in their anxiety to step up the rate of growth, are turning a Nelson's eye to the social costs of development. These costs are becoming increasingly alarming. One such cost is the high incidence of child labour. Child labour is no doubt cheap, but it implies violation of children's rights.

So serious is the situation that Senator Harkin had introduced a Bill in the American Senate, in August 1992, asking for a ban on importing goods produced by child labour. The Senator also urged the U.S. President, "to seek an agreement with other governments to secure an international ban on trade in the products of child labour". Germany had already threatened to ban import of items using child labour. The first international programme relating to the Elimination of Child Labour was adopted by International Labour Organisation (ILO) in January 20, 1993. There are 57 action programmes of the ILO already under implementation in India, while eight others have been selected for future operation[1]. As an ILO official in India puts it, "These are all demonstration projects which seek to show that can be done to combat and progressively eliminate child labour in the country"[2].

According to recent ILO document estimates, there are some 200 million children in the 10-14 age group working in the Third

World which are forced to make their own living. They naturally work under conditions of servitude. Statistics reveal that 80 per cent of all Pakistani carpets are made by children under age 15. They seldom get even a minimum wage. Their health is in fact seriously affected by wool dust. Children in India, Nepal and Afghanistan too make rugs to make living. Children pick tobacoo in Indonesia, tea in Sri Lanka and oranges in Brazil[3]. However, it has been observed that the developed countries like U.S.A and Canada are also not free from child labour problem. Several million children below the age of 15 work daily at minimum wage or less than that in MacDonal and other food companies to earn their living. Thus it appears that no region of the world today is entirely free of child labour.

Asia accounts for about 72 per cent of child labour in the world. India has the dubious distinction of having the largest number of child labourers, but the incidence of child labour is often under-estimated. Almost one-third of the world's child labour is in India. Again, in India, every fourth child in the age group of 5 to 15 is employed, and this constitute about 26 per cent of the entire labour force. "Around 33 million of the 105 million children aged between 6 and 10 years in India are not attending school : . . . rather a large number of them are engaged in child labour"[4].

Although, the percentage of poor people in India has decreased from around 50 per cent of the population to 35 per cent, yet according to World Bank Report the actual number of people living below the poverty line has increased from 164 million in 1951 to 312 million in 1993-94 due to increase in population. So the poorer sections of the population have been growing at a faster rate than the richer. Therefore, the total incidence of child labour is also on the rise. The biggest chunk of the teen-age working force comes from rural areas in India, and of them, the majority get engaged in agricultural operations or small scale industries, while a lesser percentage of them finds jobs in large industries of hazardous nature, for instance textiles, chemicals, construction, petrol pumps, saw mills, printing presses, battary, chromium plating, mica cutting, production of matches and explosives.

The World Labour Report (June 1992) has mentioned certain causes for the high incidence of child labour in both developed and developing countries. The most important cause is poverty which compells parents to send their children to work. Parents do desire to supplement their meager incomes with those of their children.

There are bonded labourers, working as virtual slaves, to pay off debts which their parents had incurred. The children are neither aware of the size of the debt they are paying off, nor they know when they will get rid off. In urban areas children are more likely to be working away from their parents, often as domestic servants in the houses of richer families. Prostitution is another type of activity in which children, especially girls, are frequently found, says the ILO study and blames this as a contributing factor, towards AIDS epidemic.

The report also speaks of contemporary forms of child slavery in terms of link between an adult's work contract and the availability of child labour. It also points out of a type of child slavery for some money often described as an advance of wages. According to ILO estimates, the number of such child slaves, could range in tens of millions in agriculture, domestic help, carpet and textile industries, quarring and brick making.

Many street children depend on rag-picking for their living. They also handle medical and radio-active waste from hospitals, discarded bottles of solvents and medicine and leaking batteries. A health study of child workers in glass and metal fabrication workshops showed the children's lungs being grossly imparied from breathing noxious fumes. Child labourers in textile industry spend long hours in crapped positions which deform their bodies. The mental and physical growth of working children is thus retarded.

The report also pointed out that many schools serving the poor are in very bad shape, or chances of upward mobility are so slim, that the expected return (on education) is not equal to the sacrifice made. It is also true that many children drop out of school because they have to work. It is equally true that many become so discouraged by school that they prefer 'to work'.

Thus, it is well known that the social cost of child labour is very high. The present study has been undertaken in view of the social and economic implications of employing child labour.

The main objectives of the study are:

(a) to examine the socio-economic profile of the child labour;
(b) to understand the motivations behind the decisions to go for jobs; and
(c) to suggest strategies and measures to regulate child labour and improve their working conditions.

Methodology

The area chosen for field work is the Patiala city of Punjab. It is one of the main transport route for most of the labour in-migrating from other states. The problem of child labour may be studied either by concentrating on the households in which the working children live or the enterprises in which they work. Choice of the household as a frame of reference seems to be more reasonable because it would be easier to collect the required information and the risk that some of the working children, who do not work on fixed location may get excluded, is also eliminated.

The present study is based on the survey carried out by the authors covering 90-sampled households belonging to Patiala and its slum areas and four villages in the periphery of the city. These households were selected at random from a list of 300 households listed from the above said area. Selected household had atleast one working child each. Each household was approached personally togather information through a set of well designed pretested schedule. The information has been collected regarding age, family size, educational level, income of the parents, and wage rates of the child workers and the impact of work on the behaviour and health of child worker.

Findings

The analysis of the data has established the following socio-economic characteristics of child workers in Patiala.

Age

It is a well established fact that age plays a dominant role in shaping the personality and values of responsibility to work and to participate in different walks of life. It was observed that most of the child-respondents belonged to the age group of 12 to 15 years followed by 10 to 11 years. However 3.2 per cent children belonged to the age group of 6 to 8 years. The child respondents were mainly from the Hindu backward classes. They were almost three-fourths of the child workers followed by scheduled caste children. A small number was of Muslim child workers.

Education

Education is of utmost importance for the proper growth and

development of the individual, it does not only shape the life pattern and living but also helps in shaping thinking, attitude and views. It is generally seen that despite best efforts made at various levels, many children in our country either do not go to schools at all or leave them soon after joining. It has been sufficiently established by different studies on the school drop-outs that the situation is alarming. Assuming that education is affected in case of the working children, information was collected on this aspect of the problem. The distribution of working children in terms of level of education showed that half of them had never gone to school. Out of the remaining 50 per cent, 37.8 per cent had schooling up to primary and the remaining 12.2 per cent up to middle standard. The parents of the children having no more desire of having money in place of education of their children.

While collecting the information, one of the mother saying, "nearly all our girls work as maid servants". Herself is a maid servant, the woman said, "Why should I waste my time and money on sending my daughter to school where she will learn nothing of use? So why not put my girl to work so that she will learn something about our work. My elder girl, who is 15 years old, will be married soon. Her mother in-law will put her to work some where. Too much schooling to girls give big ideas and then they will be beaten up by their husbands or abused by their in-laws."

Size of the Family

A family which is larger in size with less income cannot lead a happy life. As a result, the members in the family cannot have facilities of better education, recreation, health care and opportunities to be developed in healthy family atmosphere. On the other side, a family which is limited in size and is well-planned, assures all possible developmental opportunities to its members and helps them to protect themselves from insecurities of life. In view of the fact the information has been gathered through respondent child workers and observed that the common size of the family was 4-6. The information further reveals that about three-fourths of the children belong to the nuclear and the remaining to joint families. It indicates that nuclear family which keeps less number of helping hands is producing higher number of children. It may be to supplement the income of the family. During the past when we had domination of joint family, the participation percentage of children in labour force was comparatively less. It means that the increasing price rise is also compelling the children even in nuclear families to undertake work.

Hours to Work

It was also observed that the child workers were exploited to the maximum possible extent. There is no sympathy for the child workers. There is no consideration for their growth and development. The only consideration is profit only. It is really a very sad state of affairs that the child workers instead of being out to work for 5-6 hours were asked to work for 9-11 hours a day without any extra payment. This does not happen in the case of adult workers because they are able to protect their interest through trade unions and other agencies.

The data on the average number of hours worked per day by the working children shows that only 7.8 per cent of the working children worked for less than 8 hours which is the normal practice for adult workers. Some 30.7 per cent of the children worked between 8 to 10 hours, 28.5 per cent between 10 to 12 hours. One-third of the children worked even more than 12 hours a day. This shows that the working children in the unorganised sector do not enjoy any uniform practice of working for fixed hours.

Family Income

The economic position of a family plays a useful and important role in the proper welfare and development of its members. A family with better income keeps adequate resources for proper future development of its children. The children of poor families cannot think of opportunities which are availed by rich families. Therefore, in the absence of resources, children of poor families are likely to face neglect and abuse of different kinds. The information regarding the economic condition of the family of child workers gathered and it reveals that about 69 per cent of the parents had monthly income of less than Rs. 500, while the remaining 31 per cent disclosed that their income varied between Rs. 500 to Rs. 1,000. This indicates that due to the low income of the family, children were deprived of the facilities which were essential for their proper growth and development. As the parents of the working children had jobs with low emoluments, it was very difficult for them to educate their children.

Indebtedness

The economic compulsion of the parents of child workers leads them to borrow money from one source or the other. As indicated earlier, the majority of parents who are illiterate neither understand the situation they live in nor do they feel concerned about proper planning and management of their family. Therefore, whatever money they earn during the day is spent on alcohol and drugs without thinking of insecurity of income the next day.

Information gathered from the parents regarding the economic status in terms of indebtedness shows that more than two-third (67 per cent) were in debt while the rest were free from it. The actual debt conditions of the families of the child workers are that a majority of the families, owed debts between Rs. 2,000 to Rs. 10,000. This was fairly high for these people to repay. As a result, they were compelled to send their children for work. Persons with debt of Rs. 1,000 or less were only 11.5 per cent, whereas indebtedness beyond Rs. 10,000 was limited to only 5.5 per cent. This is in accordance with the general impression that the people in this class rarely needs money (loan) because of their poor standard of living.

The level of indebtedness shows that circumstances and situations of the families of the working children lead them to join the labour force at an early age.

Monthly Earning

Data relating to earnings/wages are relevant only for workers employed in establishments and the self-employed. A wide variation was observed in the income distribution of child workers. A number of, specially apprentices, did not get any money for their labour, while others get only Rs. 150 to Rs. 200 per month. The earnings of children in self-employment and family labour depend purely on the nature and place of work, and the amount of labour put in that. Some of the vendors, shoe-shiners and rag pickers informed that their average earning was more than Rs. 500 per month. An another interesting fact which emerged from the study was that nearly 30 per cent of the children did not receive their earnings themselves, rather the money was sent directly to their parents or guardians. Most of those who received it themselves gave this money to their parents to maintain their families and in turn, get some pocket allowance to meet their day-to-day expenditure.

Factors Compelling Children to Undertake Work

An attempt was also made to look into the factors compelling children to undertake work. It can be observed from the data that the maximum number i.e. 65.5 per cent of children have chosen to work because of poverty which has rather compelled them to undertake work; another 16.67 per cent have started doing work to supplement the family income followed by 11.11 per cent who joined the work out of conflict between mother and father when they failed to carry on the responsibility towards their children, 8.9 per cent of children have joined the work after the death or illness of their parents/earning members of the family. It further confirms that poverty becomes the chief factor among the various factors which compel children to work.

Effect of Work on Behaviour of Child Workers

The economic independence at an early age makes a child pseudo-mature. To differentiate himself from the non-working children and to assimilate in the adult world he develops certain bad habits, such as smoking, gambling, drug running etc. Under the spell of these habits he spends less money on his food and more on those anti-social activities. The strain of work and inadequate nutritional intake put a negative effect on his healthy development.

As regards the change in the behaviour of child workers when their parents were asked to express, about two-third of them had noticed a positive changes in the habits of children as they are becoming responsible and learning the adult behaviour. Another one-third talked about the negative changes in the behaviour of their children. These included using abusive language, smoking, gambling and, in few cases prostitution.

Suggestions

It seems that the problem and causes of child labour in Patiala are more or less same as in the case of other states of India. Therefore, the strategy for dealing with the child labour is more general in nature than specific.

So far as child labour is concerned, the Government has to take bold decisions. One way of tackling the problem is take make primary education compulsory. The move would achieve the laudable objective of universalizing elementary education, besides, reducing the incidence of child labour.

To minimize the incidence of child labour the school enrolment should be enhanced. For instance, Kerala has the lowest number of child labours as it has the highest school enrolment of 81 per cent in the age group of 5-14 years. This high enrolment holds good for both the sexes. Thus when child labour persists, the school enrolment figure will be low and vice-versa. The state of Kerala, which has the highest levels of both male and female literacy, had achieved the fastest decline in the incidence of poverty over the past 40 years.

It is also necessary that the schools should also be made attractive in terms of properly qualified and committed teachers with the required infrastructure and economic assistance in terms of books, uniforms and mid-day meals. A recent report has mentioned that the mid-day meal programmes have reduced the school drop-outs to a considerable extent.

Very recently, the Supreme Court had asked the Union Government (December 1996), to get details of child labour in all states and submit a report to the court in order to eradicate the problem of child labour in the country. The apex court also gave some definite guidelines for the survey and rehabilitation of these children. The children working in the hazardous industries were to be withdrawn immediately and the employers made to pay Rs. 20,000 per child as rehabilitation cost. The court had also instructed that the child labour in non-hazardous type units should also not be made to work for four to six hours daily and to see to it that children working as labourers should be provided education for at least two hours daily.

Abolition of child labour is no easy task in the Indian context. The offenders are not worried about deterrent punishment because they can always get away by bribing the Labour Inspectors. When the employers get advance notice to the visit of Inspectors, they entrust 'safe' jobs to the children. Of course, the Labour Commissioners are also afraid of the links between industrialists and politicians. In this way the implementation seems to be ineffective.

The problem has to be attacked on different fronts. It has been established that the practice of child labour is due to economic reasons. It is therefore, an urgent need for economic development programmes as they will raise the income of the poor families to the desired level so that the parents are able to meet atleast the minimum needs of their children.

There should be small family norms in the slum and rural areas especially among the backward classes and scheduled castes. This will automatically increase and improve the quality of the future generation. The Government has claimed a change in the attitude of married couples as majority of them desired two children.

Prevailing unemployment and under-employment in our country creates a natural apprehension about the future means of living. This fact is also responsible for the existing child labour practice. This has been identified by our planners in India.

It has also been observed that employment of children in hazardous occupations is injurious to their physical and mental development. Such occupations be carefully identified and the employment of children in these occupations should be banned through legislation.

The general public must be informed of the nature and gravity of the problem and the need to find urgent solutions so that pressure could be mounted on the authorities.

There should be legislation covering the children in organised and unorganised sectors from exploitation with provisions for welfare of these children. The enforcement of national regulations must be strengthened.

In the end, it may be said that many of the suggestions mentioned here are either being implemented or in the process of being implemented, but these are at best patch work.

References

1. Sundaram, I. Satya, 'Child Labour : Harsh Reality', *Frontier*, February 25, 1995.
2. National Labour Institute, *Newsletter*, New Delhi, No. 12.
3. *Ibid*.
4. *The Tribune*, August 27, 1997.

13

Child Labour in an Urban Setting of Kerala

—*Martin Patrick*

India, Pakistan and Bangladesh account for the highest percentage of child labour in the world. Nearly 25 per cent of World's Working Children are in India. As regards the absolute number, the estimates of child labour vary because of conceptual differences; various official estimates place the number of child labourers between 44 million and 100 million. Child labour contributes to 20 per cent of GNP and 8 per cent of work force in India. In the midst of this, Kerala can be proud of her position as she has a low incidence of child labour in India.

Indian scenario of child labour presents some salient features.

First, there is a heavy concentration of child labour in age group 10-14 with higher proportion of males. The percentage of male child labour in total children was 2.7 per cent as against one per cent in respect of females in 1991.

Second, there is high proportion of 'nowhere children' - those who are either doing household work and not classified as economic activity or are doing nothing—in the age group 5-9 years (Chaudhari, 1996).

Third, most working children are found in the unorganised sector and in marginal occupations on the streets viz urban informal sector.

Coming to Kerala, though the first and last features are quite present, the second feature is not much relevant. Moreover, in urban centres migrated labour occupies an important role in the case of child labour, particularly in certain selected activities. The low incidence, composition and features of child labour in Kerala initially invites some discussion on its demand and supply factors.

Demand and Supply Aspects

Normally, the characteristics of labour market may be manifested in the following relationships:

(*a*) changes in demand in response to wages,
(*b*) changes in supply in response to wage changes, and
(*c*) changes in wage in response to changes in demand and supply.

But the dynamics of child labour cannot be explained by wage alone; sometimes wage may be a poor variable in explaining it, particularly the case of urban child labour.

Given the competitive nature of urban labour market, it is an universally accepted truth that urban child labour is cheap. The case of rural child labour market is also not a different one. Generally, the relationship between children and work is dictated to a great extent by the stage of economic development on the system of production prevalent in a country. Consequently, a change in the economic system and the mode of production brings in a change in the structure of labour force leading to a change in the economic role of children. Thus with the onset of industrialization and the prospect of wage labour, children have been progressively employed in industry as well as domestic and commercial establishments. Government reports in 1983 showed 17.4 million children below the age of 15 in the labour force, constituting 6.8 per cent of the rural labour force and 24 per cent of the urban labour force (*Ahuja and Jain*, 1998). This large demand for child labour is attributed to two factors.

(1) employing children is a cheap and hence a more profitable one.
(2) the special characteristics of children which lead themselves to employment in certain industries.

The factors affecting the supply of child labour can be grouped into quantitative and qualitative. Natural population movements, share of children in the population, composition of children in different age-groups etc. are the quantitative factors. The income level and poverty of the family, the educational level of parents, the educational system and its quality the status of the family, caste etc. determine the qualitative factors. It is generally recognised that poverty and educational system are the two leading factors affecting the supply of child labour. In fact, there are two schools of thought in this regard - 'Poverty School' and 'Education School'. According to the former, the children who enter the labour market are compelled to do so because of the poverty of their families which restricts them to send their children to school. To them, children are economic assets in this context. But the advocates of education school argue that it is not the poverty but the inadequacy of the school system itself is the cause for child labour. The quality of schools is so poor that parents are reluctant to send their children to them and children are not motivated to attend either (Dunnu Roy, 1998). Then a question arises : which of these factors is pertinent in our situation? In fact, these two factors alongwith the social, cultural and traditional factors account for the supply of child labour. However, one can be justified if it is argued that the push factor, the poverty of the family - is the major factor among all these.

Kerala and Child Labour

Kerala's uniqueness is present even in the case of child labour. On the one hand, the problem of child labour is not acute in the state when compared with her counterparts but on the other child labour in urban Kerala is low when compared with all India average as evident from Table 13.1.

Table 13.1
Percentage of Child Labour in Urban Kerala and India

Years		*India*	*Kerala*
1961	M	3.5	2.2
	F	1.6	1.8
1971	M	2.8	1.3
	F	0.8	1.4
1981	M	2.5	0.7
	F	0.9	1.8
1991	M	2.2	0.5
	F	0.9	0.4

Source : Census of India, 1991; Chaudhari (1996).

The low incidence of child labour in Kerala can be analysed with theoretical justification. According to the advocates of 'Education School' it is absolutely necessary to make primary education compulsory for all and to reform the education system to make at more enjoyable for children. Though Kerala has not succeeded in reforming the primary education, it has exceeded in extending primary education to all. This is the major reason why Kerala has a low incidence of child labour.

Whether the percentage of child labour (be it urban or rural) is low or high, the problem does exist in Kerala and hence it need to be addressed properly. In this context, the present study is carried out in an Urban setting, *viz.* Kochi City, to look into the grave nature of the problem of child labour in urban informal sector.

Child Labour and Informal Sector in the Urban Setting of Kochi

At the outset, the study conducted in the urban setting of Kerala confirms the view that it has a low incidence of child labour. Out of 452 micro-enterprises surveyed, hardly 34 units employed some kind of child labour. It is interestingly found that most of them are associated with certain peculiar activities. The study was actually confined to manufacturing and service sectors. Job work, rubber and plastics, footwear, machine components, readymades, food products, repair and servicing etc. are the activities covered in manufacturing sector. Trade, hotels and restaurants, and personal services are the activities covered under service sector. In manufacturing sector, child labour is found to be working in three activities only *viz.* foot products readymade and repair and services. The number of children engaged in these activities are 3, 4 and 6 respectively in 8 enterprise altogether. Naturally they are mostly concentrated in service sector where they engage as salesboys in textiles and hotels and restaurants, garbage collector and finally as ironing workers in personal services. The number of children reported in these activities are respectively 5, 7, 10 and 6 in 26 enterprises.

Apart from their concentration in certain peculiar activities, child labour in urban informal sector presents some other features.

1. There is domination of males. It is reported that all child labour belong to the age group 10-14 with a high proportion of

males. Only 3 females are found to be working and that too in two activities only, viz. readymade and food products.

2. The migrated labour occupies an important position, particularly in certain activities. It is shown that ironing workers are exclusively by Tamil child labour. Their proportion is high in hotels and restaurants as they are 6 out of 10.

3. The dosage of family labour is high in other activities, especially in readymade and food products.

4. They are mainly constituted by lower castes.

In the case of both domestic and migrated child labour caste plays a decisive role. Along with this, their entry into labour market is made possible by factors like age, relation with employer, sex and activity.

These 'pre-entry' factors ultimately lead to the formation of 'fragments' of child labour in the working place. Hence, fragmentation of child labour market in a mild form is the last feature of this setting.

Consequences

Owing to the factors mentioned above, the wage packet offered to child labour in the sector is comparatively low. The average wage paid to them ranges from 1/7 to ½ of the average wage paid to an adult labour, depending on the activities they engage in. It is evident from Table 13.2.

Table 13.2
Income of Entrepreneur and Wages Paid to Adult and Child Labourers

Activities	*Income of Enterpreneur (Monthly)*	*Average Wage to Adult Labour (Monthly)*	*Average Wage to Child Labour (Monthly)*
1. *Manufacturing*:			
Food products	3650	1850	450
Readymade,	3113	2050	350
Repair and Service	5280	1800	300
2. *Service*:			
Trade in Textiles	4208	1500	600
Trade in Waste items	7000	2100	750
Hotel and Restaurant	4012	1400	300
Ironing works	2580	900	400

Source : Survey Data.

Putting in long working hours, insecurity of employment etc. are other crucial problems faced by child labour. Children in the present setting, like other situations, are expected to leave the sector before they attain the age of 15 and hence there is no security of employment. Ironically it is damned sure that they have to leave the present enterprise when they attain the age of 15 or before. In short, for the purpose of supplementing the family income or for their mere survival, child labourers are exploited in the working in different ways and several methods.

Conclusion

Generally, the problem of child labour poses two issues. The first concerns with their concentration in informal sector and the second relates to the eradication of the problem as such. To an ordinary man, the first issue has no relevance at all as The Child Labour Prohibition and Regulation Act (1986) prevent child labour from spreading to organised sector. But the fact is that there is no constitutional provision for elimination of child labour. Article 24 of the Indian constitution states that no child labour below the age of 14 will be engaged in any factory or mines or any hazardous employment. The 1986 Act also has made provisions only for regulation of child work, thereby ironically, it legitimize child labour. The second issue is really the reflection of poverty in the family. It is said that in a country like India child labour cannot end until poverty ends.

The remedy for all these issues is the eradication of poverty, but it is not easy. At this juncture Kerala's experience in minimizing the incidence of child labour by providing free and compulsory primary education has to be discussed. Of course, Article 45 of Indian Constitution makes provision for free and compulsory education to all children upto the age of 14 years, yet the ground realities are a sad reflection on the Indian policy that 50 per cent of children in the age-group 6-14 are out of school even after 51 years of Independence. As far as Kerala situation is concerned the awareness programme may be given an important role. No doubt, it has a general validity also. The focus in the awareness programme should be on a central issue: *viz,* the real cost of children. It must be noted that employment of every child labourer represents a loss of employment of adult labour. But the major fact to be considered is that their employment deprives them of the opportunity to develop themselves physically, emotionally and intellectually. Ultimately, child labour depress human capital formation. This results in enormous loss to the child as well as to the society. Starting as a child labourer, a person may derive a small sum in his entire life in relation to the income that he would have earned from the labour market after improving his skill and efficiency through human capital formation. Attempts should also be made to control the flow of migrated child labour. In this respect, the problem must be seen more of social attitude and sensibilities than anything else. What is therefore needed in an urban setting like Kochi is a package of awareness programmes so as to realise the people about real cost of child labour and to change the attitude of parents towards the child labour.

References

Ahuja, Daman and Mahavir Jain, (1998), "Economics of Child Labour—A Myth," *Kurukshetra*, May.

Chaudhari, (1996), "Dynamic Profile of Child Labour in India 1951-91," *ILO*, New Delhi.

Patrick Martin, (1996), *Urban Informal Sector : Entrepreneurship, Self-employment and Linkage*. Ph.D. Thesis, Cochin University of Science and Technology.

Roy, Dunnu, (1998), Rights of Child Labour Ethics, Production and Nation State, *Economic and Political Weekly*, Vol. 33, No. 5.

Singh, S.P., (1997), Child Labour : The Malady and The Remedy, *Yojna*, Vol. 41, No. 7.

Weiner, Myron, (1996), "Children Labour in India, Putting Compulsory Primary Education on the Political Agenda", *Economic and Political Weekly*, Vol. 31, No. 45446.

14

Problems of Child Labour: A Case Study of Goa

—*Silvia M. de Mendonca C Noronha*

This paper focusses on the problems faced by child labour in Goa. It also gives a socio-economic background of child labour in Goa and offers a few suggestions to ameliorate their working lives.

Introduction

The territory of Goa is situated on the Western Coast of India between the parallels of 15° — 47′ — 59″ North and 14° — 53′ — 54″ East and 74° — 20′ — 11″ West.[1] It was an erstwhile Portuguese colony, alongwith Daman and Diu. After liberation from the Portuguese rule on 19th December 1961, Goa, Daman and Diu were constituted as a separate union territory in 1962. On 30th May, 1987, Goa attained statehood and today it is a separate State in the Indian Union.

The territory of Goa has an area of 3,701 sq. kms. It is made up of 11 talukas, namely, Tiswadi, Bardez, Pernem, Bicholim, Sattari, Ponda, Sanguem, Canacona, Quepem, Salcette and Mormugao. For administrative purposes, it has been constituted into two districts i.e. North Goa and South Goa.

According to the 1991 census, the population of Goa was 11,69,793 out of which 6,90,041 is in the rural areas and 4,79,752 is in the urban areas. Of the total population males comprise 5,94,790 and females comprise 5,75,003.

The total labour force in Goa as per the 1991 census was 4,12,736.

This paper highlights the problem of child labour in Goa.

In Goa, child labour by and large comprises of children of migrant workers, in particular, children of migrant construction workers. Due to the boom in construction activity in Gao after liberation, there has been an influx of a large number of migrant construction workers, as, very few Goans are willing to offer themselves for this hard labour. As a result, many migrant labourers have settled in Goa, alongwith their families—some on a temporary basis and others on a permanent basis. It is the children of these workers by and large, that form the bulk of the child labour force in Goa. This paper also brings to light this aspect of child labour in Goa.

Child Labour as Per Census Records in Goa

As per the Census of India 1961, 1971 and 1981 (Goa, Daman & Diu) (Table 14.1), throughout the 1961-81 period, the percentage of child labour was low in Goa and has been on the decline. According to the census, it was 3% of the total work force in 1961, it came down to 2.6% in 1971 and declined further to 2.3% in 1981.[2] Out of this, the male children accounted for 3% of the total workforce in Goa in 1961 and females accounted for 3.6%. In 1971, male child workers were 2% of the total workforce and female child workers were 5%. In 1981, male child workers were 1% of the total workforce and female child workers were 4% of the total workforce.

From the above figures, we note that the percentage of male children working has shown a decline during the 1961-81

Table 14.1
Male-Female Comparison of the Total Child Labour Force

Years	*Percentage of Male Child Labour*	*Percentage of Female Child Labour*	*Total*
1961	3%	3.6%	3%
1971	2%	5.0%	2.6%
1981	1%	4.0%	2.3%

Source : Based on Census of India, 1961, 1971 and 1981 for Goa, Daman and Diu (Economic Tables).

period, whereas that of female child workers shows a rise in the year 1971 by 1.4% points from 1961-71 and then a 1% point fall from 1971-81. We note that, more female children are employed than males for the period from 1961-81, which shows that there is sex discrimination. When parents have to opt to send children to work, it is more often than not that females are sent to work rather than males. This is with regard to the male-female distribution of the child labour force.

With regard to rural-urban distribution of the child labour force, we find that in rural areas male children comprise 2.7% of the total rural workforce and female children comprise 3.4% of the total rural workforce, in the year 1961 (Table 14.2). In 1971, male children comprised 2% of the total rural workforce and female children comprised 4.4% of the total rural work force. In 1981, male children comprised 1.6% of the total rural workforce and female children comprised 4.2% of the total rural workforce. Here too, we note that there are more female children working in rural areas as compared to male children. Further, we note that the percentage of male child workers to the total workforce declined from 1961-81 as against that of female child workers, which shows a rise from 1961-81.

Table 14.2
Total Child Labour in Goa in 1961, 1971 and 1981

Year	Age Group	Total Child Workers					
		Males			Females		
		Rural	Urban	Total	Rural	Urban	Total
1961	0-14	3393 (2.7%)	394 (2.3%)	3886 (3.0%)	2969 (3.4%)	512 (5.8%)	3481 (3.6%)
1971	0-14	2771 (2.0%)	713 (1.3%)	3484 (2.0%)	2256 (4.4%)	772 (7.0%)	3028 (5.0%)
1981	0-14	2581 (1.6%)	874 (1.0%)	3462 (1.0%)	3575 (4.2%)	1176 (5.0%)	4750 (4.0%)

Source : Based on Census of India, 1961, 1971 and 1981 for Goa, Daman and Diu (Economic Tables)

In the urban areas, the percentage of male child workers in 1961 was 2.3% of the total urban workforce and female children were 5.8% of the total urban workforce. In 1971, male child labour was 1.3% of the total urban workforce and female child workers comprised 7% of the total urban workforce. In 1981, male child workers comprised 1% of the total urban workforce and female child workers comprised 5% of the total urban workforce. Here too, we note a fall in the percentage of male child labour in urban areas. We note too, that in urban areas, as in rural areas there are more female child workers as compared to males, although, there is a fall in this percentage from 5.8% in 1961 to 5% in 1981, a marginal fall of 0.8% points.

To conclude, we can say that the census data shows us that over the period 1961-81, there has been a decline in child labour, albeit a marginal one. It also shows that female children form a larger percentage of the total child labour force in Goa.

Given this background, we proceed to study the problem of child labour in Goa. The present study is based on primary data collected with the help of a questionnaire.

Methodology of the Study

A random sample of 113 children, representing all age groups and a variety of occupations wherein child workers are generally found, was selected for the purpose of this study. The children were interviewed with the help of a questionnaire. The interviewed children were engaged in the formal and informal sector of activity. The study covered the major cities/towns of Goa i.e. Panjim, Mapusa, Margao, Vasco, Ponda as well as villages[3] spread all over the 11 talukas of Goa. Thus, it was a sample representing a large cross section of population from the North to the South of Goa.

Out of the 113 children interviewed, 75 were boys and 38 were girls. For the purpose of analysis, the children were divided into the following broad age groups *viz.* below 10, 10-12 and 13-14.

PROFILE OF CHILD WORKERS IN GOA

Educational Background

Out of the total children in the below 10 age group, it was found that 71.43% were illiterate, i.e. had no education at all and 14.29% had 3rd and 4th standard respectively (Table 14.3). In the 10-12 age group, 42.43% were illiterate, 1.52% had finished the Ist Standard, 7.58% IInd Standard; 7.58% IIIrd Standard, 15.15% IVth Standard, 10.61% Vth Standard, 7.58% VIth Standard and 7.58% in VIIth Standard and above. In the 13-14 age group, 30% were illiterate, 2.5% finished the Ist Standard, 5% IInd Standard; 12.5% IIIrd Standard, 12.5% IVth Standard, 2.5% Vth Standard, 15% VIth

Table 14.3
Age-Wise Educational Background of Child Workers

Age Group	*Illiterates*	*IST STD*	*IIND STD*	*IIIRD STD*	*IVTH STD*	*VTH STD*	*VITH STD*	*VIITH STD and Above*	*Total*
Below 10	5 (71.43)	—	—	1 (14.29)	1 (14.29)	—	—	—	— (100.00)
10-12	28 (42.43)	1 (1.52)	5 (7.58)	5 (7.58)	10 (15.15)	7 (10.61)	5 (7.58)	5 (7.58)	66 (100.00)
13-14	12 (30.00)	1 (2.5)	2 (5.00)	5 (12.5)	5 (12.5)	1 (2.5)	6 (15.00)	8 (20.00)	40 (100.00)
Total:	45 (39.82)	2 (1.77)	7 (6.19)	11 (9.73)	16 (14.16)	8 (7.08)	11 (9.73)	13 (11.50)	113 (100.00)

Source: Field Survey.

Table 14.4
Educational Background of Male and Female Child Workers

Male/Female Children	*Illiterates*	*IST STD*	*IIND STD*	*IIIRD STD*	*IVTH STD*	*VTH STD*	*VITH STD*	*VIITH STD and Above*	*Total*
Male	25 (33.33)	1 (1.33)	4 (5.33)	9 (12.00)	12 (16.00)	6 (8.00)	11 (14.67)	7 (9.33)	75 (100.00)
Female	19 (50.00)	1 (2.63)	3 (7.89)	2 (5.26)	4 (10.53)	3 (7.89)	—	6 (15.79)	38 (100.00)
Total	44 (38.94)	2 (1.77)	7 (6.19)	11 (9.73)	16 (14.16)	9 (7.96)	11 (9.73)	13 (11.50)	113 (100.00)

Source: Field Survey

Table 14.5
Age and Sex Distribution of Working Children

Age Group	*Male*	*Female*	*Total*
Below 10	7 (87.5)	1 (12.5)	8 (100.00)
10—12	30 (75.0)	10 (25.0)	40 (100.00)
13—14	38 (58.46)	27 (41.53)	65 (100.00)
Total	75 (66.37)	38 (33.63)	113 (100.00)

Source: Field Survey.

Standard and 20% in VIIth Standard and above. Out of the total child workers interviewed, 45% were illiterate, 2% had Ist Standard, 7% IInd Standard; 11% IIIrd Standard, 16% IV Standard, 8% Vth Standard, 11% VIth Standard and 13% in VIIth Standard and above.

From the above figures, we note that a large percentage of the child labour is illiterate. The highest percentage of illiterate children is in the below 10 age group. In the other age groups, we find the percentage of school drop-outs is very high and the reason obviously is the need to work which compells them to leave school. Some of the children interviewed said that they would have liked to study, but their economic conditions did not permit it. However, some of them despite working were attending school part time, but such children complained that they could not get sufficient time to study.

With regard to the literacy rate by sex, we find that a larger percentage of female child workers are illiterate (50%) as against that of male child workers (33.33%) (Table 14.4) which confirms the fact that parents tend to sacrifice the schooling of their girls to send them to work, more than that of boys.

Age Group of Child Workers

It was found in the survey that 7.08% of the children were in the below 10 age-group (Table 14.5), 35.39% in the 10-12 age group and 57.52% were in the 13-14 age group. From these figures, we conclude that a larger percentage of the child workers are in the 10-14 age group.

Child Workers Having Living Parents

As per the data, it was found that 66.37% of the children had both parents alive; 24.78% had a single parent alive and 8.85% were orphans[4] (Table 14.6). Amongst the female children, 71.05% had both parents living; 26.32% had only one parent and 2.63% were orphans. Amongst the male children 64% had both parents alive, 24% had only one parent and 12% were orphans.

We conclude that, most of the child workers come from homes where both parents are alive, but, due to economic necessity, as is evident from their responses, they have to work. Parents are engaged in low paying jobs and some of them are unemployed. As Table 14.7 shows 82.30% of parents are working, but in menial jobs, like

Table 14.6
Male and Female Working Children Having Living Parents

Children	*Both Parents Alive*	*Either Parents Alive*	*Neither Parent Alive*	*Total*
Male	48 (64.00)	18 (24.00)	9 (12.00)	75 (100.00)
Female	27 (71.05)	10 (26.32)	1 (2.63)	38 (100.00)
Total	75 (66.37)	28 (24.78)	10 (8.85)	113 (100.00)

Source : Field Survey.

casual labourers, drivers, petty vendors, domestic servants, etc. and so their earnings do not suffice to make both ends meet. Some unemployed parents are handicapped and some have the vice of alcoholism and so do no work, forcing their children to take up jobs for survival.

Table 14.7
Child Workers and Occupation of Parents

Children	*Parents Working*	*Parents Not working*	*N.A. (Orphans)*	*Total*
Male	61 (81.33)	5 (6.67)	9 (12.00)	75 (100.00)
Female	32 (84.21)	5 (13.16)	1 (2.63)	38 (100.00)
Total	93 (82.30)	10 (8.85)	10 (8.85)	113 (100.00)

Source : Field Survey.

Place of Origin of Child Workers

With regard to their place of origin, it was found that a large percentage of the interviewed children were those of migrant workers *i.e* 61.94% and only 38.05% were Goans (Table 14.8). The highest percentage of child workers (40.71%) came from the State of Karnataka. The other States from where children come are

Bihar, Madhya Pradesh, Andhra Pradesh, etc. These are the States from where most of the migrant workers come to Goa. This provides a strong basis to say that most of the child labourers in Goa are from other States. However, we cannot ignore the fact that 38.05% (not an insignificant percentage) of child workers were Goan by origin.

Table 14.8
Child Workers According to Their Place of Origin

Children	*Goa*	*Karnataka*	*Bihar*	*Andhra Pradesh*	*Madhya Pradesh*	*Others*	*Total*
Male	26	31	2	1	1	14	75
	(34.67)	(41.33)	(2.67)	(1.33)	(1.33)	(18.67)	(100.00)
Female	17	15	—	1	—	5	38
	(44.73)	(39.47)		(2.63)		(13.16)	(100.00)
Total	43	46	2	2	1	19	113
	(38.05)	(40.71)	(1.77)	(1.77)	(0.88)	(16.81)	(100.00)

Source : Field Survey.

Occupation of Child Workers

The survey found that child workers are engaged in a variety of occupations, like helpers in construction activity, hotels and restaurants, shops and commercial establishments, automobile tinkering, domestic service, as petty vendors,[5] etc. The highest percentage i.e. 24.78% are engaged as petty vendors, followed by domestic service 23.01% (Table 14.9). The percentage of boys engaged as petty vendors is 24%, higher than in other occupations followed by employment in hotels and restaurants 18.67%. The highest percentage of girls are employed in domestic service 55.26%, followed by petty vendors 26.32%. The percentage of girls found in other employments is comparatively low. As girls are better suited for household work, they are normally preferred. In Goa, there is a great demand for domestic servants with the increasing number of families going nuclear and both husband and wife taking up jobs.

Hours of Work of Working Children

The survey also considered the hours of work put in by these

Table 14.9
Types of Job of Working Children (Males and Females)

Children	*Small Scale/ Cottage Industries*	*Auto-mobile/ Tinkering*	*Shops and Commercial Establishments*	*Hotels and Restaurants*	*Construction Activity*	*Domestic Service*	*Agriculture*	*Petty Vendors*	*Shoe Shiners*	*Other Jobs*	*Total*
Males	3 (4.00)	8 (10.67)	5 (6.67)	14 (18.67)	4 (5.33)	5 (6.67)	2 (2.67)	18 (24.00)	1 (1.33)	15 (20.00)	75 (100.00)
Females	—	—	1 (2.63)	—	2 (5.26)	21 (55.26)	1 (2.63)	10 (26.32)	—	3 (7.83)	38 (100.00)
Total	3 (2.65)	8 (7.08)	6 (5.31)	14 (12.39)	6 (5.31)	26 (23.01)	3 (2.65)	28 (24.78)	1 (0.88)	18 (15.93)	113 (100.00)

Source : Field Survey.

children. It was found that 75% of the children below 10 put in 6-8 hours of work per day and the remaining 25% below 6 hours per day (Table 14.10). 6-8 hours per day for a child below 10, is quite a lot of work. In the 10-12 age group 44.62% of the children put in 6-8 hours of work per day; 23.08% of the children put in 9-10 hours of work per day. In this age group there were also children who put in above 12 hours per day, but fortunately they were only 54%. In the 13-14 age group, 47.5% of the children worked for 6-8 hours per day; 22.5% for a 9-10 hours per day. It is generally found that, in unorganised and informal sectors of employment, where most of the children are employed, there is no legislation regulating their working hours, and hence, they are made to work for longer hours. Children who are employed in hotels and restaurants and domestic service are made to work for even longer hours.

Table 14.10
Age of Working Children and Their Hours of Work

Age Group	*Below 6 hours*	*6-8 hours*	*9-10 hours*	*11-12 hours*	*Above 12 hours*	*Total*
Below 10	2 (25.00)	6 (75.00)	—	—	—	8 (100.00)
10-12	15 (23.08)	29 (44.62)	15 (23.08)	5 (7.69)	1 (1.54)	65 (100.00)
13-14	7 (17.5)	19 (47.5)	9 (22.5)	5 (12.5)	—	40 (100.00)
Total	24 (21.24)	54 (47.79)	24 (21.24)	10 (8.85)	1 (0.88)	113 (100.00)

Source : Field Survey.

With regard to male-female children, it is found that only 8% of the boys work for 11-12 hours as against 10.53% of girls (Table 14.11). As a high percentage of the girls are engaged in domestic service, it probably accounts for this long working hours. However, many girls in Goa now prefer to work in domestic service on a daily basis, rather than as live-ins. Very few like to stay with their employers. This, to some extent, regulates their working hours to between 6-8 hours a day, as, a live-in maid is required to be at the back and call of her employers from 6.00 a.m. in the morning to the time the employers retire for the night, which means longer hours of work.

Table 14.11
Hours of Work of Working Children (Male and Females)

Age Group	*Below 6 hours*	*6-8 hours*	*9-10 hours*	*11-12 hours*	*Above 12 hours*	*Total*
Males	16	32	20	6	1	75
	(21.33)	(42.67)	(26.67)	(8.00)	(1.33)	(100.00)
Females	9	21	4	4	—	38
	(23.69)	(55.26)	(10.53)	(10.53)		(100.00)
Total	25	53	24	10	1	113
	(22.12)	(46.90)	(21.24)	(8.85)	(0.88)	(100.00)

Source: Field Survey.

Wages of Child Workers

The Survey found that those children paid on a monthly basis were in a better position to disclose their incomes. Children employed in small scale/cottage industries, automobile tinkering, shops and commercial establishments, hotels and restaurants and domestic service could give reliable figures. Those children engaged in occupations where the sales are erratic i.e. petty vendors, shoe shiners and other casual jobs, could not give their exact earnings per month. The wages in most occupations are in the range of Rs. 101 to Rs. 800. A few children earn above Rs. 800 mainly in construction activity, domestic service and in agriculture. About 20.35% children earn Rs. 101-300, 18.58% children earn Rs. 301-500; 17.69% earn in the range of Rs. 501-800; 7.08% earn above Rs. 800; 26.55% do not know how much they earn; 7.96% earn no wages and 1.77% earn upto Rs.100 per month.

In the course of survey, it was found that some children were not paid as much as they were promised by the employer *e.g.* one boy was promised a payment of Rs. 250 per month to assist in a shop, but, the owner paid him only Rs. 125 at the end of the month. The survey also found that children in the age group of 12-14 earn higher wages than those below 12 years of age.

Table 14.12
Type of Work and Monthly Earnings of Working Children

Type of Work	*No Wages*	*Upto Rs. 10*	*Rs. 101 to 301*	*Rs. 301 to 500*	*Rs. 501 to 800*	*Above Rs. 800*	*Does not Know*	*Total*
Small Scale/Cottage Industry	—	—	—	—	2 (66.66)	—	1 (33.33)	3 (100.00)
Automobile Tinkering	—	—	2 (25.00)	—	6 (75.00)	—	—	8 (100.00)
Shops & Commr. Establishments	1 (16.67)	—	1 (16.67)	2 (33.33)	2 (33.33)	—	—	6 (100.00)
Hotels and Restaurants	—	1 (7.14)	3 (21.43)	7 (50.00)	3 (21.43)	—	—	14 (100.00)
Construction Activity	—	—	—	—	1 (16.67)	3 (50.00)	2 (33.33)	6 (100.00)
Domestic Service	2 (7.69)	—	10 (38.46)	8 (30.77)	4 (15.38)	1 (3.85)	1 (3.85)	26 (100.00)
Agriculture	2 (66.67)	—	—	—	—	1 (33.33)	—	3 (100.00)
Petty Vendors	1 (3.57)	1 (3.57)	5 (17.86)	3 (10.71)	1 (3.57)	—	17 (60.71)	28 (100.00)
Shoe Shiners	—	—	—	—	—	—	1 (100.00)	1 (100.00)
Miscellaneous	3 (16.67)	—	2 (11.11)	1 (5.56)	1 (5.56)	3 (16.67)	8 (44.4)	18 (100.00)
Total	9 (7.96)	2 (1.77)	23 (20.35)	21 (18.58)	20 (17.69)	8 (7.08)	30 (26.55)	11 (100.00)

Source : Field Survey.

Problems Faced by Child Workers in Goa

The following were the problems faced by child workers:

1. *Long hours of work*: 8.8% of the children complained of long hours of work. The complaints were from children employed in hotels and restaurants and domestic services.
2. *Harsh treatment from employers*: Another 8.8% of the children complained that their employers were too severe and demanding from them. Sometimes, they were made to do work beyond their capacity.
3. *Hard work*: 12.8% of the children felt that they had to work really hard and that tired them.
4. Children engaged in selling plastic bags, lottery tickets, newspapers, peanuts, ice-creams, etc. i.e. petty vendors complained of erratic sales which affected their earnings. There were times when the sales were very poor, which meant less or no income for them, making their life miserable.
5. *Less/no food to eat*: 3.2% of the children complained that the food given to them was less and they were left unsatisfied. Ironically, this was the complaint from boys working in hotels and restaurants. Not only they were given less food, but that too, late.
6. *Not paid on time*: 2.4% of the children complained that they were not paid their wages on time. The employer took advantage of them and paid them as and when he liked.
7. They have to work in all types of weather i.e. in the hot sun or in the heavy rain. 3.2% of children had this complaint. Petty vendors were most affected by this factor.
8. 1.6% of children complained that their jobs were risky. One of the children worked as a cleaner in a bus and he complained that at times when the bus was full to capacity, he hardly had place to stand and he had to hang out of the bus, which was dangerous, as, he could have a fatal fall. Another child engaged in extracting sand from the river had to dive in the river to do his job, which again was risky.

   Rag pickers have to handle not only dirty and harmful materials but also hazardous items like broken glasses, rusted metal, etc. Children working as assistants and welders have to sometimes hold welding parts together without any protection.

9. *No proper accommodation*: 0.8% of the children complained that they were not given a proper place to live by the employer, especially, children employed in hotels and restaurants.
10. *Harassment from senior workers*: 0.8% of the children complained of being harassed by senior workers. These were children employed in hotels and restaurants. They complained that the senior workers often beat them up.
11. *Harassment from relatives*: 0.8% of children complained that their earnings were snatched by their relatives. This occured amongst children staying with relatives.
12. Non-payment for goods sold or service rendered. 1.6% of the children complained that sometimes customers did not pay for the goods sold on the pretext of having no change, etc.
13. *Exploitation by guards at the bus stand*: 3.2% of the children complained that the guards at the bus stand exploited them. They had to pay them some money to be able to sell their goods at the bus stand *e.g.* the peanut sellers at the bus stand in particular, were harassed by them.
14. *Poor working conditions*: 2.4% of the children felt that the conditions they worked-in were poor. Besides their wages, no other facilities were given.
15. 0.8% of the children complained that sometimes the employers made them do work not contracted for. Whether they liked it or not, they had to do it or else risk losing their jobs.
16. *No extra pay for extra work*: 3.2% of the children complained that their employers did not pay them extra, when they had to do more work. The payment remained the same irrespective of the work.
17. *Continuous work without a break*: 0.8% of the children complained that they had to work continuously without any rest. This happened particularly in hotels and restaurants and domestic services. The work demanded of them was endless. One child working as a domestic servant complained that she did not even have time to eat her food.

18. *Not paid the amount agreed upon*: 0.8% of the children complained that the employers often went back on their word and paid them less than that agreed upon.
19. *Low wages:* 2.4% of the children complained that they were paid low wages.
20. *No payment when sick*: 1.6% of the children complained that if they fell sick, their pay was cut. Thus, even when they were not well they had to work.
21. *Fights with other children:* 2.4% of the children complained that they had to sometimes fight with other children because of sales. This happened particularly to children engaged as petty vendors *e.g.* selling plastic bags, peanuts, etc.

The above are the problems encountered by the child workers in Goa. It is, however, interesting to note that 33.6% of the children replied that they faced no problems when approached by the interviewer. We conclude from this response that these children were afraid to tell their problems for fear of repraisal from their employers.

Suggestions for Improving the Plight of Working Children

Child labour is a phenomenon that cannot be wished away. As long as there is poverty, there will be child labour. So, what can be done is to see to it that the children who are employed are protected by effective legislations and punitive measures are taken against violators of the norms.

1. Prohibiting the employment of children in hazardous occupations. The Employment of Children Act, 1938 which was repealed in 1986 after enacting the Child Labour (Prohibition and Regulation) Act, prohibited the employment of children below 15 years in hazardous occupations. This act should be vehemently pursued.
2. Regulate the hours of work of child labour. We note from the survey that many children work for 8 hours and more which is too tedious for a young body and mind. The maximum hours a child should work should be 4-6 hours with a break in between. This has also been mentioned in the Child Labour (Prohibition and Regulation) Act, 1986.

3. The wages of child labour in various occupations should be fixed, so that there is no scope for exploitation.
4. The problem of child labour should be tackled at its root. The root cause of child labour being poverty, the government should concentrate on vigorously implementing the anti-poverty programmes in their respective States. A general rise of a large percentage of the population above the poverty line, will lead to progressive elimination of child labour.
5. Measures to promote employment-oriented development both in rural and in urban areas, adequate facilities for both formal and non-formal education, vocational education and training, social security and family welfare measures, etc. would go a long way to tackle the basic and root causes of child labour.
6. Those children who have to work to make both ends meet for their families should be allowed the facility to attend part time schools. Special schools can be set up to cater to the needs of such children. In Goa, there are some NGOs doing this, but they should be given encouragement and support to do it on a larger scale. Thus, these children do not miss out on school education and at the same time can help their families. However, committed teachers will be required to take up this type of teaching.
7. Working children should also be provided with free meals, rest room for freshening up before classes begin, as we have to remember that these children are coming to school straight from work.
8. A stipend can be given to those children who are removed from prohibited employment.
9. Health care should be provided for such children.
10. The general public should be sensitised to the plight of working children, so that they are more sensitive to the needs of such children. A large percentage of the children especially in Goa, as we see from the survey, are engaged in the informal sector activities and if people sympathise with them, then a lot of their misery can be alleviated e.g. in the case of domestic servants. If employers are sensitised, they can treat these children

in a human way and not make them work for long hours with no rest, or give them work beyond their capacity to perform and pay them less than what they would pay an adult worker for the same work done. The media, especially the television, can be used to sensitise the public to the plight of working children.

Concluding Remarks

From the foregoing analysis of data, we can conclude that child labour in Goa is a reality, though we would like to think otherwise, as Goa, is one of the most developed States in the Indian Union. However, the bulk of the child labour force comprises of children of migrant workers, but since they are working in Goa, they cannot be neglected and the Government of Goa must take steps to give these child workers a decent life.

Notes and References

1. Government of Goa, Daman and Diu, Agricultural Census, 1970-71, p. 3.
2. All the percentages have been worked out from the absolute figures given in the Census of India, 1961, 1971 and 1981, Goa, Daman and Diu, (Economic Tables).
3. The villages covered were Keri, Sanguem Honda, Mandrem, Sanvordem, Pale, Navelim, Camurlim, Bambolim and Saligao.
4. Here the word 'orphan' is used to mean children without both parents living.
5. Petty vendors refers to children selling plastic bags, lottery tickets, peanuts, newspapers, etc.

References

1. *Census of India*, 1961, 1971, and 1981, Goa, Daman and Diu (Economic Tables).
2. *Census of India*, 1991.
3. Kanbargi, R., (1991), *Child Labour in the Indian Sub-continent—Dimensions and Implications*, Sage Publications, New Delhi.
4. Patil, B.R., (1988), *Working Children in Urban India*, D.B. Publisher (P.) Ltd., Bangalore.
5. Singh, A.N., (1990), *Child Labour in India—Socio-Economic Perspective*, Shipra Publications, Delhi.

15

Child Labour in India: A Case Study of Some Selected Child Labour in Dharwad City

—*L.D. Vaikunthe*

Children are the most important asset of the society, and future of a nation depends upon how the children are educated, and trained and how their mental and physical development is taken care of. It is indeed unfortunate that the energy of the growing children which should go into their mental and physical development is exploited by owners of capital assets owing to unfavourable socio-economic setting in the country. Unless something is done to help them, they will not come out of a vicious circle of drudgery and poverty, which has been going on from generation to generation.

The most horrifying truth about child workers is that they have very little say in choosing their occupation. They have no rights as workers and they cannot join labour unions to raise their voice against exploitation.

One of the most important cause of a child labour is poverty and employment particularly in the unorganized and rural areas which compels every member of the family including children, to work to supplement the family income.

Large family size also becomes a motivating factor for the parents to send their children to work. Moreover lack of awareness and lack of educational facilities, also make the children work for anything better. In addition, orphanhood, parental rejection, broken family, disabled parents and similar other situations, in which the child has none to take care of, are also causes of child labour. And then employers generally prefer child labours, because of their sharp reflexes, greater efficiency in repetitive and fine operations, vigour, and energy and because they can take advantage of their docile nature and physical weakness. Moreover child workers are available at low wages for employment, give the employers a competitive advantage. It is true that it is difficult to obtain data pertaining to the terms of employment of child workers, partly because, the employers and sometimes, the child workers themselves are reluctant to disclose such data.

Totally we can say that illiteracy, ignorance, low wages, unemployment, poor standard of living, deep social prejudices and backwardness are some of the major factors responsible for child labour.

Child labour may be more prevalent in developing countries. But it is definitely a universal phenomena. One wonders what are the compulsions for a country like India to awake the problem of child labour now. If it because of international pressure or receding export of handicraft or a sudden love for the young and abused children in India? Elimination of the child labour system is now use or abuse is the question. If the first two appears to be the reasons then the real reason is economic, which necessiates all round efforts to eliminate child labour, otherwise, India may loose considerably in the foreign market. On the other hand, if the Government has a social cause to achieve then the cost of reforms could not only be too high but the results may be similar to what India experienced in the case of family planning and cultural centres. We would be unnecessarily playing with the time of atleast estimated 44 million children by creating a Government infrastructure, like any other Government department, which will loose its significance once the Government exhausts the funds earmarked for this programme. The National Commission on Labour, 1969 revealed in its report on child labour, that "the employment of children is indeed more of an economic problem than anything else." So, to draw an overall picture of the terms of employment applied to child workers in the industrial and agricultural sector, survey and study of labour problem is very essential.

Pakistan, India, Bangladesh have the world's largest number of child labourers. So that any effort to address the phenomenon of child labour in the third world must deal with South Asia.

According to an International Labour Organization (ILO) report an estimated fifty two million children in the world are employed in gainful occupations.

(Child labour may be more prevalent in developing phenomena.) In Naples millions of children are employed in leather industries. In Spain more than one hundred thousand children are employed in orchards and plantations.

An ILO study in the department of Madre de Dias has revealed that 20% of the workers deployed in gold production units are from 11 to 18 years of age. Thousands of children all over the western world work in fast food centres, gas stations, they sell newspapers, clean cars and work in garment and leather factories.

In 1930 M.C. Gill in his study of working children of New York and Paterson in United States concluded that among the working boys and girls of Paterson and New York, New Jersey the percentage of superior, intelligent children was about as much as among those who remained in school.

About the working children in England, Marx referred that the goods produced by those child labourers means converting immature human being into more machines.

Domestic labour particularly for young girl is the most common form of occupation particularly in developing countries. A study in urban areas of Colombo found that 40% of the 11 to 12 years city workers were domestic servants, especially in the Asian countries, a very large section of young female force is deployed as domestic servants particularly in urban areas.

According to the data provided by the ILO, more than 52 million children are employed in the world as a whole, in a variety of occupations, of which 29 million are in South-East Asia and 10 million in East Asia. Out of 52 million, 42 million work without pay in family farms and about 10 million are out for a living in workshops, tea-shops, factories and other places.

An American study conducted by the University of California at Irvine found a decrease in school performance among students who held jobs. A study written for the British Department of Health and Social Security concludes, "Pupils who spend most of their out of school time in employment tend to be less able, less industrious and less well-behaved."

The study also found that working students tends to "attend less regularly, play truant more frequently, are less punctual and wish to leave school at earlier age than those who work for fences hours or not at all."

The National Commission on labour 1969, reveals in its report on child labour, that "our evidence reveals that employment of children is almost non-existent in organised industries. It persists in varying degrees in the unorganised sector such as small plantations, restaurants, and hotels, cotton ginning and weaving, carpet weaving, stone-breaking, brick-kiln, handicraft and construction. Employment of child workers below the prescribed age is also reported to be continuing in far off places and in rural areas where enforcement of statutory provisions is more difficult."

Dale Yoder has stated in his book that in U.S.A. "states that report poorest school attendance are also states that have largest proportion of employed children."

According to 1971 census, the number of child wage earners was 10.75 million representing 4.60 per cent of the total labour force. As per the estimates of the planning commission, the number of child wage earners between the ages of five and fourteen years was 17.36 million on 1st March, 1983 and 17.58 million on Ist March, 1985.

India has the largest number of world's working children. Based on 1981 census data the estimated figure is 14.5 million children below 14 years of age or 5.5% of the total Indian child population. The participation rate in rural areas is 6.3% and in urban areas 2.5%. A 1983 estimate states that about 17.4 million children are working and 90% (about 15.6 million) of them are in rural areas. The child labour participation rate varies among the states. In rural areas the participation rate for the male child varies from 1 per cent in Kerala to 11.7 per cent in Andhra Pradesh. Among girls the participation rate in the rural areas varies from 0.3% in Punjab to 10.5% in Andhra Pradesh according to 1978 survey. On March 1978, the number of working children was estimated at 16.25 million. The committee appointed by the Government of India in 1979 headed by Prof. Gurupadswamy, has estimated the quantum of child labour in India as 20 million in 1979. According to the committee's statement, "earlier the jobs for children were confined to agriculture, and plantation where they were involved in sowing and reaping, harvesting, threshing etc. besides taking core of the cattle and fodder; but with industrialisation, their employability stretched to jobs involving much harder and harsher physical labour. In Sivakasi (Tamilnadu) children in match factories are made to work at frame filling bundles and rolling operations. In Bidi Industry, children with their nimble fingers perform the chore of rolling besides binding and closing of ends. In pencil industry children are subjected to lung disorders and diseases at an early age due to an exposure to hazardous slate dusts. In glass bangles factories, children help in katai, jalai and chunai and these chores are extremely phorene to lung diseases. In the cracker factories, a large number of children loose their lives due to fire accidents. In carpet factories, thousands of children not only loose their eye sight but also get physical deformity because of sitting at one posture for long hours.

In India very large section of young female force is deployed as domestic servant particularly in urban area. All child labourers sell some of their childhood but the worst is for those driven to prostitution. The red light areas in most major cities are full of young prostitutes, girls and boys under the age of 18 years.

A survey conducted by K. N. George in Madras revealed that children were made to work from 8 to 15 hours in certain organizations even more. This is primarily the reason why miliions of children below the age of 15 years suffer from chronic bronch. (T.B.), asthma, eye defects, slain diseases, tetanus, silicosin and deformities.

The workshop of woman and child workers in unorganised sector held at New Delhi concluded that, there is direct exploitation of the child workers in terms of very low wages, long hours of work, unhygenic conditions and sexual exploitation. This affects the growth of the personality of a child.

Most of the developing countries are having many child labourers. India has the largest number of the world's working children.

The present study deals about forty children workers in Dharwad city constituting of hotel industry, construction activities, garage and servicing centres. The paper also attempts to study what are the factors that compelled the children to work, education of the children, their wages and how the children helping their family and other aspects.

Factors Compelled Child to Work

If a person asks "why children were employing" he must look at the societies background. From long years child labour prevails to their family occupations, to those working in modern industries and in unorganised sector. Illiteracy, unemployment, poverty, population pressure, family disorganisation due to divorce, loss of parents are the important causes of emergence of child labour (Monis Raza, 1986). It is said that man is subservient to his circumstances. The rich and knowledgeable fight with their situations to change the same in the desired way, while the poor and the ignorant accept anything for their survival (A.N. Singh, 1990). Table 15.1 shows the factors responsible for employment of children in the study area.

Table 15.1

Factors Responsible for Child Employment

Factors	*Number*	*Percentage*
1. Poverty	26	32.50
2. Loss of parents	7	8.75
3. Influence of working children	2	2.50
4. To supplement family income	14	17.50
5. Lack of interest in study	8	10.00
6. Unemployment of adult members	2	2.50
7. Low status in Society	7	8.75
8. Parents desire	11	13.75
9. Other factors	3	3.75
Total	80	100.00

Note : Maximum two responses have been taken from each child respondent for analysis.

The above table shows that out of 80 responses as high as 32.5 per cent indicated that poverty is the main reason to accept work. 17.5 per cent opined that they have accepted work to supplement their family income. 13.75 per cent directly blamed their parents for sending to work. 10 per cent assigned it to the fact that child himself lacks interest in study. 8.75 per cent owing to the loss of parents.

On the basis of these findings it may be cited that the various circumstances like poverty, low family income, lack of interest in study, loss of parents lead children to work at an early age.

Education of Child Labour

In general it is observed that despite many efforts made at various levels, still drop-out rate is very high. An estimated 90 per cent of children belong to the three lowest agrarian classes, namely agricultural labourers, poor and middle class peasants (Acharya, 1982, Sahoo, 1996).

In another dimension it is observed that limited number of schools or school locations are at distant places. In many villages their is no school at all. Assuming that education of working children is affected (adversely), information is collected on this aspect of the problem. Table 15.2 shows the extent of education of working children.

Table 15.2
Education of Working Children

Education	*Number*	*Percentage*
1. Illiterate	10	25
2. Literate	2	5
3. Upto class IVth	18	45
4. Upto class VIIth and above	10	25
Total	40	100

It may be seen from the above table that 25 per cent children are illiterate and another 25 per cent children attended school upto class VIIth. It shows that for all poor families the question posed is immediate supplementary income and to use children as the source rather than postpone to an uncertain date till the completion of education (Smt. Achari 1986). As high as 45 per cent children attended school only upto class IVth and remaining 5 per cent children know reading and writing anyhow without attending school.

This shows that the underprivileged classes are economically weak and they are socially not aware of the value of education. The analysis further supports that education is secondary aspect for such classes and rich class people continue to dominate the education sector.

Wages of Child Labour

Instead of working 12 to 14 hours, in some cases it goes more than 16 hours a day, and seven days in a week. Wages of children are very low as compared to adult workers in the same establishment who work for 8 to 9 hours a day. Table 15.3 gives the idea of child workers wages in various occupations in the study area.

Table 15.3
Average Monthly Income of Child Labour

	Occupations	*Average Monthly Income (in Rs.)*
1.	Hotels & Restaurants	435
2.	Garage & Servicing centres	150
3.	Construction works	660

Children employed in construction works receiving good income as compared to others. The children employed in garages and servicing shops as learners for which they are paid less and in some cases not at all.

Table 15.4
Monthly Income of the Child Labour

	Income per Month in Rs.	*Number*	*Percentage*
1.	Upto Rs. 100	6	15
2.	101 to 300	4	10
3.	301 to 500	16	40
4.	501 to 700	6	15
5.	701 to 900	4	10
6.	901 and above	2	5
7.	No wages	2	5
	Total	40	100

5 per cent of child labourers are working without payment. Mostly these cases are of garage works where they are working as learners or trainees. 15 per cent earn below Rs. 100 which is very low. 10 per cent children earn between Rs. 101-300. The majority (40 per cent) of children earn between Rs. 301-500. Only 5 per cent children earn Rs. 901 and above. These children are employed in mason works, where the wage rate is little high than other works.

Table 15.5
How Child's Work Helping his Family

	Nature of Assistance	*Number*	*Percentage*
1.	To Educate brother/sisters	10	25.0
2.	To Care sick members	3	7.5
3.	To Supplement family income	17	42.5
4.	Others	8	20.0
5.	To learn skills (No wages)	2	5.0
	Total	40	100.00

The above table shows that major (42.5 per cent) group of child workers reported that their wages help to increase their family income whereas 25 per cent reported to educate their brothers/sisters. 20 per cent reported they are assisting for repayment of loan, to maintain his own expenses, etc. 7.5 per cent children are employed to help their family to cure sick members and the remaining 5 per cent children are not earning any wages, they are employed to learn skills to have own business in near future.

Working Conditions and Health Hazards

Working conditions of child labour in these establishments is horrible. Children have to work more than 15 hours a day or upto the satisfaction of his masters that too without rest which is a complete violation of the Child Labour (P&R) Act, 1986. The child workers employed by private contractors were paid meagre wages and were living in animal like conditions in overcrowded slums (Sujat Patel 1983).

When researcher visited hotels in search of child labour he observed that by continuous working children feeling nervousness. When he interviewed them they expressed the thing. In general children are required to work beyond their physical capacity and are paid exploitative wages. They do not get enough rest and recreation and are exposed to various pollutants and chemicals. In some cases, by the time children reach adulthood, their health has been so debited that they cannot find gainful employment as adults (Smithu Kothari, 1983). In hotels and restaurants they are to work to serve the first customers in the morning till the last customer leaves (Tripathy 1989). Not only long hours of work and low wages, children are to face many occupational health problems.

Table 15.6
Hours of Work

Occupation	Up to 5	6-8	8-10	11-12	13-14	15 & above	Total
1. Hotels and Restaurants	—	—	—	5 (25)	7 (35)	8 (40)	20 (100)
2. Garage and Servicing Shops	2 (20)	4 (40)	4 (40)	—	—	—	10 (100)
3. Construction Works	3 (30)	6 (60)	1 (10)	—	—	—	10 (100)

Note : Figures in the brackets indicate percentage.

According to Karnataka Shops and Commercial Establishment Act 1961, the child shall not be allowed to work for more than 5 hours a day.

No occupation here employed children less than 5 hours a day. In abovementioned occupations children are to work 8 hours, in some cases (40 per cent) it is more than 15 hours a day.

Only 12.5 per cent children working in between 6 to 8 hours a day which is equal to the prescribed hours of work for adults. Those who employed in construction works and garage and servicing shops working below 12 hours a day. 17.5 per cent are to work 14 hours a day.

Table 15.7
Effect of Work on Health of Child Labour

Effect	Number	Percentage
1. Headache	5	12.5
2. Nervousness	12	30.0
3. Joint pain	8	20.0
4. Skin disease	7	17.5
5. No effect	6	15.0
6. Other effects	2	5.0
Total	40	100.00

Long working hours, when the child's bones are still not fully grown and lack of play and exercise, hamper the physical growth and development of the child's body. This apart, there are accidents which can severely harm the child. (Anuradha, 1997).

It is very shameful to see the above table that out of 40 children 12.5 per cent cases are found of headache. Similarly, 20 per cent reported joint pain. It can be observed 17.5 per cent and major i.e. 30 per cent children have skin disease and feel nervousness respectively. 15 per cent of children half mindedly reported that they don't have any effect but they passed away. And finally 5 per cent reported other effects like heart ache, fever etc.

It has, to some extent, been recognised by many policies, programmes, project designers that child labour in a country like India cannot be registered out of existence overnight. Abolition may remain the long term goal. But children need protection. The government has been, therefore, concentrating on advocating public awareness, welfare projects and may tighten the law machinery for local enforcement. Till then children would continue to work, work long hours, work for little pay, work in hazardous and exploitative conditions. It is suggested that government should concentrate on enforcement of law to eliminate child labour and support NGO's and big business houses under organised sectors to have programmes relating to education, health, welfare and employment for these unprivileged children.

References

1. Myron Weiner, "Child Labour in India", *EPW*, Nov. 9-16, 1996.
2. Smithu Kothari, "There is Blood on those Matchsticks, Child Labour in Sivakasi", *EPW*, Vol. XVIII, No. 27, July 3, 1983.
3. Tripathy, S.K., *Child Labour in India*, Discovery Publishing House, New Delhi,
4. Naidu, D., Adikeshavalu, "Child Labour Participation in India: A Statewise Census Analysis," *The Journal of Family Welfare*, Vol. XXVII, June 1981.
5. Reeti Pande, "Elimination of Child Labour: Use or Abuse," *IJIR*, Vol. 32, No. 2, Oct. 1994.
6. *Government of India*, Report, National Commission on Labour, 1969.

16

Child Labour in an Informal Sector: A Case Study of Bidar District

—*Gouradevi Katnalli*

Introduction

Children are the real assets of a nation. They are the nation builders. The strength of a nation or the future of the nation largely depends upon the Children.

Childhood is a period of recreation, of enjoying everything, of School learning of physical, mental and Social development and not in bearing work, but unfortunately, children in many third world countries are deprived of this childhood. India is not an acception, Indian children are unlucky, being born in poverty, they have forced to work at an early age, it hinders, the physical, mental as well as alround development of a child.

In order to understand the child labour problem clearly, it is necessary to throw some light on the meaning and definition of child labour.

[1] "A child is defined by chronological age and also by cultural and social factors (Rogers & Standing 1981) the process of growth of the child is both social & biological. In Asia & Africa specially 8 or 9 years old is usually not considered a child, implying that it is the social status rather than age that determines who is a child (Bonnet 1993). In other words child work is not considered bad.

These societies take child's work as a socialisation process and when a child is working it learns survival skills. What is the work which the children do? It ranges from help in domestic work to work in household enterprises or farm both with and without wages (Dingwaney *et. al.* 1988) This means that to pursive child labour better the nature of the relationship between the child and the employment needs consideration. The question here is whether the relation is exploitative or not. At times in the traditional societies children have to work to repay the debt incurred by parents and in the process child gets bonded (Bonnet, 1993) An estimate of ILO (1992) reveals that there are several million bonded child labourers in South Asia. Child also gets exploited if he/she starts fulltime work at an early age, works longer hours, or the work inflicts excessive physical, social, psychological pressure which impedes his/her development." (ILO, 1992).

The problem of child labour is not merely an English or an American or an Indian problem it is an Universal problem faced by almost all the countries of the world, but the extent of child labour is relatively more in the backward and third world countries.

The economic practice of child labour in India dates back to the Industrial development in the country. Industrialisation on large scale leads to many maladjustments and one such maladjustment is the employment of children in factories, workshops and in other unregulated occupations. It may be said that children have entered all Industries from which they are not excluded by law and in which their unskilled labour and limited physical strength could be utilised.

"[2] According to World Health Organisation Report an estimated 150 million children continue to be used like animals in mining manufacturing and other dangerous jobs throughout the world. The offence largely occur in developing and third world countries.

According to Asian Monitor every third household in India has a working child and over 20% of the countries GNP is contributed by child labour". Thus India is one of the largest producer of child labour, who are working in unhealthy, unsafety and in hazardous conditions of work, inspite of all national and international conventions the child labour in India is found mostly in Agriculture and the unorganised informal sector of the economy.

As regards the determinents of child labour the number of children in the household determined the potential supply of child labour, the larger the household size, the lower is educational participation of the children and consequently increased childs participation in the labour markets.

Poverty, unemployment, low wages, illiteracy, lack of awareness are the other root causes of child labour. Besides these doorway, expenses towards social customs, bad habits of parents, unsuitable pattern of education for the first generation students of child workers are the causative factors behind the tragic phenomena of child labour.

One of the important characteristics of the child labour is that it is cheaper, they have no or poor bargaining power, they don't have any consciousness about the prevailing legislations, the employer take full advantage of exploiting them by paying low wages, so as to maximise their profits.

Child labour are found in almost all the states in India. The Karnataka State alone have approximately 11,69,402 child labours. It is observed that there are totally 14,217,588 child labours in India, who are engaged as full time workers as adults.

Andhra Pradesh rank first by possessing 21,81,462 child labours. The number of child labours in Maharashtra is 15,86;634 and in Uttar Pradesh the number of child labour is 15,85,877. Our state stands in the fourth place.

So, the efforts have been made in this regard to find out the pitiable conditions of child labour in various informal sectors of Bidar district in Karnataka.

Objectives

The main objectives of the present study are

1. To explore the conditions of child labour working in informal sector of Bidar District.
2. To know the magnitude and various dimensions of child labour in Bidar.
3. To analyse the causes for child labour.
4. To examine the Socio-economic conditions of the Child labour.
5. To study the wages and working conditions.
6. To analyse the various measures undertaken to eradicate the problem of child labour.

Methodology

The study is purely based on the primary data collected in the form of personal interview conducted by the researcher with various child labours at their working places in various parts of the Bidar District in the month of April, May 1998. Two Talukas out of five namely Bidar and Basavakalyan have been surveyed. A sample of 132 child labours have been selected from major activities such as, Hotel workers, Garrage workers, Collie workers, Mechanical workers, Maid servants, Part-time child labours and other workers. To strengthen the data base, secondary data is also collected from various books, journals and Govt. reports and also the survey conducted by C.D.P.O. and Zilla Panchayat in the chairmanship of Assistant Commissioner, Bidar in the month of May 1997.

Study Area

The study confined to Bidar District which is the small district comprising only five talukas namely Aurad, Bhalki, Basavakalyan, Bidar and Humnabad. The total population of the District according to 1991 census is 12,55,799. It is primarily a rural district with 80.43% of people living in rural areas, (see Table 16.1). The present study also attempts to highlight the various dimensions of child labour in informal sector. The child labours are found actively employed in Hotels, Collie works, Mechanical works, such as Shoe shines, Lorry cleaning, Small eatable shops and Kirana shops etc.

Table 16.1
Total Population of Bidar District 1991 Census

	Talukas	*Total Population*	*Male*	*Female*	*Rural*	*Urban*
1.	Aurad	210040	106926	103114	210041	—
2.	Basavakalyan	246340	124969	121371	203592	42748
3.	Bhalki	222918	114038	108880	196042	26876
4.	Bidar	331452	172361	159091	199044	132408
5.	Humnabad	245049	124898	120151	201378	43671
	Total :	1255799	643192	612607	1010096	245703
		(100.00)	(51.21)	(48.78)	(80.43)	(19.56)

Source : Directorate of District Statistical Office, Bidar 1996-97, Govt. of Karnataka. Figures in brackets indicates percentage.

Nature of the Child Labour

In developed countries children work to earn their pocket money, whereas in developing countries they work for their existence and for the economic need. They accept the work to assist their parents.

In a developing country like India, children work both in modern sector as well as in Agricultural sector to which they belong. The proportion of Child labour varies from situation to situation, place to place and occupation to occupation. In rural areas most of the children are engaged in Agricultural sector, whereas in cities they are engaged in unorganised sectors like street business, manufacturing units, garages, rickshaw pulling, shoe shining, car cleaning, carpenting, repair works, Hotel boys etc. Some times they do indulge in begging, black trading like smuggling etc.

Causes of Child Labour

Poverty, unemployment, low wages, large size of the family, illiteracy, lack of awareness are main causes of child labour. Besides these doorway, expenses towards social customs, bad habits of parents, unsuitable pattern of education for the first generation students of child workers are the causative factors behind the tragic phenomena of child labour.

Socio-Economic Conditions of Child Labour

The Socio-Economic background of the sample child labour is highly significant in understanding the problem of child labour in its totality in the study region.

The total labour force of child labour include both male and female of which female ratio of child labour is quite meager, they are mainly found in household sectors in private homes as domestic workers. It means that female children are restricted to go out of the house to work they are allowed to work only at houses in household work. Table 16.2 reveals that out of 132 child labours, female number is only 09 whereas the number of male is 123, *i.e.*, about 93% of the child labours are male labours. This indicates that the female participation in work is considerably less outside the house.

Child labour is common in every caste but the percentage of child labour engaged in work differs from one caste to another.

Probably all child labours hail from low income groups of the society. The survey states that about 44.69% children are belonging to Muslim community, 28.78% are belonging to SC/ST and 12.87% belonging to Forward Caste and 13.63% belonging to other castes. (Table 16.3).

Table 16.2
Sex Structure

	Occupation	*Male*	*Female*	*Total*
1.	Hotel Workers	26	—	26
2.	Garrage Workers	20	—	20
3.	Coolie	16	02	18
4.	Part-Time Child Labour	17	—	17
5.	Mechanical Workers	11	—	11
6.	Salesman	10	—	10
7.	Carpenters	07	—	07
8.	Brick Makers	08	—	08
9.	Maid Servants	00	07	07
10.	Other Workers	08	—	08
	Total :	123 (93.18)	09 (6.81)	132 (100.00)

Figures in brackets shows the percentage.

Table 16.3
Caste Structure of the Child Labour

	Occupation	*Forward Caste*	*Muslims*	*Other Castes*	*SC/ST*	*Total*
1.	Hotel Workers	04	08	05	09	26
2.	Garrage Workers	02	12	01	05	20
3.	Coolie	01	06	02	09	18
4.	Part-Time Child Labour	03	07	02	05	17
5.	Mechanical Workers	01	07	01	02	11
6.	Salesman	03	05	01	01	10
7.	Carpenters	—	04	02	01	07
8.	Brick Makers	01	04	01	02	08
9.	Maid Servants	01	03	01	02	07
10.	Other Workers	01	03	02	02	08
	Total :	17 (12.87)	59 (44.69)	18 (13.63)	38 (28.78)	132 (100.00)

Figures in brackets shows the percentage.

Educational Status of Child Labour

Education is the most efficient means by which one can protect and safeguard his interest wherever and whenever he is exploited and suppressed. It is generally agreed that child labours are always exploited by the employer by paying lower wages for long and risky work. It is partly because of their ignorance and illiteracy. But the young hands working in various types of hazardous jobs do not know how to protect their interest due to lack of education.

In the sample survey large number of working children i.e. 53.03% are illiterate, 29.54% of the child labours are having only primary education and 13.63% are having higher primary education and 5.30% are having secondary education. (Table 16.4). Thus a large number of working children are illiterate, though these child workers were sent to school to get education, but for one or the other reason they left school and joined to work. It may be due to bad performance, lack of adequate facilities, poverty, parental force etc. which deprived them of getting education even at primary level.

Table 16.4

Educational Status of Sample Child Labours

Occupation	*Illiterate*	*Primary*	*Higher Primary*	*Second-dary*	*Total*
1. Hotel Workers	15	05	05	01	26
2. Garrage Workers	14	06	00	00	20
3. Coolie	13	05	00	00	18
4. Part-Time Child Labour	04	06	05	02	17
5. Mechanical Workers	05	03	02	01	11
6. Salesman	—	04	04	02	10
7. Carpenters	03	02	01	01	07
8. Brick Makers	06	02	—	00	08
9. Maid Servants	05	02	00	00	07
10. Other Workers	05	03	00	00	08
Total :	70 (53.03)	38 (29.56)	18 (13.63)	07 (5.30)	132 (100.00)

Figures in brackets shows the percentage.

Table 16.5 states that children age at work starts from seven to fourteen. In the total sample of 132 child labours about 12.87% of the children started work at the age of 7 to 8 years, 23.48% child labours started work at 8 to 10 years; 29.54% among them started work at 10 to 12 years and 34.09% of them started work at 12 to 14 years. Thus it is clear from the table that the greater percentage of child labour is found in the age groups of 10 to 12 and 12 to 14.

Table 16.5
Age at Work

	Occupation	*7-8 Years*	*8-10 Years*	*10-12 Years*	*12-14 Years*	*Total*
1.	Hotel Workers	06	09	05	06	26
2.	Garrage Workers	03	04	05	08	20
3.	Coolie	02	04	05	07	18
4.	Part-Time Child Labour	01	03	07	06	17
5.	Mechanical Workers	—	03	04	04	11
6.	Salesman	01	02	03	04	10
7.	Carpenters	01	01	02	03	07
8.	Brick Makers	01	01	03	03	08
9.	Maid Servants	01	02	02	02	07
10.	Other Workers	01	02	03	02	08
	Total :	17 (12.87)	31 (23.48)	39 (29.54)	45 (34.09)	132 (100.00)

Figures in brackets shows the percentage.

Wage Level

The economic conditions of the child labours depends upon the wage levels. As we came to know that child labour is preferred because they are cheap, illiterate or semi-literate, who are not organised, who have no or little bargaining power so as to raise their wages. They are scattered in different types of work and it is too difficult to unite themselves in order to safeguard and protect their interest. So the employer prefer child labour than adults. Thus the employer take fuller utilisation of this situation and maximise his profits by paying lower wages to the child labour. Another possibility of employment of child labour is that children are more quicker and more obedient than the adults.

As per the information availed from the child labour through interview, large number of children were paid low wages i.e. about 34.09% of the child labours gets wages of Rs. 1-10 per day, 34.84% of the children get wages of Rs. 11-20 per day; 24.24% get wages of 21-30 per day and only 6.81% of child labours get wages of Rs. 31 and above. (Table 16.6).

Table 16.6
Wages Paid to the Workers Per Day

	Occupation	*Wages Rs. 1-10*	*Wages Rs. 11-20*	*Wages Rs. 21-30*	*Wages Rs. 31 & above*	*Total*
1.	Hotel Workers	12	10	04	—	26
2.	Garrage Workers	10	08	02	—	20
3.	Coolie	11	05	02	—	18
4.	Part-Time Child Labour	02	08	06	01	17
5.	Mechanical Workers	01	02	04	04	11
6.	Salesman	01	04	03	02	10
7.	Carpenters	01	02	03	01	07
8.	Brick Makers	02	03	03	—	08
9.	Maid Servants	02	02	03	—	07
10.	Other Workers	03	02	02	01	08
	Total :	45 (34.09)	46 (34.84)	32 (24.24)	09 (6.81)	132 (100.00)

Figures in brackets shows the percentage.

The working conditions in which the child labours have to work are worst specially in Hotel, Collie and Mechanical work. The study reveals that more than half percentage of child labours have to work for 8 to 10 hours daily in their respective work. 22% of child labours work more than 12 hours per day, who are engaged in Hotels, Coolie and Mechanical works. Apart from the work at place children are being forced to do additional work at employer houses.

Migratory Character of Child Labour

"[3]Migration is one of the most important development and demographic issue of 1990's. It is a major factor in the process of urbanisation and social change. There can be different sets of factors responsible for migration. Broadly it can be economic factor like search of jobs or better jobs, social factors like marriage or accompanying of parents or an earning member, personal reasons like pursuing of higher studies or for getting access to better educational, medical and health facility and sometimes natural calamities and political factors or lack of social security in a place."

In the study reason cases of Rural to Urban migration are predominating. (Table 16.7). About 60.60% of the child labours are migrated from nearby villages to urban areas and 39.39% are migrated from urban to urban areas. Asked about the reason for migration many of them opined that they migrate mainly in search of better employment, higher remuneration, better working conditions etc. This shows clearly the economic need and lack of employment opportunities in rural areas account for maximum migration.

Table 16.7
Migratory Character of Child Labour

Occupation	Rural to Urban	Urban to Urban	Total
1. Hotel Workers	20	06	26
2. Garrage Workers	15	05	20
3. Coolie	10	08	18
4. Part-Time Child Labour	09	08	17
5. Mechanical Workers	05	06	11
6. Salesman	03	07	10
7. Carpenters	04	03	07
8. Brick Makers	05	03	08
9. Maid Servants	06	01	07
10. Other Workers	03	05	08
Total :	80 (60.60)	52 (39.39)	132 (100.00)

Figures in brackets shows the percentage.

Asked about the Job permanency 94% of the child labourers have opined that there is no guarantee of job and only 4% of them have opined that they have job permanency.

About the future plans of the child labours, many of them have revealed that they think of starting their own business or go back to village and settle there, go for another good work.

Thus besides many problems they have to face in daily life, still they are optimistic and they have better future plans to improve their living standards.

Measures Taken to Eradicate Child Labour

Many efforts have been made by the National and International organisations recently for combating the child labour such as ILO, UNESCO, UNICEF etc., but the result is not upto the mark. ILO is the leading organisation which has taken very keen interest, so as to combat the problem. Apart from these organisational efforts Government of India has enacted a number of legislations so as to control, combat and eradicate child labour, such as Factory Act of 1948, Minimum Wages Act of 1948, the Bidi and Cigar Workers Act of 1966, Child Labour (Protection and Prohibition) Act of 1986, compulsory eradication for children etc. Thus at present more than a dozen laws are in operation. Most of the dozen laws incidentally apply to the organised sector which is not the toiling ground of 90 per cent of child labour.

Even after fifty years of our independence we are not able to protect our children at work which denies the enjoyment of precious childhood to the child workers. It affects their physical and mental development, hence sincere efforts should be made to control and eradicate child labour.

References

1. Surjit Singh, "Child Labour in India : Some Reflections" *The Indian Journal of Labour Economics*, Vol. 40, No. 4, 1997, p. 819.
2. Dr. Sukanti Priya Patnaik, "Social Security and Child Labour," An Article Presented in 38th *Annual Conference of the Indian Society of Labour Economics*, p. 3.
3. Kuntal Sensarma, "Migrant Labour in Urban Areas : Dimensions and Determinants", *The Indian Journal of Labour Economics*, Vol. 40, No. 2, 1997, p. 237.
4. Bonnet, Michel, (1993), "Child Labour in Africa", *International Labour Reveiw*, Vol. 132, No. 3; pp. 371-89.

Rodgers, Gerry & Guy Standing (eds.), (1981), "Child Labour: Poverty and Under-development", ILO, Geneva.

Dingwaney, Manjari, *et. al.* (1988), *Children of Darkness: A Manual on Child Labour in India, Rural Labour Cell,* New Delhi.

ILO, (1992), *World Labour Report*, International Labour Organisation Geneva.

Tripathy, S.K., *Child Labour in India*, Discovery Publishing House, Daryaganj, New Delhi, 1989.

Report of Convention of Working Children, (CACL), 1994.

17

Child Labour in Urban Informal Sector: A Case Study of Vijayawada City

—M. Koteswara Rao

Introduction

The alarming increase in population growth has been the main concern for developed and developing countries in the world since long time. The increase in investment and income in urban modern sectors of developing countries has attracted labour force to these urban centres resulting in phenomenal increase in urban population and labour force. Owing to lack of labour intensive type of industrialization, low levels of labour absorption capacity of the modern urban sectors was assumed and contributed to mass urban unemployment, under-employment and extreme poverty in urban areas of the Third World, causes to dual labour markets in urban economy. The pressure of labour supply gets manifested in the proliferation of certain unorganized, frequently sporadic occupations characterised by low skill, low productivity and meagre incomes. This dualistic nature of urban economy has been used as a frame of analysis of economic structures and labour markets. Researchers advocated various classifications. The most common classification is the one which divided the economy into 'organised' and 'unorganised' sectors. According to McGee, most of the cities of the Third World can be seen as "consisting of two juxtaposed systems of production—one derived from the capitalistic form of production and the other from the peasant system of production." (T.G. McGee, 1973). Clifford Gurtz described the two sectors as the "firm entered economy" and the "bazzar type economy" respectively (Clifford Gurtz, 1963). They have also been referred to as the "upper" and "lower" circuits (Milton Sentoz, 1975).

The objective of this paper is to make a probe into the causes and conditions of child labour working in informal income generating occupations in Vijayawada city. The study attempts to answer the questions like: Who are these children? What they do?, Where they live? To which caste they belong to? How do they live? etc.

This paper is organized into two sections. Section I deals briefly with the concept of Urban Informal Sector and the approaches delineated by different researchers to study this concept, and Section II gives the major findings of the case study on child labour in Vijayawada city of Andhra Pradesh.

The Concept of Informal Sector

The concept of urban informal sector in developing countries has gained considerable currency in the literature on employment and development policy. This concept was first used by Keith Hart in a study of Urban Ghana (Hart, 1973). He identified a number of income and employment generating activities in the unenumerated sector of urban areas. The study assimilated that the workers engaged in the unorganised sector are self-employed as against the wage labourers in the organised sector; the new entrants in the urban labour market are particularly the migrants from rural origin who were forced to work in the informal sector due to lack of experience and skills required for the formal sector employment. This analysis indicates that the target group or sector is described in various terms viz., informal income generating activities, unorganised sector, unenumerated sector, self-employed individuals, urban proletariate and individuals earning less than legal minimum wage.

The ILO/UNDP Employment Mission to Kenya adopted the term informal sector to analyse the employment situation and to work out a strategy for employment generation in Kenya (ILO, 1972). According to this study the informal sector has the following characteristics: easy entry for the new enterprises, reliance on indegenous resources, family ownership, small scale operations, unregulated and competitive market, labour intensive technology and informally acquired skills of workers.

Guy Standing argues that in addition to the formal and informal sectors, the informal sector itself should be broken down into two sub-sectors[1]:

(*a*) 'an irregular sector' consisting of a variety of legitimate low-status fringe activities (beginning various forms of casual labour such as regarding car washing and leaf raking) as well as many illegal activities; and

(*b*) 'the informal sector proper', consisting of small scale economic activities, commonly non-wage carried on by family concern. (Guy Standing, 1974, 1977)

Dipak Mazumdar distinguishes the formal-informal sectors based on the size of employment, security of job, and unionisation of the factory labour force. He distinguishes that the entry into the informal labour market is unrestricted by artificially raised hiring standards, norms and procedures. (Dipak Mazumdar 1974, 1977)

John Weeks provided an analytical base to the highly descriptive nature of the distinction between formal and informal sectors. His distinction is based on the unorganisational characteristics of exchange relationships and position of exchange activities *vis-a-vis* the state (John Weeks, 1975). Weeks explains that officials are favourable to the formal sector enterprises in many forms to improve their business. While the informal sector does not carry the benefits as they have outside the system of official regulations.

Heather Joshi and Vijay Joshi had analysed the formal-informal sector characteristics while distinguishing between organised and unorganised sectors in Bombay under three major heads: market structure, technology and relationship with government (Heather Joshi and Vijay Joshi, 1976). To analyse various characteristics of these sectors, the size, technology, ownership, product market, labour market and incomes are enumerated.

T.S. Papola made a distinction between the informal sector labour market and informal labour market in the urban economics. The scope of the former would be confined to the workers in the informal sector establishments while the latter would, in addition, include causal, contract, and irregular workers in the formal sector establishments. (Papola, 1980)

Steel distinguishes between the informal sector, intermediate sector and the modern sector on the basis of fixed capital. Intermediate sector firm use a small amount of fixed capital and informal sector firms use virtually no fixed capital (Steel, 1977, 1979). In a study by House carries the notion of little fixed capital to an extreme. He classifies firms as informal if they operate out of a temporary structure or building or out of no structure at all. (House, 1984)

Yap classifies certain occupational categories based on published statistics in Brazil, into formal and informal to examine the relation between rural and urban migration and the informal sector in Brazil. The modern-traditional division used in this analysis is along industry lines, according to the expectations about the concentration of small scale labour intensive and low wage activities in the industry. The modern sector activities include mining, manufacturing, public utilities, transportation and communication, finance, social and professional services and government. The traditional sector activities consist of construction, trade and personal services (Yap, 1976). Teilhert-Waldorf and Yaldorf survey takes self-employed vendors, brick workers and shop-keepers for a study of informal sector earnings in Bangkok (Saral Teilhet-Walsorf and William H. Waldorf, 1983).

The above discussion indicates that the concept of urban informal sector has been attributed to different meanings by various researchers over time *viz.*, urban poor, urban proletariate, low income households, urban population living in slums and squatter settlements, etc.

The main occupational categories generally included in the informal sector are listed as: Carpenters, Cobblers, Tailors, Sanitary fitters, Washerman, individuals employed in construction work, manufacturing of textile products, Costume, Jewellery, artificial flowers, musical instruments, metal and leather products, hawkers, peddlers, rickshaw drivers and personal services etc.

The concept is defined generally in terms of multiple criteria: Size of the Units, degree of formulation of work rules and division of labour, technology, degree of organisation and workers etc.[2] The principal criteria used in many of the studies of informal sector is the size of establishment in terms of workers. The size of the sector also varies among different sectors.

Major Findings of the Case Study

Child labour signifies employment in gainful occupation, it applies to children engaged in activities which are detrimental to their physical, mental, moral and social grooming. Children in the informal sector includes children working in tea shops, small eating places, printing presses, cycle and vehicle repair workshops, metal workshops, etc. Self-employed children such as shoe-shining boys, stall keepers, hawkers, rag-pickers are also counted in this sector. The industries, some of which are run on both, a factory and cottage industry basis, engaging child work in sizable number include: carpet-weaving, bidi making, cloth weaving, leather work, coir-making, match industry, mica, button-making, bamboo work, waste paper, reuse materials such as envelops, brick manufacturing and slate-pencil making etc. With fast spreading urbanisation, industries in small towns and semi-urban areas use child workers in large numbers.

According to recent International Labour Organisation Report about 250 million children are working in developing countries. An ILO survey published earlier estimated that 73 million children aged between 10 to 14 were working full-time in 100 countries. The new estimates suggest that 120 million children of five year and upwards are working full-time and another 130 million are working part-time. The Report also pointout that child labour is increasing in the Third World because of urban expansion. In case of India, the percentage of child labour to total population is almost stable during 1961-81. But it is declining in the case of rural areas and increasing in urban areas. The percentage of child labour to total child population declined from 8.04 to 5.17 per cent during this period. Though the percentage of child labour to total workers declined by 2 per cent during 1961-81, the absolute number is increasing. Systematic and scientific studies on children in informal sector in India are conspicuous by their absence in both rural and urban areas.

Broadly this section presents the socio-economic profile and conditions of child labour in unorganised sector on the basis of a case study of Vijayawada city of Andhra Pradesh. For the purpose of the sampling a complete list of wards in the city was collected from the office of Municipal Corporation, Vijayawada. The information provided by the Municipal Corporation authorities revealed that there are 50 Wards in the city. These Wards have been classified into 3 categories namely Residential (28), Commercial (20) and Industrial (2). Out of these 50 Wards, 13 Wards have been selected at random according to the proporation of number of Wards in each category. Thus 7 Residential, 5 Commercial and one Industrial Wards are selected at random. Two streets are selected from each ward at random and 1500 households are listed from these selected list. Appropriate questions are included in the schedule to identify the households having working children. Out of the listed households, it is found that 335 households had atleast one working child each. Children working in formal sector enterprises are observed in 35 households. These households are excluded from the sample survey. Hence, the sample constitutes 300 households having alteast one child labour. Information is solicited personally through a pre-tested questionnaire from each household.

The results presented in this chapter are based on the larger survey conducted in Vijayawada city on Child Labour and as such these results need to be interpreted carefully. There are many studies on informal sector activities conducted in different parts of India over time. But studies concerning the child labour in Informal Sector in urban areas are, however limited. Most of these studies do not lead to policy decisions too. As part of the larger project this paper briefly present the socio-economic conditions of children employed in Informal Sector of Vijayawada city. The Child Labour considered in this study are below 14 years. The official estimates state that there are 3124 child workers in Vijayawada city. But unofficially there are more than 15,000 child labourers in the city.

Results

Age and Sex Composition and Educational Attainment

The socio-economic characteristics of the sampled households belonging to the working children are analysed in relation to age, sex, caste, religion, education, residential status and employment status. It can be seen from the data in Table 17.1 that all the child workers belong to the age group of below 14 years. It is evident that more than 70 per cent of them are between the age of 10-14 years. Out of 300 sample workers 80 per cent (240) are males. In fact the children in the age group of 6-14 should be in the schools.

Table 17.1
Socio-Demographic Characteristic Features of Child Labour

Age in Years	*No. of Working Children*			
	Male	*Female*	*Total*	*Percent*
Below 8	17	8	25	8.25
8—9	22	5	27	8.91
9—10	25	5	30	10.00
10—11	35	11	46	15.18
11—12	33	8	41	13.53
12—13	46	8	54	17.82
13—14	62	15	77	25.41
Total	240	60	300	100.00

Religion

Religion	*Number*	*Percent*
Hindus	145	48.23
Muslims	50	16.38
Christians	105	35.49
Total	300	100.00

Social Status

Social Status	*Number*	*Percent*
O.C.	71	23.43
B.C.	122	40.26
S.C.	58	19.14
S.T.	49	16.17
Total	300	100.00

Education

Level of Education	*Number*	*Percent*
Illiterate	101	33.64
Primary	147	49.09
Upper Primary	38	12.73
High School	14	4.54
Total	300	100.00

Since the children are sent to the work, it is expected that they are deprived of even the elementary education which may lead to low level of education of the households from whom these children have withdrawn.

The caste-wise break-up of child labour indicates that about 80 per cent of them belong to weaker sections like SC, ST & OBCs. Fifty per cent of child labour are Hindus followed by Christians and Muslims. The educational levels of children show that majority of them have not even completed primary education. Only a small portion of them had studies (4.54%) upto school final. It is striking to point out that no one in the sample had studied beyond 10th class and also none of these worker had acquired any technical qualification in the formal institutions.

Child labour force in the informal sector is mainly employed as wage-worker. Besides, some of them are working such as shoe-shine boys, hawkers and peddlers in a number of informal sector activities. Children are found working in a variety of occupations in Vijayawada city like dyeing, toy making, welding, gold work, weaving, printing press, helper in bakeries, hawkers, peddlers, helpers in shops, stores and mills, construction industry and in service activities. These children are not protected either by legal regulations or by strong trade unions.

Residential Accommodation

With regard to the type of residential accommodation, it is found that 46.36 per cent of the sample workers lived in rented accommodation, 25.45 per cent lived in own houses, 1.00 per cent lived in rent free accommodation provided by the employer and 27.20 per cent are living in vacant places occupied by these people (Table 17.2). More than 80 per cent of them are living in sheds and huts. About 50 per cent of them are in slum areas. It is found that 30% child labour are migrants. About 80 per cent of the migrants are living in rent free accommodation provided by their employers and also at public places. The provision of electricity in the houses of workers shows that 50.08 per cent of the child workers are living in electrified houses and the remaining 49.92 per cent are living in non-electrified.

Occupation of Child Labour

The multiplicity of occupations in which these children are engaged

Table 17.2
Type of Residential Accommodation Used by the Child Labour

Status of House	*Number*	*Per cent*
Rented house	139	46.36
Owned house	76	25.45
Provided by Employer	3	1.00
Occupied (other)	82	27.19
Total	300	100.00

Type of Dwelling	*Number*	*Per cent*
Pucca Building	46	15.18
Sheds	124	40.92
Huts	130	42.90
Total	300	100.00

Place of Living	*Number*	*Per cent*
Slums	144	48.52
Non-slums	156	51.48
Total	300	100.00

Migrant Status	*Number*	*Per cent*
Migrants	90	30
Non-migrants	210	70
Total	300	100

has been classified into five industrial categories based on the homogenity of these activities. They are:

(a) Manufacturing,
(b) Trade and Commerce,
(c) Transport,
(d) Services; and
(e) Construction.

(i) *Manufacturing*, which include manufacturing of food products, metal products, plastic goods, furniture,

paper covers, leather products, printing and publishing etc.

(ii) *Trade and Commerce* include hotels and restaurants, wholesale trade and retail trade in finishing goods, fruits and vegetable, timber, general goods, kerosene, provisions etc.

(iii) *Transport* which includes transporting by motor vehicles, animal transporting and transporting by man, carrying of luggage etc., hand car driving, rickshaw pulling, cycle rickshaw driving etc.

(iv) *Services*—community, social and personal, including repair services like repair of bicycles and tricycles, laundry services, hair dressing etc., can be grouped under service sector.

(v) *Construction* includes construction and maintenance of building, including electrical and sanitary installation.

The data on the type of enterprises in which the working children are employed reveals that it is the trade and commerce activity, which is providing largest share of employment to the children (25.74%); followed by Manufacturing (23.10%); Services (21.12%); Construction (19.47%); and Transport (9.57%) respectively (Table 17.3). The sex-wise break-up shows, that majority of the girls are working in households. They do such work as house cleaning, utensils cleaning, clothes washing, cooking, child keeping etc. Very few girls are working in factories, construction work, hotels and shops in the study area.

Table 17.3
Distribution of Workers by Industrial Category

Industrial Category	*No. of Workers*	*Per cent*
Manufacturing	70	23.10
Trade and Commerce	78	25.74
Transport	29	9.57
Services	64	21.12
Construction	59	19.47
Total	300	100.00

Nature of Employment

The data on the nature of employment of the sampled working children is presented in Table 17.4. The data explains that about 50 per cent are employed on regular and part-time basis. The proportion of working children employed on casual basis and contractual basis is 17.67 per cent and 7.33 per cent respectively. Among the children working in different industrial categories, it is observed that more than 55 per cent of the child workers are engaged in construction activity on casual basis, while more than 65 per cent of the child workers in service activity are employed on regular part-time basis. The larger share of child workers working on regular part-time basis is engaged in manufacturing, trade and commerce and transport categories. It is observed that majority of these part-time workers are school going children.

Table 17.4
Distribution of Working Children by the Nature of Employment and Industrial Category

Industrial Category	*Nature of Employment*				Total
	Regular (full-time)	*Regular (part-time)*	*Casual*	*Contractual*	
Manufacturing	22 (31.42)	31 (44.02)	9 (12.78)	8 (11.36)	70 (100.00)
Trade and Commerce	29 (37.18)	42 (53.85)	7 (8.97)	0 (0.00)	78 (100.00)
Transport	0 (0.00)	27 (93.10)	2 (6.90)	0 (0.00)	29 (100.00)
Services	17 (26.56)	42 (65.63)	3 (4.69)	0 (0.00)	64 (100.00)
Construction	7 (11.86)	6 (10.17)	32 (54.24)	14 (23.73)	59 (100.00)
Total	77 (25.67)	148 (49.33)	53 (17.67)	22 (7.33)	300 (100.00)

Causes of Child Labour

In a developing country like India, chronic poverty is the strongest factor responsible for the prevalence and perpetuation of the child labour. Owing to backwardness and labour intensive type of technology there is a search for cheap labour which is available in the form of child labour. Further the absence of state sponsored special schemes for family allowances to enable parents to ensure their childrens proper and adequate nutrition and living conditions, the poor parents are forced to send their children to work, and on the other hand, the lack of protective child labour legislation and the evasion of existing laws for the protection of child labour, keep the child labour growing and getting exploited. In addition to these reasons sudden death of father, mother or both parents in a poor or low middle class family, big size of family, and sometimes childs desire to work make them work during childhood. All these factors provide ample scope for the employers to exploit the working children in whatever the manner they could.

The causes of child labour surveyed in Vijayawada city are given in Table 17.5. The results indicates that poverty is the major reason for the prevalence of child labour in the city. Nearly 65 per

Table 17.5
Distribution of Child Labour by Causes for Taking up Employment

Causes	*Male*		*Female*		*Total*
	Number	*Per cent*	*Number*	*Per cent*	
1. Poverty	167	66.80	25	41.75	192 (63.36)
2. Children not interested in studies	10	4.20	8	13.36	18 (5.94)
3. Parents not interested to send school	5	2.10	11	18.37	16 (5.28)
4. To learn work	9	3.78	1	1.67	10 (3.33)
5. To clear debts	9	3.78	2	3.34	11 (3.63)
6. Father not alive	5	2.10	2	3.34	7 (2.31)
7. Mother not alive	2	0.85	0	0	2 (0.66)
8. Traditional causes	21	8.82	2	3.34	23 (7.59)
9. Large families	8	3.36	3	5.01	11 (3.63)
10. Unemployment or under-employment of parents	4	1.69	6	10.02	10 (3.33)
Total	240	100.00	60	100.00	300

cent of the children have to work because of poverty and unemployment or under-employment of parents. About 8 per cent of children are persuing their own traditional caste based occupations indicating the absence of occupational mobility inspite of the developmental efforts launched in the light of modernization. Similarly, about 6 per cent of the child labour are working due to reluctance of parents to send the children to schools and about 6 per cent of children are not interested to go to schools. The other reasons of child labour are to learn work (3.33%), to clear debts (3.63%), large size of the family (3.63%) and death of parent. (Table 17.5)

Working Conditions of Child Labour

In the formal sector, the workers enjoy formulised working conditions including fixed working hours. They are also protected in respect of their wages. On the other hand the workers in the informal sector do not enjoy fixed working hours. The working hours also vary from one occupation to another occupation depending upon the nature of occupation. The data or the average number of hours worked by the working children in the informal sector enterprises are furnished in Table 17.6.

The data indicates that about 33 per cent of the working children in informal sector worked for less than 8 hours which happens to be the normal practice for adult workers in the formal sector. About 27 per cent of the children worked between 8-10 hours, 28 per cent worked between 10-12 hours and 11 per cent worked between 12-14 hours a day. This analysis shows that the working children placed in informal sector enterprises do not enjoy any uniform practice of working for fixed hours. The analysis of the data indicates that the practice of working more than 8 hours existed in all types of industrial categories. In the industrial categories like manufacturing, construction, trade, transport and services more than 60 per cent of the working children are found to be working about 8 hours. For example, in services nearly two-thirds of the working children attended to their work more than 10 hours a day. Most of them are domestic servants. Further, it is noticed long hours often lead to accident, especially when children are working with poorly maintained and dangerous machinery.

The information regarding the distance of the place of work from the place of living explains that nearly two-thirds of the

Table 17.6
Distribution of Working Children by Average Number of Working Hours Worked Per Day and Industrial Category

Industrial Category	Average No. of Working Hours						Total
	Less than 4	4-6	6-8	8-10	10-12	12-14	
Manufacturing	—	—	26 (37.14)	21 (30.00)	17 (24.29)	6 (8.57)	70 (100.00)
Trade and Commerce	—	4 (5.12)	25 32.05)	26 (33.33)	11 (14.12)	12 (15.38)	78 (100.00)
Transport	—	3 (10.34)	9 (31.03)	12 (41.40)	5 (17.23)	—	29 (100.00)
Services	—	7 (10.94)	8 (12.50)	10 (15.62)	26 (40.63)	13 (20.31)	64 (100.00)
Construction	—	3 (5.08)	16 (27.12)	25 (42.37)	12 (20.34)	3 (5.09)	59 (100.00)
Total	0 (0.00)	17 (5.67)	84 (28.00)	81 (27.00)	84 (28.00)	34 (11.33)	300 (100.00)

working children have to cover the distance of 1 to 2 kilometres to reach their place of work. These children, who are living away from the place of work, had to reach there and go back to their houses on foot. Children engaged in construction work are found to be living at the place of work or very close to the place of work. Regarding the rest-interval of working children 56.34 per cent did not get any rest-time, 19.47 per cent got upto half-an-hour rest interval. The remaining 24.19 per cent workers got 1/2 to 1 hour rest. None of these working children do not have any fixed length of rest interval. Further, the information regarding the wages for the period of absence from work reveals that more than 95 per cent of the children had to loose their wages if they absented from work.

Working children are also more succeptable to infectious diseases, including tuberculosis, as long as they suffer from malnutrition, anemia, fatigue and inadequate sleep. Similarly, the other physical health hazards including bone lesions and postural deformity and other chronic diseases are noticed in the survey.

Levels of Living

The distribution of working children by level of wages in different activities has been calculated and presented in Table 17.7. It can be observed from the Table that out of 300 child labour, 51 per cent received less than Rs. 400 per month. About 31 per cent of working children are receiving Rs. 400 to 500 per month. Only 15 per cent of the working children are earning more than Rs. 500 per month. Among the industrial category, child labour working in Trade and Commerce and construction activities are paid higher wages than the other categories. It is interesting to point out that the children engaged in construction activity are having more than one job to earn extra income. As such, about 10 children are earning more than Rs. 600 per month. As the working hours for children working in informal sector are not fixed, normally the question of over-time payment does not arise, but in case of the activities like dyeing, printing, toy making units of manufacturing activity, it is found that these children sometimes worked over twice during nights and getting wages for this extra time in some cases Re. 1 per hour, while Rs. 1.50 per hour in some cases.

Payment of Wages

An attempt is also made to examine whether the payment of wages

Table 17.7
Distribution of Working Children by Monthly Wages and Industrial Category

Industrial Category	*Wages Per Month*							*Total*
	100–200	*200–300*	*300–400*	*400–500*	*500–600*	*600–700*	*700–800*	
Manufacturing	2 (2.86)	5 (7.14)	22 (31.43)	29 (41.43)	3 (4.29)	8 (11.43)	1 (1.43)	70 (100.00)
Trade and Commerce	0 (0.00)	14 (17.95)	31 (39.74)	22 (28.21)	0 (0.00)	5 (6.41)	6 (7.69)	78 (100.00)
Transport	0 (0.00)	0 (0.00)	10 (12.82)	16 (20.51)	2 (2.56)	1 (1.28)	1 (1.28)	29 (100.00)
Services	7 (10.94)	11 (17.19)	22 (34.38)	13 (20.31)	8 (12.50)	2 (3.13)	1 (1.56)	64 (100.00)
Construction	0 (0.00)	3 (5.08)	26 (84.69)	14 (45.60)	7 (22.80)	6 (19.54)	3 (9.77)	59 (100.00)
Total	9 (3.00)	33 (11.00)	111 (37.00)	94 (31.33)	20 (6.67)	22 (7.33)	12 (11.76)	300 (100.00)

Table 17.8
Distribution of Working Children by Practice of Wage and Industrial Category

Industrial Category	*Wages Paid*			*Total*
	Daily	*Weekly*	*Monthly*	
Manufacturing	29 (41.43)	22 (31.43)	19 (27.14)	70 (100.00)
Trade and Commerce	36 (61.02)	11 (18.64)	12 (20.34)	59 (100.00)
Transport	32 (41.03)	11 (14.10)	35 (44.87)	78 (100.00)
Services	24 (82.76)	3 (10.35)	2 (6.89)	29 (100.00)
Construction	23 (35.94)	17 (26.56)	24 (37.50)	64 (100.00)
Total	144 (48.00)	64 (21.33)	92 (30.67)	300 (100.00)

is daily, weekly or monthly. The information on payment of wages is calculated and presented in Table 17.8. It reveals that about 50 per cent of the working children are being paid daily. However, 30 per cent of the children are getting their wages on monthly basis. The practice of payment of wages on daily and weekly basis is prevalent in Manufacturing sector (73 per cent), Trade and Commerce (55 per cent) and Services (60 per cent).

It may be concluded from the foregoing analysis that the main causes of child labour are poverty and unemployment and indebtedness of the households. Informal sector income generating activities are the major source of income for the child labour.

The problem of child labour cannot be solved by prohibiting the employment of children, unless the household to which the working children belong are provided with basic human needs such as food, shelter, clothing and free education facilities. Provision of gainful employment to adult members of the family would solve this problem to a certain extent. As there is no legal protection for the child labour a comprehensive legislation for child labour in informal sector be enacted and implemented effectively. Further child workers should be provided free compulsory schooling during the night time. Further, immediate attention should paid for total elimination of child labour in hazardous employment within a time frame.

References

Louis Emmerji objects to the use of the 'traditional' as a term of disparagement. He feels that it is the product of an alien culture that seel 'tradition' as detrimental to development rather than an integral part of nation's culture and identify (see Louis Emmerji, 1974).

For a critical review on the concept of urban informal sector in developing countries, see S.V. Sethuraman (1976 and 1981): T.S. Papola (1980a and b): R.K. Wishwakarma (1980): and Portes, A. (1983).

Aziz, Abdul, (1984), 'Urban Poor and Urban Informal Sector,' Ashish Publishing House, New Delhi.

Breman, John, (1976), "A Dualistic Labour System—A Critique of the Informal Sector," *Economic and Political Weekly*, Vol. XI, No. 5, 48, 49 and 50 of Nov. 27, Dec. 4 and 11, pp. 1870-76, 1905-08 and 1939-44.

Dandekar, V.M. and N. Rath, (1971), 'Poverty in India' *Indian School of Political Economy*, Bombay.

Dhesi, Autar S. and Urvashi Wadhwa, (1980), "The Informal Sector in Nangal, 1980 (Punjab): An Over Review," *Indian Journal of Regional Science*, Vol. XV, No. 1, pp. 38-47.

—— (1984), "Productivity, Earnings and Employment Potential of Informal Sector: A Case Study of Nangal (Punjab)," *Indian Journal of Industrial Relations*, Vol. XX, No. 1, pp. 1-16.

Gurtz, Cliffford, (1963), 'Peddlers and Princess: Social Change and Economic Modernisation in Two Indonesian Towns,' University of Chicago Press, Chicago and London, Ch. 3.

Guy, Standing, (1974), "A Trichotomous Model of Urban Labour Markets," Paper presented at the *Research Conference on Urban Labour Markets*, Geneva, September (Geneva, International Institute for Labour Studies, Doc. ULM/DP 12, 1974).

—— (1977), "Urban Workers and Patterns of Employment" in Subbaiah Kannapan (eds.) *Studies of Urban Labour Market Behaviour in Developing Areas*, International Institute for Labour Studies, Geneva.

Hart, Keth, (1973), "Informal Income Opportunities and Urban Employment in Ghana," *Journal of Modern African Studies*, London, March, pp. 61-89.

House, William, J., (1984), "Nairobi's Informal Sector: Dynamic Entrepreneurs or Surplus Labour? *Economic Development and Cultural Change*, January.

International Labour Organisation, (1972), 'Employment, Income and Equality Strategy for Increasing Productive Employment in Kenya,' Geneva.

Joshi, Heather, and Vijay Joshi, 1976, 'Surplus Labour and the City—A Study of Bombay,' Oxford University Press, Delhi.

Louis, Emmerji, (1974), "A New Look at Some Strategies for Increasing Productive Employment in Africa," *International Labour Review*, September, p. 202.

Lakadawala, D.T. *et. al.*, (1963), 'Work Wages and Well being in an Indian Metropolis: Economic Survey of Bombay City', Bombay, pp. 483 and 528.

Mc. See (1973), "Peasants in Cities: A Paradox, a Paradox, a Most Ingeneous Paradox," *Human Organisation*, Washington, Summer.

Milton, Santos, (1975), "The Shared Spare: The Two Circuits of Urban Economy and their Spatial Repercussions," London, Methuen.

Mitter, Vishwa, (1986), "Income Distribution and Poverty in the Urban Informal Sector," *Margin*, NCER. Vol. XVIII, No. 2, January, pp. 29-41.

Mazumdar, Deepak, (1975), "The Urban Informal Sector," *World Bank Staff Working* Paper No. 211, Washington.

—— (1977), "Notes on the Informal Sector" in Subbaiah Kannapan (eds.), *op. cit*.

Mazumdar, Atreji, (1980), 'In-migrants to Urban Informal Sector: A Case Study of Urban Delhi'.

—— (1981), "Employment in Urban Delhi—Role of Informal Sector," *Economic Times*, April 30.

Papola, T.S. (1980a), "Informal Sector: Concept and Policy," *Economic and Political Weekly*, Vol. XV, No. 18, May 3, pp. 817-24.

—— (1980b), 'Urban Informal Sector in Developing Economy', Vikas Publishing House, July, New Delhi.

Paul, Linda A., (1985), 'The Urban Informal Sector in Economic Development', Unpublished Ph.D. Thesis, Faculty of Graduate School, University of Maryland, Maryland.

Portes, A., (1983), "The Informal Sector, Definition, Controversy and Relation to National Development," *Review*, Summer, pp. 151-74.

Pothana, V., (1983), "Approaches to the Study of Urban Poverty in India: Need for Integration," *Bulletin*, Madras Institute of Development Studies, Seminar Series, Vol. XIII, No. 12, December, pp. 5150-73.

Saral, Teilhet Waldorf and William H. Waldorf, (1983), "Earnings of Self Employed in an Informal Sector: A Case Study of Bangkok," *Economic Development and Cultural Change*, April.

Sen, Gupta and P.D. Joshi, (1981), "On the Concept of Poverty Line and Estimates of Poverty at Regional level in India," a paper presented at the Indian Association of Social Science Institutions, 12-15 January. Quoted from Vishwa Mittar (1986).

Sethuraman, S.V., (1976), "The Urban Informal Sector: Concept Measurement and Policy," *International Labour Review*, Vol. CIV, No. 1, July-August, pp. 69-81.

—— (1977), "The Urban Informal Sector in Latin America," *International Labour Review*, Vol. CVI, No. 3, November-December, pp. 343-52.

—— (1981), "The Urban Informal Sector in Developing Countries, Employment, Poverty and Environment', *ILO*, Geneva.

Government of India, (1985), 'Seventh Five Year Plan, 1985-90,' Vol. II, Planning Commission, New Delhi, October.

Steel, William, F., (1977), 'Small Scale Employment and Production in Developing Countries', Praeger Publications, New York.

—— (1979), 'Small Enterprises in African Development: A Survey' World Bank Staff Working Paper No. 363, Washington D.C.

Thomas, W. Merrick, (1976), "Employment and Earnings in the Informal Sector in Brazil: The Case of Belo Horizonte," *Journal of Developing Areas*, April, pp. 339-40.

Weeks, John, (1975), "Policies for Expanding Employment in Informal Sector of Developing Countries," *International Labour Review*, Vol. CXI, No. I, January, pp. 1-13.

Yap, Lorens, Y.L., (1976), "Rural-Urban Migration and Urban Development in Brazil", *Journal of Development Economics*, 3, pp. 227-43.

Section - III

CHILD LABOUR IN DIFFERENT INDUSTRIES

18

Child Labour: Diagnosing the Problem and Rehabilitation of Garage Child Workers Through HRD Approach

—Kalyani Mohanty

Introduction

With the advent of 21st century when one part of the world is busy in ensuring best of human rights, living conditions, social justice and development, the other part kneels with abject poverty, illiteracy, poor health and misery of life. There thousands of poor children are forced to come out for their livelihood and working in poor and hazardous conditions. Their rights for life, good health, food, education and a loving childhood remains like a dream unfulfilled. Their inquisitive eyes in search of a lovely vision stints in the horizon of employers whims. Hence the issue of child labour has gained attention and more important is the steps now being taken to abolish the system. No doubt it is a social evil which is weakening the society but also as an economic necessity sometimes it compensate some of the weaknesses of the society. However, the paper has focused a light on different aspects of child labour alongwith an empirical study for rehabilitating a section with a constructive view.

Concept

Coming to the concept of child labour it is universally accepted that a 'child' is below 14 years of age. The term 'Child labour' sometimes understood as 'working child' or 'employed child'. However here in the age group of 6-14 years, who is doing labour either paid or unpaid. It is co-extensive with any work done by child for gain or a child engaged in gainful occupation is called child labour.

Extension of the Problem

In agrarian economy the jobs for children were confined to agriculture and plantation extended to the work, sowing, reaping, harvesting, threshing etc. alongwith the jobs like taking care of the cattle and fodder. But with the advance of industrialization it is stretched to hazardous jobs in match factory, bidi industry, glass work, bangles making, carpet making, garment and leather factories, cracker factories, garages, hotels and restaurants and even prostitute business. The health hazardousness with all such jobs in developmental stage causes various physical deformity, loss of eye sight, asthmatic problem and various diseases as identified which can be found from the appendix.

National and International Scenario

According to an I.L.O. Report it is estimated that 52 million children in the world are employed in gainful occupation out of which one-third of the working children are Asians and one-fourth of the working children are Indians. It is nothing other than poverty and uneven distribution system which forces millions of poor parents to send their children in search of their livelihood. Child labour[2] in India significantly contributes to the Indian Economy i.e. to 20 per cent of GNP and 8 per cent of workforce. Most of our export industries like carpet, brassware and diamond etc. are based on mainly child labour. Around 13,600 children are engaged in cutting and polishing small diamond pieces. Nearly 8,000 to 50,000 children are working without shoes, gloves, goggles or personal protective equipments near the furnances and other heat emitting machines and equipments in various factories. Besides, poor young girls are dragged to be prostitutes. According to Campaign Against Child Labour in Bombay, 20% prostitutes are minor and large number of them are HIV positive and suffer from various other veneral diseases[4]. K.N. George in Madras revealed that children are forced to work for 8 to 15 hours per day. Besides thousands are working as bonded labourer particularly in rural areas[5].

It is not only a problem with India. In Nepal millions of children are engaged in leather industry. In Spain 100 thousands children work in orchards and plantations. In U.S.A[6]. the United Farmers Workers Union in 1985 reported that millions of young hands are employed in farms and plantation. An I.L.O. study[7] revealed that 20% of the workers deployed in gold production are from 11 years to 18 years of age. A study in urban areas of Colombo found that 40% of 11 to 12 years city workers were domestic servants[8]. Another study in 1990 revealed that there were nearly 4000 children in Chile working as prostitutes[9]. Besides, thousands of children all over the western world work in fast food joints, gas station, sale newspapers, clean cars and work in garment and leather factories.

Efforts for Eliminating Child Labour

The Reformists, political and social thinkers, various Governments and International bodies like ILO, UNICEF, Child Right activists all are quite serious to protect the interest of the children and to stop exploitation of the child labourer. Senator Tom Harkin introduced a legislation in the U.S. Congress about banning of import of goods made through child labourer. France and Germany are also banning the import of goods manufactured through child labourer. If the International Child Labourer Elimination Act, introduced by Chris Smith is enacted it will prohibit importation into U.S. of products manufactured in countries and industries that engage child labour.

In India, there is neither any law which can prohibit children participation in various jobs nor any constitutional provision for elimination of child labourer. Article 24 prohibit the employment of the children below age of 14 in factory, mines and other hazardous job. Again Article 45 makes provision for free and compulsory education to all the children upto the age of 14 years. But in the event of 50 years of independence celebration, 20% of GNP is contributed is by child labourer. Nearly 50% children in the age group of 6-14 (90 million out of a total 179 million) are out of school which are assumed to be working children in one way or the other.

The Child Labour (Prohibition and Regulation) Act (1986), has made provision for regulating working hours of children, restriction of employment during night, prohibition of overtime work etc. Inspite of these enactments 2 million child workers are working in hazardous jobs. Recently under National Child Labour Project[10] (NCLP) the Govt. has sanctioned for 63 districts alongwith 12 on going, 140 thousand children for their rehabilitation and strengthening the economic condition of the family. NCPL projects are for setting up of special schools with provision for educational and vocational training in addition to an incentive consisting of monthly stipend mid-day meal, health care for children drawn from work place.

Research Findings

UNICEF Report "The State of the World's Children 1997" emphases "The end of hazardous child labour should not wait for poverty to end. The world poverty cannot be eliminated by the end of the decade, but the hazardous child labour and the grave violation of the rights of children involved can be." C.P. Chandrashekhar's study that finds no correlation between poverty and child labour. He stated that five states i.e. Andhra Pradesh, Rajasthan, Tamilnadu, Karnataka and Maharashtra have more number of child labour in comparison to poor states like U.P., Bihar and Orissa. In another study Kailash Satyarthi the Chair-Person of SACCS (South Asian Collation of Child Servitude) viewed child is not a necessary consequence of poverty. Rather it is the rampet menance of child labour that perpetuates poverty". UNICEF holds similar view also, United Nations International Childrens' Emergency Fund recorded "Not all work performed by children is harmful to their development".[14] Citing the case of deployment of 75% child labour working in garment industry of Bangladesh. The respective families were exposed to acute financial crisis. Taking world view, I.L.O. concluded that "any society which wants its children free to learn and play; must first free the entire population from fear of want. So instead of making them jobless, they should be empowered with skill, knowledge and self-dependent.

II

However, Dr. V.V. Giri has rightly said that child labour is an economic necessity as well as a social evil. So simultaneous effort for strengthening economic condition and proper education along-with a positive reformative attitude is essential for its remedy.

The second part of the paper deals with the extension of HRD approach as an alternative for remedy and rehabilitation of child labour. It is based on a pragmatic study conducted in the field of motor garages and automobile workshops engaging child labour.

Scope

This piece of work is undertaken on the garage child workers working in various big and small garages registered and unregistered, operating in Bhubaneshwar, the capital city of Orissa, approximately 550 to 600 children are working.

Methodology

For the purpose of present study 40 garages as sample were choosen on a random basis. Both the working children and the owners of the garages were interviewed with the help of a well structured questionnaire and the views were taken in 4 and 5 point scale. The total number of working children interviewed were 80 and number of owners were 40. The Table 18.1 presents the distribution of respondents.

Findings

The distribution of child labour engaged in various garages were mainly of rural background with an average size of 8 members. Most of the respondents were having 2 or less than 2 earning members. The leading family occupation was found by marginal farmers (Table 18.1A & 18.1B)

Emphasising on the economic necessity most of the working children and garage owners viewed they were sent by their parents to earn and supplement their family income.

It was also found that the jobs assigned to the child workers were quite interesting and liked by them and 50% refused to take any job other than that are assigned. Almost all the owners have also same view as they observed the "attitude" of the child labour.

Taking the training facilities for acquisition of skill most of the respondents viewed, the senior mechanics are quite co-operative. Asking on hostile attitude of the senior mechanics 80 per cent viewed that they were rather quite concerned and recognise their performance when they do a good job. They need stipend to maintain themselves and supplement the family income if they were to be rehabilitated through any private or Government agency by vocational training centre.

Table 18.1 (A)

Distribution on Family Size and Earning Members

Background	*Distribution of Respondents*						
	No of Respondents	*Average Size of their Family*	*With Working Mother*	*Without Working Mother*	*No of Earning Member*		
					Less than 2	*2*	*More than 2*
Urban	2	9	2	Nil	2	—	—
Semi-urban	8	6	—	8	4	4	—
Slum	14	5	6	8	6	8	—
Rural	64	8	10	54	24	34	6
Total	88	18	70	36	46	6	

Table 18.1 (B)
Distribution on Occupation

Background	*Number of Respondents*				
	Marginal Farmer	*Daily Labour*	*Service*	*Small Business*	*Self-Employed*
Urban	—	2	—	—	—
Semi-urban	—	4	—	—	4
Slum	—	6	—	—	8
Rural	22	16	12	6	8
Total	22	28	12	6	20

Keeping the rehabilitation of such child worker it was found most of them couldn't believe whether they can be rehabilitated through some vocational training centre with food and clothing.

Asking on the length of training most of them viewed it should be stretched from minimum 6 months to more than a year. The owners have also the same view on the matter.

Taking the views of the owners except two, all 38 owners disagreed to the proposal to convert their garage to a training centre. But all of them were ready to accept the proposal with financial assistance from the Government. Besides though they do not assure the job to the child labour after training, but most of them had shown positive attitude to guide the working children directly or through their senior mechanics. However, they expressed a positive view to ban and abolish the child labour and assured to co-operate with Government for abolition. So far the nature of the garage child worker is concerned, the owners expressed a very positive view about this. The details of the view as tabulated can be witnessed from the Annexure II.

Conclusion

The children, who are engaged in garages, undoubtedly they are sent by their parents or some other relatives, but they are aware of the advantage of skill for future employment and they realized that it is better than formal education. Considering the Human Resource Development of the nation, the children those who are engaged in such occupation can be rehabilitated in more constructive way. It will increase the supply of more number of skilled workers to the economy. But duration of working hours, health and working condition of the training centres should not affect the physiological and psychological development of the working children.

Though the National Child Labour Projects provide for setting up of special schools with provision for education and vocational training in addition to an incentive consisting of monthly stipend, mid-day meal and health care etc. it cannot reach to the working children and in the same of rehabilitation intermediaries are enjoying the advantage of such schemes. So child labour abolition in a country like India is a dream where the budgetary provision for education is 9 per cent and roughly 40% people live below poverty line. It is better to prevent the ignorance and poverty than curing the problem with legal framework.

References

1. Madak, A., "Child Labour Some Issues, Some Suggestions", *Yojna*, May 1996.
2. Singh, S.P., "Child Labour : The Malady and Remedy", *Yojna*, July 1997.

3. Madak, A., "Child Labour Some Issues, Some Suggestions", *Yojna*, May 1996.
4. *Ibid.*
5. *Ibid.*
6. *Ibid.*
7. *Ibid.*
8. *Ibid.*
9. *Ibid.*
10. *Ibid.*
11. Mahapatra, S., "Steps to Check Child Labour", *Yojna*, July 1997.
12. Singh, S.P., *Child Labour : The Malady and the Remedy.*
13. *Ibid.*
14. UNICEF.

ANNEXURE I

Hazards and Occupational Diseases in Different Occupations in Orissa (1995-96)

	Hazardous Occupation	*Diseases*
1.	Agriculture	Hand and Leg injury during Ploughing and Grasscutting
2.	Bidi rolling	T.B., Asthma, Cough, Allergic, Itching
3.	Construction	Body injury
4.	Firework/match making	Burning due to explosion, Cardiotic problem
5.	Fisheries	Dawning
6.	Garage workshop	Loss of eye sight, body injury
7.	Gudakhu making	Tuberculosis, Cough, Heart and lungs problem
8.	Hotel/restaurant	Heart and lungs problem, Skin disease
9.	Minor engineering work	Eye injury
10.	Rag picking	Physical disability, Skin diseases
11.	Rice mill	Hand and Leg injury, Dust allergic
12.	Stone breaking and crushing	Dust allergic, Body injury

Source: Child Labour Survey in Orissa—1995-96. Newsletter Vol. III, No. 5, July, 1996.

ANNEXURE II

Response of the Owners of the Garages

	Questions	*Alternative Answers*	*Response in Numbers*
1.	Who Supplied them Child labour	Sent by Parents	30
		Come their own	10
		By other source	Nil
2.	You find the nature of the child labour is good	Strongly Agrees	16
		Agrees	22
		Indifferent	02
		Disagree	Nil
		S. Disagree	Nil
3.	The C.L. one interested to learn the job assigned	Very much	18
		Much	20
		Indifferent	02
		Not interested	Nil
4.	You take initiative to guide the children working in your garage	Strongly Agree	2
		Agree	28
		Indifferent	10
		Disagree	Nil
5.	You like to send the nothing children to training centre	S.A	2
		A	2
		Undecided	30
		D.A.	2
		S.D.A.	
6.	You like to engage the Children working with you after their training	Agree	4
		Undecided	34
		No response	2
7.	You guide the children to expand their salary they receive from you	Always	10
		Often	14
		Rarely	14
		No response	2
8.	You like to change your garage to a training centre with some monetary assistance form the Govt. & Private agency	S. Agree	8
		Agree	28
		Undecided	4
		Disagree	Nil
		S. Disagree	Nil
9.	The child workers usually leave your garage after training	Mostly	4
		Sometimes	12
		Rarely	14
		No response	10
10.	You like to Co-operate with the steps taken to ban the child labour	S. Agree	12
		Agree	20
		Undecided	8
		Disagree	Nil
		S. Disagree	Nil

(Contd.)

Questions	*Alternatives answers*	*Response in Numbers*
Response of the Child Labour Working in Garages		
1. How did you come to the garage	Sent by parents	80
	By relations	2
	By their own	6
2. You like the job	Very much	22
	Much	58
	Indifferent	8
	Not at all	Nil
3. You find the job interesting	Very interesting	14
	Interesting	34
	Indifferent	34
	Some times difficult	6
4. Your master appreciates when you do a good job	Always	24
	Sometimes	54
	Rarely	10
	Never	0
5. Your senior mechanic likes you	Very much	6
	Much	66
	Indifferent	4
	No response	12
6. Your senior mechanic allows to learn the job well	Strongly Agree	2
	Agree	68
	Undecided	10
	Disagree	6
	S. disagree	2
7. Your senior mechanics gives you hard punishment when you commit some mistake	Strongly Agree	Nil
	Agree	2
	Undecided	10
	Disagree	74
	S. disagree	12
8. You like to join in the school with the amount you receive now	Yes	6
	No	74
	Undecided	8
9. You like to join in a formal training school to learn the skill well	Very much	2
	Much	6
	Indifferent	54
	Never	22
	No response	4
10. You like to join in a workshop cum training centre with stipend or some monetary assistance	Very much	8
	Much	60
	Indifferent	9
	No response	5
	Never	6

(Contd.)

	Questions	*Alternatives answers*	*Response in Numbers*
11.	Your salary is adequate to maintain yourself	Strongly Agree	Nil
		Agree	40
		Indifferent	15
		Disagree	23
		S. Disagree	Nil
12.	You spend major portion of your wage	Supplement	62
		The family earning	16
		Maintain your self	..
		Spend otherwise	2
13.	You want the training period should be	More than a year	Nil
		No response	33
		6 months to 1 yr	24
		Less than 6 months	21
		No such limit	10
14.	You want to enroll yourself in training centre with food and clothing	Strongly Agree	Nil
		Agree	16
		Undecided	68
		Disagree	6
		Strongly disagree	Nil
15.	You want to have your own garage after acquiring the skill	S.A	4
		A	20
		Indifferent	60
		D.A.	4
		S.D.A.	Nil

19

Child Labour in Diamond Cutting and Polishing Units in Gujarat: A Case Study of Bhavnagar City

—A.D. Saramma

Introduction

It is said that every child is God's gift to mankind. With the birth of every child the society is offered one more chance for a better tomorrow for the whole community. But is our treatment of children in conformity with this? Regrettably the answer is 'no'.

With the economic conditions of the society plummeting and consequently more values taking a back seat, not only are the needs of the children ignored, but the children are exploited in every sense. Child labour is only one facet of this situation. Today the problem of child labour is assuming serious dimensions in poor countries. India is not an exception, where every field of unorganised activities, the children are employed. Despite the enactment of various laws for banning child labour and defining a child's rights are on paper, the reality is still very grim. In order to prevent the under-aged children from working, various international bodies like UNO and ILO and many national Governments have passed many resolutions.

"The child shall not be admitted to employment before an

> appropriate minimum age, he shall in no case be caused or permitted to engage in many occupations or employment which would prejudice his health or his education or interference with his physical, mental or moral development" (UNO, 1959).

However, this declaration has not any impact on the employment of child labour. The abolition of a child labour is still a distant dream and its persistence of the world community (ILO, 1983).

Government of India also appointed a National Commission on labour during 1966 to study the various problems of different types of child labour. This commission analysed the problem of child labour and made recommendations on this issue. The main recommendation was that child labour should be given the necessary educational facility alongwith their work. Further, the Government of India set up a committee in 1979 headed by Gurupad Swamy to initiate the concrete policy measures for the protection of working children (Gurupad Swamy, 1979). Later on another act *viz.* the Child Labour (Prohibition and Regulation) Act 1986 prohibits the engagement of children in certain employment and regulates the conditions of work of children in certain other employment. During August 1987 the National Child Labour Policy has also been formulated with the object of bringing certain facilities like non-formal education, health care, vocational training, recreation facilities etc. Beginning of the year 1997 Supreme Court has passed a law that any children who is working in any factory or store is caught by the concerned authority, then the concerned owner of the factory or the store has to pay a fixed amount to the welfare of the child ranging from Rs. 25,000 onward. However, none of these Acts and Resolutions have been implemented effectively. Still child labour is visible every where and became an unending problem.

Child Labour and Their Exploitation

Child labour are exploited in many ways *viz.* economically, exploitation in terms of health, education etc. The exploitation of child labour is reflected in terms of long working hours, low wages, casual nature of work, absence of holidays, absence of social security, poor working environment etc. As a result, some times, they are thrown to extreme sufferings too. The health of the children will affect adversely when he works in hazardous occupations, or when they work for longer hours in difficult postures, in unhealthy and unsafe surroundings or by straining their tender body. Apart from this, the low wages and poverty do not provide them sufficient food, results into under nutrition and malnutrition. Illiteracy or low educational levels keep them unskilled or semi-skilled and thereby limit the opportunities of upward mobility. Besides there are some additional areas of deprivation which, though serious, are generally ignored by governments. These are:

(*a*) psychological deprivation due to early exposure to adult life and absence of free childhood. If too much discipline is imposed in tender age, it will result into adverse effects.
(*b*) physiological consequences of children using machines, tools etc. designed for adults, and
(*c*) misuse of children for illegal and immoral works.

Child Labour in Diamond Industry

The most serious problem facing poverty stricken economies in this regard is that—children are forced to go to work to earn when they should be in schools. Today many industries like carpet weaving, diamond cutting, automobiles, bidi making, brick making, domestic work and agricultural operations where more children are employed. In Bhavnagar city, the main industrial activity is diamond cutting and polishing stands second in diamond production in Gujarat. In this activity more children are also employed. Thus, an attempt is made to examine the extent of child labour in these units, their social and economic status, their working environment etc. by surveying 50 diamond cutting and polishing units in Bhavnagar city. 100 child labour are included in this study.

Peculiarities of Diamond Cutting and Polishing Industry

The diamond cutting and polishing unit is a small enterprise and its owner is transient in nature. It is an extremely interesting industry evolving a variety of aspects; covering imports, exports, manufacturing and processing operations, technological choices, size of operations, investment, employment, training, skill formation, business dealings, marketing and market structures and government policies and above all the common sense and risk bearing capacity of the entrepreneur who undertakes this type of business.

The main peculiarity of the industry is that it is an "Owner-cum-manager" type of production unit as owner keeps only an informal type of relation with the employees and quite often employees are the members of the same family. The requirement of capital for the unit is very less. The success of one unit inspires others to start the same type of activity.

A small diamond unit can be established with four polishing machines, two motors and two lathes. It is a labour intensive unit. Generally four workers can work on one polishing machine, polishing the bottom, top and facets. Two lathes would provide employment to ten workers. The technology of these units is indigenous. The Law of Constant Returns is applicable to this industry. This activity can be started in small residential areas also. The energy requirement of the unit is very nominal. The workers do not need any formal education to enter into this activity. The workers can be easily trained within a short period of three to four months on jobs of cutting and polishing. The operations of diamond production and trade are based on trust. The very important feature of these units is that the unit can be closed for months and can be restarted without any hindrance. Three types of diamonds are generally produced *viz.* single cut, double cut and fancy cut.

A Profile of the Surveyed Diamond Cutting and Polishing Units in Bhavnagar City

In order to study the various aspects of the activities of diamond and the child labour, two questionnaires were prepared. The profiles of fifty surveyed units were made by circulating a questionnarie to the owners of the units and regarding child labour in these units, the questions were directly asked to the child labourers.

1. *Year of Establishment*

Out of the surveyed 50 units, 2 units were established during 1982-85 and the remaining after 1985 and thus majority of the units are of recent origin.

2. *Types of Work Done in the Units*

The diamond units could be engaged in single cutting, double cutting and fancy cutting. The surveyed units of Bhavnagar city are classified one the line of work done by them. Out of 50 units, 27 units are engaged in fancy cutting.

3. *Form of Ownership*

Out of 50 samples surveyed, 28 units are partnership firms and others are under single ownership.

4. *Caste Composition*

70% of the owners of diamond cutting and polishing units under consideration belong to Patel community 15% Rajputs, 12% Kolis, 2% Bharwad and the remaining belong to Brahmins and other lower class community. It is revealed that Patel community is dominant in this activity.

5. *Size of Investment*

Table 19.1 denotes the size group in the sample of Bhavnagar city. The distribution indicates that 50% of the units belong to the investment size Rs. 10,001 - Rs. 2,50,000 and 30% belong to the size Rs. 4,000 - Rs. 10,000.

Table 19.1

Size of the Investment in Diamond Units in Bhavnagar City

	Size of Investment (in Rs.)			*Number of Units*	*Percentage*
1.	4,000	—	10,000	15	30
2.	10,001	—	25,000	25	50
3.	25,001	—	50,000	06	12
4.	50,001	—	1,00,000	03	06
5.	Above 1,00,000			01	02
	Total Investment		Rs. 25 lakhs		

Source : Based on the survey.

6. *Size of Employment*

The total employment in diamond cutting and polishing units under consideration is 1200. Both males, females and children are working in all the units. Educational qualifications of these workers ranging from illiterate to Post-graduation.

7. *Wage Rate*

The wage rates of the workers of these units vary depending upon the type of cutting and polishing as well as it varies across the units and also from place to place. The wage rate of single cutting in Bhavnagar city varies from Rs. 4.50 to Rs. 7.00, double cutting from Rs. 6.00 to Rs. 14.00 and fancy cutting from Rs. 10.00 to Rs. 25.00.

8. *Working Period*

The average working period of these units vary from 8-11 months during an year.

Magnitude of Child Labour in Diamond Cutting and Polishing Units in Bhavnagar City

Table 19.2 presents the magnitude of child labour in diamond units in Bhavnagar city.

The total employment of child labour in all the 50 units surveyed are 103, consisting of 8.58% of the total employment. The surveyed units where only male child labourers were employed. For examining their social and economic conditions, only 100 child labourers were considered.

Table 19.2

Magnitude of Child Labour in Diamond Units in Bhavnagar city

	Size of Investment (in Rs.)			*Number of Units*	*Employment in Each Investment Group*	*Total No. of Child Labour Employed*
1.	4,000	—	10,000	15	45	08
2.	10,001	—	25,000	25	180	22
3.	25,001	—	50,000	06	250	20
4.	50,001	—	1,00,000	03	370	43
5.	Above 1,00,000			01	355	10
Total Investment			Rs. 25 lakhs	50	1200	103

Source : Based on the survey.

Socio-Economic Conditions of the Child Labour in Diamond Units

1. *Age Profile of Child Labourers*

Table 19.3 shows the age profile of the child labourers under consideration in the diamond units in Bhavnagar. It is revealed that 56% of child labourers are under the age group 13-14 years.

Table 19.3

Age Profile of the Surveyed Children in Diamond Units in Bhavnagar City

	Age Group	*Number*
1.	Below 12	—
2.	12 - 13	44
3.	13 - 14	36

Source : Based on the survey.

2. *Caste of the Child Labourer*

Table 19.4 depicts the caste of the child workers surveyed. It is observed that maximum number of working children are belonging to Patel community followed by Kolis, Rajputs etc. All the child labourers belong to Hindu religion.

Table 19.4

Caste of the Child Labourers of the Diamond Cutting Units in Bhavnagar City

	Caste	*Number of Child Workers*
1.	Brahmin	15
2.	Patel	25
3.	Koli	35
4.	Bharwad	08
5.	Mali	05
6.	Others	02

Source : Based on the survey.

3. *Presence of Parents*

The presence of parents of the surveyed child labourers are given in Table 19.5. Sixty per cent of the child workers have both parents. 20 per cent have only father alive, whereas 13% have only mothers alive. Thus most of the child labourers have to work inspite of the fact that both their parents are alive. Still 33 per cent of the child workers in diamond units are suffering from the absence of atleast one parent.

Table 19.5

Presence of Parents of the Child Labourers of Diamond Cutting and Polishing Units in Bhavnagar City

	Status	*Number*
1.	Only father alive	20
2.	Only mother alive	13
3.	Both alive	60
4.	Both dead	07

Source : Based on the survey.

4. *Size of Family*

Table 19.6 presents the family size of the surveyed child labourers. It is realised that most of the child workers belong to 7-8 family size group followed by 20 in 9-10 size group. Very big and very small family size are comparatively less prevalent in the study.

Table 19.6

Size of Family of the Child Workers of Diamond Units in Bhavnagar City

	Size of Family	*Number*
1.	Below 4	04
2.	4 - 6	30
3.	7 - 8	42
4.	9 - 10	20
5.	Above 10	02
	Total	100

Source : Based on the survey.

5. *Occupation of the Parents*

The occupation of the parents of the child workers are presented in Table 19.7.

Table 19.7

Parents' Occupation of Child Workers in Diamond Units in Bhavnagar City

	Occupation	*Father's*	*Mother's*
1.	Diamond workers	20	—
2.	Construction workers	25	15
3.	Household work	02	35
4.	Others	10	08
5.	Not working	23	15
	Total	80	73

Source : Based on the survey.

Thirtyone per cent of the fathers of the child labourers considered in the study are construction workers, 25% working in diamond units, whereas most of the mothers are working in households. About 29% of fathers and 20% of the mothers are not working.

6. *Education*

The educational status of the child workers and their heads of the family are outlined in Table 19.8. It is indicated that 37% of the heads of the family are illiterate; 50% of the heads were having education upto primary level and those heads falling under the educational between primary and secondary levels are only about 8.6%. However, all the child workers are literate. Eightysix percent of the child workers are having education upto primary level and the remaining have the educational status between primary to secondary level. They have expressed their unwillingness to study along their work.

Table 19.8

Educational Levels of Child Workers and their Heads of Family in Diamond Units in Bhavnagar City

Educational Level	*No. of Heads of the Family*	*No. of Children Below 15 Years*
1. Illiterate	35	—
2. Upto Primary level	57	86
3. Above Primary and upto Secondary level	08	24
4. Above Secondary level	—	—
5. All levels	100	100

Source : Based on the survey.

7. *Working Hours*

The working hours of the surveyed child labourers are shown in Table 19.9. It is observed that 65% of these children work 4 hours to 6 hours and 35% children work 6 to 8 hours per day.

Table 19.9

Working Hours of Child Workers in Diamond Units in Bhavnagar City

Working Hours	*Number*
1. Upto 6 Hours	65
2. 8 to 10 Hours	35
Total	100

Source : Based on the survey.

8. *Monthly Production of Diamonds by Child Labour in Diamond Units in Bhavnagar*

Table 19.10 depicts the monthly production of diamond by the child workers in diamond units in the study. It is observed that five child labourers produce diamonds at the range of 101-125 units per month, 30 child labourers from 76-100 diamonds and 45 child workers at the range of 51-75 diamonds per month.

Table 19.10

Monthly Production of Diamonds by the Child Workers in Diamond Units in Bhavnagar City

	Production of Diamonds/Month	*No. of Child Workers*
1.	15 - 20	—
2.	25 - 50	20
3.	51 - 75	45
4.	76 - 100	30
5.	101 - 125	05
	Total	100

Source : Based on the survey.

9. *Monthly Earnings*

The monthly earnings of the child labourers under consideration are shown in Table 19.11.

Table 19.11

Monthly Earnings of the Child Labourers of Diamond Units in Bhavnagar City

	Earnings/Month (Rs.)	*Number*
1.	Below 500	25
2.	501 - 600	55
3.	601 - 700	20
	Total	100

Source : Based on the survey.

It is evident from the table that 5 per cent child labourers have monthly income of more than Rs. 750, 30 per cent of them fell in the range of Rs. 601 to Rs. 750, 45 per cent are earning a monthly income ranging from Rs. 301 to Rs. 600, the remaining 20 per cent are getting less than Rs. 300 per month and these 20 per cent child workers are just beginners in this activity. These child workers give 85-90 per cent of their earnings to the heads of the family. The remaining spend for the consumption of tabacoo, smoking etc.

Reasons for Working

In the course of the survey the reasons for working of these child workers are also examined. The same is presented in Table 19.12. The data in the Table show that 30 per cent of the working children belong to poor families and they work in order to supplement family income for subsistance. 26 per cent of the sample population work for acquiring skill. The rest of them are working for wages for other reasons such as not having parents, inability of parents to earn an income and ill habit of the fathers etc.

Table 19.12

Reasons of Child Workers Working in Diamond Units in Bhavnagar City

Educational Level	*Number of Child Workers*
1. Poverty	30
2. Death of father	07
3. Death of mother	13
4. Death of both parents	07
5. Ill habituated father	05
6. Parents handicapped	12
7. To acquire skill	26
Total	100

Source : Based on the survey.

Working Conditions of the Diamond Units

The working conditions of these units are not on the basis of the norms of Factory Act 1948 and therefore crowding is there in these units. Weekly washing, yearly white washing, repairing and revarnishing once in five years is not done as per the Factory Act norms. This will negatively affect the health conditions of the workers and especially child workers in the long run. Adequate window and door facilities are not there in these units and therefore adequate natural light and free air circulation are not getting in these units. Generally humid climate is experienced in these units. Moreover, adequate toilet facilities, safe drinking water, waste disposal facilities, and any type of recreational facilities are lacking in these units. This will adversely affect the health of these child workers in future. The main health problems experienced by the workers in these units are loss of eye sight due to long years service in diamond cutting and polishing, T.B., allergy problems etc. Generally a person can work only upto 40-45 years in diamond units due to these health problems.

Conclusion

Despite many legislative measures taken by the government the child labour have been growing and are being exploited in many activities and diamond cutting and polishing units are not an exception. The main reasons for the child labour in diamond units is to earn to supplement income for subsistence. These children neither get any facility for education nor willing to study alongwith their work. Therefore, horizontal mobility of work is not possible. Besides, there is no scope for vertical mobility of work in future as they do not have adequate income for starting their own diamond business. There is no financial organisation to help them financially for starting diamond business or any other business. There is no organisations like trade unions to protect their rights. If this is the case, then vicious circle of poverty will be operated in their life too. As these child workers will be forced to send their children also for this type of work and thus will result into an unending problem. Therefore, to avoid the child labour, the Government should avoid inherent problems of poverty, illiteracy, unemployment and other social evils.

References

1. Government of India, [1986], *Child Labour Act of 1986*, Prohibition and Regulation.
2. Gurupad Swamy, [1979], *Committee on Child Labour*, Govt. of India.
3. International Labour Organisation, [1983], *Report of the Director General, ILO*, Geneva, 69th Sessin.

20

The Working Children: A Case Study of Brick Industry in Nandyal

—I. Narendra Kumar & A. Prasad

"Every child is an experiment, an adventure into noble ··ᶜe, an opportunity to change the old pattern and make it new."

—S. Radhakrishnan

Child labour is refer to work undertaken by a child, who is below 15 years of age, for wage of it refers to employment of children in gainful occupations. Child labour today, is a global phenomenon and a harsh reality. The Human Development Report 1993 indicates a 250 per cent increase in violation of child labour laws in U.S. Between 1983-90, reportedly in New York city alone, 1,50,000 children are employed in the garment industry, some of them as young as 10 years[1].

The UN General Assembly declared 1979 as the International Year of the Child and aimed "to encourage all countries, rich and poor, to review their programmes, for the well-being of children and to mobilise support for national and local action programmes according to each country's conditions, need and priorities". The Government of India in its National Plan of action for international year of child 1979 acknowledged the importance of children by quoting "A Nation's children are its supremely important asset and the nation's future lies in their proper development. An investment is children is indeed an investment in the nation's future. A healthy and educated child of today is the active and intelligent citizen of tomorrow.[2]

In India although Government sources report the child labour to be below 18 millions, non-government organisations claim it to be not less than 40 million. The percentage of child population in the zero to 14 age group in 1991 was 37.2 per cent. Moreover the World Health Organisation's estimation depicted that by 2001 out of the estimated population of 1003 million, child population would be about 33 per cent of the total population of India[3].

The prevalence of children's work is marked in Andhra Pradesh the child labour recorded 1.75 million in 1981 census[4]. The child labour in 1991 census—2.18 millions. The magnitude of child labour is far higher in Andhra Pradesh than in any other state in India. Child labour were 3.28 per cent of the total population in Andhra Pradesh in 1981[5]. The percentage of child workers to the child population was 8.50 in the state, twice the figure for India. The percentage of child workers in Kurnool District[6] is about 10.92, which is highest in the state.

Purpose of the Study Area

The present study attempts to analyse the conditions of child labour, work participation of child labour in various operations, the structure of wage payment, monthly income they get from the profession, the total income of their family members in the brick industry of Nandyal in Kurnool District of Andhra Pradesh. For the purpose of the study a survey has been conducted in 20 brick industries of Nandyal. The result of the study is presented.

The average investment in brick industry is Rs. 50,000 to Rs. 2,00,000. As per the direct observation of the researcher, the total work performed by the labourers occur in four different phases. In percentage terms, each phase involves 25% of the total works contributed by the labourers.

Ist phase: Involves making paste like clay from suitable soil and suitable earthen falls as required for single brick. At this phase, adult females and children are employed.

2nd phase: Involves making raw bricks. Only adult males are employed in this phase.

3rd phase: Involves carrying raw bricks from the place of

manufacturing to the drying-pit, where raw bricks are allowed to dry in sun-stroke. In this stage again the adult females and children are employed.

4th phase: All the bricks setting the square type and fired the bricks in the stage. In this stage all the workers participated.

The total number of the children employed in brick industry in Nandyal (Ponnpuram) is 184 out of which 102 are male child labour and 82 are female child labour which has been shown in Table 20.1. It reveals that 55.43 per cent of the workers in the brick industry are male child labour and the remaining 44.57 per cent of the workers are female child labour.

Table 20.1

Distribution of Child Labour Working in Brick Industry on the Basis of Sex

Category	*Industry*	*Percentage*
Male	102	55.43
Female	82	44.57
Total	184	100.00

Source : Field Data.

From Table 20.2 it is found that out of the child labour 8.7 per cent belong to OC, 46.7 per cent belong to BC, 31.5 per cent belong to SC, and 13.1 per cent belong to ST category.

Table 20.2

Distribution of Child Labour Working in Brick Industry on the Basis of Caste

Caste	*Industry*	*Percentage*
OC	16	8.7
BC	86	46.7
SC	58	31.5
ST	24	13.1
Total	184	100.00

Source : Field Data.

The average number of days in a month the child labourers get work in manufacturing brick industry is presented in Table 20.3. We find that 22.28 per cent children do their work within the range of 1-10 days. 47.83 per cent child labourers get their work for 11-20 days and 29.89 per cent children get their work for 21-30 days in brick industry.

Table 20.3

Distribution of Child Labour Working in Brick Industry Average Number of Days of Working in a Month

Category	*1-10 Days*	*11-20 Days*	*21-30 Days*	*Total*
Male	22 (21.56)	52 (50.98)	28 (27.46)	102
Female	19 (23.17)	36 (43.90)	27 (32.93)	82
Total	41 (22.28)	88 (47.83)	55 (29.89)	184 (100)

Note : (parenthis) shows the percentage of the average working days in a month.
Source : Field Data.

Usually piece-wage system prevails in all the brick manufacture industries. From the sample study it has been found that on an average Rs. 120 is given per 1,000 dried raw bricks. The distribution of child labour working in brick industry weekly average wages is presented in Table 20.4. Sometimes the brick industry owners followed the weekly wages system. The weekly average wages of male child labour is Rs. 120 and female child labour is Rs. 90 in the industry.

Table 20.4

Distribution of Child Labour Working in Brick Industry on the Basis of Weekly Average Wages

Category	*Wages*
Male	120
Female	90

Source : Field Data.

Table 20.5 gives information regarding child labours families monthly whole income. It is found that 10.33 per cent children's families monthly whole income is within the range of Rs. 500-1,000, 15.22 per cent children's families monthly whole income is within the range of Rs. 1,001-1,500, 31.52 per cent children families monthly whole income is within the range of Rs. 1,501-2,000, 35.87 per cent children's families monthly whole income is within the range of Rs. 2,001-2,500 and 7.06 per cent children families monthly whole income is above the Rs. 2,500 and more.

Table 20.5

Distribution of Child Labour Working in Brick Industry on the Basis of Family's Whole Income

Category	*500-1000*	*1001-1500*	*1501-2000*	*2001-2500*	*2500 & above*	*Total*
Male	12 (11.76)	16 (15.69)	32 (31.38)	34 (33.33)	8 (7.84)	102
Female	7 (8.54)	12 (14.63)	26 (31.70)	32 (39.02)	5 (6.10)	82
Total	19 (10.33)	28 (15.22)	58 (31.52)	66 (35.87)	13 (7.06)	184 (100)

Source : Field Data.

A good and congenial work environment boosts the efficiency of child labourers and raises the productivity. It has been observed that the work environment of brick industries is not proper and congenial since the majority of child labourers belong to BC, SC community, due to the taboos of caste by stem, they remain neglected subject to some degree of hatred and antagonism by the local workers and the employers.

Thus even in the absence of sympathy and pleasure in their work environment, desperately they continue their struggle for their bare survival.

Though there are huge constitutional provisions and a number of legislative enactments from time to time to the provisions, problem of child labour rampathy exists. According to article 24 of the constitution children below the age of 14 are not to be employed in any factory or mine or engaged in any other hazardous employment?

There are plethora of laws for the protection of child labourers.

(*a*) The Factories Act, 1948.
(*b*) The Mines Act, 1952.
(*c*) The Plantation Labour Act, 1951
(*d*) The Contract Labour (Regulation & Abolition) Act, 1978
(*e*) The Child Labour (Prevention and Regulation) Act, 1986

Merely all the constitutional provisions, legislative enactment and different government policies remain as the paper-tigers only.

On the basis of foregoing study the following recommendations may be forwarded.

1. Poverty alleviation programmes like JRY, IRDP, DWACRA, EAS, [PMRY, CMEY] must be effectively implemented in the child labourer prone regions.
2. Universalization of primary education should be accompanied with special emphasis of child labourers prone regions.
3. Nearly 80 per cent of child labour force belong to rural areas. Therefore the objectives of rural development should improve as well as minimum acceptable food, clothing, shelter, education and health for the people.

References

1. Mehta, Jaya, *My Name is Today*, Vol. II, No. 1, Jan.-March, 1994, p. 10.
2. Dr. B.K. Dattanaik, *Yojna*, July, 1998, p. 45.
3. *Ibid.*, p. 45.
4. Sumi Krishna, *Restoring Childhood*, Konark Publishers Pvt. Ltd., New Delhi, 1996, p. 34.
5. *Ibid.*
6. *Ibid.*
7. 'Right of Children' *Yojna*, September 1994.

21

Child Labour: Status and Gender Bias in Brick Industry

—*C. Muthuraja*

Child Labour in India

Child labour in ancient India existed in the form of child slaves. The Cruel practice of purchasing children of less then 8 years existed in ancient India. These budding and blooming flowers were treated a commodity which could be bought or sold, used or abused according to the whims of their masters. To accord protection to these working children whose plight was miserable by all standards, Manusmriti and Kautilya have pointed out the need and practice of giving protection to these working children.

It has been a tradition in our country that children from the very beginning have been participating in work both within and outside the family. In the earliest times children used to be engaged in the work relating to agricultural and grazing of animals. In the Medieval period they used to be involved in various types of crafts and trades, besides the agricultural activities. In the present complex social set-up, characterized by the use of energy and technology for mass production of different kinds of commodities with maximum speed, children can be seen performing a number of jobs which, by their very nature, are hazardous to their physical and mental growth and development. Agriculture continues to be the most dominant occupation, engaging an overwhelming majority of the working population. Despite its becoming nechanized and commercial day-by-day it is characterized by the employment of a large number of children performing a wide variety of jobs.

Child labour continues to be an important constituent of the workforce engaged in both the organised and unorganised sectors of our developing Economy. Constitutional provisions and other legal safeguards notwithstanding, the lopsided development process in the backdrop of an exploitative socio-economic structure has resulted in the marginalisation of the poor for whom children are the main economic assets.

Economist's Point of View

Some economist consider that working children involve labour at the point of its lowest productivity, and is thus an inefficient utilisation of labour. Some go further and assert that if child labour were abolished altogether, it would release countless jobs for our currently unemployed manpower. Neither argument, however, is basically tenable for the simple reason that children often work harder and for longer hours and for less money then a feckless adult and are not involved in political or union games which waste millions of man-hours of work all over the country. Both women and children continue to constitute a low-cost labour resource. Can legislation really alter this? It is a well-known fact that the feminist demand for equal pay for equal work, alongwith maternity benefits, has tended to reduce than rather enhance women's wage earning capacity. It would, therefore, be unwise to try to protect children against labour exploitation by abolishing their right to work if, in the process, we destroyed their role in helping their family economy.

The ILO has estimated the number of child workers to be around 100 millions in the world as a whole. The bulk of them are from the under-developed countries, with Asia's contribution to the maximum extent. Most of the child labour is concentrated in South and South-East Asia. A vast majority of child labours are employed in the informal sector, where they are subjected to prolonged hours of hard labour for minimal wages and without weekly off or proper rest intervals. Apart from poverty, the low educational and occupational status of the parents, and inadequacy of the legislative system as well as its insufficient enforcement are the other reasons for the persistence of child labour.

Child labour, which has its origin in the exploitative systems operating at both the national and international levels, has defied all solutions for its complete eradication. Even the industrialised economies could, at best, only reduce the level of its incidence but not fully get out of this syndrome. In the case of LDC's the problem has assumed serious dimensions. The lop-sided development process in the backdrop of an unevenly balanced Socio-economic structure, has resulted in the marginalisation of the poor who are left with no option but to use child labour as a survival strategy.

Female Child Labour

About 54 per cent of girls in rural India worked as agricultural labour in 1991 and about 33 per cent worked on family operated farm cultivators. These two categories combined accounted for 88 per cent of rural female child labour in 1981 and 87 per cent in 1991. Rural manufacturing activities employed 7 per cent of child labour in 1991. The absolute number in this category grew during 1971-81 and declined during 1981-91.

In absolute terms, the total number is less than 10 million children with a labour force participation rate of less than 5 per cent urban, industrial child labour which is the focus of global interest and rural wage based non-agricultural child labour combined, is about one million children. Variations across states in the incidence of child labour and its rates of decline over the last three decades are rather large. States such as Kerala, Tamilnadu, Himachal Pradesh and Punjab are leading in substantially reducing the incidence of child labour while others such as UP, Bihar, Rajasthan, MP and AP continue to have a rather sluggish decline though variability among laggards also is quite substantial.

There is a huge gender bias in the incidence of child labour. In urban India more boys than girls work as child labours though in percentage terms, they are substantially lower than in rural India. In rural India, the proportion of boys working as child labourers has declined from over 10 per cent in 1961 to over 5 per cent in 1991. The gender difference is substantially larger in the states of the northern India but relatively smaller in the rest of India. A large majority of girls still work within the agricultural sector of rural India.

The brick industry is an important segment of the industrial/ Infrastructure Sector, earning huge amount of income and fulfilling the increased demand for housing materials at the state level as well as the national level. Incidentally, the brick industry is also reported to be one among the largest employer of children as a workforce.

The researcher is mainly concentrating on the status of child labour and Gender bias in brick industry, for this study. The researcher made a lot of visits to observe the condition of child labour in various brick kilns. Brick industry is a very powerful sector in Madurai and Ramnad Districts of Tamilnadu. It provides a lot of employment opportunities to men and women, who are mostly illiterate and uneducated. These districts have only poor agricultural performance, because of failure of mansoon and improper distribution and utilisation of water resources. So most of them, have to find employment in non-farm activities. Brick industry is one sector which absorbs more men and women and also widely utilize child labour. The findings of the study will be useful in formulation of policies for future course of action, for complete eradication of child labour in the industry.

Child labour is rooted in poverty, precarious incomes and insufficient opportunities. They work for their own survival and that of their families. Economic compulsions weigh so heavily that the poor parents do not hesitate in violating the laws and putting their children to exploitation. It is still a widespread and perhaps an ever growing phenomenon in the world today.

Today, there are millions of children in the world, who are forced to seek survival on the streets of towns and cities. They work and live alone without adequate food, shelter, education, affection and social security. Though the physical deprivations faced by them are of a very distressing nature, more damaging are the psychological and social deprivations.

Causes for Child Labour

- Main cause, for child labour appears to be utter poverty, unemployment and under-employment of parents in the family. Utter poverty conditions compel parents to send their children to work.
- Vested interest of employers is another factor. In their greed to maximise profits and minimise cost they flout factory regulations. Employers prefer children, as they are cheap labour, honest, hard working, easy to control and disciplined. It is found that pockets of child labour concentration are also

draught prone areas and areas of high adult unemployment.

- Parents attitudes and socio-cultural factors are another set of factors responsible for child labour.
- Limited success in providing compulsory education to all boys and girls in 5-14 age group is another important factor for child labour. A child sent to school is a child saved from exploitation. It can enter the labour market with better skill.
- Failure of legislation. Government effort is equally responsible for child labour particularly in the hazardous occupations. Legislation remains on paper, loop-holes in the law are easily availed off by the employers. Government administrators and factory Inspectors often fail to do their job successfully, with the result, children continue to be exploited as child labour.

Status of Child Labour in Brick Industry

Most children work in brick industry because poverty forces them to earn money and the survival of their families depends upon it. In more prosperous societies, where survival is less precarious, children can be spared from some work to go to school or to play. But where families need their help, children will continue to work.

The exploitation of child workers in terms of remuneration is prevalent all over the states in India and particularly in Tamilnadu. Where they are paid, they almost invariably receive low wages. This appears to be one of the reasons for the widespread use of child labour. Children are also subjected to many types of remuneration, such as piece rates, that place undue strain upon them.

Another major problem is hours of work. Children in brick industry are working more than 8 hours per day. Girls in this industry are also working more than 8 hours per day. Other problems relating to working time are the absence of insufficiency of rest-breakes during the day, or weekly rest and of annual holidays with pay.

The large size of the family, uneconomic and unproductive farming operations and dwindling employment opportunities in farm and non-form operations, etc., have compelled the parents of the brick industry children to accompany their children.

Educational Status

The constitution of Indian democracy adopted in 1950, declares that the state shall endeavour to provide within a period of ten years from its commencement free and compulsory education for all children until they complete the age of 14 years. A number of measures have been taken by the Government for achieving constitutional provisions. Unfortunately, all the efforts of the Government have had only a limited impact in achieving universalisation of primary education. Wide variations in literacy levels are discernible not only at the inter-state level but also at the intra-state levels, and at the rural/urban level with a strong gender bias. Schooling and work participation activities that are often competitive, lead to higher dropout rates and greater illiteracy among working children. Such a phenomenon appears to be true of the brick industry of these areas, where a large number of children continue to work on brick cutting and its allied activities either as a part of the family labour or as wage labour.

Economic Status

Brick industry was still the principal source of income of the households. A relatively large proportion of the population has ended up as labourers in agricultural and non-agricultural occupations in recent times.

The meager income of the head of the family is insufficient to meet the requirements of the fairly large size of the family and this is the principal reason for child labour in brick industry. The employers laying no condition of employment of the children employed they can leave the job at any time on their own will. There are no pre-conditions in service matters.

Monetary benefits had always been the major attraction for the illiterate parents to send their wards to the brick industry. The child labour gets wages of Rs. 20 to 30 per day (approximately). There is a discrimination between a girl worker and a boy worker. For some kind of job the girl worker is able to get only less wages than boy worker. In some other jobs girl workers manage to get more wages than boy workers, because the nature of work is more suitable to girl workers only.

Parents are well aware that engaging the children in brick industry is not fair and amounts to denial of developmental opportunities. Some of the households justified the phenomenon stating that their children are not interested in studies.

Nature of Work

There are several stages in brick making. The first stage involves the preparation of clay out of various kinds of soil. Then the clay is used for cutting of bricks. The workers have to wait for a minimum of three days of hot sun light and dry air, after that the bricks will be transferred into chamber for heating. To bury the bricks, firewood, lignite and waste of cashew shell. Then after 2 or 3 days the heated bricks will be taken out from the chamber. Now the brick is ready for sale. The price of bricks will be decided by the market forces. Since this is a seasonal (during non-rainy season only) business, the price of brick will be high during the time of rainy seasons. The brick cutters and other workers involved in brick making are engaging in agricultural occupation during this season.

Working Hours

Children are working in brick industry for about 8 hours per day on an average. Children in the wage labour segment continue the same monotonous job. Monotony of the job often results in lower levels of productivity which in turn necessitates longer hours of work.

Other than wages, brick industry are not paid any other incentives or benefits in cash or in kind. But the workers can get the benefit in the form of clothes, once in a year.

Brick industry can be less monotonous if the working environment is conducive to health. Unfortunately children work on brick making and transport amidst dust and heat and constantly get exposed to health hazards.

According to the children, there is some satisfaction in the availability of basic amenities in the work places. Many basic facilities such as proper lighting, drinking water, First aid facilities and toilet have been created in recent years.

Gender Perspective in Child Labour

The existence and dimension of child labour in India has become a matter of universal concern during the present decade. More than 80% of the working children in India belong to the rural areas and work in the un-organised primary sector of the economy. They enter the labour market to help poverty affected families, to repay long standing family debts, due to sudden death of bread-winner of the family or sometimes when they run away from the families due to personal or caste exploitation. No single cause can be identified or isolated for the prevalence of child labour, as it is inherent in the vicious circle of poverty and unemployment.

Both women and children are never consulted in policy-making or planning for their own future. They are never part of any policy making even in cases of the so-called best interest of their groups. They are almost always treated as minorities. As a result of these manifestations of isolation, most often the marginalised are deprived of a large range of resources, opportunities and power. Within these marginalised groups are the girl-working child, who has layers of oppression pressuring them. The girl worker in India requires special mention in the context of child labour, as she is a child, a girl and a labourer and faces discrimination on all counts.

Gender Bias in Child Labour in Brick Industry

In most economically dis-advantaged families, the greater the poverty, the more aggravated is the situation of the girl child. Denied educational, nutritional and health care, her growth and development is further restricted by the process of socialisation.

Despite their significant contribution to the family income, the girl's economic participation goes unnoticed as they are employed in either family labour or domestic work or in the un-organised sector, particularly in brick industry.

Conclusion and Suggestive Measures

Entry of children into the brick industry was not a matter of choice but a matter of economic compulsion to supplement the family income. Hence, taking a child away from brick industry unit will amount to a loss of family income which the family of the child can ill afford.

Approach to Child Labour

Poverty is the prime cause behind children setting out or being sent forth to join the working force. Poverty exists in rural as well as urban areas. Fighting child labour is part of the fight against poverty.

By focussing attention on the exploitation of the working child and the long-term ill-effects of working, groups of conscious individuals and organisation could join hands in bringing about necessary amendments in legislations as well as welfare policies.

The working child has missed out on education and it needs to be brought to him/her in an informal form with large components of vocational/skill training which could equip him/her for better jobs. Keeping in mind the economic necessity to earn for many of these children, it would not be a miss here to suggest that education could be imparted at their places of work.

Need for recreation cannot be overlooked. Any child and more so, the working child, in order to relieve him/her from the drudgery of long monotonous working hours needs recreation. Organised cultural and recreational activities either by the employer or a social welfare agency would help prevent these children from drifting into delinquency and vagrancy.

The health status of the working child needs immediate attention for a sense of total well-being. This nutritional level could possibly be enhanced by the employer by providing them nutritious food at subsidised cost. Measures also need to be taken to safeguard their health against the occupational hazards that they face. Some of the working children need immediate medical attention in terms of regular medical checkups.

Strategies for Dealing with Gender Bias in Child Labour

The various socio-economic factors combine to give most girl children lack of self-esteem and confidence. So it becomes much more challenging to initiate mobilisation of woman and children. But once the process is set in motion against discrimination, experience has shown that women and children take much easily to the concept of partnership and collective strength. However, they need continuous protection from exploiters of various categories during the entire period of mobilisation. No strategy for eradication of child labour would be successful, unless in involves the weakest amongst this section like girl children, working in unorganised sector particularly in brick industry, in the decision-making process. This is the only way to bring about a sustainable change in the ethos of a truly developed society.

Social and Other Measures

Free and compulsory elementary education for all children upto the age of 14 should be ensured immediately through the formal school system. Compulsory Education Act should be enacted in states wherever it is not done. This will be the most effective method of abolishing child labour of all kinds. If parents are guaranteed wage-employment the need for sending the child to work will be reduced.

Since formal education does not appear to be favourable with the children or the parents, the vocational (training) education contents is proposed to be made part and parcel of the general syllabus in all schools. It will be desirable if special schools are set up in as many villages as possible in the brick industry belt for this purpose. The co-operation and assistance of Non-Governmental organisation and brick manufacturers in organising such school may prove useful.

Some specific actions that are urgently needed are as follows:

- Immediate elimination of hazardous and exploitative child labour.
- Governments must fulfil their responsibility to make relevant primary education free and compulsory for all children and ensure that all children attended primary school in a full time basis until completion.
- Laws on child labour and education should be consistent in purpose and implemented in a mutually supportive way. Such legislation must encompass the vast majority of child work in the informal sector of the economy.
- All children should be registered at birth. Registration is essential to permit the exercise of the child's rights.
- Data on child labour are scarce. National and international systems must be put in place together and analyse globally comparable data on child labour, if the problem is to be addressed effectively.
- National and international corporations are urged to adopt codes of conduct guaranteeing that neither they nor their sub-contractors will employ children in conditions that violate their right.

Brick industry suffered due to existence of corruption practices between the manufacturer and Government officials. This is the reason for the absence of effective implementation of laws. The Government should form a committee under the chairmanship of retired academician (University Professor), inclusive of members from brick manufacturing, Government officials, brick workers, and few members from NGO'S. This committee will act as "suggestive body" for eradication of child labour in this industry.

References

"Child Labour in Carpet Industry", (1994), *Margin*, Vol. 27, No. 1.

Chaudhri, D.P., "Female Child Labour and Gender Bias in School Education in Indian States—1961-91 (1997), *The Indian Journal of Labour Economics*, Vol. 40, No. 3.

Chaudhri, D.P., "A Policy Perspective on Child Labour in India with Pervasive Gender and Urban Bias in School Education (1997), *The Indian Journal of Labour Economics*, Vol. 40, No. 4.

Kamala Srinivasan & Veena Gandotra (eds.) (1993), "Child Labour—Multi Dimensional Problem", Ajanta Publications, New Delhi.

Kalsi, C.L. (1989), "Tackling the Problem of Child Labour", *Yojna*, Vol. 32, No. 24.

Mohd. Mustafa & Onkar Sharma, (1996), *Child Labour in India: Bitter Truth*, Deep & Deep Publications, New Delhi.

Mookherjee, S. & Pushkar Pandya (eds.), (1985), "Child Labour in India", Gandhi Labour Institute.

Muthuraja, C. (1997), "Child Labour in Brick Industry : A Case Study (Abstract)", *The Indian Journal of Labour Economics*, Vol. 40, No. 4.

Muthuraja, C. (1997), "Socio-economic Status of Child Labour in Brick Industry", *Social Science Abstract*, Vol. 21.

Muthuraja, C. (1990), "Rural Women in Indian Agriculture", *Khadi Gramodyog*, Vol. 36, No. 8.

Muthuraja, C. (1997), "Womenfolk in Indian Agriculture: An Analysis of their Participation and Contribution" in Basant Mehta & Prakash Chandra Mehta (eds.), *Perspectives of Tribal Economy*, Intellectual Publishing House, New Delhi.

Nazir Ahmad Shah, (1992), *Child Labour in India*, Anmol Publications, New Delhi.

Neeti Mohanti (1997), "Gender Perspective in Child Labour", *Social Welfare*, Vol. 44, No. 1.

Report of the National Committee on Rural Labour: An Overview (1993), *The Indian Journal of Labour Economics*, Vol. 36, No. 1.

Subramaniyam, Y.S. & Poonam Sandhi, (1990), "Child Porters : Psycho-social Profile of Street Children", *The Indian Journal of Social Work*, Vol. LI, No. 4.

Tara Ali Baig (1979), *Our Children*, Publications Division, GOI, New Delhi.

UNICEF, (1979), *The State of the World's Children 1997*, Oxford University Press, New York.

Vijayagopalan, S. (1993), *Child Labour in Carpet Industry*, National Council of Applied Economic Research, New Delhi.

World Bank (1991), "Gender and Poverty in India".

22

Problems of Migrant Girl Child Labourers in Brick and Tiles Industry—A Case Study of Malur

—*A.C. Komala*

Introduction

Migration is a common factor in recent times. Apart from the natural increase in population, migration is a major factor in the process of urbanisation and social change. It can change the demographic feature of the region.

The reasons for migration can be many. The important factors are:

1. Economic factors like search for jobs or better jobs.
2. Social factors like Marriage, accompanying of parents or an earning member of the family.
3. Personal reasons like pursuing of higher studies or for getting access to better educational, medical and health facilities.
4. Sometimes natural calamities and political factors or lack of social security in a place (Kuntal sensama).

It is observed that the abovementioned factors also cause the Migration of rural labourers to urban areas. In addition, the programme of economic development in India which gave rise to the growth of new industrial areas pushed the tempo of migration of rural workers. So rural-to-urban migration is a pushed factor (Dandekar and Rath-1971).

When we are talking about migrant labourers particularly in an informal sector, we can certainly come across girl child labourers. Girls in rural areas associated with agriculture sector have always been participating in economic activities in one way or the other. They help their parents in cooking, fetching water, collecting fuel wood, looking after younger sisters and brothers, rearing animals and participating in agricultural activities. These activities are not considered as economic activities except their wage work.

The recent trends also witnessed the increase in the absorption of female child labour in the labour market, as it is relatively easier to offer them wages lower than the ongoing market rates (Indrani Gupta and Arup Mitra) while the work of the girls in rural India is very significantly visible in all walks of life. In urban unorganised sector girls are found to be working in some concentrations of child labour only (K. Ramachandran and others). One of such concentration which we have considered in our present study is Brick and tiles industry in Karnataka. It is attracting more migrant rural agricultural families. In this the importance of economic and social factors of migrant girl child labourers are taken into consideration. Poverty and migration with parents are the main causes for child labourers in brick and tiles industry. Acceptance of lower wages is another reason for increase[1] in girl child labourers.

In this paper, Section II highlights the reasons for taking up this topic for the study and Section III deals with background about the study area. In Section IV the working and living conditions of these migrant girl child workers is discussed. Summary and conclusions are presented in the final section.

Importance of the Present Study

Very few studies analyse the problems and prospects of female child labourers. Therefore the direct impact of any problem on their living and working conditions and on their households has not been measured. In fact to my knowledge, there are no empirical studies of migrant girl child labourers in brick and tiles industry in our country. One reason for this may be that such studies are difficult to come, because the industry is scattered in nature.

In the present study an attempt is made to correct this by using a unique set of data collected by employing ethnographic methods alongwith a survey instrument. The interview schedule was specially constructed to collect information on migrant girl labourers in brick and tiles industry. The data is from the child labourers working in different brick and tiles factories in Malur town of Kolar District in Karnataka. It is a Micro-level study. Data were collected during the period of December 1993 to March 1994.

Study Area and the Sample

Malur is one of the Municipal towns located in the Kolar District of Karnataka State. It is approximately 50 kms. away from Bangalore. It is a drought prone area with a moderate climate throughout the year. It is known for being the major concentration of brick and tiles industry because of the suitability of clay[2]. There are about 22 registered brick and tiles factories around Malur town. These units employ very simple technology with a huge manual labour. At present 2000 labourers are working in these units comprising of 40% male, 46% female and 14% child labourers. Among child labourers 80% are girls.

As far as industrial activities are concerned, the study area has an industrial estate where large number of small and medium scale industries are concentrated. It is providing employment opportunities at a bigger scale and attracting the labourers from different parts of Karnataka and neighbouring states. It has got good communication network, and basic infrastructure facilities like railways, road transport, and good educational institutions.

Working and Living Conditions of Girl Child Workers

In the present study, children aged between 5-15 years are taken into consideration. It consists of mirgant households working at brick and tiles units in Malur Town. For intensive investigation 100 girls were selected in different factories in a random order. Girls were asked about working, living and earing conditions. Girls answered clearly for some questions, and often parents answered on behalf of the younger girls. Thus the interview schedule was prepared in such a way to make convenient for them.

The literacy rates of these girls are shown in Table 22.1. As can be seen from the table 25 girls are illiterate, 63 girls have the education level of 4th std or less, and 12 girls studied upto 7th standard. This data implies that these girls must be working as productive workers inside or outside the families with or without the remuneration.

Table 22.1
Age-wise Education Level

(in Percentage)

Education Level	*Age Groups*		*Total*
	5-10 Years	*11-15 Years*	
Illiterates	12	13	25
4th std or less	24	39	63
5th-7th std.	—	12	12

Source : Field data.

The study also revealed that none of them are continuing education, and they are working on full-time basis. All these children live below poverty line. They must have stopped their education because of poverty and started as suppliers of regular income to their families.[3]

The most important aspect of child labour is their hard work. This can be revealed through the number of working hours undertaken by these girls. It can to seen from Table 22.2 that the majority of them work for long hours.

Table 22.2
Number of Working Hours Undertaken by the Sample

(in Percentage)

Working Hours	*No. of Girls (in %)*
6-7 hours	11
7-8 hours	34
More than 8 hours	56

Source : Field data.

It shows that 56% of the girls work for longer hours. Their extra work is not paid, and there is a lot of exploitation.[4]

The living conditions of these workers are measured through their wage rate and personal expenditure criteria. According to Table 22.3, 28% of the girls earn upto Rs. 100 a week, 53% of them earn between Rs. 200-300 a week.

Table 22.3
Weekly Wage Earnings of the Sample

Class Size (in Rupees)	No. of Girls (in Percentage)
Up to Rs. 100	28
Rs. 100–200	53
Rs. 200–300	09
Rs. 300–400	—

When we compare their wage earnings with the working hours, it is very much clear that they are not paid according to their labour. Their work is under-estimated. They are over-exploited by the owners.[5]

Table 22.4 shows the right of the girls over their own earned income. It reveals that their per capita personal expenditures[6] are very limited. Their highest per capita personal expenditure is Rs. 21-30 per month.

Table 22.4
Per capita Personal Expenditure of the Sample (Per Month)

Size of the Expenditure	*No. of Girls (in Percentage)*
Rs. 0–10	78
Rs. 11–20	19
Rs. 21–30	03
Rs. 31–40	—
More than Rs. 40	—

Source : Field data.

It is clear from the above table, that these girl's personal needs are very limited. They earn wage income to fight their family's poverty. Owners of brick and tiles units are not providing any welfare facilities to them. Government or the NGO's are not taking any steps to improve their condition.

Summary and Conclusion

This study is a Micro-level study. It consists of migrant household girl child workers working at brick and tiles industry in Karnataka. Due to the failure of agriculture sector and poverty, they migrated with their parents to urban areas.

They started working as wage earners to augment their family incomes. These girls are over-exploited by forcing them to work for longer hours with lower wages. These girls are working as manual labourers without having any future plans, aims or goals of their own. They are keeping away all their childhood dreams in order to supplement the income by their wages to reduce the poverty of their families.

The Micro-level studies like this are subjected to both advantages and disadvantages. Further research will have to examine if these results are more generally applicable. However, this study provided evidence to the problems of migrant girl child labourers.

Notes

1. Most of the time these girls work is not considered as wages work, instead considered as free assistance.
2. The other reasons are availability of cheap labour and fuel wood. Most of the owners of these brick and tiles units belongs to pottern community where they have got some special skills in running these production units.
3. Most of the children in this sample survey stated that they started this work as supplement labourers during their mother's or siblings ill health, or during their mother's pregnancy or delivery period. Their work is considered as wage work in the place of their mothers absence. They were not getting equal wage but job guarantee is there.
4. Since the industry is seasonal in character. During full reason summary these girls work 12-13 hrs. a day and during off season they work 8-9 a hrs. a day regularly. Their extra work during full season is not paid but employment guarantee will be there. Another important factor is all these girls families are located within the factory premises. During early morning and late evening they work as housemaids in there owners houses.
5. The employment guarantee is depended on the sweat nature of the employer. If they demand for higher wages, there is a chance of loosing job. So they never demand for higher wage. The wage rate, can increase only at the mercy of the owner.
6. Their personal expenditure consisted of Kumkum Bindis, Ribbons, Hair Bands, Bangles, flowers, some snackes and Bananas.

References

1. Chaudhri, D. P., (1997) " Policy Perspective on Child Labour in India with Pervasive Gender and Urban Bias in School Education," *Indian Journal of Labour Economics*, Vol. 40, No. 4, pp. 789-808.
2. Duraisamy, Malathy, (1997), *Changes in Child Labour Over Space and Time in India—1981-91*, IJLE, Vol. 40, No. 4, pp. 809-18.
3. Komala, A.C. (1994), *Working Women and their Problems in Brick and Tiles Industry in Kolar District*, Unpublished M.Phil. Dissertation, Bangalore University, Bangalore.
4. Gupta, Indrani & Mitra, Arup, (1997), *Child Labour a Project in Delhi Slums*, IJLE, Vol. 40, No. 4, pp. 841-47.
5. Oberai, A.S. and Singh, Man Mohan H.K., (1984), "Migration Employment and the Urban Labour Market—A Study in the Indian Punjab," *International Labour Review*, Vol. 123, No. 4, July-Aug. 1984.
6. Swamy, Nathan Madhura, (1997), *Do Child Workers Acquire Specialised Skills? A Case Study of Teenage Workers in Bhavnagar*, IJLE, Vol. 40, No. 4, pp. 830-39.
7. Sensarma, Kuntal, *Migrant Labour in Urban Areas—Dimensions and Determinants*, IJLE, Vol. 40, No. 20, 1997.
8. Stretton, Alan, (1983), "Circular Migration, Regranted Labour Markets and Efficiency—The Building Industry in Manela and Post Moresby," *International Labour Review*, Vol. 122, No. 5, Sept.-Oct. 1983.

23

Child Labour in Handloom Industry: A Case Study

—*N. Narayana*

Child labour means the employment of children (5 to 14 years of age) in gainful occupations, which are injurious to their physical, mental, moral and social development. The children belonging to meagre family incomes are compelled to join the labour force to supplement the family income. Generally, people from lower strata of our society send their children for work instead of sending them to school for education. The growing number of child labourers all over the world causes serious concern to those who are interested in child welfare both in developed and developing countries. In India the size of the child labour force is not only large but has increased from year to year inspite of International Labour Organisation's conventions, labour legislations and India's commitment to universal and compulsory education upto the age of 14 years.

According to International Labour Organisation's recent report about 250 million children are working in developing countries. An ILO survey published earlier this year estimated that 73 million children aged between 10 to 14 were working full-time in 100 countries. The new estimates suggest that 120 million children of five year and upwards are working full-time and another 130 million are working part-time. The report also point out that child labour is increasing in the third world because of urban expansion. In case of India, the percentage of child labour to total population is almost stable during 1961-81. But it is declining in the case of rural areas and increasing in urban areas. The percentage of child labour to total child population declined from 8.04 to 5.17 per cent during this period. Though the percentage of child labour to total workers declined by 2 per cent during 1961-81, the absolute number is increasing. Majority of the child labourers are engaged in the agricultural sector as cultivators and agriculture labour while the rest are in the manufacturing and other industrial activities. The census data indicates that the component of employment of child labour in the non-agricultural activities like manufacturing, trade and commerce etc., has been increasing over the last two decades. It is evident from the census data that highest per cent is registered in Andhra Pradesh (3.28%) in 1981, while it is 1.68% for all India, followed by Meghalaya (2.98%), Madhya Pradesh (2.63%), and Karnataka (2.60%). The lower percentage of child worker to total population are found in Lakshdeep (0.08%), Kerala (0.27%), Delhi (0.40%), Chandigarh (0.43%) and Andaman and Nicobar Islands (0.45%). Over 90 per cent of child labourers are to be found in eleven states.

Poverty forces the parents to send their children to seek employment because augmentation of their income is essential for the survival of the families which are invariably large. Illiteracy, ignorance, low wages, unemployment, poor standard of living, deep social prejudices and backwardness are some of the major factors responsible for child labour. The children work in various sectors like agriculture, plantation, match factories, zari industries, glass factories, firecracker industries, shoe-making factories, eating joints, domestic servant, prostitutes and other areas and subjected to very harsh working conditions. The largest share of employment of children in Andhra Pradesh is found in rural agrarian sector, household industry and followed by different activities within urban informal sector.

The prominent age old household industry in India is the handloom industry. The handloom industry is an important constituent of the decentralised sector of the Indian economy which contributes not only to employment generation and cloth production but also to the national exchequer. Despite the eminent position enjoyed by this sector, it is beset with a series of problems which ultimately culminated in starvation and suicide deaths of handloom weavers in Andhra Pradesh recently. This paper has particular relevance in view of the recent death toll due to hunger and starvation of weavers in Mangalagiri mandal.

Handloom industry, with its vast network of about 5 million handlooms, occupies a predominant place in India today, providing employment to about 15 million people mostly drawn from rural areas and the handloom industry alone accounts for more than one-third of the total exports of the country. Handloom Industry in Andhra Pradesh occupies most important place in the economy next to agriculture. Andhra Pradesh weavers produce the finest silk brocades and cotton fabrics. Among the silk weavers the Dharmavaram silk, Gadwal and Kottakotha Sarees are famous in the world. Among cotton sarees, the most prominent varieties are the Venkatagiri Sarees and Siddipeta Sarees.

Mangalagiri cotton Sarees are also very famous at nation level. Recently, 'punjabi dresses' produced in Mangalagiri are moving in markets very fastly. Andhra Pradesh, has nearly 8.30 lakhs of handlooms constituting more than one sixth of the total handlooms in the country.

Guntur District is having nearly, 40,000 looms, while there are 3,800 looms in Mangalagiri. Mangalagiri town is purposively selected to study the socio-economic conditions of child workers engaged in different stages of production of cloth in the handloom industry. The objective of this paper is to probe into the causes and conditions of child labour working in handloom industry in Mangalagiri town of Andhra Pradesh. Broadly this study explains socio-economic profile, conditions of child labour, nature and type of employment, levels of living and reasons for taking up employment in this sector.

According to information furnished by the Mandal Revenue Office and Mangalagiri Weavers Co-operative Society, more than 40 per cent of the town population is engaged in this handloom industry. Out of 26,000 weavers about 4,000 children are directly or indirectly working in this industry. This activity is predominantly concentrated in the areas like Damarla Ramakantha Rao Colony, Indira Nagar, Koppuravuru Nagar Colony, and Bhargavapet. These four localities are purposively selected to identify the working children in each household. Appropriate questions are included in the schedule to identify the households having working children. 5 per cent random sampling is selected constitutes 200 households having atleast one child labour below 14 years of age. Information was solicited personally through a pre-tested questionnaire from each household.

Major Findings of the Study

The socio-demographic features of the sample households of working children are studied in relation to age, sex, caste/religion, level of education, family size, type of residential accommodation etc. The survey result reveals that about 54 per cent working children are girls (Table 23.1). About 90 per cent of the child workers belong to the age group of 9 to 14 years in the study area. The peculiar feature that can be observed in this study is that most of these working children are school going children. In the sense that these are regular (part-time) workers assisting their parents in various stages of production to supplement the family income. Most (48.5%) of the children belong to a big size of family of 6-8 members, followed by 4-6 members size family (27%). Very small size of family are comparatively less prevalent in the study area. All the households belong to the same community namely 'Padmasali', who are listed under Backward Class in Hindu religion, indicating their continuation in their own caste-based professional occupations. In the sense that the question of occupational mobility doesn't appear in the light of modernization. Regarding the residential accommodation it is found that 70.25 per cent of the sample workers lived in own accommodation, 23.40 per cent lived in rented accommodation and 6.35 per cent are in vacant places occupied by these people. About 65 per cent of the families are living in huts in slum areas, while 30 per cent are in sheds and only 5 per cent of the sample workers are staying in pucca buildings. 60.82 per cent of child workers are living in electrified houses and the remaining 39.18 per cent are staying in non-electrified houses.

Broadly child workers in Handloom industry are found to be working in 4 types of works. They are namely winders, pern winders, sizers and helpers. It is evident from the data that majority of the child worker are winders (35%) followed by pern winders

Table 23.1

Socio and Demographic Characteristics of Working Children

Age Group	*Male*	*Female*	*Total*
5 - 6	1 (1.09)	2 (1.85)	3 (1.5)
7 - 8	7 (7.61)	11 (10.19)	18 (9.00)
9 - 10	19 (20.65)	37 (34.26)	56 (28.00)
11 - 12	36 (39.13)	31 (28.70)	67 (33.50)
13 - 14	29 (31.52)	27 (25.00)	56 (28.00)
Total	92 (100.00)	108 (100.00)	200 (100.00)

Education Level

Literacy Level	*Male*	*Female*	*Total*
Illiterate	2 (2.17)	5 (4.63)	7 (3.50)
Primary	28 (30.44)	37 (34.26)	65 (32.50)
Upper Primary	39 (42.49)	47 (43.52)	86 (43.00)
High School	23 (25.00)	19 (17.60)	42 (21.00)
Total	92 (100.00)	108 (100.00)	200 (100.00)

Size of the Family

Size of the Family	*Number*	*Per cent*
Below 4	21	10.50
4 - 6	54	27.00
6 - 8	97	48.50
8 - 10	28	14.00
Total	200	100.00

(32%), sizers (27%) and helpers (6%) respectively (Table 23.2). Among the above four types of works sizers are called as skilled workers, constituting only 27 per cent of the workforce compared to winders and pern-winders. Regarding the nature of the employment of these workers, the results show that more than 55 per cent are regular part-time workers. Within this category more than 87.39 per cent (Table 23.3) of child workers are unpaid family workers, who are school going children. The children are contributing to enhance the earnings of their family while pursuing their studies regularly. The data also reveals another important feature that more than 65 per cent of the regular full-time child workers are wage earners who are identified as school droputs. This distribution of working children by the type of employment and working hours explain that these workers have no fixed working hours. Also it varies from one to another type of work. For example, more than 70 per cent of the winders, who are regular part-time workers, are working for less than 6 hours per day. But more than 90% of the skilled sizers who happen to be the regular full-time wage earners (piece rate) are working for 6 to 12 hours a day (Table 23.4)

As per the results furnished in Table 23.5 on the causes of child labour in household industry in the study area, 56.5 per cent of them are pursuing in this industry due to poverty and unemployment or under-employment of parents and to clear their family debts. Similarly, about 26 per cent of child workers are owing to the socio-demographic reasons such as their willingness to continue in their own caste profession, big size of family, death of father, death of mother or both etc. Only 17.5 per cent of them are due to lack of interest to go to school and the reluctance of their parents to send them to school.

With regard to the levels of earnings of child labour in this industry, out of 200 sample workers more than 51 per cent of them are earnings less than Rs. 200 per month and the remaining are receiving between Rs. 200 to Rs. 350 per month (Table 23.6). The distribution of household income including and excluding income from child labour is furnished in Table 23.7. The data in the table shows that 23.5 per cent of the households had an income of less than Rs. 2,000 per month. But none of the household receive an income of less than Rs. 1,000 per month. On the other hand, when the income from the child labour is excluded, it is found that 37.5 per cent of households received an income of less than Rs. 2,000

Table 23.2

Distribution of Working Children by the Type of Work

Type of Work	*Male*	*Female*	*Total*
Winders	31 (33.70)	39 (36.11)	70 (35.00)
Pern-winders	27 (29.35)	37 (34.26)	64 (32.00)
Sizers	31 (33.70)	23 (21.30)	54 (27.00)
Helpers	3 (3.26)	9 (8.33)	12 (6.00)
Total	92 (100.00)	108 (100.00)	200 (100.00)

Table 23.3

Distribution of Working Children by their Type of Employment, Nature of Employment and Employment Status

Type of Employment	*Nature of Employment*				
	Regular Full-time		*Regular Part time*		*Total*
	Wage Worker	*Unpaid Family Worker*	*Wage Worker*	*Unpaid Family Worker*	
Winders	9 (15.52)	4 (12.90)	1 (7.14)	56 (57.73)	70 (35.00)
Pern-winders	22 (37.93)	8 (25.81)	5 (35.71)	29 (29.90)	64 (32.00)
Sizers	24 (41.38)	17 (54.84)	6 (42.86)	7 (7.22)	54 (27.00)
Helpers	3 (5.17)	2 (6.45)	2 (14.29)	5 (5.15)	12 (6.00)
Total	58	31	14	97	200

Table 23.4
Distribution of Working Children by their Type of Employment and Working Hours

Working Hours	*Type of Employment*				Total
	Winders	Pern Winders	Sizers	Helpers	
0 - 2	1	0	0	1	2
	(1.43)	(0.00)	(0.00)	(8.33)	(1.00)
2 - 4	19	3	1	7	30
	(27.14)	(4.69)	(1.85)	(58.33)	(15.00)
4 - 6	28	8	3	4	43
	(40.00)	(12.50)	(5.56)	(33.33)	(21.50)
6 - 8	17	12	9	0	38
	(24.29)	(18.75)	(16.67)	(0.00)	(19.00)
8 - 10	4	21	21	0	46
	(5.71)	(32.81)	(38.89)	(0.00)	(23.00)
10 - 12	1	16	11	0	28
	(1.43)	(25.00)	(20.37)	(0.00)	(14.00)
12 - +	0	4	9	0	13
	(0.00)	(6.25)	(16.67)	(0.00)	(6.50)
Total	70	64	54	12	200
	(100.00)	(100.00)	(100.00)	(100.00)	(100.00)

Table 23.5
Reasons for Taking up of Employment by Child Labour

Type of Reason	*Number*	*Per cent*
1. Economic		
(a) Poverty	72	36.00
(b) To clear debts	24	12.00
(c) Desire to Earn money	17	8.50
2. Socio-Demographic		
(a) To continue tradition	8	4.00
(b) To learn work	19	9.50
(c) Big size of family	12	6.00
(d) Father is not alive	3	1.50
(e) Mother is not alive	1	0.50
(f) Both are not alive	9	4.50
3. Education		
(a) Not interested in studies	16	8.00
(b) Parents are not interested to send school	19	9.50
Total	200	100.00

Table 23.6

Distribution of Working Children by their Monthly Earnings

Earnings per Month (in Rs.)	*Male*		*Female*		*Total*	
	Number	*Per cent*	*Number*	*Per cent*	*Number*	*Per cent*
100-150	14	15.23	11	10.19	25	12.50
150-200	31	33.70	46	42.59	77	38.50
200-250	35	38.04	32	29.63	67	33.50
250-300	7	7.61	12	11.11	19	9.50
300-and above	5	5.42	7	6.48	12	6.00
Total	92	100.00	108	100.00	200	100.00

Table 23.7

Distribution of Households by Household Income (Including and Excluding Child Labourer's Income)

Household Monthly Income size (in Rs.)	*Including Child Labourer's Income*		*Excluding Child Labourer's Income*	
	No. of Households	*Per cent*	*No. of Households*	*Per cent*
500 - 1000	—	—	9	4.50
1000 - 1500	9	4.50	32	16.00
1500 - 2000	38	19.00	34	17.00
2000 - 2500	97	48.50	92	46.00
2500 - 3000	48	24.00	30	15.00
3000 - 3500	8	4.00	3	1.50
Total	200	100.00	200	100.00

Mean	2270.00	2027.50
C.V.	94.90	188.87

and 20 per cent received less than Rs. 1,500 per month. This analysis indicates that child labour tends to raise the levels of household income, especially the weaving community which has been figured in the low income brackets. The mean households income of the sample households is raised by Rs. 242.5 per month through the contribution of child labour. Further, the co-efficient of variation is also substantially reduced indicating that the child labour not only increases the household income but also reduces the variations in it.

through the contribution of child labour. Further, the co-efficient of variation is also substantially reduced indicating that the child labour not only increases the household income but also reduces the variations in it.

As the above analysis indicate the child labours contribution towards household income, it is pertinent to examine its contribution as a percentage to total household income. This has been computed and presented in Table 23.8. The results indicate that in nearly 55 per cent of the households, the contribution of child labour towards households is more than 20 per cent. But 7 per cent of the households are found to be receiving an income where the contribution of children is more than 40 per cent. However, the results reveal that in about 80 per cent of the households the contribution of child labour to total household income is between 20 to 40 per cent. Thus the child labour placed in the household industry seems to contribute significant amount to the family earnings.

Table 23.8

Contribution of Child Labour in Total Household Income

Contribution of Child Labour to Total Household Income (per cent)	*Number of Households*	*Per cent*
Less than 10	17	8.50
10 - 20	73	36.50
20 - 30	85	42.50
30 - 40	11	5.50
40 - 50	8	4.00
50 and above	6	3.00
Total	200	100.00

It can be concluded from the foregoing analysis that the handloom industry is providing employment and income to the child workers in the study area. The major reasons for the child labour are poverty and unemployment or under-employment of the parents and indebtedness of the households. As there is no legal protection to the workers in this sector a comprehensive legislation is to be enacted and implemented effectively to safeguard the interests of the child workers in the handloom industry. Provision of non-formal education during night times and establishment of training centres to enable the child labour to work with improved technology, and implementation of Minimum Wages Act and regulation or working hours alongwith basic minimum facilities can improve significantly the contribution of child labour to his family earnings.

Section - IV

CHARACTERISTICS OF CHILD LABOUR IN INDIA

24

Socio-Economic Dimensions of Child Labour in India

— Raghuraman Narayan, T. Karunakaran & Sriman Narayanan

SECTION I

Introduction

Child labour in India is a grim reality. All know that it cannot be done away with legislation as it involves complicated socio economic problem. We cannot say that the problem is purely economic. As many studies have proved that social aspect of the problem is also prominent.

Our approach to the problem of Child Labour in India would analyse the problem from various angles.

Child Labour is a passing phase during the period of economic development. Even in England, during 18th Century the children were forced to hard, long hazardous work. (South Gate: Modern Economic Development of England).

Children were tied to a pole, wrapped on with sack were asked toclaim thechimneys of the smoke chimney to clean them. Whipping the boys when they were about to fall asleep, was not uncommon during the 18th century England.

However, the child labour problem came to limelight when the World Trade Organisation protested against the child labour employment in Third World Countries.

B.B.C. through it's telecasting a feature on child labour employment in carpet weaving caught the attention of the world.

UNICEF and some Non-Government Organisations highlighted the problems of child labour concentrated areas. (Indian examples, Sivakasi in Tamilandu and Carpet weaving in U.P.)

The Nobel Laureates (1996) made call to eradicate child labour.

The U.S. Senator, Tom Harkins brought Child Labour Deterrent Act in U.S. Senate (1996).

The sequence of events show a western bias on child labour problem in developing Third World Countries.

Legislations cannot solve the problem of child labour, as already said it is multi-faceted issue.

It is a complex problem involving economic growth, demographic transition, poverty, social set-up and other inter-linked complex issues.

Poverty, demographic transition, lack of employment generation, hurdles in mobility of labour, social fabric result in Child Labour. A multi-dimensional approach to child labour is necessary. Irrelevant education, unimpressive teaching at primary level and another dimension to the problem.

SECTION II

Supply Theory and Labour

The general supply and demand theory deviates when applied to labour. We treat labour as a commodity. Unlike other commodities; labour is wanted only when the goods produced by labour are wanted. In Economics, we call it as derived demand. Commodities get prices. Labour get wages. Wage is the price of labour.

The general commodity market act with change in prices. When the prices shrink, the supply comes down. When the prices increase the supply goes up.

In labour market when the price increases (wage) the supply decreases. For example, when the husband earns enough money he may stop his wife from going for employment. Likewise when the price (wages) comes down the supply of labour goes up. When the adult income is low, he may send his wife and children for employment.

In my opinion the child labour is an indicator of low adult wages.

There may be a number of reasons for low adult wages. Increase in supply of labour due to population increase, or increase in supply of labour in the particular area due to immobility of labour to migrate from one area to another, mechanisation may reduce the demand for labour (technology) and other factors.

Malthus and Supply of Labour

According to Malthus or Physiocrates, the labour should get wages at a level in which he and his family can subsists. When the wages fall below the level, the population may shrink and wages may increase.

When the population increases due to low death rate and higher birth rate, the supply of labour increases and the wages fall. If the adult wages are high, children get married at an early age and get children. It would push the population level. As a consequence wages may come down for adults. Such a situation may force the adult to send his wife and children for employment to reach subsistence level.

Income of labour is determined by many factors. Labour cannot move from low wages area to higher wages area freely.

As an economist commented, among the goods, labour is more difficult to be transported. Women may get higher wages at a distance from their place of living. She may not be able to go for physical security reasons. That is one of the reasons of low women wages. Language, climate, religion may create an impediment in movement of labour. For example, the Muslim women in Tamilnadu do not move out of their house for employment. They seek some work to be done in their houses itself. It is exploited by the employers. (*e.g.* low wages offered in beedi rolling).

A study conducted among workers (unmarried) in Tirupur, Bombay and Coimbatore by a group of sociologists revealed that many prefer to remain single due to low wages. The theory of shrinking family size when wages are low is proved.

Poverty may not be the sole cause for child labour. In a consumer economy children may be sent for employment to buy more of consumer goods. In middle class families women are sent for employment to buy the consumer durables. At what cost? (social)—is a separate issue.

Why International Objection to Child Labour?

According to Americans (US), when child labour is used, the prices are lower by 30%. Under such a situation, countries with higher labour standard cannot compete with goods manufactured using child labour. According to Marshall (1994) bad labour standards drive good labour standards out. It is an extension of Gresham's Law.

The Child Labour Deterrence Act of U.S. is nothing but a protectionists policy. Sri Subramaniam Swamy's report on Child Labour Standard is more realistic. He suggested social security measures at par with adult labour (1996).

Grootsert and Kambur (1995), emphasise that child labour standard could alter the bargaining power and welfare of the children; while weakening the economic position of the families.

There is another view by Basu and Van (1996). According to them the abolition of child labour will push the adult wages, possibly to the point where families are wealthy enough that they no longer need their children to work. (My first part of the paper deals with emergence of child labour due to low adult wages is confounded. I have quoted D. H. Robertson (1955) to substantiate the point).

There is another view on abolition of child labour without making a birth for them. It says that a legislation to that effect may push the children from one sector to another; which may be socially undesirable. Only relevant schooling will attract children to school.

Prof. D.H. Robertson in his book on 'Principles of Economics' related wages; cost of living; supply of labour. According to him the wages are inadequate for an adult due to high cost of living. The supply of labour will increase as men and women are offered in job market. The population increase results in increased supply of labour and the consequent low wages. As the wages are low the unskilled workers try to enhance their income by getting more children.

It is like a vicious cycle. Workers get more children to meet the kitchen cost. More children add pressure on food. Increased demand for food lead to increase in the prices of food articles.

Market Failure

Low wages for adults keep the pressure on family for more income and the tender hands are put to work. A recent research paper (Finance & Development) on 'International Labour Standards and

Trade', explains the sequence. The Labour Market fails due to low adult wages leading to the entry of child labour. Information in the labour market is imperfect. For example, employees may have adequate information on safety conditions. Employer may have an incentive to conceal risks. It happens in casual labour market. For example the worker engaged in hazardous work are not covered by insurance.

The employer may not bring them under insurance coverage either due to lack of information or to avoid expense.

Another example—child labourers are often imperfectly mobile, which confers some monoposony powers to the employers. When employers have monoposony powers over workers, a skillfully set minimum wage could increase wages, employment and welfare. If minimum wage is set too high, it could reduce employment and efficiency; even in monoposonist labour market. Such a situation may lead to the award of wages unrelated to productivity differentiating sex, race, age—extend the logic. (In real world it happens. Non-Muslim workers are paid lower wages in middle - east). Wages are differentiated between sex and age in real World Labour Market (Unorganised).

Unless labour standard is set, it will lead to reduction of labour standard in other countries. It will further lead to unemployment.

For example, in low-income countries child labour may be used to manufacture export goods (*e.g.* Carpets—Knitwear). The price will be lower by 30% when compared to goods produced by the adult worker (unskilled) in other countries. As a result the importing country may not be able to sell it's own goods. It will result in unemployment in importing country. The importing country should accept either low wages or face unemployment.

SECTION III

Child Labour—Today's India

Nearly 40% of 226 million children below five years are living in developed countries. In India correct figures of children working in hazardous and non-hazardous industries in not spelt out. 1981 and 1991 census put the figure of child labour in the country as 13 million and 11 million. (The decrease of 2 million has been shown in 1981 and 1991 census. The Baroda based operation research group puts it as 44 million. Recently (8-7-97) the official figures in 14 States and 3 Union Territories put it 5 lakhs).

The figures are confusing, whether it is from Government or Private Research Organisation.

In this unit an attempt has been made to highlight the problems of child labour in different parts of the country. More than numbers, the plight of the children will help the researchers to understand the depth of the problem.

Case Studies

Tiruchirapalli

It is a corporation around 300 Kms. south of Chennai. It is more a pilgrim centres. 40 years ago, now hubbing with industrial activity due to the establishment of BHEL, Central Government rifle factory etc.

Murugan, a boy of 10 years, working in a gem (artificial) factory for the past six years as his father has borrowed Rs. 600 from its owner. The loan is yet to be repaid. It is a case of 'Bonded' child labour. The boy earns Rs. 15 a day (1997).

In Trichy district 6000 child workers are employed in hazardous industries like, synthetic gem cutting, quarrying, stone-crushing and beedi rolling.

Coimbatore

It is a very big industrial city in Tamilnadu. It has become very famous after series of bomb-blasts during general elections. According to Non-Government Organisation the total number of child labour in Tirupur (Part of Coimbatore District) is around 30,000-60,000. If the figures are to be believed, it is next to Sivakasi of Tamilnadu, internationally famous for Child Labour. As too many publications have come about it, the place has been left out in our paper.

The official version is 10,600 child labourers are working in this area (1996).

Many work in hosiery units. It is a place in Tamilnadu where there is no employment for unskilled. But many could not survive as water availability is only 4 lts. per head as standards fix it as 40 lts. for good living.

Madurai

In this section I have taken only the case of street children. A NGO has fixed up the figures as 6,000 (1997).

The NGO has contact with street children from 1990. Among them 4,000 are boys and 2,000 are girls. (figures rounded up). Their earnings are between Rs. 30-60 a day. Many are the victims of the society. Drunkard parent, broken families, bad environment drives them to Madurai from neighbouring villages.

The unique feature of these children is that they do not like regular employment in establishments. When the NGO got them placement in workshops, hotels they ran away after a month and went to street back.

They say the income is enough for their living and enjoy independence. (The trade-off regular employment to breath the air of independence).

Surprisingly their income is more than that of adult workers in the villages.

The 'gang' rivalry and trafficking are part of their life. Dadas in making, if steps are not taken.

Salem

It is at the foot-hills of Western Ghats, famous for its steel factory. The famous 'brigand' Veerappan is operating only in the region around. Kollimalai, a hill near the town (city) is famous for herbal medicines.

Child labour is an issue to be noted. Many parents 'bond' their children for Rs. 1,000—3,000. Likewise nearly 60,000 bonded children are working in powerlooms (1997 June). Night shift for children is a special feature of child labour. Children between 5-6 years are only preferred for work. 'SMILE' an NGO is trying to bring the problem to an end.

There are many places in Tamilnadu which employ child labour in manufacturing. Vellore is the first area which adopted the bonded child labour practice. Beedi rolling is the main spot for employing child labour.

Kanchipuram, a famous silk centre near Madras (more nearer to Sriperumbudur, the place of Rajiv Gandhi's assassination) employs several thousands of child workers in weaving. It is similar to Carpet Industry of Northern U.P.

In my opinion child labour in organised sector alone is taken for our study.

No attempt has been made to identify non-working and non-school going children in villages. Their number may outnumber the child workers under our focus.

In agriculture several thousands are working at home doing cattle rearing, household chores etc.

SECTION IV

International Views on Child Labour

The Child Labour problem is entering into International Agenda of 21st Century. In 1977 a conference on child labour was conducted in Oslo of Norway. The conference pointed out as a first step bonded and hazardous industries employment of child labour should be eliminated.

The Oslo conference stressed the need for affordable, accessible, relevant education alone keep them off from working. (we will discuss it under Indian conditions in the latter part of the paper).

The mobilisation of social awareness is stressed.

International Voluntary Organisations like 'Save the Children Alliance' opined that poverty is the main cause of child labour.

NGO's recommended the following steps to eradicate child labour at International level. They are:

(a) Faster debt relief to poorer countries.
(b) Slow pace of structural adjustment.
(c) Ensuring living wages to adults. (refer Section-I of the paper)
(d) Poverty eradication.

Poverty eradication is a long-term measure. Short-term measures should be taken to relieve bonded child labour and children working in hazardous industries. In UN convention the children's right to work has no place. In the 'Rights of the Child' document, right to work has no place. Neera Bura a researcher on children says that the child has got right for education and childhood. The theme of the conference is to mobilise social opinion for child education and against child labour. Unless it is done legislations and enforcement will fail (in the latter part of the paper the Indian situation is studied).

The Government should give financial assistance to parents to send their children to school.

Bura says paying the parents to send their children to school will not work sustainably. Poverty is linked to child labour and formal education is necessary to eradicate it.

Indian representative of the conference at Oslo brought the following resolutions:

(a) Define children being out of school is intolerable form of child labour.
(b) Impose International standards and monitoring and time frames for elimination of child labour.
(c) Adopt social labelling of products from countries having child labour.

However, the fourth clause was opposed that it is another form of protectionists policy.

The language of 'rights' by developed countries by introducing the International labour standard will affect the sovereignty of many poor countries.

Human Rights Watch pointed out child labour in hazardous industries of India.

'The Small Hands of Slavery' a book on child labour say that there are 15 million bonded child labourers in India (17th January, 1998). They work from the age of 2 till growing into adult to pay the loan of Rs. 2,000 (average) got by parents. If the Government minimum wages act is implemented, their loans would have been wiped off within 6 weeks. Many of the workers are working in export industries. Children were affected severely not out of poverty, but exploitation of poverty. Stopping exploitation will remove poverty. (a case study of such an act has been given at the end of the paper).

Indian View on Child Labour

Child Labour (Prohibition & Regulation) Act of 1986 made provision for the rehabilitation of child workers from Child Labour Rehabilitation and Welfare Fund. In India many child workers are employed in hazardous industries, like match making, fireworks, carpet weaving, hosiery, powerlooms, diamond cutting, polishing etc.

Many studies pointed out poverty as the main cause of child labour. It is at macro level. At micro level family is responsible.

If poverty is the only reason we may find it difficult to prove it as child labour is also growing in developed countries also.

UNICEF pointed out that many advanced countries also employ child labour and their number is increasing.

Kalpana Sharma has written in one of her articles in The Hindu that there are many variables accounting for child labour. (Hindu, December 20, 1996) Poverty is linked to child labour in some countries and not all the countries.

Even Indian researchers have pointed out many causes for child labour. A Madurai (Tamilnadu) study says that other than poverty, drunkard parents, broken families, childhood friends also matter in driving a child as labour.

A researcher came out with following facts on school dropouts (study area Coimbatore):

- *(a)* The education and environment is uninspiring. (the same reason was spelt out in Sivakasi, Tamilnadu)
- *(b)* Alphabets and numerals are rebaffling. (in one case a boy who has finished primary education could not write in his own mother tongue).
- *(c)* No scope for trade learning which would give him better life. (Studies unrelated to life).

International confederation of Free Trade Unions, said that child labour employment is illegal and the use of child labour in unregistered units cost the exchequer several million dollars, which could be used for providing schooling for children. Simple one per cent tax on carpet exports from India is sufficient to educate child labour. They suggest the 'RUGMARK' carpets (no child labour involved) is acceptable even at a higher price by the foreign consumers. One per cent tax is sufficient to rehabilitate them. ICFTU says that Multi-national companies in India exploit child labour in diamond cutting. It happens in Surat. The children should be removed from their jobs and paid compensation. The MNC and their sub-contractors should respect International Labour Standard and should keep off from children.

Beneficiary Pays Concept

It is similar to polluter pays concept.

A memorandum of Understanding was signed by Bangladesh Garment Manufacturing and Export Association (BGMA) and the Sialkot Chamber of Commerce and Industry (SCCI) with the ILO and UNICEF for planned and phased removal of child labour from garment and soccer ball stitch industry.

It is suggested instead of passing resolution, it is time to bring the local and multi-national employers to table and make them commit.

In Oslo conference, the Indian delegation did not make single concrete commitment, but got removed uncomfortable clauses from the Agenda of Action.

Japan, Sweden and Norway promised more fund to Egypt, Indonesia and Philippines.

The main outcome of the Oslo conference was to make countries accept minimum age for employment and phased out eradication of child labour but without agreeing to any time frame.

However, the Oslo conference on 'Small hands of Slavery' has created International awareness to eradicate child labour.

Indian Exercise in Eradication of Child Labour

Child Labour (Prohibition & Regulation) Act was passed in the year 1986. It was due to Supreme Court's intervention. More than 10 years have passed till then. Many theoretical analysis were conducted to find the root of child labour. Poverty was found guilty. Further studies said that poverty is not the only variable promoting child labour. Child Labour Rehabilitation and Welfare Fund was initiated by Sri Narasimha Rao. The allocation was insufficient for any quick remedy. The Supreme Court ordered, children working in match industry, fireworks, diamond cutting should be rehabilitated. Hotels and automobile workshops should keep children off. (I wish to differ from this opinion. Hotels are the first place to entry for destitutes. In automobile workshop they learn some trade which would foot them at a higher pedestal of life. Learning mere numericals and alphabets will not lead them to a job).

Tamilnadu conducted a State Level conference on child labour. (1977 March). The children said, "Either let us live or give us our way". In Tamilnadu the problem of child labour has been left to non-Governmental Organisation.

The conference was different. They allowed the children working in organised and unorganised sector to speak.

The children deposed before a five member jury. The 'Campaign Against Child Labour' said that more than 3 million children are working in Tamilnadu. (Let us recall the Government's estimate of child labour is only 2 million in the whole country. We are baffled with figures by Government and non-Government).

Most of the children are working in hazardous industries. 12 such sectors were notified. They are: dyeing, bleaching, handlooms, powerlooms, knitwear, metal works, fisheries (processing units) tanneries, gem cutting, match industries, fireworks, and construction.

The over-worked and under-nourished children (girl) are sexually abused in Tourists centres. (Even boys are abused in Kovalam resort (beach of Kerala). They are all under-paid and aired their desire to study.

We have given here few cases to strengthen our statements.

A 13 year old Alamelu from Senur near Vellore from the age of 10. She gets Rs. 10 to roll 1000 beedies a day (1997). Beedi rolling cause lung problems at a tender age. She attends a night school run by child welfare department. She says poverty is the reason.

Vinayagamoorthi, another boy 10 year old, was sent to beedi rolling to redeem his father's debt. He say he must work for his food.

Thousands of children in eversilver polishing units of Chennai work in ill-ventilated rooms and often suffer from cuts by the sheets.

Tamilnadu Act of Compulsory Primary Education (1994) failed to have any impact.

Life of Child Labour in Various Cities of Tamilnadu

An attempt has been made to focus the problems of child labour through narration of specific cases. The World Bank in one of it's publication said that poverty cannot be understood by providing figures, like calories of intake, housing, clothing etc. They described the life style of few families in different parts of the country to explain the plight.

Likewise examples of Child Labour employment from various centres of Tamilandu are given below.

More than money, productive and creative thinking is not found in many school dropouts. Though full meal is provided some dropouts prefer to keep off from the school and ear the leftovers at home. Why such a thinking? Uninteresting classes and ill-motivated teachers are responsible for such a situation.

A boy in Madurai, working in a workshop gets only Rs. 5 for the work from dawn to dusk. Besides low wages he is ill-treated in the workshop.

Shakunthala, aged 12, a girl child working in a beedi rolling centre in Tirunelveli for the last three years. Her father died three years ago. She has to earn alongwith her mother to make out a living. She joined the work after completing primary schooling.

Drunkard husband drove Shakunthala's mother to leave the family with her daughter. The old women wants to lead a peaceful life without a man's help.

Nine year old Kesavan (boy) from Nilakottai (Madurai district) is working with a flower trader. He wakes up by 2.30 AM (wean hours). He completes his job of plucking the flowers by six. Then assists to pack the flowers to be transported. He gets Rs. 15 a day (1997). Reason—drunkard father.

Lakshmi, a twelve year old girl (Trichy district) is working as a baby sister at Madurai. She is also cooking. She says that she is happy with shelter and wholesome food. She says that she may not be going to school even if she is with her parents. She is satisfied that she gets good food. The reason for her childhood job is that her father has deserted her mother. (I myself has seen several cases in my village, Royampettai, Thanjavur District, Tamilnadu).

Ramu, an office boy in Nagapattinam, was deserted by his father after his mother's death. He would have eloped somebody in that area and simply disappeared leaving his 6 years old son in the street. Result he works as a child labour. He gets a wage of Rs. 3 a day.

The above case studies from different parts of Tamilnadu (representative) make us conclude, as follows:

The main problem is attitudes. Lack of family attachment, fall in moral values, wrong priorities, attitude towards education, absence of human dimension in decision taking of parents regarding the children, poverty and loss of bread winner make people to take this hard decision.

This part of the paper concludes that main cause of child labour is more than poverty. I have witnessed parents beating the boy who fails go to school. Still beating fail to drive him to school in many more numerous cases; more in number than the poverty driven childhood labour. With no compulsions many, many children do not go to school. Why? The question is unanswered.

SECTION IV

Steps Taken to Eradicate Child Labour

Central Government

In 1955, Sri Narasimha Rao's Government announced (August 15) to rehabilitate 2 million child labour working in hazardous industries by 2000 and so set up a fund of Rs. 850 crores. Only 4% of this fund was allotted during 1995-96. At this rate only 2% of the child workers will be rehabilitated in the course of 25 years; not two years. Government even refused ILO and IPEC funds and said it is going to stand on it's own resources.

In December, 1996 Supreme Court sent a directive to the Government asking all the States to conduct surveys on child labour and present a report. (A false report was presented in 1997, December that the number is only 20 lakhs in the entire country, attributing 15 lakhs to Orissa and the rest to other States (26 States and UT).

Supreme Court further said that Rs. 20,000 should be collected from employers and the money should be used for rehabilitating children. The survey excluded hazardous industries and even the survey was a farce. (see, earlier para inside brackets). We need a minimum of Rs. 40,000 crores to rehabilitate them.

Impact of Supreme Court Order

The Supreme Court Order (December, 10, 96) resulted in the closing of door to children in Noida and Okhla of New Delhi surroundings. Children who were earning something are virtually on the streets. They have no option. ILO estimated full time child employees as 12.7 million (1997).

Child Labour Eradication In Tamilnadu

Tirunelveli

In Tamilnadu only NGO's do something to eradicate child labour. As per 1995 records the total number of child labour in the district was 70366. Among them 23,488 are employed in beedi, 43,340 in the match industry, and 3538 in other industries.

Factors of child labour as identified by the study group are as follows:

- *(a)* Poverty,
- *(b)* Unemployment of adults,
- *(c)* Social Problems like broken families, alcoholic parent, uncongenial environment to go to school, etc.

A core group consisting of Non-Government Organisation was formed to prepare a proposal and the Government would give financial assistance. Assistance will be offered to the parents of working children, so that their child may be withdrawn from jobs and put in school. Loans can be obtained from Banks under Government schemes.

Ten non-formal educational institutions are to be run with the help of teachers and unemployed graduates. It would be set up in child labour dominated areas. District Rural Development Agency will impart technical education. 800 will receive it. It has been estimated that there are 1.25 lakhs child workers in the district.

M.S. University Sociology department studied this problem and brought out the following inferences.

Besides unemployment and poverty, the high rate of interest collected by money-lenders in rural areas is responsible for forcing the children to earn. The department suggests liberal loans to the parents of child workers to withdraw their wards from employment.

It was suggested to create awareness in villages about the importance of education. (It can be done only through teachers who work with dedication. Faulty selection of teachers resulted in empty class-rooms in villages. It cannot be corrected unless they retire and the right type of teachers with motivation are appointed at Primary level).

Ramanathapuram District

It is one of the child labour concentrated district of Tamilnadu. Madras High Court Judge, Sri Ramamurthy said 'Child Labour is a cancer to the society'. It is an area with numerous match and fireworks units employing child labour. The judge suggested a mental approach to eradicate the evil.

The district has started 82 schools under National Child Labour Project with a strength of 4500. Two core projects, with the assistance of ILO, are be started from this year (1998-August 8, Newspaper Report).

Virudhunagar (Kamaraj District)

National Child Labour Elimination Project (NCLEP) to be intensified in Kamarajar District (1997-July report). Fiscal and financial restrains the working of the project more speedier. Now 42 schools are functioning under this scheme. As per the Collector's statement, still large number of children are working in hazardous industries.

The school timings are changed. The boys will get mid-day meals. Doles will be given to children's parents.

According to a recent survey conducted (1997, Jan.-Feb.) there are 2500 small and big factories employing 1.5 lakh workers among them 45,000 are child workers. A house to house survey was conducted and found that in rural areas the number of children going to school is less than UNICEF survey.

In the present survey 14970 children are working in factories.

Teachers will be selected from the villages with vocational knowledge.

Trichirapalli District

Child Labour Elimination and Effective Rehabilitation Society (CHEERS). 13 NGO have started 30 schools to trace child workers from their places of work and rehabilitate them. They have estimated 600 children are working in hazardous industries. CHEERS project will get Rs. 100 a month from Government for their parents to withstand the loss.

SECTION V

In this section an attempt has been made to draw the final lines for war against the child labour.

The empire cause of child labour is population increase. The claim is still under dispute. The theory says that child labour is a passing phase when the development and demographic transition are in cross-roads. Experts say when the country reaches 'replacement' fertility the problem will get automatically solved.

The key milestone of demographic behaviour is the replacement level fertility. This is called as total fertility rate. That is, an average number of children a women will have if the women experiences the current fertility pattern throughout her reproductive span. The magic number of TFR is 2.1. After about 20-25 years the population growth figures will reach zero.

Kearla had already reached the stage of magic number or TFR. It is possible because of 90% literacy rate among women. But, now Tamilnadu has reached Kerala level.

The ideal demographic figures of life expectancy of higher order (70 in Kerala) infant mortality 13 per thousand population and the population growth rate is 1.2 per annum. Kerala has attained replacement rate of fertility in 1988.

In Tamilnadu this rate was achieved in 1997. The growth rate is 1.3 (not far away from replacement fertility). Female literacy rate is 56%. Infant mortality rate is 54 per thousand, it is 52 in Punjab.

Our question is, why the child labour problem is more in Tamilnadu than Kerala and Punjab. So, population growth has got nothing to do with child labour.

Literacy may not be a prominent reason for child labour. Even female literacy is around 54, is more than 52 in Punjab.

Poverty

It has been sighted as the chief cause of Child Labour. If so why child labour is on the increase in advanced countries also?

Broken Families

Broken families are very high in advanced countries like, U.S. Then why Child Labour problem is not prominent there?

We conclude the child labour is a complex problem. The problem may be due to certain specific causes in areas of concentrated child labour.

In Madurai, the rag pickers do not choose to work in regular establishments. Why? Unemployment may not be the sole cause. Even when employment is offered, they do not choose regular employment.

How will you classify non-school going and non-working children? Do we have any figures. Are they not our social problems, needing our attention?

Making Primary Schooling Compulsory will Eradicate Child Labour

It is a suggestion to eradicate child labour. In Madurai 90% of the child workers have completed their primary schooling.

(Report by St. Joseph Girls' High School study presented at Children's National Science Conference in 1996).

Poverty of Parents

In Kamarajar District both parents earn more than sufficiently by working in match, litho, fireworks factories. Then, why they do not send their children to school.

We need more in-depth study on child labour—regionwise.

Notes

1. The study on child labour gained momentum only after passing the Child Labour Deterrence Act in U.S. Senate in 1996. So no official date is a available for our study. The statistics given in the paper are collected from Newspapers over a period of two years. There is a wide difference between the official data and date published by Non-Government Social Organisations.
2. The paper is based on mainly newspaper clippings and magazines. Besides, personal observations in my village.

Reference

Sir. D. Robertson—'Lectures on Economic Principles' Collins—Fontana Library (1996).

Paper clippings.

1. TNSCB Scheme to Eradicate Child Labour, *Hindu*, dt. 30-7-98.
2. Stunted Growth in Children may Affect their Success, *Hindu*, dt. 23-5-98.
3. NGOs' Role in Eliminating Child Labour, *Hindu*, dt. July 23, 1998.
4. Child Labours, Cancer to the Society, *Hindu*, dt. 11-8-1998.
5. Small Hands of Slavery, *Hindu*, dt. Jan. 25, 1998.
6. Bundles of Joy, *India Today*, August 15-30, 1998.
7. Where will the Vicious Cycle End, *Economic Times*, March 30, '97.
8. More States Want Ban on Child Labour, *Hindu*, dt. 8-7-97.
9. Net Working Needed to End Child Labour, *Hindu*, 9-2-97.
10. Ban on Child Labour End Children Jobless, *Hindu*, May 6, '97.
11. I.L.O. Sings MOU on Child Labour Awareness, *Hindu*, 9-5-97.
12. Smile that Makes the Difference, *Hindu*, dt. June 13, 1997.
13. Child Labour Elimination Project is to be Intensified, *Hindu*, dt. 1-9-97.
14. Cheer in the Lives of Child Labourers, *The Hindu*, August 15, '97.
15. Child Labour in Knitwear Industry, *The Hindu*, May 3, '97.
16. On the Streets for Survival, *The Hindu*, dt. 6-11-97.
    (All the Hindu Editions are printed at Madurai).

25

Socio-Economic Conditions of Child Labour in Coimbatore Hotel Industry

— *V. Ambumani & S. Ganesan*

Introduction

India today has the dubious distinction of having the largest number of child labourers in the world (about 27.4 million). Child labour constitutes a sizeable proportion of the total labour force in hotel industry and hence this paper attempts to examine the socio-economic conditions of child labour in Coimbatore hotel industry with reference to the following objectives:

Objectives

1. To estimate the proportion of child labour in the total labour force.
2. To analyse their income, expenditure and savings pattern.
3. To identify their nativity details and family background.
4. To study their motivations and to examine the reasons for taking to job so early in their life, and
5. To analyse factors conducive for child labourers in hotel industry.

Methodology

Scope

The study covers ten branches of prominent five mediumsized hotels in Coimbatore city. While selecting samples we have chosen only restaurants, even though lodging houses also employ child labourers for some menial work.

Child Labourers

For the purpose of this study child labourers include all those who have completed 7 years of age but not completed 15 years of age. In all, 10 branches we have surveyed, only boys were employed and hence no girl child labour is included in this study.

Data Collection

The study is based on the data collection from the hotel management as well as from the labourers. Some personal information like native place, educational qualifications, parentage details, wages, etc.; have been collected directly from the labourers. For data collection one full day has been spared for one branch since there were change of labourers due to shift operation. The entire process of data collection has been completed between 2nd June and 20th June 1997.

Data Analysis

Since it is only an explorative study we have used only simple arithmetics for working out the proportion, percentage, etc.

Results and Discussions

No. of hotels studied	:	5
No. of branches surveyed	:	10
Total table capacity	:	212

Significance of Table Capacity in Work Allocation

During the course of our investigation we find that the work allocation for servers, water boys, cleaners, and tumbler pickers is purely based on the number of tables and each table contains seating capacity for four customers. We were surprised to know that table capacity acts as a standard allocative mechanism and helps the supervisor for equitable distribution of workload among the various categories of labourers.

Proportion of Child Labour to Total Labour Force

The following Table 25.1 presents the details of total labour force, number of child labourers etc.

It may be observed that in the total labour force, the proportion of child labour is 42.46 per cent and the jobs like watering, table cleaning and tumbler picking have been done exclusively by the child labourers in all branches of the hotels surveyed.

Table 25.1
Proportion of Child Labour to Total Labour Force

Category	*Total Labour Force (No.'s)*	*Child Labourers (No.'s)*	*Proportion %*	*Average No. of Customers to be Served*
1. Server	142	—	—	12
2. Waterboy	54	38	70	32
3. Table cleaner	48	48	100	36
4. Tumbler pickers	42	42	100	40
5. Others*	112	41	37	NA**
Total	398	169	42.46	

* Others include cooks, Asstt. cooks, parotta Master, etc. child labourers in this category are vessels cleaners, kitchen assistants, vegetable cutters etc.

** Average number of customers is unascertainable because it includes customers getting parcel also.

Wage Structure	*Average monthly Income*
1. Server Rs. 175-225 p.m. + 3% bonus based on collection in his servicing area	775-825
2. Waterboy Rs. 75-125 p.m. + Daily Beta Rs. 2	160
3. Table cleaner Rs. 75-125 p.m. + Daily Beta Rs. 3	190
4. Tumbler picking Rs. 75-125 p.m. + Daily Beta Rs. 2	160
5. Others Rs. 100-150 p.m. + Daily Beta Rs. 3	215

For the categories 2 to 4 the work assignment would be on rotational basis. For all labourers the total working period is 8 hours a day and rest at a stretch 4 / 3 hrs. depending upon the situation.

Non-monetary Benefits

For all categories: Food (only prescribed items) and shelter. It seems the labourers are not allowed to eat all that is available in the hotel. They can eat only the prescribed items.

It is clear from the above, that the average monthly income of the child labourers ranges between Rs. 160 and Rs. 215 besides food and accommodation. The vessel cleaners and kitchen assistants are getting a little higher income because of the hazardous nature of work.

Overtime Work

When somebody is on leave and if the same labourer is asked to work continuously, for the extra work he is paid overtime wages which is two times of the normal wages. We do not find any evidence of leave compensation in lieu of overtime work.

Age Composition of the Child Labourer

Table 25.2 presents the details regarding the age composition of the child labourers.

Table 25.2
Age Composition of the Child Labourer

Category	*Age*			*No Response*	*Total*
	7–10	*10–13*	*13–15*		
Waterboy	—	7	29	2	38
Table cleaner	8	20	15	5	48
Tumbler picking	19	10	9	4	42
Others	4	19	16	2	41
Total	31 (18%)	56 (33%)	69 (42%)	13	169

It is evident that nearly 74 per cent of the child labourers are in the age group of 10 and 15 years. It seems immediately after the completion of their elementary school education they leave their home for some job.

Parentage Details

Table 25.3 presents the detail regarding their parents.

Table 25.3
Details Regarding their Parents

Category	*Both Parents Alive*	*Only One is Alive*	*Both are not Alive*	*No Response*	*Total*
Waterboy	19	10	7	2	38
Cleaner	24	12	7	5	48
Tumbler picking	26	6	6	4	42
Others	26	8	5	2	41
Total	95 (56%)	36 (21%)	25 (15%)	13	169

Contrary to the common belief we find that in case of 56 per cent of the child labourers both parents are alive and they are also hale and healthy. Only in case of just 15 per cent of child labourers both the parents were not alive and hence as the above details show orphanage cannot be the reason for child labour.

Nativity

Native State

Table 25.4 indicates the native state of the child labourers.

Table 25.4
Native State of the Child Labourers

Category	*Native State*				*Total*
	Tamilnadu	*Kerala*	*Others*	*No Response*	
Water boy	29	4	3	2	38
Table cleaner	33	7	3	5	48
Tumbler picking	29	5	4	4	42
Others	27	10	2	2	41
Total	118 (70%)	26 (15%)	12 (7%)	13	169

It is evident from the table above that more than 70 per cent of the child labourers are from Tamilnadu and another 15 per cent from Kerala. Thus in Coimbatore Hotel Industry, more than 85 per cent child labourers are from Tamilnadu and Kerala.

Native District

Since more than 70 per cent child labourers are from Tamilnadu we wanted to find out from which district sizable number of child labourers are emerging. To our surprise, we find that more than 65 per cent child labourers of Tamilnadu are from Pudukkottai and undivided Ramnad district (Pasumpon, Kamarajar and Ramnad) as shown below: Tirunelveli/Kanyakumari and Trichy/Salem contribute equal number of 13 each. It is even more surprising that though Madurai and Dindigul are equally drought districts and depends mostly on well irrigation, the number of child labourers are less as compared to many other district as shown in the table. It is interesting to note that no child labourer is from Coimbatore District.

Table 25.5
Native District of the Child Labourers of Tamilnadu

Category	*PDK RMD*	*TNL KNK*	*TRY SEL*	*MDU DGL*	*Others*	*No Response*	*Total*
Waterboy	20	3	1	1	2	2	29
Table cleaner	19	4	3	3	2	2	33
Tumbler picking	19	3	3	2	1	1	29
Others	19	3	3	1	—	1	27
Total	77 (65%)	13	10	7	5	6	118

PDK = Pudukkottai, RMD Ramnad, TNL = Tirunelveli, KNK = Kanyakumari, TRY = Trichy, SEL = Salem, MDU = Madurai, DEL = Dindigul.

Native Place

An attempt has been made to identify their native place. We have divided the places into three categories viz: Rural, Semi-Urban and Urban and grouped the child labourers according to their native place. From the information received we find that more than 84 per cent of the child labourers are from rural areas (Table 25.6).

Table 25.6
Native Place of the Child Labourers from Tamilnadu

Category	*Rural*	*Semi-Urban*	*Urban*	*No Response*	*Total*
Water boy	22	4	1	2	29
Table cleaner	28	3	—	2	33
Tumbler picking	25	1	2	1	29
Others	24	1	1	1	27
Total	99 (84%)	9	4	6	118

Occupation of the Parents

Table 25.7 presents the details of occupation of the parents of the child labourers.

Table 25.7
Occupation of the Parents of the Child Labourers

Category	*Land Holder*	*Coolie*	*Others*	*No Work*	*Total*
Water boy	5	21	1	2	29
Table cleaner	3	29	1	3	36
Tumbler picking	3	27	2	—	32
Others	2	28	1	3	34
Total	13	105 (73%)	5	8	131

It is astonishing to note that more than 73 per cent of the parents of the child labourers are coolies eking out their lives on daily wages and probably this could be one of the significant reasons for sending their children to job at an early age.

Education Qualification

It is surprising to note that nearly 66 per cent of the child labourers had completed their elementary school education as shown in Table 25.8.

Table 25.8
Educational Qualification of the Child Labourers

Category	*Elementary Education*	*No Education*	*No Response*	*Total*
Water boy	25	11	2	38
Table cleaner	28	15	5	48
Tumbler picking	27	11	4	42
Others	29	10	2	41
Total	109 (66%)	47	13	169

Reasons for Taking Up This Job

We wanted to ascertain the major cause for leaving the home at this young age and take up this job. Majority of the boys have cited three reasons *viz.* Insufficient food, frequent quarreling between parents and hardwork as coolies.

Table 25.9
Reasons for Taking Up This Job at Young Age

Category	*No Food*	*Quarr-Eling*	*Hard Work*	*Others Orphanage*	*No Response*	*Total*
Water boy	13	8	8	7	2	38
Table cleaner	17	9	10	7	5	48
Tumbler picking	14	9	9	6	4	42
Others	14	10	10	5	2	41
Total	58 (34%)	36 (21%)	37 (21%)	25 (15%)	13	169

However, we find that insufficient food and orphanage seems to be the single most reason (about 49 per cent), for taking up this job besides frequent domestic quarreling and danger of hard work as coolies.

Desire for Higher Education

We wanted to know whether the boys are really interested in education, given the facilities. And the answer was really astonishing. More than 60 per cent of the child labourers said they would study if facilities are given.

Table 25.10
Desire for Higher Education

Category	*Interested in Studies*	*Not Interested in Studies*	*No Response*	*Total*
Water boy	26	10	2	38
Table cleaner	29	14	5	48
Tumbler picking	23	15	4	42
Others	23	16	2	41
Total	101 (60%)	55 (33%)	13	169

Mode of Appointment

Relatives who are already working in the hotels happened to be the dominant mode (about 62 per cent) of getting employment as shown below:

Table 25.11
Mode of Getting Employment

Category	*Relative*	*Friends*	*By Own Trial*	*No Response*	*Total*
Water boy	26	4	6	2	38
Table cleaner	26	8	9	5	48
Tumbler picking	28	6	4	4	42
Others	25	8	6	2	41
Total	105 (62%)	26	25	13	169

Motivation

The prospects of becoming a server and subsequently supervisor seems to be the single most dominant motivation from the view of these young boys. Even though some boys wanted to go for higher studies they were unable to say how they are going to achieve their objectives.

Table 25.12
Motivation Sticking to the Job

Category	*To Become*		*To Study*	*To get Some Other Job*	*To go Back Home*	*None*	*Total*
	Server	*Cook*					
Water boy	20	4	4	4	4	2	38
Table cleaner	25	4	6	5	3	5	48
Tumbler picking	19	3	5	6	5	4	42
Others	15	6	5	8	5	2	41
Total	79	17	20	23	17	13	169

Average Monthly Expenditure

Table 25.13 presents the details of the average monthly expenditure of the child labourers.

Table 25.13
Average Monthly Expenditure

Category	*Average Monthly Income*	*Average Monthly Expenditure*				
		Cinema	*Cosmetics*	*Food*	*Parents*	*Saving*
Water boy	160	60(37%)	10	30	50	10
Table cleaner	190	60	15	35	50	30
Tumbler picking	160	60	10	30	50	10
Others	215	65	15	40	50	45

It may be observed that expenditure on cinema happens to be the single dominant item of expenditure (abour 37 per cent) of the boys working in the hotels. It is distressing to note that hard earned money at the budding stage is not being used in meaningful purpose but is wasted. All boys said they are sending Rs. 50 every month to their parents. Though the contribution is meager compared to cinema, it is encouraging to note that they are supplementing their family income too.

Job Satisfaction/Mental Satisfaction

Table 25.14
Job Satisfaction/Mental Satisfaction

Category	*Fully Satisfied*	*Satisfied*	*Not Satisfied*	*No Response*	*Total*
Water boy	24	8	4	2	38
Table cleaner	29	11	3	5	48
Tumbler picking	22	11	5	4	42
Others	21	13	5	2	41
Total	96 (57%)	43 (25%)	17	13	169

Finally we wanted to know whether the boys are satisfied with the present job, wages, food and other facilities. To our surprise we found that 82 per cent of the child labourers are satisfied with three things i.e. food, wages and other facilities. Their view is that in their native place they would not get such a food. Besides food they are also getting good wages. The satisfying factor above all is that they are independent, devoid of their parents control and they have money to spend.

Summary

The study is exploratory in nature and has been conducted with particular reference to socio-economic conditions of child labourers in hotel industry. The major conclusions are:

1. The proportion of child labourers to total force is 42 per cent and the average monthly income range between Rs. 160 and Rs. 215 besides food and shelter.
2. 74 per cent of the child labourers are in the age group of 10-15 years. After completion of their elementary school education they leave their home for job.
3. In case of 56 per cent of the boys, both parents are alive and hence orphanage could not be the reason for child labour.
4. 70 per cent of the boys are from Tamilnadu and 65 per cent of the child labourers of Tamilnadu are from Pudukkottai and Ramnad District. 84 per cent of the boys are from rural areas and 73 per cent of their parents are

coolies. Thus coolies in rural areas mostly send their children for job at an early age.

5. Insufficient food followed by domestic quarreling and hard work are the prominent reasons for taking up job.
6. More than 60 per cent of the boys expressed desire to study if facilities are given. Thus lack of facilities for education could also be a valid reason for child labour.
7. Relatives happened to be the dominant mode of getting employment and the prospects of becoming server is the single most dominant motivation of these young boys.
8. Cinema is the single dominant item or expenditure and 82 per cent of the boys are satisfied with the job based on i.e. food, wages and independence from parents.

Conclusion

Thus like a moth flying around a lamp burned by its brightness without knowing its consequences, these young boys are happy with the food, cinema and their freedom without bothering about their future. Time alone will say whether they are right?

26

Migrant Child Labour in Vijayawada City: A Case Study

—*P. Venu Gopal & E. Singa Rao*

Migration refers to the movement of workers from one place to another. It is used to denote the movement of workers from the agricultural to non-agricultural, mainly from industrial sector. Migration implies a change in the occupation of workers. Generally it is difficult to change occupation without changing the place of work. Therefore, migration results in an occupational as well as geographical redistribution of population. Change in the place of work is mainly responsible for many of the evils associated with migration. Migrant workers in the Indian context do maintain close relation with agriculture and their villages. They continue to regard the villages as their homes because the villages are their native places. They are accustomed to village atmosphere, usually they keep their families in villages.

Studies on Migration

Several studies used two-sector model to explain the rural-to-urban migration of labour at the aggregate or regional level, and the labour supply and demand conditions in the urban areas (Todaro 1969; Sjaastad 1961, 1962; Sahota 1968; Berry 1970; Mehmet 1976; and Benerjee 1981). In most of the models, the focus is on the individual, who is assumed to maximize his or her utility or income while deciding about whether and where to migrate. Mincer (1978) has also drawn attention to family consideration in migrant decision in the context of an entire family in which both husband and wife work, and migration decisions may involve the movement of the entire family.

The studies on migration have tried to explain reasons and wage differentials between origin and destination. (Hoselitz 1953, 1955, 1957) had argued that unfavourable employment conditions in rural areas has fostered the process of rural-urban migration. Dandekar and Rath (1971) treated rural poverty as a 'push' factor. Benerjee and Kunbur (1981) take an opposite view. Other studies by Yeshwant (1962), Sovani (1966), Connel *et.al.* (1976) as cited indicated a higher propensity to migrate among middle income groups rather than in the lower and upper income groups. A number of studies both for LDC's and advanced countries found 'distance' to be an important factor for migration viz., Beals, Lefry and Moses (1967), Sahota (1968), Greenwood (1971), Benerjee and Kunbur (1981). Distance act as a proxy for cost of transportation and psychic costs. Increased distance raises both these costs and since information decline with distance, migration usually falls with greater distance.

In LDC's a good deal of migration occurs between rural and urban areas. But what is not so commonly recognised is that considerable degree of migration between urban areas also occur (Greenwood, 1971). According to his study a kind of in-sight process occurs in India whereby rural persons first migrate to nearby small towns, become acclimatized, then shift to larger cities and towns. Similarly Yap (1977) found that urban-to-urban migration is substantial in LDCs. Kundu (1986) noted the growth of large number of small towns and emergence of several new towns around big cities because of such step-wise migration. There are various social and economic constraints which prevent migrants from going directly to big cities.

The migratory character of the workers in the Indian Industry has often prevented them from joining any permanent labour union or unions. The majority of workers have not liked to pay their monthly or annual membership subscription to the existing unions or take any active part in the formation of a new union because they did not intend to live in the industrial town permanently. This tendency among the industrial workers in India has largely been responsible for unhealthy growth of the trade unionism in this country.

The migratory character of the industrial workers has also been one of the causes of frequent absenteeism which is largely found in the Indian industries. Another evil effect of such migration has been the fact that the health of immigrant workers is often subjected to a heavy strain in big cities and towns. The workers in the industrial cities has to live generally in dark, narrow and congested quarters in various 'bustees' lacking sanitation. The factory operative has to work for long hours under strict discipline whereas in the village the work is intermittent with long hours of rest. Thus the changes in the climate, conditioning and conditions of work, seriously impair the health and efficiency of the workers. Then the work of the industrial workers also effected adversely by the extremely low quality of diet.

The workers in the city easily indulge themselves in various unhealthy and immoral practices such as drinking, gambling and immorality. Not only the above, it also is, increasing the child labour. Poverty of the migrant parents forces to send their children to seek employment and earn more incomes atleast to feed their large size of families. The growing number of child labourers all over the world causes serious concern to those who are interested in child welfare in both developing and developed countries.

The child labour which faces restrictions to entry in the formal sector activities, is comparatively more easily absorbed in the informal sector activities, which are not guided by the legal restrictions. Therefore, it would be interesting to study the socio-economic characteristics of the working children belonging to the migrants.

Studies on Child Labour in India

The empirical research on child labour shows that the conditions of work at the place of their employment are highly unsatisfactory especially in unregulated factories and other informal sector enterprises. They have to work for long hours in il-lighted and absolutely dirty environment. Since many children are shown to be working as apprentices to avoid legal actions, they are also badly treated by their employers. In many cases they are forced to be domestic work for their employers (J.C. Kulshreshtha, 1978).

Vishwa Mittar (1987) argued that the wages paid to workers

in the informal sector in general and to children in particular are very low. He denied the normal statutory protection available to an adult worker. The introduction of child labour, normally as apprentices, permits a reinforcement of segmentation while at the same time applying pressure on wage levels in other segments of the labour market (Gerry Rodgers and Guy Standing, 1979)

Abundant literature on child labour is available in the Indian context. Among others the notable studies are Sharma (1979), Verma (1979), Rao (1980), Mohsin (1980), Mukherjee (1981), Kothari (1983), Kumar (1983), Murthy and Rani (1983), Smolowe (1984), Patel (1987), Ali (1987) and Iyenger (1987). These studies broadly points out the problems of working children like working hours, wages, rest interval, nature of work and the reasons for the child work, some of these studies also analysed the legislative facilities.

The economic factors are the main reasons for child labour. The poor parents sending their children for work, in some cases the children are becoming bonded labour. In some cases the families are compelled to migrate their children temporarily to the nearest cities or urban areas of adjoining states to earn the necessary income (Vishwa Mittar, 1984).

The studies which have attempted to analyse the nature, causes, problems of child labour and remedies to curb the problem of child labour. However, the studies emphasizing the problems of migrant child labour in the Indian context are however, conspicuous by their absence. Hence, it is proposed to study the problems of migrant child workers in Vijayawada City.

Objectives

The main objectives of the study are :

1. to examine the causes for migration in general and child worker in particular.
2. to study the employment aspects of the migrant working children.
3. to study the level of earnings of migrant child labour.

Methodology

The official estimates shows that there are 3,124 child labour in Vijayawada city. We have taken 10 per cent of the total i.e. 310. Out of the listed 310 households, it is found that 220 are natives. Those are excluded from the survey. Hence, the sample constitutes

90 households. For the purpose of sampling, a complete list of wards in the city was collected from the office of the Municipal Corporation, Vijayawada. The information provided by the Municipal Corporation authorities reveals that there are 50 wards in the city. These wards have been classified into three categories namely—Residential (28), Commercial (22) and Industrial (2). Out of 50 wards, 13 wards have been selected at random according to the proportion of number of wards in each category. Thus 7 Residential, 5 Commercial and 1 Industrial wards are selected at random. Two streets are selected from each ward at random. The information was solicited personally through a pre-tested questionnaire from each household. The results of the study are broadly presented in the following paragraphs.

Major Findings of the Study

Reasons for Migration

The study reveals that both push as well as pull factors are responsible for migration of parents of the working children. Attraction of the city life and comparatively higher income opportunities are among the pull factors and inferior conditions of living in the sending areas alongwith lack of work opportunities are among the push factors responsible for migration. Besides, the another push factor is that the economic compulsion of parents may induce them to send children to work to the nearest or even far off urban centers. The adverse financial position of parents compels them to borrow from the village money-lender, who charges exhorbitant interest rates on the loans advanced to the villagers. A pressure from the side of money-lender to repay the debts is likely to compel the parents to send their children to earn, since no work is available in the village. Thus financial factors in addition to large family size with low family income seems to be responsible for child migration. Lack of interest in studies, non-availability of work in the village and liabilities are other factors responsible for child migration. Information has been sought from the working children to enlist the various factors responsible for their move to the city. These responses are contained in Table 26.1.

The data show that the economic factors dominate the decision for the migration. Debts and financial liabilities, economic compulsion were amongst the most important reasons of migration. To seek better employment, to learn technical work, no work at

Table 26.1
Distribution of Migrant Children by Reasons of Migration

Reasons of Migration	*No. of Children*	*Per cent*
I. Economic Factors		
1. Debts and financial liabilities of parents	16	17.78
2. Economic compulsion of the parents	29	32.22
3. Interested to earn	05	5.56
II. Employment Factors		
1. No work at place of origin	7	7.78
2. To get better employment	4	4.44
3. To learn technical work	9	10.00
III. Sociological Factors		
1. Social/traditional problems at the place of origin	8	8.89
2. To follow family	4	4.44
3. Liked the city life	1	1.11
IV. Other Factors		
1. Discouraging behaviour of parents	2	2.22
2. Lack of interest in studies	4	4.44
3. A run away child	1	1.11
	90	100.00

the place of origin, were the other reasons responsible for the child migration. 20 per cent of migrants were under this reason i.e. employment causes. The remaining 20 per cent of the migrants migrated due to the social factors.

Distribution of the migrant children by industrial category shows (Table 26.2) that among variety of industrial categories, migrant children were concentrating mainly on construction (35.56%), followed by service industry (26.67%). Thus, the migrant children absorb themselves in all types of jobs which would provide them more salaries. A small portion of the child labour (8.89%)

Table 26.2
Industrial Category and Migrant Child

Industrial Category	*No. of the Children*	*Per cent*
Manufacturing	12	13.33
Trade and Commerce	[illegible]	15.56
Transport	8	8.89
Service	24	26.67
Construction	32	35.56

were working in transport industry.

Employment Status

Distribution of migrant children by the employment status (Table 26.3) shows that migrant children were mostly engaged as wage-workers. More than half-of the child labour were engaged as wage workers. Nearly one-fourth were engaged as own-account workers. They were hawkers, shoe shine boys, balloon sellers, flower-vendors, peddlers etc. Only 2 per cent working children are engaged in other status, i.e. as beggars etc. 20 per cent of the migrant child labour were working as unpaid family workers in Vijayawada City.

Table 26.3
Distribution of Migrant Children by the Employment Status

Employment Status	*No. of Children*	*Percent*
Wage-workers	49	54.45
Own-account workers	21	23.33
Unpaid family workers	18	20.00
Others	2	2.22
Total	90	100.00

Payment of Wages

The distribution of working migrant children by level of wages in different activities has been calculated as presented in Table 26.4. It is observed from the table that out of 90 migrant working children, 22 received less than 400 rupees per month. The table reveals construction workers are receiving more incomes, when compared with other activities.

Conclusion

The National Commission on Labour viewed the employment of children as indeed more of an economic problem than anything else. It observed that "while the economic difficulties are real, a way has to be found to give the child the necessary education in his more receptive years. We feel this can be ensured by fixing the employment hours of children so as to enable them to attend to school where the number of children is adequate, the employees, with the assistance of State Governments, should make

Table 26.4
Distribution of Migrant Working Child by Monthly Wages and Industrial Categories

Industrial category	*Wages Per Month*							*Total*
	100-200	*200-300*	*300-400*	*400-500*	*500-600*	*600-700*	*700-800*	
Manufacturing	—	—	4 (23.56)	6 (40.02)	1 (4.00)	1 (4.55)	—	12 (13.73)
Trade & Commerce	1 (50.00)	1 (33.33)	6 (35.34)	2 (13.34)	3 (12.00)	1 (4.55)	—	14 (15.56)
Transport	—	2 (66.67)	3 (17.67)	1 (6.67)	1 (4.00)	1 (4.55)	—	8 (8.89)
Service	1 (50.00)	—	3 (17.67)	2 (13.34)	6 (24.00)	11 (50.05)	1 (16.67)	24 (26.67)
Construction	—	—	1 (5.89)	4 (26.68)	14 (56.00)	8 (36.40)	5 (83.33)	32 (35.56)
Total	2 (100.00)	3 (100.00)	17 (100.00)	15 (100.00)	25 (100.00)	22 (100.00)	6 (100.00)	90 (100.00)

arrangements to combine work with education". Hence, the problem of child labour cannot be solved by prohibiting the employment of children, unless the household to which the working children belong are provided with basic human needs.

Government should take steps to create and develop employment opportunities within the rural areas. Secondly, job seekers migrating to urban areas must be regulated. Their flow also must be directed properly. For this purpose the Government must adopt a policy on migration. Therefore, the urban migrating people will have a chance of getting some knowledge on employment opportunities and conditions in the urban areas. Similarly, preference must be given to those who have aptitude for industrial way of life. As there is no legal protection for the migrants, a comprehensive legislation in urban areas be enacted and implemented effectively to eliminate the migrant and non-migrant discrimination.

References

Banerjee, Biswajit and S.N. Kanbur, "Some Methodological Aspects of Analysis of Data on Internal Migration" in Ashish Bost *et al. Population Statistics in India,* Vikas Publishing House Pvt. Ltd., New Delhi, pp. 307-16.

Connell, J. B. Dasgupta; R. Laishley; M. Lipton, (1976), *Migration from Rural Areas,* Oxford University Press, New Delhi.

Gosal, G.S. (1961), "Internal Migration in India: A Regional Analysis", *Indian Geographical Journal,* 36, pp. 106-21.

Greenwood, M.J. (1971), "A Regressive Analysis of Migration to Urban Areas of a Less Developed Country : The Case of India", *Journal of Regional Science,* Vol. II, No. 2, August, pp. 253-62.

Lewis, W. A., "Economic Development with Unlimited Supplies of Labour", *The Manchester School of Economic and Social Studies,* Vol. 22, No. 2, May, pp. 547-54.

Ravenstein, E.G., (1895), "The Laws of Migration", *Journal of Royal Statistical Society,* June, 167-227.

Sahota, G.S., (1968), An Economic Analysis of Internal Migration in Brazil", *Journal of Political Economy,* March/April, pp. 218-45.

Sovani, N.V., (1966), *Urbanization and Urban India,* Asia Publishing House, Bombay.

Yap, L.Y.L., (1975), *Internal Migration in Less Developed Countries : A Survey of Literature,* World Bank Staff Working Paper No. 215.

Yeshwant, T.S., (1962), "Rural-Migration—A Case Study in Four Ramanathapuram Villages", *Agricultural Situation in India,* Vol. 17, No. 6, September, pp. 655-63.

27

Migration and Child Labour: A Case Study

—*K. Gangadhara Rao & K. Sreelakshmamma*

Child Labour is a global phenomenon, but is rampant in developing countries such as India due to economic compulsions and retrogade socio-cultural perceptions. Inspite of lofty constitutional provisions and legislative measures, more than 17 million children are forced to work in various industrial and non-industrial occupations. Child Labour, anywhere, truly reflects dehumanization. In India its incidence is growing in volume and intensity. Child labour in India lack basic facilities which exert a directly negative effect on the physical and mental development in children. The child labour in India is of two types — legal child labour and illegal child labour. Legal child labour includes the child labour which is above the minimum, but not adult. Illegal child labour includes all such child labour which is below the minimum age of 14 years, working in the unorganised sectors which are not covered by child labour legislation.

This paper focuses mainly on the socio-economic characteristics of illegal child labour with particular emphasis on migrant child labour. An attempt is also made to study the causes, conditions and problems of migrant child labour in the Ongole Town, which is one of the fast growing town of Andhra Pradesh. For this, a sample of 100 child labourers have been studied purposively in Ongole Town in August, 1999.

The working children in the Ongole Town are mostly found in a variety of unorganised sector occupations. Based on the homogeneity. All these activities are classified into the following five sub-sectors for the purpose of analysis:

(a) Trade : Trade and commerce include wholesale trade, retail trade and petty trade, hotels, wayside mobile canteens and messes (eating places of students, employees and low income groups).

(b) Repair Works : Repair works include repair works of scooters, motor cycles, mopeds, autos, cars, tractors, lorries and all other heavy motor vehicles. This also includes of repair services of bicycles, tricycles and home appliances, etc.,

(c) Domestic Services : Servant boys and girls in residential houses and offices come under this category.

(d) Construction : Children working in construction activities of residential houses and other buildings including apartments come under this category.

(e) Others : Children working in brick making, tailoring, rickshaw pulling and poultry come under this category.

Socio-Economic Characteristics

Religion and Caste

Table 27.1 presents the proportion of sample child labour in different employment categories by religion and caste. It is evident that the working children who belong to Hindu Religion account for 66 per cent. Next in order comes the group of Muslims, their share being 24 per cent in the total child workers and Christians form only 10 per cent. It is also observed that no single child worker belonging to other religion is found the entire sample.

The data show that within the Hindu community, the proportion of child labour belonging to backward class/community is large with 26 per cent. If working children belonging to SC/ST, Muslims and Christians are added to this, the urban unorganised sector appears to have attracted backward community/castes persons into it on very large scale. This observation ties up with findings of similar studies carried out elsewhere too the on caste composition of child labour. It is found that among upper castes (OCs) Balija/Telega child workers are in majority whereas Vysyas are in minority. But, no single child worker belonging to Brahmin caste is found in the entire sample.

Table 27.1

Percentage Distribution of Child Labour by Religion and Caste

Sectors	*A Trade*	*B Repair works*	*C Domestic Services*	*D Construction*	*E Others*	*All Sectors*
1.	2.	3.	4.	5.	6.	7.
I. Muslims	19.05 (8)	42.86 (12)	—	—	80.00 (4)	24.00 (24)
II. Christians	4.76 (2)	7.14 (2)	25.00 (4)	12.22 (2)	—	10.00 (10)
III. Others	—	—	—	—	—	—
IV. Hindus	76.19 (32)	50.00 (14)	75.00 (12)	77.78 (7)	20.00 (1)	66.00 (6
Backward of which classes	28.57 (12)	21.43 (6)	25.00 (4)	44.45 (4)	—	26.00 (26)
SC/ST	19.05 (8)	—	50.00 (8)	—	—	16.00 (16)
Other castes	28.57 (12)	28.57 (8)	—	33.33 (3)	20.00 (1)	24.00 (24)
Total :	100.00	100.00	100.00	100.00	100.00	100.00

Note : Figures in brackets are Numbers of Child workers.

Across the employment categories, the distribution of child labour by social stratification is quite interesting. It is found that Hindu children are in majority with 77.78 per cent in construction and trade with 76.19 per cent followed by domestic services (75%). But Muslim children are concentrated in repair works with 42.86 per cent. A point that cannot be missed is that upper caste children are not found in domestic services but lower caste children are found concentrating in Domestic services, trade and construction followed by repair works in order. It is also observed that there is no single SC/ST child in repair works and also no single Muslim child is found in domestic services.

Age and Sex Composition

Distribution of sample child labour by age and sex and employment category is furnished in Table 27.2. It reveals that the average age of working children is comparatively low being 12.06 years. This figure varies across the employment categories. The average child worker in repair works (B) is youngest (10.57 years) and he is the oldest in construction (D) being 12.83 years of age, followed by others (E) with 12.44 years of age. It is found that the average age of child workers in domestic services (C) is less with 11.49 years when compared to the average age of child worker in Trade (A) with 11.78 years of age. It is observed from the data depicted in the table, a quite sizable proportion of child labour belongs to working age group of 9 to 12 years, whereas only 12 per cent of child workers are aged between 6 to 9 years. It is also observed that a significant proportion of child labour (40%) belongs to working age group of 12 to 14 years.

Further, the data indicates that the unorganised sector in the study area is male dominated being 68 per cent and female child workers are 32 per cent which is also significant. The dominance of male is much pronounced in repair works (100%) followed by Trade (71.43%) and Construction (57.14%). It is also observed that no single female child worker is found in repair works but a quite sizable proportion of male child workers (87.50%) are engaged in domestic services, followed by Construction (42.86%) and others (42.86%) in order.

Table 27.2
Distribution of Child Labour by Age and Sex and Employment Category

Employment Category	*Average of Child Labour*	*Children 6-9 Years*	*Children Age Group 9-12 Years*	*Working Age Group 12-14 Years*	*All Workers*	*Per cent*	*Workers by Sex*	
							Male	*Female*
A	11.78	6 (14.29)	22 (52.38)	14 (33.33)	42 (100.00)	42.00	30 (71.43)	12 (28.57)
B	10.57	4 (14.29)	14 (50.00)	10 (35.71)	28 (100.00)	28.00	28 (100.00)	—
C	11.49	2 (12.5)	6 (37.5)	8 (50.00)	16 (100.00)	16.00	2 (12.5)	14 (87.50)
D	12.83	—	2 (28.57)	5 (71.43)	7 (100.00)	7.00	4 (57.14)	3 (42.86)
E	12.44	—	4 (57.14)	3 (42.86)	7 (100.00)	7.00	4 (57.14)	3 (42.86)
Total :	12.06	12 (12.00)	48 (48.00)	40 (40.00)	100 (100.00)	100.00	68 (68.00)	32 (32.00)

Note : Figures in Brackets are percentages.

Age-wise Education Levels

Table 27.3 gives the percentage of child labour by their age-wise education levels. As can be seen from the first row, 83.33 per cent and 16.67 per cent of the working children in 6 to 9 and 9 to 12 age categories have no formal education at all. It means 18 per cent of the total sample child labour are illiterate. It is found that a vast majority (50%) of sample child workers got middle school education whereas a significant proportion (30%) of child labour attained primary school education. There are only 2 per cent of working children who are between 12—14, got highest middle school education with 77.50 per cent, whereas children between 9—12 years got lowest with 39.58 in getting middle school education. But the percentage of children between ages 9—12 is highest with 43.75 per cent in attaining primary school education, whereas it is lowest with 16.62 per cent in the children aged 6—9 category. It is interesting to note that all working children between the ages of 12—14 are literates.

It is also observed from the table that on an average unorganised sector child worker is found to have undergone only 4.66 years of schooling. But it is high with 6.41 years in the age group of 12-14 years, whereas it is low in the ages 6-9 with less than one year. But the average years of schooling is 4.17 in the children between ages 9-12. It is further observed that non-schooling of 6.12 than migrant working children who got average years of schooling of 3.63.

Structure of Employment

Generally it is held that majority of child labour in the unorganised sector are engaged on a semi-permanent or temporary basis. The working children in Ongole Town are engaged in a variety of activities. Table 27.4 contains information regarding structure of employment of sample child workers by the employment categories and migrant status. The data reveals that out of the total 100 sample working children nearly two-thirds of them are migrants and the remaining one-third are natives. It is found that 42 per cent of total working children are engaged in Trade including hotels and messes. Repair work is another important employment category which has employed 28 per cent of the total sample. Domestic service is the next important employment category in

Table 27.3
Age-wise Educational Levels of Child Labours

(In Percentage)

Educational levels	*Ages 6-9*	*Ages 9-12*	*Ages 12-14*	*Total*
1. No formal education	83.33 (10)	16.67 (8)	—	18.00 (18)
2. Primary	16.62 (2)	43.75 (21)	17.5 (7)	30.00 (30)
3. Middle	—	39.58 (19)	77.5 (31)	50.00 (50)
4. Matric/Technical	—	—	5.0 (2)	2.00 (2)
Total :	100.00 (12)	100.00 (48)	100.00 (40)	100.00 (100)
Average years of schooling	0.58	4.17	6.41	4.66

Note : Figures in Brackets are Numbers of child workers.

Table 27.4
Distribution of Child Labour by the Employment Category and Migrant Status

Employment Category	*Number of working Children*			
	Migrant	*Non-Migrant*	*Total*	*Percent*
(1) Trade	34 (80.95)	8 (19.05)	42 (100.00)	42.00
(2) Repair works	12 (42.86)	16 (57.14)	28 (100.00)	28.00
(3) Domestic services	12 (75.00)	4 (25.00)	16 (100.00)	16.00
(4) Construction	5 (55.56)	4 (44.44)	9 (100.00)	9.00
(e) Others	3 (60.00)	2 (40.00)	5 (100.00)	5.00
Total :	66 (66.00)	34 (34.00)	100 (100.00)	

terms of the number of working children employed (16%) followed by construction (9%). Other category is the least important employment category in terms of employment, where children are working in brick making, rickshaw pulling and poultry, where only five children are found to be working as casual workers.

The data in the table shows that among a variety of employment categories migrant child workers are concentrating mainly on trade, including hotels and messes (80.95%) and domestic services (75%). The free entry condition in the trade and domestic sector is possibly the reason of a large percentage of migrant working children being employed in them. The non-migrant working children are concentrating mainly; in repair works (57.14%), followed by construction and others (40.00%).

Causes and Problems of Migrant Child Labour

Migration to urban areas is a common experience of almost all towns and cities in India. Push as well as pull factors are responsible for migration of people to urban centers. The push factors refer to the poor economic conditions and the resultant economic misery or lack of opportunities for advancement which push the people out of the origin areas in search of a livelihood or better economic opportunities. Pull factors refer to the factors which encourage migration to urban areas as employment and other economic opportunities, and eminities etc. The influx or migrants brings with them a number of children to help their parents or relatives in raising their level of earnings by employing them in a variety of activities of the urban economy.

The data on percentage distribution of in-migrant child labour by place of origin reveals that, if an in-migrant is defined as the one who was not born in Ongole Town, then a vast majority of the sample child labour (66%) were in-migrants. It will be seen from the table that out of these in-migrants a significant proportion (60.61%) originated from Prakasam District other than Ongole Town. It is interesting to note that the proportion of those who migrated into the town from other states takes the second place. It is surprising that the same number of migrant child workers originated from Nellore and Guntur. In-migrant working children originated from other districts from a small proportion (6.06%) of the total in-migrant child labour.

Across the employment categories, percentage distribution of the in-migrant child workers is slightly different. It is found that all the in-migrant child workers engaged in construction and others category originated from Prakasam District and Nellore District.

Causes for Working of Migrant Child Labour

Table 27.5 explains the causes of working of migrant child labour. It is observed from the table that poverty is responsible for the growth of child labour. All the sample working children are working due to poverty. Big Size of the family happens to be the next important cause for working of Migrant Children (51.52%). More than one-fifth of migrant children are working because of death of father. Death of father (9.09%) death of both (9.09%) and ill-habituated father (9.09%) are other causes responsible for the working of migrant children.

Table 27.5
Causes of Working of Migrant Child Labour

Cause of Working	*Boys*		*Girls*	
	Number	*Per cent*	*Number*	*Per cent*
1. Poverty	42	100.00	24	100.00
2. Death of father	8	19.05	6	25.00
3. Death of mother	2	4.76	4	16.67
4. Death of both parents	2	4.76	4	16.67
5. Big size of family	26	61.91	8	33.33
6. Illhabituated father	4	9.52	2	8.33
7. Illegality of child	—	—	—	—
8. Child's desire to work	—	—	—	—

Working Hours

A number of acts state that no child should be put to work for more than 4-6 hours a day. But in the study area more than three-fourths of the migrant working children are working more than 10 hours a day. Only about 10 per cent of the children are working 6-8 hours a day. It is observed from the study that no child is working below 6 hours a day (Table 27.6).

Monthly Income

An attempt is made to examine the monthly income of the migrant working children. It is observed from the data that about 40 per cent of the working children are earning about Rs. 200 per month (including Bata and Tips). One-third of the migrant child workers

Table 27.6
Working Hours of Migrant Child Labour

House of Work	*No. of Child Workers*	*Percent Age*
6 - 8	6	9.09
8 - 10	10	15.15
10 - 12	32	48.49
More than 12	18	27.27

are earning between Rs. 200-300 per month. Only 12.12 per cent of the migrant child labour are earning more than Rs. 400 per month. It is also observed from the study that no child is earning more than Rs. 600 per month (Table 27.7).

Table 27.7
Monthly Income of Migrant Child Labour

Income in Rs.	*No. of Child Workers*	*Per cent*
Below 100	6	9.09
100 - 200	20	30.30
200 - 300	22	33.33
300 - 400	10	15.15
Above 400	8	12.12

Type of Residential Accommodation

An attempt is also made to examine the type of residential accommodation used by the child labour (Table 27.8). It can be observed from the table that about 70 per cent of the non-migrant children are living in own house and only 21 per cent migrant working children are living in own houses. Most of the migrant children (30.03%) are living in rented houses. Total 212 working children are living in the houses, which were provided by their employer, 81.82% of these are provided to migrant child labourers.

Some of these migrant children migrated alongwith their friends/relatives. Some of these children are living in the rented houses, but the rent will be shared. The remaining migrants are not having any fixed place of living. They used to live at the place of work.

Table 27.8
Type of Residential Accomodation Used by the Child Labour

Status of House	*Migrant*	*Non-Migrant*	*Total*	*Per cent*
Owned	14 (36.84)	24 (63.16)	38 (100.00)	38.00
Rented*	20 (76.92)	6 (23.08)	26 (100.00)	26.00
Provided by the employers	18 (81.82)	4 (18.18)	22 (100.00)	22.00
Rented but shared	8 (100.00)	—	8 (100.00)	8.00
Others**	6 (100.00)	—	6 (100.00)	6.00
Total :	66 (66.00)	34 (34.00)	100 (100.00)	100.00

★ Includes children living with their parents in rented house.
★★ No fixed place of living.

Conclusions and Suggestions

The main cause of migration of labour is the poverty of family, which forces them into the labour market. The following few suggestions are offered to reduce the intensity of the problem of the child labour to a considerable extent:

1. To respect the provisions of the constitution of India as laid down in Article 24, no child under the age of 14 years be permitted to be employed and if found so, the employer as well as the father/guardian of the child both, be punished severely.
2. A statutory Board with executive powers, including the three main departments concerned—labour, social welfare and works and housing as well as other employing departments, where necessary at local or project level should be set up. Putting teeth into this Board would be the only way for efficient implementation.
3. Specialized migrant labour cells should be set-up through this Board, staffed by qualified people, to act as laision with migrant labour, convey employment and other information, provide access to facilities, and build-up a network of facilities through existing municipal and other agencies etc.

4. Wide publicity through mass media be made about long term consequences and dangerous impact on society about employment of children of tender age.
5. Care should be taken to improve health of working children. Similarly safety measures should be adopted at work places to protect the life of the working children.
6. Educational and recreational facilities should strengthened.

28

Landholding, Child Labour and Schooling

— *R. Nagarajan*

Introduction

The availability of empirical evidence from the number of demographic surveys conducted recently in rural areas of less developed countries (LDCs) led to a debate on the nature and extent of relationship between landholding and fertility behaviour (Stokes and Schutjer, 1984; Cain, 1985, 1986; Stokes *et al.*, 1986; Thomas, 1991; Clay and Johnson, 1992). These debates have raised several issues on the cause-effect mechanism of the relationship, viz.,

(i) large farm size may raise household's need for labour and consequently fertility (land-labour demand hypothesis);

(ii) land is adjusted to accommodate change in the labour force of the household (reverse causation);

(iii) ownership of land reduces the importance of children as a source of old age security and thus fertility (land-security hypothesis);

(iv) farm size increases fertility not by raising demand but by increasing supply of children i.e., couples who live on large

farms have access to better nutrition and health care for themselves and their children and this raises their natural fertility and child survival (supply effect); and

(v) extent of land-fertility relationship depends on institutions like market for land, labour and produce. Certainly, the relationship is quite complex and needs further investigation separately on each of these dimensions.

It is generally realised that fertility in rural areas of LDCs is high because children often make important economic contributions to the household (Mamdani, 1972; Cain, 1977; Nag et al., 1978; De Tray, 1983). Land as a production factor needs adequate labour input to produce. In agricultural households children often make a direct contribution to production. The participation of children in agricultural production activities starts as early as of age six (Cain, 1977, 1978). For example, children often herd and take care of livestock, gather wood for fuel, bring food and water to those working in the farm, take care of younger siblings (thus freeing adults to productive activities), help around house, and fetch water. Under these circumstances, the direct labour contribution of children to the household production is an important factor determining fertility behaviour of households. Hence, it has been suggested by many researchers that there is a complementarity between landholding and child labour, and this is responsible for the observed consistent positive relationship between landholding and fertility in many LDC settings (Rosenzweig and Evenson, 1977; Mueller and Short, 1983; Lee and Bulatao, 1983; Stokes and Schutjer, 1984).

It is stated that, farm families with access to large amount of holdings have greater labour requirements, and are able to employ profitably more family labour in the family farm and thus can raise its income. This income in turn increases the demand for children by making children more affordable and more profitable as a source of family labour. This explanation has been termed as 'Land-Labour Demand Hypothesis' (Stokes and Schutjer, 1984; Stokes *et al.*, 1986). However, only very few empirical studies have examined this important hypothesis. Hence, this paper focuses the 'Land-Labour Demand Hypothesis' with the help of household level data collected from the farm families in rural Tamilnadu.

Literature

Some empirical evidence that relates land and labour contribution of children is available at the aggregate and household level studies conducted in LDCs. It should be mentioned that these studies are not primarily aimed to investigate the land-child labour connection. Land is included as one of the independent variables. Some of these studies are reviewed here.

In Brazil, farm size is found to have a positive and significant relationship with proportion of children aged 5-14 working as unpaid family labourers and significant negative relationship with proportion of children aged 5-14 attending school (Merrick, 1981). The opposite effects of farm size on child labour and schooling suggest a substitution between child labour and schooling with respect to land. In rural Egypt, there is a positive significant relationship between child labour force participation and size of land devoted to cotton, and significant negative relationship between age specific school enrolment and land size, profit per acre, and modernisation (Levy, 1985). These opposite effects suggest that the shadow price and the market value of children's time discourage formal schooling. In India, Rosenzweig and Evenson (1977) found significant positive relationship between labour force participation of male and female children aged 5-14 and size of farm. On the other hand, school enrolment ratio of children aged 5-14 of both sexes was found to be negatively related with landholding. Similarly, the relationship between child wage and child school enrolment ratio was also found to be negative. All these macro-level studies reveal the land-child labour complementarity.

At the household level, in rural Botswana school enrolment and average time spent per day in school were observed to be significantly lower in households with more land. But the amount of time spent by children in school was higher among households wealthy of cattle, since these households could hire labour and keep children in school on a more regular basis (Chernichovsky, 1985). In Pakistan, school enrolment and cropped area tend to have a 'U' shaped relationship for male children and positive relationship for female children. This result suggests that wealth effect dominates in the case of female but opportunity costs in the case of male schooling (Irfan, 1989). Cain (1977) in his intensive time-use study in rural Bangladesh found that among children aged 10 and older, those from landless households did considerably more work than those from landed classes. By contrast, he observed, boys below age 10 from landless households worked fewer hours overall than boys from landed households; and they also spent proportionately less time in directly productive work. Further, Cain (1978) argues that boys are more valuable to landowners, particularly to the large landowners. Because, not only landless generate fewer surviving children and thus less child power relative to landowners, they also have less control over each child's output. Since, ownership of land provides a father leverage over his sons, which gives him a degree of control over the timing of son's departure from his household and may enable him to expropriate their labour and output. A landless father does not have this leverage. He found that among large landowners son's mean age of leaving home is much greater than among the landless. Further, the large landowners have a much smaller proportion of sons living away from home than landless ones in Bangladesh.

Vlassoff (1979) reported that in rural Maharashtra children were economically active only among rich families and he argued that, the rich families who owned more land also provided more opportunities for economic contributions of their children. In rural Karnataka, average time input per day by schoolgoing and non-schoolgoing children in different household and productive activities was found to increase with landholding and number of livestock at home. Further, landholding is found to significantly decrease the amount of time spent in school by the child (Kanbargi and Kulkarni, 1986). Visaria *et al.* (1993) found that the probability of a child aged 10-14 becoming a worker tends to rise if the family possesses per capita land of more than 1.00 acre in Gujarat or more than 0.5 acre in Maharashtra.

Yotopoulos (1983) reported higher marginal productivity of child labour in large farms than in small and tenant farms in Philippines. In Ruanda, support of children from outside the household was found to be negatively related with landholding, but significant positive relationship between landholding and support of children within the household was observed, suggesting families with large landholding are able to employ their family labour effectively (Clay and Harr, 1993). In Thailand, Arnold and Pejaranonda (1977) reported that more parents with large landholding found children's help in family farming advantageous than parents with small holdings.

In contrast to the above studies, land variables (size of land owned, proportion of land suitable for high yielding variety of rice and proportion of cultivable land irrigated) in West Bengal are found to have an insignificant effect on schooling of boys aged 5-14 and significant positive effect on schooling of girls aged 5-14 (Mukhopadhyay, 1994). Nadkarni (1976) in rural Maharashtra observed a negative association between size of landholding and economic contribution of children and positive association between size of landholding and schooling of children. Labour force participation and school attendance of children in dryland farming areas of India is reported to have negative and positive association, respectively, with landholding (Jodha and Singh, 1991). However, Rosenzweig (1982) did not find any relation between farm size and school enrolment of children in the districts chosen for Intensive Agricultural Development Programme in India. An analysis of data from the village level studies conducted in India by the International Crops Research Institute for the Semi-Arid Tropics (ICRISAT) shows that with increase in size of land both boys and girls aged 5-17 are less likely to participate in wage labour and household production activities and more likely to participate in schooling (Skoufias, 1994).

The abovementioned theoretical discussion and empirical studies show that, with some exception, labour force participation of children increases with land. This is consistent with the notion that farm households with access to larger holdings have greater labour requirements, and that there is a complementarity between child labour and productive assets of the household. However, it has been pointed out that the child labour factor by itself may not strongly influence fertility, and that the direction of causation may not necessarily be from child labour to fertility (Dyson, 1991; Vlassoff, 1991). Moreover, an analysis of the National Sample Survey data in India also indicated that the wage contribution of children from land-owning households may not be as important as in the case of landless households (Vemuri and Shastry, 1991). Hence, a complementarity between land and labour may not necessarily mean a positive effect of land on fertility as assumed by many demographers. Clearly, the land-child labour linkages needs to be examined carefully.

The differentials in the level of schooling among different size of farm households have generally been attributed to differing opportunity costs of sending children to school due to relatively higher utilisation of children in productive activities of the farm households. School age farm children can readily participate in farm production activities and thus contribute to family income. Also, the level of schooling a child completes directly influences the farm family's income. Further, the labour force contribution of farm children implies that an increase in the level of schooling to the children is the value of the income of profit sacrificed as a consequence of the child's school attendance. The empirical studies reviewed above show that the school age farm children's potential contribution to the farm production activities is substantial. The positive relationship between landholding and labour force participation of farm children reveals that the value of children's time influences their level of schooling and that an increase in farm size reduces the enrolment rate of farm children.

Taking into consideration the issues discussed above the objectives of this paper on the relationship between landholding and child labour are :

(*i*) to assess the actual labour contribution of children from farm families in terms of their work input in household and productive activities in farm; and

(*ii*) to assess the effect of farm size and farm income on actual labour contribution of children and schooling of children.

The Data

Data analysed in this paper pertains to the farm households selected for a landholding-fertility survey in Periyar district of Tamilnadu by the author. Since land-child labour relationship is relevant for a population that is purely dependent on agriculture, this study was specifically restricted to the Kongu Vellala community, which is the predominantly agrarian community in the north-western region of Tamilnadu.

The nature of land-child labour relationship could vary, among various other factors, by source of irrigation. In particular, this relationship in assured irrigated areas (more cropping intensity) could be different from that in non-assured irrigated areas (less cropping intensity). But the scope of this study is restricted to the non-assured irrigated areas only. Open wells are the main source of irrigation besides rain-fed cultivation. Major crops cultivated are groundnut, vegetables, millet, pulses, mulberry, cotton and to a limited extent paddy. Kongu Vellala agricultural households, in the primarily well irrigated and rain-fed portions of Dharapuram taluk of Periyar district, was the universe of the study. Currently, married men aged 20-25 with wife in the reproductive age of 15-45 and with atleast one living child at the time of the survey form the unit of analysis for the study.

A two-stage self-weighing sampling scheme was adopted to select the sample households. In the first stage, five villages were selected with probability proportional to size. In the second stage, all the Kongu Vellala agricultural households in the selected villages were listed and from each village, a sample was selected systematically. An interview schedule was specifically developed to meet the data requirements of the study. Information from 360 respondents was obtained from personal interviews by the author. Data for the study were collected during the months of July 1991-February 1992.

To assess the relationship between landholding and labour contribution of children, data on actual time inputs (in hours per day) in household and productive activities have been obtained for children aged 6-17 years in the selected households. There are 323 children in this age group (177 boys and 146 girls) in the 360 sample households.

Analysis

In the analysis of child labour, 'household work' of children includes bringing drinking water, cleaning the utensils, taking care of younger children, cleaning the house, collecting firewood, washing clothes, shopping provisions, running errands, activities related to preparation of food, *etc.* 'Productive work' includes work on own family farm, livestock, family enterprise and wage work. Labour contribution of children to productive activities directly contributes to household income. Contribution to household activities is valuable for household maintenance, besides, it relieves the elder members of the household to work more on directly productive activities.

The association between landholding and child labour has been examined separately for male and female children. For this purpose, cross tabulations have been presented to illustrate the pattern of labour contribution of children by landholding and some other background variables. Further, since the labour contribution would depend on whether a child is in school or not, the results are also given separately for schoolgoing and non-schoolgoing children. No tests of significance of associations have been performed in this preliminary analysis; the regression analysis presented later would provide results on the significance of effects controlled for other factors.

Labour Contribution of Children

The labour contribution of children (in terms of number of hours per day) aged 6-17 years by sex in household and productive activities is presented in Table 28.1. The data indicate that children in these households are engaged in various activities which are useful to the household. Girls spend more time on household activities than boys, whereas boys spend more time on productive activities than girls. School-going children naturally spend less time on work and non-schoolgoing children contribute a considerable amount of their labour time to the household in various activities.

About 80 per cent of the children in the 6-17 age group are in school indicating the Vellalas' strong desire to educate their children rather than keep them outside the school for household and farm work atleast in these younger ages. Boys outnumber girls in schooling reflecting the typical Indian gender bias in educating the children.

Labour contribution of children by age and sex of children (Table 28.2) reveals that these two demographic factors play an important role in determining the extent of participation in activities. Children put in an increasing amount of time on productive as well as household activities as they grow older. The average time spent increases substantially after the age of 14. This large increase is due to the large number of dropouts in this age group (Table 28.3). About 53 per cent of boys and 66 per cent of the girls are outside the school in this age group and spend considerable time on productive and household activities.

The age-wise data on schooling and labour contribution of children indicate that schooling is almost universal among children up to age eleven (Table 28.3). Substantial labour contribution starts only after the age of 11. There are large differences in labour contribution among schoolgoing and non-schoolgoing children. Total time spent on all work by schoolgoing boys and girls increases from less than half an hour at age 6-8 to more than two hours at ages 15-17. Total time spent on all work by boys and girls going to school in each age group is almost the same. At the same time total time input of children who do not go to school increases from less than three hours at age 9-11 to more than eight hours at ages 15-17.

Table 28.1
Average Time Input of Children Aged 6-17 in Household and Productive Activities

	Boys	*Girls*	*Both*
Number of children	177	146	323
Per cent attending school	84.75	70.55	78.33
Time input (hours per day)			
Household work	.44	1.33	.85
Productive work	1.99	1.88	1.94
Total	2.44	3.21	2.79
N	177	146	323
Time input: Schoolgoing children only			
Household work	.39	.85	.57
Productive work	1.04	.60	.86
Total	1.43	1.45	1.44
N	150	103	253
Time input: Non-Schoolgoing children only			
Household work	.74	2.49	1.81
Productive work	7.28	4.93	5.83
Total	8.02	7.41	7.65
N	27	43	70

Table 28.2
Average Time Input (in Hours) Per Day by Age and Sex of Children Aged 6-17 in Household and Productive Activities

Sex	*Age Group*	*Household Work*	*Productive Work*	*Total Work*
Boys				
	6 – 8	.13	.37	.49
	9 – 11	.35	1.06	1.41
	12 – 14	.57	1.89	2.46
	15 – 17	.72	5.00	5.73
	6 – 17	.44	1.99	2.44
Girls				
	6 – 8	.18	.22	.40
	9 – 11	.88	.59	1.47
	12 – 14	1.66	2.09	3.75
	15 – 17	2.17	3.94	6.11
	6 – 17	1.33	1.88	3.21

Table 28.3
Average Time Input (in Hours) Per Day by Schoolgoing and Non-Schoolgoing Children in Household and Productive Activities by Age and Sex

Sex & Age	*%in School*	*Schoolgoing Children*			*Non-schoolgoing Children*			*No. of Children*
		HH	*Prod*	*Total*	*HH*	*Prod*	*Total*	
Boys								
6 – 8	100.00	.13	.36	.49	—	—	—	44
9 – 11	97.50	.36	1.01	1.37	0	3.00	3.00	40
12 – 14	89.09	.57	1,39	1.96	.58	6.00	6.58	55
15 – 17	47.37	.61	1.81	2.41	.83	7.88	8.71	38
6 – 17	84.75	.39	1.04	1.43	.74	7.28	8.02	177
Girls								
6 – 8	100.00	.18	.22	.40	—	—	—	26
9 – 11	92.31	.83	.53	1.36	1.50	1.33	2.83	39
12 – 14	67.50	1.31	.83	2.15	2.38	4.69	7.08	40
15 – 17	34.15	1.25	1.04	2.29	2.65	5.44	8.09	41
6 – 17	70.55	.85	.60	1.45	2.49	4.93	7.42	146

HH : Household work.
Prod : Productive work.

Differentials in Child Labour and Schooling

School enrolment and labour input of schoolgoing and non-schoolgoing boys and girls by landholding and some other background variables are presented in Tables 28.4 and 28.5. Size of landholding seems to decrease the non-schoolgoing children's productive activities, but does not have any meaningful association with the schoolgoing children's activities. Land and income are positively associated with the school attendance of male children but rather surprisingly negatively with the attendance of female children. Higher the education of father lower is the labour contribution and higher the schooling of both male and female children suggesting the educated father's higher educational aspirations for their children. Other variables included in the table, like value of livestock and agricultural implements, and education of mother, do not have any systematic association with the labour contribution of children.

Regression Analysis

The preceeding discussion is based mainly on cross tabulations and shows only gross association. Therefore, regression analysis is carried out to assess the net influences of land and other factors on labour contribution and schooling of children. For this purpose two dependent variables are used *viz.,*

(*i*) labour input of children and
(*ii*) schooling status of children.

Table 28.4
Average Time Input (in Hours) Per Day of Schoolgoing and Non-schoolgoing Boys Aged 6-17 in Household and Productive Activities by Background Variables

Background variables	*%in school*	*Schoolgoing Children*		*Non-schoolgoing Children*		*No. of Children*
		HH	*Prod.*	*HH*	*Prod.*	
	Average time input (in hours) per day					
Landholding (in acres)						
< 5	81.48	.43	1.19	.70	8.40	54
5 – < 10	78.85	.28	.80	.77	6.80	52
10 – < 15	91.67	.39	1.45	.50	6.00	24
15 +	91.49	.45	.91	.88	6.38	47
Farm income (in Rs.)						
< 25000	80.00	.41	.98	.73	7.44	55
25000 – < 50000	85.14	.40	1.19	.77	7.45	74
50000 +	89.58	.36	.88	.70	6.50	48
Value of livestock (in Rs.)						
< 5000	77.78	.38	.90	.50	7.50	27
5000 – < 10000	87.76	.41	1.03	.75	8.11	49
10000 – < 15000	87.23	.35	1.15	1.58	7.50	47
15000 +	83.33	.41	1.02	.33	6.44	54
Value of agricultural implements owned						
0	93.75	.53	.97	0	9.00	16
< 10000	78.48	.40	1.08	.97	7.35	79
10000 – < 15000	86.05	.35	1.08	.33	7.19	43
15000 +	92.31	.36	.97	.50	6.50	39
Education of father						
Illiterate	84.00	.48	1.30	.75	8.34	25
1 - 5 years	80.22	.40	1.09	.64	7.54	91
6 – 8 years	90.91	.30	.89	.83	6.33	33
9 + years	92.86	.40	.87	1.50	4.25	28
Education of mother						
Illiterate	80.22	.42	1.15	.50	7.72	91
1 - 5 years	90.63	.37	.97	1.00	6.61	64
5 + years	86.36	.32	.87	1.67	6.00	22

Table 28.5
Average Time Input (in Hours) Per Day of Schoolgoing and Non-Schoolgoing Girls Aged 6-17 in Household and Productive Activities by Background Variables

Background Variables	*%in School*	*Schoolgoing Children*		*Non-schoolgoing Children*		*No. of Children*
		HH	*Prod.*	*HH*	*Prod.*	
	Average time input (in hours) per day					
Landholding (in acres)						
< 5	82.35	.99	.53	2.58	5.75	34
5 – < 10	68.63	.83	.81	2.75	5.50	51
10 – < 15	65.22	1.10	.67	2.13	4.88	23
15 +	65.79	.58	.34	2.35	3.88	38
Farm income (in Rs.)						
< 25000	72.55	.86	.47	2.29	5.29	51
25000 – < 50000	73.02	.95	.79	2.56	5.06	63
50000 +	62.50	.63	.40	2.63	4.33	32
Value of livestock (in Rs.)						
< 5000	76.19	.88	.58	2.30	7.40	21
5000 – < 10000	67.65	.63	.61	2.95	4.59	34
10000 – < 15000	80.95	1.02	0.74	2.25	4.56	42
15000 +	61.22	.82	.45	2.37	4.63	49
Value of agricultural implements owned						
0	64.29	.83	.42	2.20	6.70	14
< 10000	74.03	1.00	.82	2.45	5.23	77
10000 – < 15000	52.38	.77	.27	2.15	4.10	21
15000 +	76.47	.58	.33	3.19	4.13	34
Education of father						
Illiterate	55.00	.73	.61	2.06	4.44	20
1 – 5 years	67.90	1.02	.72	2.67	4.94	81
6 – 8 years	81.82	.75	.39	2.75	3.63	22
9 + years	82.61	.53	.45	2.00	7.25	23
Education of mother						
Illiterate	63.86	1.00	.63	2.43	4.78	83
1 – 5 years	82.98	.56	.54	2.50	5.50	47
5 + years	68.75	1.13	.68	2.80	4.90	16

Labour input is measured by the number of hours per day working in productive activities by the child. Schooling status of child is a dichotomous variable measured as 1 if child goes to school (enrolled and regularly attends), and 0 otherwise. The means and variances of the variables included in the regression analysis are give in Appendix.

For labour input of children, age and schooling status of child are used as control variables. The regression results (Table 28.6) show that there is a significant negative relationship between size of landholding and labour input of children. Sex-wise analysis shows that the size of landholding has significant negative effect on labour contribution of female children but not of male children. The other background variables (education of parents and farm income) included in the regression equation other than control variables did not show any effect on labour input of children. Thus, the data do not support the complementarity between landholding and labour contribution of children, instead the amount of land tends to decrease the labour input of children, especially girls. This is perhaps because large landholders enjoy higher status in the society and hence would not want their daughters to work on farm.

Table 28.6
Regression of Labour Contribution of Children (in Hours) Aged 6-17 in Productive Activities on Landholding and Background Variables

Independent variables	*All Children*	*Male Children*	*Female Children*
Size of landholding	–0.024***	–0.005***	–0.035***
	(2.994)	(0.951)	(2.654)
Annual farm income	–0.003	–0.003	–0.003
	(1.092)	(1.081)	(1.616)
Education of father	0.021	–0.042	0.053
	(0.859)	(1.591)	(1.268)
Education of mother	–0.030	–0.021	–0.004
	(1.165)	(0.853)	(0.096)
Number of living children	0.073	0.059	0.261*
	(0.837)	(0.663)	(1.712)
Age of child	0.180***	0.190***	0.131***
	(7.505)	(7.853)	(3.084)
Sex of child (= 1 if male)	0.869*** (6.156)	—	—
Schooling status of child (= 1 if in school = 0 otherwise)	–4.376*** (22.449)	–5.316*** (24.233)	–3.809*** (12.111)
Constant	2.969	4.639	2.614
R^2	0.77	0.88	0.70
Number of observations	323	177	146

*** significant at the .01 level.
** significant at the .05 level.
* significant at the .10 level.
t – values are given in parenthesis
Note : The means and standard deviations of the variables are given in Appendix.

Table 28.7
Regression of Labour Contribution of Children (in Hours) Aged 6-17 in Productive Activities on Landholding and Background Variables

Independent Variables	*All Children*	*Male Children*	*Female Children*
Size of operational holding	–0.024***	–0.004	–0.040***
	(2.816)	(0.428)	(2.704)
Annual farm income	–0.003	–0.003	–0.002
	(1.085)	(1.115)	(0.519)
Education of father	0.021	–0.043*	0.059
	(0.836)	(1.653)	(1.377)
Education of mother	–0.029	–0.021	–0.005
	(1.159)	(0.844)	(0.115)
Number of living children	0.071	0.059	0.267*
	(0.819)	(0.657)	(1.749)
Age of child	0.179***	0.189***	0.132***
	(7.460)	(7.843)	(3.095)
Sex of child (= 1 if male)	0.868***	—	—
	(6.139)		
Schooling status of child (= 1 if in school = 0 otherwise)	–4.370***	–5.322***	–3.813***
	(22.429)	(24.265)	(12.113)
Constant	2.975	4.651	2.594
R^2	0.77	0.88	0.70
Number of observations	323	177	146

*** Significant at the .01 level.
** significant at the .05 level.
* significant at the .10 level.
t – values are given in parentheses.

Note : The means and standard deviations of the variables are given in Appendix.

The landholding variable used above includes both cultivated holdings and land leased-out. However, child labour is more likely to depend on operational holding, *i.e.*, the total land being actually cultivated. Therefore, the regression analysis has been redone using size of operational holding (land owned and cultivated + land leased-in for cultivation) in the place of landholding (land owned and cultivated + land leased-in + land leased-out); all the control and background variables are retained. The results are shown in Table 28.7. It can be seen that the results are almost identical to those obtained in Table 28.6 *i.e.*, with landholding as the measure of land. The reason for this is that in this region the extent of land leased-in is quite small and size of landholding and size of operational holding are nearly the same even at the individual level; the zero order correlation between these two land measures is. 982.

Landholding and Schooling Status of Children

Since schooling status is a dichotomous variable, the logistic regression approach is used. The results (Table 28.8) show that size of landholding significantly increases male children's schooling. Usually in the typical rural Indian conditions parents prefer to put

Table 28.8
Logistic Regression of Schooling Status of Children (Aged 6-17) on Landholding and Background Variables
Dependent variable: Schooling status of child
Measured as = 1 if the child goes to school
= 0 otherwise

Independent variables	*All Children*	*Male Children*	*Female Children*
Size of landholding	0.007	–0.094**	–0.060
	(0.337)	(2.259)	(1.561)
Annual farm income	–0.000	–0.002	0.009
	(0.026)	(0.212)	(0.704)
Education of father	0.086	–0.093	0.261***
	(1.306)	(0.857)	(2.740)
Education of mother	0.063	0.000	0.082
	(0.982)	(0.002)	(0.908)
Number of living children	–0.549**	–0.027	–0.907***
	(2.486)	(0.065)	(2.643)
Age of child	–0.603***	–0.770***	–0.608***
	(7.297)	(5.053)	(4.964)
Sex of child (= 1 if male)	0.652*	—	—
	(1.807)		
Log likelihood	-106.99	-45.09	-52.45
Number of observations	323	177	146

*** significant at the .01 level.
** significant at the .05 level.
* significant at the .10 level.
t – values are given in parenthesis.

Note : The means and standard deviations of the variables are given in Appendix.

a male child in school for a longer time than a female child. But an increase in education of father significantly increases the schooling status of female children as well. The effect of size of landholding on schooling of female child is negative but not significant.

Landholding and Aspirations for Children's Education

Aspirations for children's education determine the desired quality of children and in turn influence desired quantity. Various factors including land could influence parental aspirations toward the quality of children. Hence, to assess the effect of land on quality of children, aspired level of education for them was obtained from the fathers. Instead of asking a general question about aspirations, respondents were asked about the aspirations for specific children, who were going to school. Out of 323 children in age group of 6-17 years, 253 (150 boys and 103 girls) were going to school at the time of survey. For each of these, father's aspirations were recorded.

Table 28.9 shows the aspired level of education for children separately for sons and daughters. More than 90 per cent of respondents want their children to have atleast high school level education, and over 30 per cent want their children to have college education. Their aspirations towards their children's education are high as compared to their own level of education. The parents clearly want their children to have higher level of education than themselves. There is, however, a clear sex bias in that, aspirations on son's education are higher than daughter's.

Table 28.9
Educational Aspirations of Parents About Schoolgoing Children

(Percentage Distribution)

Aspired Level of Education	*Sons*	*Daughters*	*Combined*
Below high school	2.7	13.6	7.1
High school	20.7	27.2	23.3
Higher Secondary	36.0	38.8	37.2
College	40.7	20.4	32.4
Total	100.0	100.0	100.0
Mean (years of schooling)	12.75	11.47	12.23
Number of children	150	103	253

Regression analysis is performed to analyse the effect of land, income and background factors on aspired level of education for children, expressed as years of schooling, as the dependent variable (means and standard deviations of the variables used in this analysis are given in Appendix). The results (Table 28.10) show that land has a significant positive effect on educational aspirations for male children (note that this regression is based on only children in school). This finding is particularly important because even after controlling for income and parental education, the effect of land is positive and significant, suggesting that land has an independent effect on changing tastes and aspirations. Education of father significantly increases educational aspirations for both sons and daughters. The effect of education of mother is in the expected direction though not significant. The results also reflect the significant higher educational aspirations for male children.

Table 28.10
Regression of Aspired Level of Education for Schoolgoing Children (Aged 6-17) on Landholding and Background Variables

Independent Variables	*All Children*	*Male Children*	*Female Children*
Size of landholding	0.033*	0.004**	0.016
	(1.948)	(2.155)	(0.547)
Annual farm income	0.003	0.004	0.013
	(0.447)	(0.631)	(1.322)
Education of father	0.186***	0.168***	0.237***
	(3.530)	(2.656)	(2.602)
Education of mother	0.094*	0.068	0.127
	(1.771)	(1.113)	(1.311)
Age of child	0.113**	0.066	0.172**
	(2.440)	(1.176)	(2.115)
Sex of child (= 1 if male)	1.277***	—	—
	(4.480)		
Constant	8.590	10.690	7.386
R^2	0.23	0.16	0.23
Number of observations	253	150	103

*** significant at the .01 level.
** significant at the .05 level.
* significant at the .10 level.
t – values are given in parenthesis.

Note: The means and standard deviations of the variables are given in Appendix.

Conclusions

The objective of this paper was to examine the nature and extent of labour contribution of children to the farm household and determinants of it. The results indicate that on an average children in the age group of 6-17 years contribute 2.79 hours per day to the household in various activities, and their contribution increases with age as expected. Girls contribute more to household work, whereas boys contribute more to productive work. Overall girls contribute more than boys because relatively fewer girls go to school than boys. Further, the results indicate that in the Kongu Vellala households, education is universal for children up to age 11. Hence, only after the age of 11 do children start to make a notable contribution, and only after age of 14 is the contribution substantial. This result is contrary to what Cain (1977) observed in nearby Bangladesh where children start working at an early age and become net producers by the age of 13.

The regression results clearly show that size of landholding does not increase labour contribution of children, on the contrary it reduces the contribution of girls. Thus, land-labour demand hypothesis does not get support atleast in this study area. Landholding does increase the tendency to send boys to school. Moreover, the aspired level for sons' education also rises with the size of landholding. Note that these effects are found in the regression equations and are thus net effects of education and income. This indicates that landholding has an independent effect on changing tastes and educational aspirations. This tendency towards the higher quality of children could in turn raise the cost of child rearing and have a fertility depressing effect.

The Land-Labour Demand hypothesis is one of the most prominently and frequently mentioned hypothesis in demographic literature. It is true that empirical evidence in the past was generally in favour of land-labour complementarity. The demand for child labour was naturally presumed to create a demand for higher family size. In the present study, we find that the link between size of landholding and child labour itself is very weak. In this situation land obviously cannot have any notable impact on demand for family size because of the child labour factor. The possibility of a strong land-child labour link in other agrarian settings within India and other LDCs cannot, of course, be ruled out.

In the past, schooling was less common among the agricultural communities, child labour was perhaps considerably higher. However, now that schooling has become nearly universal atleast during early childhood, the contribution of children is no longer perceived to be important. Moreover, large landowners have a greater tendency to send children to school even during later years of childhood. Thus, though there may be greater scope for child labour in large landholding families, the actual prevalence is not so. This is probably one of the reasons why the land-child labour complementarity does not appear to exist in the study population.

Child labour is economically advantageous to the landholder only in the absence of cheap and dependable labour market. If a fairly dependable labour market is available, there is no need for the farmer to have more children to work on farm. The farmer would be able to employ wage labourers and send their children to school or off-farm activities. Hence, the complementarity between land and labour depends on the labour market. Our analysis of the labour market in the study area shows that most of the farmers are cultivating with the help of hired labourers and some even employ permanent labourers (20 per cent of the households). This indicates that the farmers are able to employ permanent labourers at affordable wage rates. The availability of hired labourers and ability of farmers to pay for them together may have an influence on the labour contribution of children to the farm household.

References

1. Arnold, F. and C. Pejaranonda, 1977, Economic Factors in Family Size Decisions in Thailand Bangkok, Institute of Population Studies, Chulalonkorn University and National Statistical Office, Hawaii, East-West Population Institute.
2. Cain, M., 1977, The Economic Activities of Children in a Village in Bangladesh, *Population and Development Review,* Vol. 3, No. 3, pp. 201-27.
3. Cain, M., 1978, The Household Life Cycle and Economic Mobility in Rural Bangladesh, *Population and Development Review,* Vol. 4, No. 3, pp. 421-28.
4. Cain, M., 1985, On the Relationship Between Landholding and Fertility, *Population Studies,* Vol. 39, No. 1, pp. 5-15.
5. Cain, M., 1986, Landholding and Fertility: A Rejoinder, *Population Studies,* Vol. 40, No. 2, pp. 313-17.
6. Clay, D.C. and J.Mc Allister, 1991, Family Development Cycle, Social Class, and Inequality in *Rwanda, Rural Sociology,* Vol. 56, No. 1, pp. 22-40.

7. Clay, D.C. and J.E.V. Harr, 1993, Patterns of Inter-generational Support and Childbearing in the Third World, *Population Studies*, Vol. 47; No. 1, pp. 67-83.
8. De Tray, 1983, Child Labour in Malaysia, *Population and Development Review*, Vol. 9, No. 3, pp. 437-55.
9. Dyson, T., 1991, Child Labour and Fertility: An Overview, An Assessment and An Alternative Framework, In: R. Kanbargi (Ed.), Child Labour in the Indian Sub-continent: Dimensions and Implications, New Delhi, Sage Publications.
10. Irfan, M., 1989, Poverty, Class Structure and Household Demographic Behaviour in Rural Pakistan, In : G. Rodgers, (Ed.), Population Growth and Poverty in Rural South Asia, New Delhi, Sage Publications.
11. Jodha, N.S. and R.P. Singh, 1991, Child Labour in Dryland Agriculture in India, In : R. Kanbargi, (Ed.), Child Labour in the Indian Sub-continent: Dimensions and Implications, New Delhi, Sage Publications.
12. Lee, R.D. and R.A. Bulatao, 1983, The Demand for Children : A Critical Essay, In : R.A. Bulatao and R.D. Lee (Eds.), Determinants of Fertility in Developing Countries: Supply and Demand for Children, Vol.1, Studies in Population, New York, Academic Press.
13. Levy, V., 1985, Cropping Pattern, Mechanisation, Child Labour, and Fertility Behaviour in a Farming Economy : Rural Egypt., *Economic Development and Cultural Change*, Vol. 33, No. 4, pp. 777-91.
14. Mamdani, M., 1972, *The Myth of Population Control : Family, Caste, and Class in an Indian Village*, New York, Monthly Review Press.
15. Merrick, T.W., 1981, Land Availability and Rural Fertility in the North-Eastern Brazil, In : J.L. Simon and P.H. Lindert (Eds.), *Research in Population Economics*, Vol. 3, pp. 93-121.
16. Mueller, E. and K. Short, 1993, Effects of Income and Wealth on the Demand for Children, In : R.A. Bulatao and R.D. Lee (Eds.), Determinants of Fertility in Developing Countries: Supply and Demand for Children, Vol. I, Studies in Population, New York, Academic Press.
17. Mukhopadhyay, S.K. 1994, Adapting Household Behaviour to Agricultural Technology in West Bengal, India : Wage Labour, Fertility, and Child Schooling Determinants, *Economic Development and Cultural Change*, Vol. 43, No. (1), pp. 91-115.
18. Nadkarni, M.V., 1976, Over Population and Rural poor, *Economic and Political Weekly*, Vol. 11, Nos. 31-33, pp. 1163-72.
19. Nag, M., B.N.F. White and R.C. Peet, 1978, An Anthropological Approach to the Study of the Economic Value of Children in Java and Nepal, *Current Anthropology*, Vol. 19, No. 2, pp. 293-306.

20. Rosenzweig, M.R. and R. Evenson, 1977, Fertility, Schooling and Economic Contributions of Children in Rural India : An Economic Analysis, *Econometrica,* Vol. 45, pp. 1065-79.
21. Skoufias, E., 1994, Market Wages, Family Composition and the Time Allocation of Children in Agricultural Households, *The Journal of Development Studies,* Vol. 30, No. 2, pp. 335-60.
22. Stokes, C.S. and W.A. Schutjer, 1984, Access to Land and Fertility in Developing Countries, in : W.A. Schutjer and C.S. Stokes (Eds.), *Rural Development and Human Fertility,* New York, MacMillan.
23. Stokes, C.S., W.A. Schutjer and R.A. Bulatao, 1986, is the Relationship Between Landholding and Fertility Spurious? A Response to Cain, *Population Studies,* Vol. 40, No. 2, pp. 305-11.
24. Thomas, N., 1991, Land, Fertility and the Population Establishment, *Population Studies,* Vol. 45, pp. 379-97.
25. Vemuri, M.D. and U.V.K.V. Shastry, 1991, Participation of Children in Economic Activity: A Regional Analysis of Rural India, In: R. Kanbargi (Ed.), *Child Labour in the Indian Sub-continent: Dimensions and Implications,* New Delhi, Sage Publications.
26. Visaria, Pravin, Anil Gumber and Chinnam Gopinath, 1993, Child Labour, Family Life and Fertility in India, *Working Paper No. 55,* Ahmedabad, Gujarat Institute of Development Research.
27. Vlassoff, M., 1979, Labour Demand and Economic Utility of Children: A Case Study in Rural India, *Population Studies,* Vol. 33, No. 1, pp. 415-28.
28. Vlassoff, M., 1991, An Assessment of Studies Linking Child Labour and Fertility Behaviour in Less Developed Countries, In: R. Kanbargi (Ed.), Child Labour in Indian Sub-continent: Dimensions and Implications, New Delhi, Sage Publications.

APPENDIX

Means and Standard Deviations of the Variables Used in Tables 6, 7, and 8

Independent variables	*All Children*		*Male Children*		*Female Children*	
	Mean	*Std.*	*Mean*	*Std.*	*Mean*	*Std.*
Size of landholding (in acres)	10.91	9.79	10.71	9.25	11.15	10.43
Size of operational holding (in acres)	10.43	9.16	10.26	8.99	10.66	9.39
Annual farm income (in '000 Rs.)	38.81	29.12	40.08	29.92	37.28	28.14
Education of father (in years)	4.94	3.24	4.97	3.24	4.90	3.25
Education of mother (in years)	2.35	3.05	2.48	3.17	2.19	2.91
No. of living children	2.13	0.83	1.93	0.76	2.38	0.84
Age of child	11.68	3.30	11.45	3.28	11.96	3.33
Schooling status of child (=1 if in school)	0.78	0.41	0.85	0.36	0.71	0.46
Productive activities of children (in hours)	1.94	2.45	1.99	2.49	1.88	2.46
Sex of child (=1 if male)	0.55	0.50	—	—	—	—
N	323		177		146	

Means and Standard Deviations of the Variables Used in Table 10

Independent variables	*All Children*		*Male Children*		*Female Children*	
	Mean	*Std.*	*Mean*	*Std.*	*Mean*	*Std.*
Size of landholding (in acres)	10.94	9.89	11.25	9.60	10.51	10.34
Annual farm income (in '000 Rs.)	39.27	28.80	40.46	28.26	37.54	29.61
Education of father (in years)	5.20	3.25	5.10	3.30	5.34	3.19
Education of mother (in years)	2.47	3.06	2.58	3.18	2.35	2.89
No. of living children	2.04	0.72	1.93	0.80	2.20	0.55
Age of child	10.78	3.05	10.77	3.01	10.80	3.11
Sex of child (=1 if male)	0.59	0.49	—	—	—	—
Aspired level of education (in years)	12.23	2.50	12.75	2.18	11.47	2.73
N	253		150		103	

Section - V

CURBING CHILD LABOUR

29

The Child and The Law

—M. Koteswara Rao & P. Venu Gopal

Children are recognised as the most important asset for the future of any society. The children are the most important factors to fulfil the requirements of society from time to time. But now-a-days, children are facing so many problems for their survival. In a country like India, a large number of children are at work for their survival as well as their families. They are becoming earning members of the families of low incomes and poor. Poverty forces them to go for work instead of going to schools. Though State responded to this problem there is no cohesive thought on this issue, half-heartedness and disinterest of the policy makers, legislators and intellectuals make this problem difficult. A number of acts and legislations were enacted to allieviate the child labour. They can be divided into two parts i.e.

(A) Constitutional Provisions, and

(B), Legal Provisions.

(A) Constitutional Provisions

The Constitution of India itself guarantees many rights to the child labour. This is two-fold : The Fundamental Rights and Directive Principles. Article 24 states that ' No child below 14 years of age shall be employed in any factory, mine or any other hazardous industry.

Article 39 (e) states that the State ensure that the health and strength. of workers, men and women, and the tender age of children are not abused, and that citizens are not forced by economic necessity to enter avocations unsuited to their age or strength.

Article 39 (f) states that the children are given opportunities and facilities to develop in a healthy manner and in conditions of freedom and dignity and that childhood and youth are protected against exploitation and against moral and material abandonment.

(B) Legal Provisions

A number of Acts were enacted to protect the interest of working children. Broadly these Acts deal with the following aspects:

(a) Children working in Hazardous Employment,
(b) Maximum hours of work and rest interval,
(c) Prohibition of children working at nights,
(d) Minimum age for employment of children,
(e) Medical Examination of children, and
(f) Minimum wage for the child worker.

To deal with the above provisions, Government had enacted different acts over a period of time. The following Acts aimed at protecting the interests of children as listed above:

1. The Workmen's Compensation Act, 1923
2. The Trade Unions Act, 1926
3. The Children (Pledging of Labour) Act, 1933
4. Employment of Children Act, 1938
5. Factories Act, 1948
6. The Minimum Wages Act, 1948
7. The Plantations Labour Act, 1951
8. The Mines Act, 1952
9. Merchant Shipping Act, 1958
10. Apprentices Act, 1961
11. Motor Transport Act, 1961
12. Beedi and Cigar Workers (Conditions of Employment) Act, 1966
13. The Bonded Labour System (Abolition) Act, 1976
14. The Child Labour (Prevention and Regulation) Act, 1986.

The provisions laid down in different acts listed above are discussed at length in the following pages.

(a) Children Working in Hazardous Employment

Different sections of Acts prohibit children from working in hazardous occupations. Under section 23 of Factories Act (1948) 'no young person can be employed on dangerous machines unless he/she is fully instructed, and is under adequate supervision. The Employment of Children Act (1938) prohibits employment of children in any workshop, where the process of beedi making, carpet weaving, cement manufacturing, cloth printing, manufacture of matches, explosive and fire-works, mica cutting and splitting, soap manufacturing, canning is carried out. Under Beedi and Cigar Workers Act (1966) 'no person can be employed in industrial premises'. According to the Mines Act (1952) ' no person below 18 years shall be allowed to work in any mine Apprentices and other trainees, with the permission of the Child inspector/inspector may work, provided they are above 16 years'. The Child Labour (Prohibition and Regulation) Act, 1986, intends to ban the working children in hazardous occupations and processes as listed in the Act and regulate the conditions of their work where they are not prohibited from working.

(b) Maximum Hours of Work and Rest Interval

The Child Labour (Prevention and Regulation) Act, 1966, regulates the major conditions of work of children, such as total six hours of work, including the time spend in waiting for work, rest interval of one hour after three hours paid weekly holiday and maintenance of register of child workers. The Factories Act and Mines Act provide four hours as the maximum limit for a child between 14 and 15 years, who is working in a Factory. Acts related to shops and other establishments, recommended 5 to 7 hours of work. The maximum hours of work as prescribed by the Transport Act and The Plantation Act are forty hours a week. The Minimum Wages Act (1948) decided a maximum period of four hours for children.

The working child is assumed by law, a rest interval of half-an-hour after every four hours of work (Motor Transport Workers Act). Rest for atleast one hour after every three hours of work [Child Labour (Prevention and Regulation) Act], half-an-hour's rest after five hours work (Plantation Labour Act and Shops and Commercial Establishments Act). Most of these Acts also assure one day a week leisure after every six days' work, and also annual paid leave after a period of 240 days of work.

(c) Prohibition of Children Working at Night

In all the Acts, night work between 7 PM to 6 AM is banned for children. Overtime is not permitted, and after work for 3-5 hours (depending on the Act) there should be a rest period of half-an-hour. The Factories Act mentions that children between 14 and 17 years cannot be asked to work i.e. between 10 PM to 6 AM. The Child Labour (Prevention and Regulation) Act has not allowed children for work at night (7 PM to 8 AM) and overtime is also not allowed. Motor Transport Workers Act mentions that no child (below 15 years age) is asked to work between 10 PM to 6 AM.

(d) Minimum Age for Employment of Children

Almost all the acts define child as a person below 14 or 15 years. The minimum age prescribed for employment of children differ in various acts. The Child Labour (Preventions and Regulation) Act, specifies that a child is one who has completed his 14th birthday. The minimum age of employment in Shops and Commercial Establishments Act in various States varies from 12 to 15 years. Under Section 67 of Factories Act, 'no child below 15 years can work in a factory' and under Section 23 'no young person can be employed in dangerous machines, unless he is fully instructed, and is under adequate supervision. A young person could be either a child (below 15 years) or an adolescent (15-18 years). No child (below 15 years) can be employed to work in any capacity: in any motor transport undertaking (Motor Transport Workers Act, 1961). Children are not allowed to work in plantations till they complete 12 years (Plantations Act). Till they complete 14 years, they are not allowed to work in industrial premises or undergo apprenticeship training in any designated trade (Section 3 (a) of Apprentices Act). No person below 18 years shall be allowed to work in any mine (The Mines Act). A young person is defined as one under 18 years of age (Merchant Shipping Act). Sections 109-113 of this Act are dealing with employment of young persons and the act prohibits children below 15 years of age to work in any capacity in any ship unless it is a school/training ship, or a ship in which all persons employed belong to one family, or in a home-trade ship of less than 200 tonnes gross, or where such a child is to be employed on nominal wages, and is under the charge of his father or other adult near male relatives. All young persons under 18 years of age have to produce a medical certificate of fitness by a certifying surgeon.

(e) Medical Examination of Children

The Indian laws lay 18 years as the minimum age upto which the certificate of fitness would be required, whereas, International Labour Organisation Conventions clearly recommend that no person upto the age of 21 years should be employed in health risk establishments without a certificate of fitness. In India, a certificate of fitness for the employment of a particular child was prescribed by the Factories Act, Motor Transport Workers Act, Plantations Labour Act, and some other Acts also provide for medical examination of the child at annual intervals.

(f) Minimum Wage for the Child Worker

The Minimum Wages (Central) Rules were made under the Minimum Wages Act. The Minimum Wages Act defined the child, adolescent and adult as the same meaning in the Factories Act. Under Section 17 of this Act, each employer shall maintain registers and records giving details of employees, wages etc. The State Government will fix a minimum wage in all scheduled employments.

The foregoing analysis on child labour leads to suggesting some suitable suggestions to eleviate the working conditions and prevent the child labour.

Suggestions

The following suggestions may be given to eleviate the child labour from India as well as from Andhra Pradesh:

1. Most legislations pertaining to children need to be revised. Apart from the lacunae in the laws themselves, several areas have been left unlegislated,. A Uniform Civil Code has yet to be enacted. In the laws relating to health, education, housing and employment, compromises are made which are contrary to the principles of the Constitution and the CR.

2. The necessity for a comprehensive legislation prohibiting all child labour, child being defined as one below 16 years. Andhra Pradesh State Government should also initiate this.
3. Section 9 of the A.P. Education Act should be made operate by the Government by creating facilities for Free and Compulsory Education.
4. Regarding implementation, we must remember that a law is only as good as its enforcement in fracture. Our many laws give the appearance of being a well-regulated society whose state is devoted to the protection of the child. Law has a symbolic value of setting norms, but there is little concern with law as a means of inducing compliance.
5. There should be a single department of the Government that oversees and guides all aspects of child-related laws. Various other departments may or may not handle individual laws, like those of labour or police, but it should be the department alone which is answerable to all laws relating to children.
6. The Bonded Labour System (Abolition) Act should be implemented vigorously, and all offending employers should be prosecuted.
7. Special drive with prior publicity should be initiated to implement the Child Marriage (Restraint) Act in the State: Leading politicians should start with their constituencies first.
8. Government should stop leakages in the Welfare Programmes. All the programmes should have transparency. And the financial allocation for Child Welfare and rehabilitation programmes should be increased.

30

Elimination of Child Labour: A Blueprint for Action

—*A.K. Verma*

Child Labour! the moment we hear this word, a picture emerges in our mind—a boy or girl, deprived, weak, uneducated, semi-clad, harrassed child—may be working as rag-picker on the city street, may be as 'chottu' in a road-side hotel, may be as shoe-shine boy on a railway station etc. etc. Such a perception and image of working child will vary depending upon our own background and area from which we come from. A person from northern city of Aligarh will perceive it as child worker in a lock industry whereas a person from South may visualise it as a child working in match and fireworks industry. East or West, North or South it is a very unfortunate reality that child labour in one form or the other is present around us and most people have become either immune to it or have accepted it as a 'reality of life'.

It is not to suggest that nobody thought of child labour as a problem in yesteryears but it is a stark reality that it has become an ever growing menace. Academicians, bureaucrats, law makers, social activist and all persons with concern who saw working child around them, raised their voices against the menace of child labour in their own way. Inumerable workshops, seminars, symposia, conferences and similar academic get-together are held on the subject. There is no dearth of publications of research papers, books, articles and Ph.D's on this subject. In addition, Legislative enactments, rules and regulations, guidelines are also in plenty but despite all these great efforts the problem of child labour has become an ever-increasing menace.

There are international interventions, too, to weed-out this evil phenomenon from our society. ILO's International Programme on Elimination of Child labour (IPEC) is a recent example in case. In addition to such general programmes there have been international assistance programmes at the industry/area specific level. From its very inception in 1919, the International Labour Organisation (ILO) has been concerned about the employment of children. This concern has been reflected in the series of conventions and recommendations adopted by ILO from 1919 onwards. Convention number 5, "Fixing the Minimum Age for Admission of Children to Industrial Employment" was first of them. Similarly, IPEC is a recent global initiative of the ILO launched in 1992 to support participating member countries in their national efforts to combat and eliminate child labour progressively, while simultaneously creating a world-wide movement against it. There are a number of other UN agencies also which are helping the countries to fight against this evil practice of child labour.

The Confusions

What is Child Labour ? Giving a universally acceptable definition of child labour is not easy as it may appear. Because, it encompasses three difficult-to-define concepts 'child', 'work' and 'labour'. These concepts have different connotations in different societies. Therefore, child labour could mean different things to different governments, social and other organisations and individuals—depending upon the context. Moreover, there is a perceived difficulty of drawing a distinction between positive and negative child work. However, a working definition of a 'child labour' may be:

> "a person below the general limit of 15 years or in special circumstances 14 years, who is not attending school and is engaged in either paid or unpaid occupation, either within or outside the family, that is detrimental to his/her physical and mental growth".

Further, various child labour laws and regulations have defined such concepts as 'child', 'labour' and 'workplace' to reflect a number of situations and assumptions. They assume, for instance, that working for one's parents, inside the home, or without pay is more acceptable than working for others, outside the home, or for money. Moreover, children's work in small-scale enterprises is less harmful than their work in large-scale enterprises; and that work in closed spaces is more harmful than work in the open air. However, whatever may be the arguments and assumptions about child labour, the important aspect of child work which is always overlooked is that the intervention agencies/departments never go for the opinion of the children at work to define the concept of 'child labour'. Because, the kind of work situation seen by intervention agencies as acceptable or relatively unproblematic are often, from the child's point of view, precisely the kind of work which bring the most problems. But one thing is clear that children at work occupy a relatively more vulnerable and easily exploitable position in the work relations and in the labour market.

The Magnitude

Magnitude of child labour is difficult to measure. Till date there are no firm estimates as to how many children are at work. The fact remains that since child work is illegal, hence there is deliberate attempt to conceal it. Often, this leads to gross under-estimation of the actual number of children engaged in. wage and/or non-wage employment in the country. This problem basically owes its origin to the absence of standardised definitions of 'child' and their 'work' i.e. child labour. Non-availability or comparable time series data on the volume of child labour and the pattern of their employment in various sectors including the household sector further adds to the problem of under reporting of the magnitude of child labour phenomenon.

Given the definitional and conceptual ambiguities and the resulting complexities of enumeration it is not surprising that the available official and non-official estimates of working children vary greatly. According to 1971 census, there were 10.7 million children in the workforce which was 4.6 per cent of the total child population. In 1981, the figure on child labour increased to 13.6 million which was 5.2 per cent of all children. Out of 13.6 million child workers, there were 8.1 million males and 5.5 million females. Again, of these, 11.6 million children were engaged in agriculture and more than a million were working in manufacturing, processing, repairs, trade and commerce, transport, construction, and other services. An overwhelming number of children were also engaged in household industries. These census figures are consistent with the NSS data, which reported 16.3 million child labourers in 1972-73 and 17.4 million in 1983. Moreover, if we extrapolate the figure of the 43rd round of the NSS data, the volume of child labour would reach an alarming 20 million by the year 2000.

However, if we take into account other estimates of child labour, it would seem that the official figures grossly under-estimate the actual magnitude of the problem. For instance according to the Operation Research Group, Baroda, there are 44 million children in the 5-14 age group in the labour force. And, a subsequent assessment has placed the figure of child labour even much higher at 114 million. Apart from this, if we assume that children who are not attending schools and those who are dropping out of the school system are joining the workforce, then the actual estimate of working children will be still much higher. For example, as per the official estimate, the percentage of children in the age group 6-14 who are attending schools is around 44. The projected population in the age group for 1994-95 is around 179 million which implies that nearly 90 million children do not go to school. Even after assuming that all working children do not go to school there is an unexplained gap of atleast 72 million children whose status is that of non-working, non-school going in the country. Such children are called as 'No-where Children' by some experts. This segment is prone to fall in the child labour network.

The Constitutional Safeguards

Our constitution makers, had known that India of their vision would not be a reality if the children of the country are not nurtured and educated. For this, their exploitation by different profit makers for their personal gain had to be first indicated. It is this need, which has found manifestation in Article 24, which as one of the two provisions in Part IV of our Constitution on the fundamental right against exploitation. The framers were aware that this prohibition alone would not permit the child to contribute its might to the national building work unless it receives atleast basic education. Article 45 was therefore inserted in our paramount parchment casting a duty on the state to endeavour to provide free and compulsory education to children. Our constitution containing some other provisions also desiring that a child must be given opportunity and facility to develop in a healthy manner.

Despite the above, the stark reality is that in our country, like many others, children are an exploited lot. Child labour is a big problem and has remained intractable, even after about 50 years of our having become independent, despite various legislative enactments prohibiting employment of a child in a number of occupations or avocations.

The Remedy

Despite all above rules and regulations, facts and figures, child labour is accepted as a "harsh reality". However, it is widely accepted that there is a very dubious nexus between illiteracy, poverty and child labour. India is a significant exception to the global trend in making education compulsory and banning of child labour. Poverty has not prevented many governments in the world from banning child labour. Countries like Myanmar, Thailand, Indonesia, etc. have achieved high literacy levels by completely banning child labour. Many African countries with income levels lower than India have, through proper planning and effective implementation of labour laws, been able to achieve higher levels of literacy. These include Botswana, Gambia, Ghana, Ivory Coast, Libya, Mauritius, Zambia, Zimbabwe, Rwanda, etc. Even a highly populous country like China has achieved double the literacy rate of India. India is the largest producer of illiterates in the world.

The Indian Government has been unable to deal with urgent problems like rising illiteracy, low school enrolments, high dropout and rampant child labour. India instead of putting a complete ban on child labour, passed legislation as late as in 1986 regulating employment of child workers in non-hazardous occupations and

carefully the contents of this piece of legislation we find that government has actually legalized child labour in the garb of regulating the same. It is difficult to understand these policies in the context of avowed declaration of welfare state in Article 38 of the Constitution.

This is inspite of explicit and categorical assertion in the Constitution calling for a ban on child labour and for compulsory primary education. Although a ban on child labour is our objective as acknowledged by more than several committees over the past four decades since independence, yet there is a gap between what we profess and practice. India's low per capita income and economic situation is less relevant as an explanation for a lack of ban on child labour.

The Pull and Push Strategies

We can adopt two types of strategies to eliminate the problem of child labour—the pull strategies and the push strategies. The pull strategies are such instruments as legislative enactments, rules, regulations and enforcements etc. which essentially attempt to pull-out the child labour from the society. In such a strategy there is very low/limited support and co-operation from the society to do away with the problem of child labour. On the other hand there could be push strategies to tackle the problem of child labour. Such strategy would aim to generate a societal pressure from with-in the system to push out the evil. Such a strategy attempts to build-up support and co-operation from the society to weed-out the menace.

If we look-back at our child labour eradication programmes, rules, regulations, acts, guidelines etc. and try to categorise them under push/pull strategies, it may be seen that all these programmes, primarily, fall under the pull strategies where we tried to weed-out the problem without initiative of the society from with-in. And that is the primary reason for all failures of child labour laws and enactments in our country. This is also a reason for underestimates of child labour figures due to concealment by the society.

If we want to seriously attempt to tackle the problem of child labour, our strategies at national and governmental level will have to take a U-turn from the present pull to push strategies. Without participation of the society, for which all rules and regulation are being made, all our efforts are liable to remain on paper and can even become the source of corruption.

Elimination of child labour from our society need to be tackled under an integrated time-bound programme. Since the child labour is a many faceted problem it cannot be done away with, if isolated efforts are made. If we are serious about the menace of child labour we have to deal it with the fervour of 'Pulse-Polio' programme. If anti-pollution drives can be launched in big cities of India with target dates why can't we have child labour elimination programmes with a target date ?

The following paragraphs attempt to give a blueprint of time bound 'SCOOP' programme for elimination of child labour.

The 'SCOOP' Programme

The main components of the SCOOP programme are as under:

Sensitisation of the parents and society.

Co-operation of local people.

Organisation of adult literacy programmes.

Opportunities (alternative) to the children.

Placement of adults in the jobs (vacated by Children)

All above components of SCOOP will have to be simultaneously operated. The 'SCOOP' programme will have the following pre-requisites. Subsequently each component of 'SCOOP' programme shall be discussed independently.

Time Target

An important aspect of the 'SCOOP' programme will be the time period. It is proposed that the programme be operationalised for a period of five years from its date of initiation in any area. A five year action programme may be designed specifically for the target group and meticulously implemented. However, an upper time point may be fixed for completion of all such programmes, it could be, say, 31st December 2005. This means that programmes at all locations will be initiated by turn of the century.

Involvement of NGOs

Since the very basic character of the SCOOP programme is involvement of local people, role of NGOs cannot be under-estimated. Wherever possible NGOs be actively involved in the operation of the programme. However, the activities to be controlled by NGOs and the government officials may be clearly demarcated in a co-ordinated manner so as to achieve the objectives within a time frame. If deemed appropriate, NGOs may be allowed to adopt the specified area in collaboration with government functionaries.

The 'SCOOP' Components

(i) Sensitisation

In order to generate the push force to eliminate the child labour with-in the specified time period it is important to sensitise the parents and society about the ill effects of child labour. They need to be explained with the programme in its totality and their specific queries be responded to. *It is extremely important to sensitise mothers of children to withdraw their children from the labour force for their bright future.*

Role of media and specially television is very important in sensitising people. There should be special programmes, prepared in local language, during the primetime on television. These programmes should have greater involvement of local people and interview of such parents who withdraw their children from the labour force to prompt others to follow.

Awareness could also be generated through local language songs composed to denigrade the ills of child labour, slogans, pledge by the parents (for not sending their children to work) street shows etc. to name a few. Role of print media is also important but given the illiteracy among the masses, and specially in the child labour households, use of print media may be kept selective.

(ii) Co-operation

Co-operation of local persons will be core of the 'SCOOP' programme. This co-operation will be built up at two levels.

First level of co-operation would be generated for all groups in the society to support the programme. Over the period of time, this co-operation would be given a formal structure and co-operative shall be constituted to sustain the anti-child labour movement once Govt./NGO support is withdrawn after the specified period. Such a co-operative may also take-over the production of goods which were earlier produced with the help of child labourers. This would not only help improve their economic condition but also explode the myth that such an economic activity cannot be sustained without child labour's involvement.

(iii) Organisation of Adult Literacy Programmes

It has been repeatedly said and has been established that

illiteracy among parents is one major cause of sending their children to work place instead of school. Illiterate parents also succumb to the trap of local factory owner/money-lender and in turn send their children as bonded labour in lieu of the small amount of money taken. This is one very big menance in rural India, giving rise to bonded child labour system in our country.

After 50 years of independence our country cannot further wait for yet another generation to come in the hope that our next generation would be educated one and shall refrain from sending their children to work-place. Hence, under the 'SCOOP' programme the problem of adult illiteracy would have to be tackled immediately.

Secondly these adult schools can also be used as a platform to generate awareness against child work. It is once again asserted that more and more attention be paid on the mothers to stimulate the eradication of child labour. Let us not forget the old saying :

> 'When we teach the child, we teach a persons,
> when we teach the father, we teach a family, but
> when we teach the mother, we teach a nation.'

(iv) Opportunities (alternative) to the Children

'SCOOP' programme will lay specific emphasis on providing alternative avocations to the children specially those who have been pushed out of the child labour force. 'SCOOP' programme will lay emphasis on rejuvenation of schools in the area and facilitate to provide necessary help to children so that they may attend schools. This, in turn, may require some initial incentive schemes to the school going children in the form of mid-day meal or cash incentive to the family of the child. However, modalities of such schemes could be decided from situation to situation and from time to time.

'SCOOP' would attempt to lay emphasis on girl child in the matters of schooling too. Higher incentive may be offered for the girl child to attend the school. The programme may also use the platform of adult schools to prompt the parents to send their children, specially the females, to school.

'SCOOP' would also endeavour to provide free medical check-up of the children attending school. It will also attempt for provision of some minimum basic medicine to the ill children. It is important to note that this will not only act as an incentive for child to attend the school but would also help to build a healthy and happier nation.

(v) Placement of Adults

It has been often observed that in industries where child labour is prevalent, incidence of adult unemployment is very high. 'SCOOP' programme would attempt to replace the adult population of the area as replacement to child labour. Such a step would call for two fold strategies. *Firstly*, in some cases some minimal training need be given for the adults to do the work, and *secondly*, SCOOP would have to combat the local vested interest groups which would attempt to foil this effort.

The myth of necessarily involving children in some activities would have to be broken and electronic media would have to play a significant role in this regard. The cases of industrial establishments which would have replaced their child labour with the adult work force need be given some duty/tax benefits in the form of incentives. An atmosphere need to be created where all other establishments follow such industries.

Consolidation of Child-labour Eradication Efforts

A very important factor for success of SCOOP programme would be to pool our resources and bring them under one roof. This would mean that many isolated efforts had and are being made here and there wherein a lot of resources are involved. Let us now stop such isolated efforts, and replan our strategy and make a concentrated effort to do away with child labour under an integrated time bound programme like 'SCOOP'.

Post-SCOOP Programme Period

There is built-in provision in the 'SCOOP' programme so that society could look-after its own interests and children do not revert to the child labour situation. It is believed that during the five years of operation, 'SCOOP' would generate enough social awareness among masses that they would not let their children return to the drudgery of child labour. Still some additional safety mechanisms are to be built for the post-SCOOP period to prevent incidence of such isolated occurrences.

First tier of safety mechanists would be build up with growth of the SCOOP over the period of five years through formation of co-operatives. Such co-operatives would not only indulge in collective industrial activity but also act as watch-dogs that no child reverts back to the older profession as child labour.

Second tier of safety mechanists would be a 'SCOOP Committee' consisting of social activities, government officials, police and enforcement officials, etc. as its members and the District Magistrate as the patron. The access to such a committee should be easy and in case of any information related to child labour, the 'SCOOP Committee' should act promptly and give relief and rehabilitation to the victim (the child).

Penalties for involvement of child-labour be imposed on both the sides during post-'SCOOP' period. Both sides mean that where there should be heavy penalty on the employer to employ the child, some penalty should also be levied on the child's family (the parents/guardians) for sending the child to work. Such an act would warn the parents, and they would be alert to send their children to school than to work place. Employment of children should be made cognitive non-bailable offence for the employers.

Areas which are slightly developed and telephone facilities exist the information to the 'SCOOP Committees' may be given on telephone. A uniform three digit telephone number be selected for such committees (say '105') similar to the pattern of police-fire-ambulance telephone numbers, which are uniform all over the country.

Conclusion

Elimination of child labour is no easy task. Governments have adopted various measures to root-out this evil. Government even softened its attitude by attempting to improve the working condition of child labours in various activities. A lot has been said about the problem, its dimension, its gravity, its geographical distribution etc. but now the time has come when we should pool our energies and efforts under a single programme like 'SCOOP' which would act as a catalyst and generate pressure from with-in the society to do away with the evil practice of child labour. The child labour can be better pushed away than pulled-out.

The review document of IPEC programme in India, too, has very significantly underlined the need of generating local genius for elimination of child labour, "IPEC on its own cannot eliminate child labour—the outwardly visible symptom of a deeper and more complex social malaise. Nor is IPEC alone capable of improving the quality of support to the working children and their families. These inputs have to be found, in the long-run, locally, and harnessed through local genius. By pointing out possibilities and limitations, IPEC, has indicated the need for a renewed search for alternatives, and implementation of radical thinking for ultimate elimination of child labour".

If a time bound multifaceted determined push strategy (like SCOOP programme) is adopted for elimination of child labour, Indian society can also proudly call the child labour as the 'phenomenon of the past' in the years to come.

Bibliography

Champaklaxmi, R. & Verma, A.K., (1983), Measures for Improving the working conditions of Children in the Carpet and Glass Bangle Industries : Study conducted by Institute of Applied Manpower Research for Ministry of Labour, *Government of India,* New Delhi.

Chaudhri, D.P., (1996), *Female Child Labour and Gender Bias in School Education in Indian States 1961-1991,* Department of Economics, University of Wollongong, Australia.

International Labour Organisation, (1980), *Children at Work* (Ed:) by Elias Mendelievich, ILO, Geneva.

International Labour Organisation, (1996), IPEC in India (1992-95) : Looking Back (Ed:) by M.P. Joseph, *International Programme on the Elimination of Child Labour,* (IPEC), New Delhi, India.

Jain, Mahaveer, *(1996), "Child Labour : A Growing Phenomenon in India", in Poverty & Employment : Analysis of the Present Situation and Strategies of the Future,* New Age International Publishers, New Delhi, (pp. 295-318).

Jain, Mahaveer, (1996), "Child Labour : Cause and Combat Strategies", in *Health for the Millions,* Jan.-Feb., 1996, pp. 31-32.

Kitchlu T.N., (1996), *Exploited Child—A National Problem,* M.D. Publications Pvt. Ltd; New Delhi.

Nangia, Parveen, (1987), *Child Labour : Cause-Effect Syndrome,* Janak Publishers, New Delhi.

National Labour Institute, (1993), *Working Children in India,* Child Labour Cell, NLI, NOIDA (U.P.)

National Labour Institute, (1996), *Towards Eliminating Child Labour : A Report of Workshop of District Collectors/District Heads,* National Resource Centre on Child Labour, NLI, Noida (U.P.).

National Labour Institute, (1996), *Manual for Trainers of Enforcement Officials in Child Labour Legislation*, National Resource Centre for Child Labour, NLI, Noida (U.P.).

Supreme Court of India, (1996), *Judgment on Writ Petition* (c) No. 465 of 1986 between M.C. Mehta (Petitioner) : Vs State of Tamilnadu and Others (Respondents), New Delhi.

UNICEF, (1995), *The State of World's Children 1995* by James P. Grant, Executive Director UNICEF, Oxford University Press, New Delhi.

Verma, A.K., (1985), "Child Labour in India", in *The Manpower Journal*, Vol. XXI, No. 1, April-June, New Delhi (pp. 89-108).

31

Combating Child Labour

—S. Velayudha Perumal

The phenomenon of Child Labour mirrors a social curse. If one accepts the fact that the 'society is a living organism' then the practice of employing a child instead of providing him with the basic necessities to develop his personality (education, health services, recreation facilities etc.) is obviously a blow to the edifice of the society. How the exploitation of such tender, innocent but illiterate and poor child is conducive to dehumanisation. Marx has gone so far as to proclaim that the result of purchasing children at an immature age by the capitalist is not only a physical deterioration but a social degeneration as well.

Though employment of children is a global phenomenon its incidence is heaviest in South Asia.

Child labour is an area of reform that was amongst the earliest subjects of ILO conventions (Conventions 5 & 6, 1919) and its elimination is one of the organisation's core goals. In 1973 the ILO codified its previous conventions on child labour into a single convention (Convention 138) but because the new standard was so prescriptive it received ratification from only 46 countries over the following two decades with no country in the Asia-Pacific including Australia By contrast, the convention on the Rights of the Child (1989) for which UNICEF has responsibility and which is much less prescriptive has already attracted ratification from 155 countries with the USA being the only major nation not to ratify.

Employment of Child Labour

Children are engaged into a variety of employments in factories or mines or self-employment in street trades. They are the final link in a long chain of sub-contractors. Some receive wages in kind and some are paid on piece rate. Many are unpaid and work for kin in the home or on the land. They form an important part of migrant labour. Of late, there has been a marked growth in urban child labour and the whole increase has been absorbed in non-agricultural activities where deprivation is more than in agriculture. Child labour free adults for wage labour and facilitate adult migration. They are more often casual labour and more transient in the labour force.

Children in industry face serious risk to their health and physical development and are required to undertake tasks for which they are entirely unprepared physically. They also work for long hours. There are the possibilities of special risks associated with the working environment. Children are more liable to suffer occupational injuries, fatigue, poor judgement and insufficient knowledge of work processes mainly because the equipment and machinery, tools and layout of most work places are designed for adults. Similarly, the incidence of malnutrition and other health related problems among street children are especially high.

Children are widely exploited at work and subjected to harassment by peers and adults. Since the work is poorly organised and remunerated they are forced to work for very long hours to earn the meagre income they need for their livelihood. Many engage in activities like crime and prostitution under the control of anti-social groups and work and live under the constant threat and reality of violence, even from public authorities.

Though child work has a social and economic function there is no social recognition to it and a marked tendency to under-value it. Children rarely receive an income even approaching the minimum wage, and their earnings are consistently lower than those of adults in similar tasks. They receive no fringe benefit, insurance, or social security payments, an added saving for the employer.

Employers exercise considerable power and control over their under-aged workers. Labour laws are openly flouted in view of poor labour inspection and existence of large number of illegal and unregulated enterprises in big cities. The problem is not one of law enforcement alone. Children must work since the survival of their families often depends on it. Absence of alternative sources of employment increases the hold employers have over them. Much of this evil is due to the precapitalists forms of recruitment and the very personal link they have with their employers.

Children's recruitment is more responsive to social obligations than to market forces. Labour relations involving minors are part of an extension system of oppressive patronage. The manner in which child labour is embedded in the fabric of society presents a serious obstacle to its abolition and introduction of protective measures. Ultimately, children have very little say when choosing their occupation, this decision is the prerogative of adults.

It is extremely difficult to obtain precise data on levels of remuneration among child labourers in view of the sensitive nature of information and they themselves are extremely reluctant to divulge information on the subject.

India's Efforts to Combat Child Labour

Though the prevalence of child labour and its evils were made known by the Reports of the Royal Commission on Labour 1931 and the Labour Investigation Committee, 1942 it took four decades for the Government to take steps to regulate child labour employment, leave alone its eradication.

The thrust of the government action consisted of three complementary measures. The first involved dealing with the legal hurdles which impeded practical action which resulted in the enactment of the Child Labour (Prohibition and Regulation) Act, 1986. This Act prohibits the employment of children below 14 in hazardous occupations, regulates the conditions of work in activities permitted by law, and provides for a Child Labour Technical Advisory Committee to review and advise on hazardous occupations.

The second step involved is the formulation of a National Policy to deal with the socio-economic factors of child work and to provide a frame work for programming. The policy anticipates the development of an extensive system of non-formal education. A target has been set whereby all children who attain the age of 11 years by 1990 will have received five years of schooling and all children will by 1995, be provided with free and compulsory education upto the age of 14. Bordia (1987 : 101). The policy also anticipates employment intensification and income generating schemes where the incidence of child labour is high.

The National Policy provides for specific pilot projects to establish the basis for a programme of action. The plan also anticipates the establishment of structures at both—national and state levels for implementation. An additional feature is the important role given to non-government organisations in the delivery of welfare services and non-formal education and in raising public awareness. NLI (1992).

A National Authority on Elimination of Child Labour (NAECL) was created in 1994. In 1995, at the behest of the NAECL, Child Labour Cells were created in all states with some states establishing a Task Force to eliminate child labour. The NAECL identified 137 administrative districts (out of a total of 362) in 11 states which had a high incidence of child labour and established District Committees in each of these areas to promote the campaign with their membership including NGOs, Members of Parliament and Local Officials. The committees have a mandatory obligation to report to the NAECL. In addition, assistance is being made available from International agencies like the UNICEF and UNESCO.

The Government of India, Ministry of Labour had launched a major programme in 1994 for *withdrawal of children from hazardous occupations and their rehabilitation through special schools.* Under this programme 76 National Child Labour Projects were sanctioned for rehabilitating 1.5 lakh children. Funds were released to 123 districts for carrying out surveys on child labour and to 133 districts for generation of awareness at the district level Arunachalem (1997:25).

Suggestions

The Confederation of Indian Industries (CII) suggested to create a national fund for rehabilitation of child labour and institute a machinery for their rehabilitation (CII : 1996)

The UNICEF Report stresses the vital importance of primary education in preventing future generations of children from joining the workforce.

The National Human Rights Commission (NHRC) : Stresses co-ordination between government, judiciary, media, legal professionals and NGOs. In January 1997 the NHRC recommended that government servants be prevented from employing children below the age of 14 years as domestic servants and urged the union government to amend the Central Services (Conduct) Rules, 1964 that no government servant shall employ to work any child below the age of 14 years and breach of this rule shall be misconduct attracting a major penalty. The commission also wants that the relevant service rules of the State Governments also be amended on the above lines. (Venkatachaliah : 1996).

Trade union in India, though late, have taken up the child labour issue. With the sensitisation of the women work force, the under payment of wages of women workers has become an issue which the trade unions are fighting jointly with the women's movement. But *the child, till lately, seemed lost somewhere in the massive workforce Patro* (1997 : 33). A consensus is evolving on this issue among all central trade unions. There is a need for ensuring physical, legal and financial protection to both the trade unions and the working children, by the government. The Central Government has sanctioned Rs. 850 crores for eradication of child labour from hazardous industries but the money was pumped through NGOs without any tangible results.

For any concerted effort to sensitise both parents and employers, for a long time to come, one of the best medium will remain the trade union movement since unions alone can more easily identify child labour. The pressure which needs to be brought on the employers of child labour can only come from unions.

According to the *Commission on Labour Standards and International Trade*, child labour force, which at present is estimated at 25 millions, has an annual growth of 4 per cent which requires an outlay of Rs. 15,000 crores to abolish it in reality (GOI : 1996). Another estimate is 14 million with another 10 million children are marginal workers. Growth of child labour in different states varies from 7 per cent in Uttar Pradesh to minus 0.7 per cent in Tamilnadu (Chaudhari : 1996). National level growth during 1981-1991 was 1.2 per cent and projections to 2001 AD suggest an annual decline of -1.44 per cent.

The Supreme Court's recent judgement in M.C. Mehta Vs State of Tamilnadu and others has directed creation of a Child Labour Rehabilitation-cum-Welfare Fund, to be set up at the district level in each State. Employers who engage child labour in violation of the Child Labour Act are required to pay Rs. 20,000 to the fund. The Court has further directed that for child labour in non-hazardous jobs, the working hours should be between 4 to 6 hours only and it should receive atleast 2 hours of education each day with the cost to be borne by the employers. The labour inspectors are required to ensure compliance of the directions of the Court.

The implications of judgement are as follows:

(i) Simultaneous action in all Districts of the Country.
(ii) Survey for identification of working children (to be completed by 10.6.1997)
(iii) Withdrawl of children working in hazardous occupations and ensuring their education in appropriate institutions.
(iv) Contribution of Rs. 20,000 per child to be paid by the offending employers to a welfare fund to be established for this purpose.
(v) Employment to one adult member of the family of the child so withdrawn from work and if that is not possible, a contribution of Rs. 5,000 to the welfare fund to be made by the State Government.
(vi) Financial assistance to the families of the children so withdrawn to be paid out of the interest earnings on the corpus of Rs. 20,000-25,000 deposited in the welfare fund as long as the child is actually sent to the schools.
(vii) Regulating hours of work for children working in non-hazardous occupations so that their working hours do not exceed six hours per day and education for atleast two hours is ensured. The entire expenditure on education is to be borne by the concerned employer.

Conclusion

The Supreme Court Judgement has given several responsibilities to the Ministry of Labour for eliminating child labour. This will be a massive exercise and much depends on the co-operation of the people at large. The Common Minimum Programme of the Government pledges to eliminate child labour in all forms. To this, we have to make education a fundamental right.

Education of children to be withdrawn from hazardous occupations is to be assured in suitable institutions. There are children of various ages, different skills and qualities. All cannot be fit in one basket. Unlike formal education, in this case we need a multi-pronged strategy considering education, psychological rehabilitation and skill upgradation. Curriculum content has to correspond to the multi-age, multi-skilled strategy with a package where the child feels reassured. In non-hazardous industries employers have to bear the responsibility of education of child labour.

In view of the widespread poverty and a formidable array of institutional constraints, the immediate abolition of child labour is not possible. Neither the parents are interested in sending their kids to the schools, nor the children develop a liking to it. They simply learn the art which the adults perform. There is no political will or political approach for eradicating child labour. The immediate solution is that child labour be covered under the Minimum Wage Act, stipulate six hours of work daily and equal wages for equal work and a health scheme for child labourers.

References

Arunachalam, M. (1997), "Mandate of the Government", *Labour File,* Vol. 3, Nos. 1 & 2, January-February.

Bordia, A., (1987), "Child Labour in India : Implications for Educational Planning" in *ILO, Proceedings and Working Papers,* Asian Regional Tripartite Workshop on Practical Measures to combat Child Labour, Bangkok.

Castle, Robert, Chaudhri, D.P., Nyland, Chris & Nguyen, Tarang; (1997), "Labour Classes, the World Trade Organisation and Child Labour in India", *The Indian Journal of Labour Economics,* Vol. 40, No. 1.

Chaudhri, D.P., (1996), *Dynamic Profile of Child Labour in India* 1951-91, CLASP, ILO, New Delhi.

Confederation of Indian Industries, (1996), *Economic Implications of Abolition of Child Labour in India,* CII, New Delhi.

Government of India, (1986), *Child Labour (Prohibition and Regulation) Act,* 1986, Ministry of Labour and Employment, New Delhi.

Government of India, (1996), *Commission on Labour Standards and International Trade,* Ministry of Labour and Employment, New Delhi.

National Labour Institute, (1992), *Awards Digest,* Vol. XVIII, Nos. 3-6, March-June.

Patro, B.V., (1997), "Child Labour : Trade Unions Woke up to the Challenges", *Labour File,* Vol. 3, Nos. 1 & 2, January-February.

Rohde, Jan. E., (1997), *State of the World's Children Report,* UNICEF.

Venkatachaliah, M.N., (1996), *NHRC Annual Report* 1995-96, New Delhi.

Weiner, Myron, (1995), Burra, Neera, *Born to Work-Child Labour in India,* Oxford University Press, New Delhi.

32

Child Labour in India: Problems and Methods of Abolition

—Shyam Nath Nandkeoliyar

Introduction

Child labour is a worldwide problem. It is existing more or less both in developed and developing countries. But the problem is more acute in the developing countries than developed countries. In developing countries, the children are exploited, deprived of educational, mental and physical growth, put to hazardous nature of work and forced to work basically in order to maintain living conditions of their families. In most of the developed countries, it is claimed that child labour from hazardous units have been eliminated and children work there to meet their pocket expenses and not to meet their families' food. But according to International Labour Organisation, World Labour Report 1992, in USA in three days enquiry in 1990, Labour Department had found 11,000 child labour working illegally. So is also in England, 36 to 66% of total child population below the age of 15 years work there. But it is also a truth that developed countries have to a greater extent solved and controlled the problem of child labour while developing countries are still facing the problem.

In the third world countries, child labour is the highest in Africa, then comes Asia and Latin America. It is why the South

Asian Coalition of Child Servitude (SACCS), an organisation dedicated to eradication of child labour has undertaken a "world tour against child labour" in 1998. The Global March against child servitude was flagged off from Manila on January 17 this year and after criss-crossing three continents-Asia, America and Africa, it concluded at Geneva in May to participate in the ILO Convention from June 1 where the first time ever, non-governmental organisation representatives were invited to attend and air their views on child labour.

The march was organised in three phases. In the first phase, children from South East Asian countries started their journey from Manila, in the second phase from Capetown, the capital of South Africa and in the third phase from Lima (Peru) in Latin America. Altogether 200 children from the three continents participated in the march which was supported by over 2 lakh people who also walked along the marchers while passing through various countries of the world. The ILO convention will pass several resolutions to check the scourage of child labour rampant in the countries of Asia. The chief of the SACCS, Mr. Kailash Satyarthi estimates about 25 crore child labourers in the world.

So far India is concerned, child labour in total labour force is the maximum and the highest one accounting both boys and girls. The report of the UNICEF says that in India the number of child labour is equal to the total population of Holland and Spain.

According to Child Labour (Prohibition and Regulation) Act 1986, a child is a labour if he is below 14 years of age. A child below the age of 5 years is not considered so matured that for the sake of payment and profit, can be absorbed in profitable economic activities, therefore a child regarded as labour is under 5-14 years of age.

In India, the number of working children according to Census of 1961,1971, 1981 and 1991 were 145 lakh, 107 lakh, 135.9 lakh and 126 lakh respectively. The centre for concern of child labour has estimated that the total number of child labour in India is 10 crores. At least half this number are engaged in hazardous industries like fire-crackers, glass making and querries. Many of them succumbs to the harsh environment they function in and those who survive are physically and mentally shattered. The government's response has always been to frame more legislation earning India the dubious distinction of having the maximum number of laws to combat this evil. Periodically target dates are set by which the problem will cease to exist, the latest is 2000 A.D. As the century comes to a close these hollow promises stand exposed—nothing at all has changed the ground.

The Supreme Court in its order of December 10, 1996 had directed all concerned to release children under 14 employed as child labour in any hazardous units. By its order any employer found employing such children shall be penalised Rs. 20,000 per child and release the children. Also the State concerned was to pay Rs. 5,000 in each case. All these amounts together would be deposited into a fund for rehabilitation and welfare measures of such released children. State concerned would have to submit a compliance report in the form of affidavit to the apex court regarding the status of the child labour. As a result, the governments of several States has launched a statewise survey to find out about child labour employed in the hazardous industries in the State. As many as 5,54,970 children have been identified as working in both hazardous and non-hazardous occupations after the first phase of survey (1998) being conducted following the Supreme Court directives.

Position and Problems

Indian economy is witnessing a rapid growth of population since 1921 and every effort to control it has not given a result which is earnestly required in the country. This has led the economy employment-stringent one, which has increased the poverty. The larger proportion of population is in rural areas where poverty, deprivation and illiteracy is a permanent feature. In the situation parents are not capable of providing adequate food, cloth and basic necessities of children. A large portion of population living in urban areas have also the same fate of distinction. Thus in the country, most of the inhabitants of rural and urban areas are under poverty line. A total of 32.03 crore people of the country live below poverty line as per the 1993-94 estimates of the Planning Commission, as informed in Rajya Sabha on July 17, 1998. This poor population have increased the proportion of have-nots and their living conditions are worst than the miserable. The members of the family in these poverty stricken families have the only desire and ambition i.e. to increase the income to combat starvation. And for the purpose, entire members of the family are put to work save and except those who are either below 5 or above 70-75 years of age.

They never resist the exploitation of their children and never think in terms of their proper growth. Their freckled faced and heavy hands belie their tender age as does their capacity to toil for existence.

Thus, child labour is an outcome of such a pathetic situation. The Labour Investigation Committee has remarked that the government owes a duty to the future generation of workers to see that childhood is not wasted in the dingy corners of factories and workshops instead of being educated in schools and brought up in nurseries and on playgrounds. But the situation is quite reverse. In our country childhood is not only wasted in dingy corners of factories but also on footpaths, thus proving it worth that their childhood is a saga of exploitation.

In a study, it has been found that the numbers of male child labour has reduced while that of female child labour has increased.

Table 32.1
Percentage Index of Child Labour in India (1971-81)

State	*Male Child Labour*	*Female Child Labour*
Andhra Pradesh	-3.30	29.02
Bihar	-21.44	-0.76
Gujarat	-11.88	-2.85
Haryana	-9.30	99.71
Karnataka	5.47	54.24
Kerala	-41.12	-32.56
Madhya Pradesh	9.69	52.81
Maharashtra	13.43	49.05
Orissa	-8.40	84.58
Punjab	-24.21	132.62
Rajasthan	-10.05	31.78
Tamilnadu	-0.12	69.88
Uttar Pradesh	-2.31	-22.68
West Bengal	-4.86	57.68
All India	-3.51	32.23

Source : Analysis of workforce in India, Occasional Paper No. 8, 1988, Registrar-General, India and Commissioner of Census, Indian Government, Home Ministry, New Delhi.

This figure shows the trends of child labour and it depicts that in India the percentage of male child labour has decreased to 3.51 while female child has increased to 32.23 between 1971-81.

In the under-developed countries of the world one child in every fourth child is labour and out of 19 crores children in these countries of the age of 10-14 years, three-fourth works 6 days or more in a week and about 50% works more than 9 hours daily.

In India, the highest proportion of child labour is in agriculture sector but they are more exploited in manufacturing and industrial production sectors where production process is generally risky and dangerous. They work there on the temperature of 800°—1200° Celsius.

In India, out of the total population of child labour 88.64% are in rural areas and 11.36% are in urban areas and the child labour in India is only 5.2% of total labour force while it is 19.5% in Bangladesh, 18.8% in Brazil, 27.3% in Turkey, 16.6% in Pakistan, 4.9% in England, 11.5% in Mexico. But this 5.2% child labour of total labour force has increased the number of child labour in our country as the highest one in the world because of increasing population and highest percentage of labour force.

The child labour in our country has increased much after industrialisation. As industrialisation took a rapid momentum, the industrialist in order to gain more profit in less cost started employing child labour who were paid less wages compared to adult male labourers. Besides employer found much benefit in employing them because they had no union, they were disciplined, they could be put to any job without resistant and so on. The poverty of the economy or poor economic factors were also prevalent in the country to increase the child labour. Poor parents, failing to meet the needs of their children and families usually compell their sons and daughters to go on work for wages. The government or the administrator even did not concern much of their employment because the aim of independent India was to prosper agriculture and industry, to build up an economy on sound footings and so a fringe of efforts were made in this regard. They had little time to think seriously on the pathetic conditions of the children. Their efforts were also nullified by law evaders. Whatsoever the reasons may be assigned, the child labour is having an increasing trend in our country so much so that it has outweighed every country of the world in the total number.

Methods of Abolition

Children must be valued and for this, every effort be made to provide chances for their mental and physical growth. It is urgency of the time that child labour is eliminated from every sphere of employment and be directed towards education to become such an adult on whose shoulders the nation can rest and prospect. Kailash Satyagrahi, Chief of the SACCS has rightly observed, "If we try to make a child an asset for 5 years in the formative years of childhood, he will become a sure liability for 50 years. On the other hand, we accept a child as a liability for 5 years in his childhood, he will become an asset for the next 50 years.

The complete elimination of the child labour in India is a daunting task. The issue is very cumbersome, complex and complicated. It seems very hard to get all through success in the mission of elimination of child labour. India is an agricultural country. In agriculture, children are seen as a rule to work and help their parents. In certain other unorganised sectors also, their existence cannot be avoided. In our country, the strong demonstration effect, the desire of living a comfortable and luxurious life by the high-ups families also lead to the creation of child labour. Children of poor family are kept in their homes as domestic servants to discharge their household liabilities. The law-makers cannot prohibit this affluent or high class employing child labour. Women of this rich growing class, too, play an active role in promoting child labour. They want to spend their times in clubs, playing Rummy and gossiping than to perform household affairs like cooking, washing and cleaning of the homes. These tasks are being performed in their houses from the children of tender ages. Besides children in many villages or towns, small hotels, tea shops, sweet shops, scooter repairing shops etc. are found working for hours together. In such unorganised sectors, laws are bravely evaded and the existence of child labour is bound to continue.

A research based report of Centre for Indian Trade Unions (CITU), Calcutta District Committee presented to the Government in March-April 1997 says the children faced with the rigors of life, come to work from Howrah, Nadia, Midnapore, Murshidabad for a salary as meagre as Rs. 200 a month. The other ones working in brick kilns get 20 paise per 8 bricks carried to the furnace. They make hundreds of such trips to the furnace to earn some money. This condition of child labour is existing in our country.

Unless the economy is not revitalised, its growth is not fastly increased, a fully employed situation in the economy is not brought, a developed gesture of the economy is not achieved, the problem of child labour cannot be solved completely. The country has enough potential resources to be developed provided the policies are framed and implemented to achieve them honestly, sincerely, spiritually and with dedication. Flaming Larsen, IMF deputy Director in 1997 has rightly observed in a special briefing on globalisation that with more reforms, India can grow faster than her present 7% growth rate and reduce significantly the time it will take to catch up with the living standards of developed countries. Thus, it seems that the complete elimination of child labour can be possible only when the country reaches the level of developed countries, otherwise, all the programmes and policies can eliminate child labour in organised sectors and not in unorganised sectors, where the number is more and where the necessity is more.

In India, the government and non-government organisations have been active in taking many potential measures to meet the problems of child labour. In March 1931, in Lahore Session of the Congress Mahatma Gandhi presented, over 20 resolutions were presented to protect the rights of children. The Constitution of India also lays down that" no child below the age of 14 years shall be employed to work in any factory or mine or engaged in any other hazardous employments", and the State shall see that "the tender age of children is not abused" and that "childhood and youth are protected against exploitation and against moral and material abandonment".

As regards child labour, first of all, the British Government has made rules in 1938. After then, Coal Mica Act in 1946, Factory Act in 1948, Plantation Act in 1951, Mines Act in 1952 etc. were passed to protect child labour.

Considering the seriousness of child labour Gurupadswamy Committee was set up which submitted its report in 1997 with various recommendations. In 1986, Child Labour Act was passed to prohibit children from employment in some specific places and hazardous units. In 1987, National Child Labour Policy was made to safeguard the child labour from exploitation and emphasis was laid on education, entertainment, health and general development works. Sri P.V. Narasimha Rao, the then Prime Minister of the country on 15th August, 1994 in his speech had announced a large national programme to eliminate child labour. In order to increase and attract the children to schools, they are to be provided with noon meal in the school since 15th August, 1995. Supreme Court's recent decisions, as mentioned earlier, has also proved a positive step in its detection and elimination.

Besides, many non-governmental organisations are also trying in this perspective. The prominent among these have been "The Concern for Children", Bangalore, "Iyper", Calcutta, "Prabhat-Tara", Delhi, "Chetna Vikas", Maharashtra, "Butterflies", Delhi, "Sewa" (Service) Ahmedabad, "Shakti", Delhi, "Raids", Bangalore.

But inspite of these efforts and steps, the existence of child labour in the country cannot be ignored. Certain future policies are essential to be framed and implementation of these are required seriously, the important methods or steps needed to abolish or eliminate child labour from our country are summarised as follows:

1. *Restriction to Job Market:* It must realise that the only way to contain child labour is to ensure that children do not enter the job market in the first place. If this is not done, today's illiterate child labour will become tomorrow's illiterate and unskilled adults.

2. *Poverty Elimination Programme*: The root cause of growth of child labour is poverty. So poverty elimination programme be launched widely. In the districts, where poverty is more, proper employment opportunities be provided there. In the unorganised sectors, minimum wages be strictly implemented. This will help the parents to maintain their family and send their children to schools.

3. *Free Compulsory Education:* Half the battle will be won when compulsory education becomes available to all children up to the age of 14 years. In states like Kerala where the 'education for all' mantra has been made a reality, child labour is unheard of. Yet in India, the government is far more committed to universalisation of education for the age group of 11-14 years.

4. *Increase in Income:* Attempts must be directed towards raising the income of the poorer sections of the community because poverty and deprivation force children to work. Children will be valued only when they are not a burden on the parents and this requires that their incomes are adequate to feed, clothe and rear their children in an adequate fashion . It is the most cruel form of hypocrisy to pay insufficient wages to fathers of families and then to show sympathy by employing child workers and by contributing to child welfare agencies to feel that duty has been done.

5. *Adult Education:* Adult Education Programmes should be widely launched. This will help in changing the attitude of parents and recognise the value of children for themselves and for the nation.

6. *Strengthening of Inspection:* One reform which can be carried out immediately is the strengthening of inspection so that provisions of law are not violated. The penalty for the breach of the Act should be both imprisonment and huge fine. Whatever policy is made to eliminate child labour, that needs the fullest enforcement through proper inspection and provision of educational and other facilities to children.

7. *Producers' Co-ordination:* The producers of the country should make the provision of mentioning on the product that this commodity has employed 'no child labour'. The consumer should also purchase those commodities only where such statements stand.

8. *Increase the Age Limit:* The age limit of the child labour should be increased than that defined in Factories Act, 1948 of 14 years and Mines Act 1952 of 15 years. As suggested by V.V. Giri, the age limit of employment of children should be raised to 16 years. But even this age should be subject to prohibition of work in hazardous units or likewise.

9. *Need of a Comprehensive Legislation:* There should be consolidation to the existing laws relating to prohibition and regulation of employment of children into a single comprehensive law. This legislation should include employment, regulation, training, welfare and development of child labour.

10. *Recreational Facilities:* Necessary recreational facilities besides education must be provided to children to develop their mental and physical status. The facilities of extra nutrition and health care be also provided.

11. *Evaluation:* Unless a systematic evaluation is made from time to time in respect of jobs in which children are employed and certain purposeful policy decisions are taken to meet the deficiencies, the existing situation is not likely to undergo any dimensional, qualitative and quantitative changes.

12. *Strictures:* The State High Court and the Supreme Court must take steps seriously in liberating and rehabilitating child workers and pass strictures to be forcefully implemented. A heavy fine and punishment should be imposed on both the employer and parents if they evade the orders.

13. *Need of Change in Employers' Attitudes:* Quite often it is the feeling of sympathy than the desire to exploit which weighs with employers in employing child workers. They also plea that employment of children increases the earning of the family and

it keeps children away from the mischief. Such arguments be not advanced by the employers to hide their ill-motives. Conservation of human resources should also be their responsibility. But for the sake of more profit, employer should not exploit them on whom the future of nation stands.

14. Consciousness of People: Laws can be enforced when individuals are guilty. When the society exploits the children by tolerating their employment, nothing can be done. So children should be valued and society should be vigilant enough to save them from exploitation. Basically it is the lack of awareness among the public that situation has much worsened.

Awareness against child labour is gaining ground in every States of India. Therefore, it can be presumed that scenario will change in near future.

References

1. J.C. Kulshrestha, *Indian Child Labour.*
2. S. Kothari, Exploiting the Young, *India Today*, January 15, 1983.
3. Sharma, Subhash, *Child Labour in India* (H), Prakashan Sansthan, Delhi.
4. B.B. Patel and Raksha Alagh, *Child Labour in India.*
5. UNICEF, *An Analysis of the Situation of Children in India* (1994), New Delhi.
6. Saxena, R.C., *Labour Problems and Social Welfare*, K. Nath & Co., Meerut.
7. Dass, R.K., *Child Labour in India.*
8. *The Hindustan Times*, Several Issues.

Index